The Giant Jigsaw Puzzle

Kenneth A. Shepsle

The Giant Jigsaw Puzzle

Democratic
Committee
Assignments in the
Modern House

The University of Chicago Press   Chicago and London

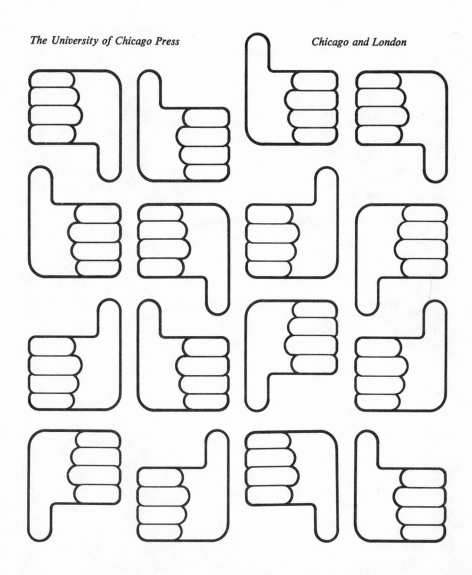

KENNETH A. SHEPSLE is professor of political science at Washington University. He has served as the editor of *Public Choice* since 1975 and is the coauthor of *Politics in Plural Societies: A Theory of Democratic Instability.*

The University of Chicago Press, Chicago 60637
The University of Chicago Press, Ltd., London

82 81 80 79 78   5 4 3 2 1

Library of Congress Cataloging in Publication Data

Shepsle, Kenneth A
    The giant jigsaw puzzle.

    Bibliography: p.
    Includes index.
    1. United States. Congress. House—Committee.
2. Democratic Party. I. Title.
JK1429.S5   328.73′07′65   77-16036
ISBN 0-226-75268-2

Contents

Acknowledgments

Acknowledgments are among the more pleasant writing assignments we scholars have. They allow us to reflect publicly on many of the values most of us hold dear—collaboration, collegiality, intellectual growth and accomplishment. Like others, I, too, have accumulated an enormous number of intellectual debts during the course of this project, both in the tranquil groves of academe and the busy corridors of Capitol Hill.

My earliest interest in the Congress generally, and committee assignments in particular, was stimulated by a graduate seminar at the University of Rochester in 1967. Its instructor, Richard Fenno, has remained my teacher, critic, and friend for a decade. He has read the entire manuscript, making numerous notes and suggestions; he has assisted me in the Washington-based aspects of my research, sharing his ideas about interviewing congressmen with me, lending me some of his own interviews that related to committee assignments, and providing me with a number of useful contact points in Washington; he (together with John Manley) provided me with a portion of the data set employed throughout this study; and, from time to time, he "took my confession" and otherwise assisted in the resolution of my intellectual doubts and concerns. His influence on this study will be obvious to the reader throughout. I can only add that I now understand, as anyone who has met the man does, why congressmen spill their guts to him!

Professor David Rohde of Michigan State University has been a valuable friend, collaborator, critic, and sounding board throughout the life of this project. His general enthusiasm about things congressional has been contagious, indeed.

Numerous others have read and criticized portions of this manuscript or have discussed aspects of their own related work with me. I list them here and

Acknowledgments

thank them for their ideas, many of which I have lifted and claimed as my own: Keith Acheson, Yoram Barzel, Thomas Borcherding, Richard Brody, Charles Bullock, John Ferejohn, Morris Fiorina, Irwin Gertzog, Robert Inman, John Jackson, Richard McKelvey, John Manley, Donald Martin, Nicholas Masters, Robert Peabody, Nelson Polsby, Bruce Ray, Robert Salisbury, Herbert Weisberg, and Peter Wissel.

On Capitol Hill, many congressmen and staffers have kindly given me their time and shared their knowledge. James Healey, former administrative assistant to Representative Dan Rostenkowski, should be singled out in this respect for, in my case, he appreciated and reduced the one problem all students of Congress have—access.

Several institutions have provided me with forums in which to think aloud about my research. I am most appreciative of their hard criticism and good will and would like to thank the staff and students of the Departments of Political Science at Washington University, the University of Chicago, and Occidental College; the Division of Humanities and Social Sciences at California Institute of Technology; the Center for the Study of Public Choice at Virginia Polytechnic Institute; the *American Political Science Review* editorial interns at Stanford University and the University of California, Berkeley; and the Hoover Institution.

Financial benefactors have been most generous. A National Science Foundation grant (GS–33053) in 1972–73 provided me with the time to think and learn about mathematical assignment problems and other aspects of mathematical programming. The Hoover Institution provided a stimulating environment in 1974–75, where, as a National Fellow, I was able to complete much of the empirical work and some of the writing. A Carthage Foundation grant in 1976–77 permitted me to complete the empirical work and put the finishing touches on the manuscript. During the entire period Washington University provided me with reduced teaching loads, a sabbatical leave, computer facilities, secretarial assistance (in the person of Mrs. Lillian Ehrlich), and a great deal of flexibility without which this project would still be on the drawing board.

Neither intellectual nor financial benefactors should be held accountable for my (mis)use of their generosity. One person who should share generously in any praise this study receives is my wife, Risë. I dedicate this book to her and thank her for the interest she continually expressed, the insightful suggestions she made, and the sympathy for a harassed author she displayed. I trust these have paid dividends in this final product.

Finally, let me thank Professor George Goodwin, whose fourth chapter of *The Little Legislatures* provided the title for this book.

K.A.S.
St. Louis, Missouri

Part 1

Overview

Chapter 1

The House has become **Introduction**
not so much a legislative
assembly as a huge panel
from which committees
are selected.
James Bryce (1911)

For students of social organizations in general, and the House of Representatives in particular, committees have long had an ambiguous status. On the one hand there is a familiar catalogue of virtues of small groups: they benefit from and encourage the division and specialization of labor; they are sifters and refiners of the larger organization's agenda; they are the instruments of decentralized decision-making; they are repositories of expertise within their specialized jurisdictions; they become relatively autonomous units with standard operating procedures that sometimes serve to insulate them from shortsighted and narrow external influences; and they are more expeditious and efficient in the molding of detailed proposals than the larger parent organization. On the other side of the ledger there is the folk wisdom that defines a camel as a horse built by a committee and an elephant as a mouse designed by one; there is the Wilsonian concern (a reflection of an earlier Jeffersonian concern—see Chapter 2) with the veto power of small groups;[1] and there is the modern reformer's concern with the biases inherent in committees that are unrepresentative of the parent body.

Where one stands on these alleged virtues and vices of committees depends, to some extent, on where one sits. In any event, they reflect the belief that committees exert a powerful influence on the collective choices of the parent body. Since ultimate decisions by the parent body confer benefits on some and impose costs on others, evaluations of these items are bound to be controversial. Thus, at the same time that a young, reform-minded scholar named Woodrow Wilson castigated congressional committees as "dim dungeons of silence," the minority leader and soon-to-be Speaker of the House, Thomas Brackett Reed, fondly described the congressional

3

committee as "the eye, the ear, the hand, and very often the brain of the House."

The ambivalence of students of the House regarding the appropriate role of that chamber's subunits has provided still another confirmation of the First Law of Social Science, namely, "Sometimes it's this way, sometimes it's that way." Committee-based research of the last two decades has added an important corollary to this theorem.[2] Fenno (1973, p. xiii), articulates the corollary:

> Most of our empirical generalizations [about committees] are of the same order. Each one is uttered as if it were equally applicable to all committees. And taken together, they convey the message that committees are similar. Our recent studies of individual committees have taught us, to the contrary, however, that committees are markedly different from one another.

Perhaps the most important thing to know about committees in the House of Representatives—and what, at bottom, is most responsible for the differences Fenno and others have documented—is that they are *jurisdiction-specific* subunits of their parent chamber. Jurisdictional differences have induced structural-organizational, procedural, and output differences among committees because they have identified where conflicts are resolved and whose interests are at stake. Jurisdictional distinctions, as a consequence, direct the flow of interested parties, members of the chamber as well as external actors, to the appropriate arena in which they seek to have an influential voice. This flow of influence and the complex fabric of motives and interests that clash with and complement one another are decisive in forming the character and operational style of each congressional committee. In his comparative study of six House committees, Fenno (1973, pp. xiv–xv) takes essentially this point of view:

> The members of each congressional committee have certain goals that they want to achieve through membership on a committee. If there is a high level of consensus on goals, they will organize their committee internally in ways that seem likely to aid them in achieving these individual goals. However, each committee operates within a distinctive set of environmental constraints—most particularly the expectations of influential external groups. Committee members will, therefore, also organize their committee internally in ways that seem likely to satisfy the expectations of these groups that make up their environment. The members of each committee will develop strategies for accommodating the achievement of their individual goals to the satisfaction of key environmental expectations. These strategies become the proximate premises on which each committee's internal decision-making processes are based. From these strategies, operationalized as decision rules, flow

committee decisions. In our explanatory scheme, then, member goals and environmental constraints are the independent variables; strategic premises (or, decision rules) are an intervening variable; and decision-making processes and decisions are dependent variables.

To this explanatory scheme, I would simply add that it is the jurisdictional characteristics which attract the distinctive membership and environmental constraints distinguishing committees from one another (see Hinckley 1975).

In light of the committee-based research of the last two decades, and the discovery that committees differ from one another as a result of the different congeries of interests they attract, a good deal of scholarly attention has been devoted to who gets assigned to which committees, how they are assigned, and why.[3] The main purpose of this study is to articulate and test a theory of congressional behavior that addresses these questions. While the abstract form of the theory is actually quite general, being a close cousin to constrained maximization theories commonly found in economics, in its particulars it is tailored to the legislative context.

More precisely, a theory of committee assignments in the House of Representatives is articulated and tested with data from the period 1958–74. The principal focus is on Democratic committee assignments during this period, though occasional references to Republican assignment practices, and to Democratic practices in other eras, are sprinkled throughout the text.

The Approach of
This Study

At the level of observation, the committee assignment process culminates in three separate House resolutions. The first, moved by the majority leader, establishes committee sizes and apportions committee berths between the majority and minority parties. The second and third resolutions, moved by the chairman of the Democratic and Republican Committees on Committees (CC), respectively, determine how committee slots are to be distributed among party members. With the passage of these resolutions, ordinarily "without objection," the committee structure for a new Congress is created.

The several weeks preceding these official decisions witness a complex set of interactions among a variety of interested parties, coordinated both by explicit institutional rules of the game and by implicit, occasionally idiosyncratic, informal practices. Observable behavior in this setting is motivated by the private goals and objectives harbored by the participants but is constrained by the sometimes competing goals and objectives of others and the formal rules that define the process.

The committee assignment process, in fact, may be analyzed from the perspectives of three distinct sets of actors whose behavior and interests are described in table 1.1.

Table 1.1　　　　　**The Committee Assignment Process:**
Actors, Behavior, Objectives

Actors	Behavior	Objective
Rank-and-file members	Submission of requests for initial committee assignment, transfer assignment, dual-service assignment; lobbying and campaigning activity aimed at securing desired assignments	"Good" committee assignments
Party leaders	Negotiation of a committee structure: committee sizes and party ratios established	Strategy of accommodation
Member of the party CC	Assignment of rank-and-file members to committees	Quid pro quos; "pipelines" into committees; chamber influence

1. Rank-and-file members are motivated by a desire for "good" committee assignments, where "good" is determined by introspective value judgments, an assessment of the likelihood of obtaining particular assignments, and the opinions, advice, and preferences of interested others. Emerging from these interactions are the *revealed preferences* of members.

2. Party leaders, engaged in the early forms of coalitional activity required of partisan leadership, are chiefly interested in accommodating member requests, though they do take a more particular interest in the money committees (Appropriations, Ways and Means) and the agenda committee (Rules). The "strategy of accommodation" is succinctly stated by Westefield (1974): "committee positions are given the status of a currency, a basis of exchange between leaders and followers. The leaders...perceive they can use the currency to accommodate the members and thereby induce the members to behave in ways the leaders desire. Indeed, the leaders can 'manufacture' this currency and add to the resource base at their disposal."

3. Members of the party CC are interested chiefly in chamber influence; their activities in behalf of rank-and-file members, party leaders, and interested others are calculated with an eye to eliciting specific quid pro quo behavior and more general forms of reciprocity.

The important point of departure for this study that can be extracted from these observations is this: each actor in the committee assignment process entertains interests, possesses behavioral alternatives, chooses from among the latter with an eye to the former, and is constrained in his choices by the interests and choices of others and by formal institutional rules. Behavior in this context is instrumental; it may be characterized as "constrained maximization in an institutional setting." The underlying approach of this study, then, is one of rational behavior in politics; it is, however, rich in institutional detail. The chapters that follow represent an attempt to examine how self-interest is manifested, channeled, and redirected in an institutional environment.

A Note on the Data

While the approach employed in this study is quite general, the empirical focus is on *Democratic* committee assignments, 1958–74. The somewhat narrower empirical focus is necessary for several reasons. First, the Democratic party in the House has become an almost permanently entrenched majority. Consequently, both journalistic and scholarly attention to committee assignment practices has been heavily weighted in favor of the Democrats. The empirical foundation upon which to construct a behavioral theory, that is, is virtually absent for the Republicans. Although the descriptive materials of this study are primarily related to the committee assignment process of the majority party, I believe the theoretical forces at work are of a more general nature. I do hope that scholars undertake separate studies of the committee assignment process for the Republicans. Their CC, their minority status, the role of their party leaders—in sum, the "parameter" values of the theory I articulate in this study—differ from those of the Democrats, and from these differences additional insights may be gained.

The second and probably more determining reason for restricting attention to Democratic committee assignments in this study derives from the availability of a certain body of data for the Democrats. Each freshman Democrat seeking an initial committee assignment and each nonfreshman seeking a transfer or dual-service assignment submits a request list of committees to his member on the party CC. This request list takes the form of a *preference ordering*, revealing the member's judgments about his own interests (electoral, policy, chamber influence, ambition, and so on) and his evaluations of the committees on which they will best be served. These data, because they tap subjective perceptions and evaluations, are extremely useful as empirical measures of private motives. Through the good offices of others, and some work of my own, preference data for every Congress between 1958 and 1974 (except the Ninety-first Congress, 1968–70) have been made available to me.[4] These data provide the empirical base for a theory of requests, a theory of the negotiated committee structure, and a theory of assignments.

A third rationale for focusing on Democratic assignment practices follows from the second. In order to breathe some life into these request data, as well as to track down a number of specific descriptive details of the committee assignment process not available in the public record, I took a month-long research trip to Washington in December 1974–January 1975. During that time, I conducted semistructured interviews with a number of actors in and observers of the committee assignment process. Interviews were obtained with members and administrative assistants in twelve of the offices of the thirteen Democrats on the Ways and Means Committee (the Democratic CC) who were returning to the Ninety-fourth Congress. The average length of the interviews was about an hour (despite the fact that, at that time, members of the House were involved in the confirmation and swearing in of Nelson Rockefeller as vice-president, leadership of the Ways and Means Committee was in transition as a result of the hospitalization of Wilbur Mills, and the early politicking for the upcoming Democratic Caucus, in which a number of changes involving the Ways and Means Committee were to be considered, was underway). The interviews usually took place in the member's office, though occasionally they were conducted over lunch or just off the House floor in the Ways and Means committee room. Additional interviews were conducted with the chief counsel of the Ways and Means Committee, members of the House press corps, the three Democratic freshmen who organized the freshman class of the Ninety-fourth Congress, and the one freshman appointed by the Speaker to the new Democratic CC.[5] The lack of access to committee-request data from the Republican side reinforced my earlier decision to restrict the scope of this study to Democratic committee assignments.

In later parts of this study, discussions of requests, structure negotiation, and assignments are presented. There I focus on theoretically motivated descriptions of these pieces of the giant jigsaw puzzle, behavioral implications, and empirical assessments of these implications. First, however, there is a historical interlude. The House of Representatives, like any other social institution, has a history. Committees and committee assignments have evolved historically from rather meager origins. Inasmuch as an organization like the House has a "memory," its history serves both as a constraint on current ways of doing things and as a source of insight about contemporary organization and modes of operation. It is to these historical issues that I now turn.

What is "the House"? An aggregation of vigorous elements, having different objectives, antagonistic notions, and selfish interests, centered about indefinite party policies and moved by personal, political, and sometimes patriotic purposes.
DeAlva Stanwood Alexander (1916)

Committees and Committee Assignments: A Historical Perspective

Committee assignments in the contemporary House are matters of utmost importance to congressmen, party leaders, and the people who must deal with the legislative process, for congressional committees today, like Wilson's "dim dungeons of silence" of a previous time, nurture, protect, and at times expand the jurisdictions in which their voices are decisive. Though committees today vary in their effectiveness on the floor (see Dyson and Soule 1970), it is nevertheless the case that most of the time the legislative action recommended by a committee is the legislative action taken by the House. And it is especially rare for the House to reverse a committee's negative judgment on a bill or, in any other fashion, to discharge a committee of its authority over a piece of legislation. Committees, that is, are effective *veto groups* within their legislative jurisdictions. They are one of the necessary (although not always sufficient) hurdles a bill must clear on its way through the legislative process.

The importance of committee assignments in the legislative process has varied historically with the changing attitude of the representative toward his role and his career, the effectiveness of party- and administration-led coalitions in guiding the business of the House, and, most important, the changing status of the standing committees as the principal agencies of legislation. From a reading of the extant literature on the historical evolution of legislative practices in the House of Representatives,[1] five "principles of composition" for the standing committees of the House emerge:

1. committees as favorably disposed translators of the "will of the House";
2. committees as mirrors of partisan and sectional divisions in the House;

3. committees as impartial and expert boards;
4. committees as vehicles for party government;
5. committees as instruments for individual members in the pursuit of their personal objectives.

Residues of all five principles appear in every historical period; however, each appeared to dominate committee assignment practices at a different time. The first was most prominent in the very early Congresses but had probably been replaced by the second by the beginning of the Jeffersonian period. The third committee assignment principle emerged during the Jefferson administration, if not earlier, and commanded more respect than the others until the 1840s. The fourth principle had its roots in the Clay speakership, was reflected in a number of pre–Civil War speakership elections, was given explicit recognition by the time of the Blaine speakership in the 1870s, and gained ascendancy in the late nineteenth century; then the so-called "Reed Rules" provided the majority party in the House with the instruments to legislate a party program (as defined and interpreted by a then powerful speaker). The fifth principle is of more recent vintage, descending directly from the Democratic-Progressive revolt against Speaker Cannon in 1910. It has accompanied the growing "institutionalization" of the House (see Polsby 1968; Abram and Cooper 1968), the increased seriousness with which the representative has taken his job as a career (see Price 1971, 1975; Fiorina, Rohde, and Wissel 1975), and the representative's strong desire to protect the source of his individual influence from the discretionary judgments of others.

The methods by which committee berths are allocated reflect the importance accorded each of these principles in different historical periods. To set the stage for my treatment of the contemporary committee assignment process in the House of Representatives, my focus in this chapter is on historical origins.

Committees in the Early Congresses

The Constitution provides each legislative chamber with considerable organizational flexibility. In the House, during the early Congresses, experimentation with organizational forms was constrained by two important principles having their origins in English legislative history: conventions surrounding the Committee of the Whole and the concept of committee.

Fearful of authority of any sort, the House retained for itself both the initial and the final say on legislation. It did this through the Committee of the Whole procedure, a practice by which the House convened itself into a committee for the purposes of general debate and the eventual hammering out of detailed legislation. Only after a consensus on general guiding principles, and often on specific detail, was reached by the Committee of the Whole, was a select committee appointed with instructions to mold the principles into a bill. "Rational discussion" by the full House, it was believed, served both to inform and enlighten the majority decision that emerged and to protect the rights of individual members. As Cooper (1970, p. 19) has observed, "fear of the distorting effects reliance on smaller committees might have on majority rule related not simply to the manner in which such reliance could infringe equal influence over outcomes, but also to the grave infringements of discussion and mutual enlightenment that such reliance could easily involve."

The Committee of the Whole was the primary legislative instrument of the House. Complementing it, and reflecting again the basic distrust of authority in the hands of a few, was a system of *select* committees. Once a consensus on general principles was reached by the Committee of the Whole, a committee was appointed whose sole charge was to render the general principles into the form of a bill or resolution and to suggest alternatives and amendments. The committee was short lived (when it completed consideration of the legislation for which it was appointed, it was required to report back to the House and its life then ended); it could not pigeonhole or otherwise veto the "will of the House"; and its membership was controlled by the House.[2]

In fact, the term "committee" had a singular as well as a collective usage. In its singular form, a committee was a member of a panel committed to a particular point of view (McConachie 1898). Since the purpose of a select committee was to render the "will of the House" into legislative form, it was assumed that those who made up the committee would be sympathetic to its purpose:

> when it became necessary to place resolutions or bills in the hands of smaller committees, these committees and their chairmen should be favorable to the object of the resolution or bill committed to them.... The general practice [was to make] the man who moved the appointment of a committee with regard to a particular resolution or bill its chairman. [Cooper 1970, p. 22]

The normal procedure—

1. debate in the Committee of the Whole;
2. appointment of a select committee to codify the general principles arrived at in the Committee of the Whole debate;
3. Committee of the Whole consideration of the select committee's report—

was rarely altered during the first several Congresses. In particular, only one *standing* committee, the Committee on Elections,[3] originated in the First

Congress, and no others were established until the beginning of the Fourth Congress (Galloway 1961, pp. 66–67). The House, during nearly its first decade, remained skeptical of permanently empaneled bodies and ordinarily guarded its prerogative as the sole repository of legislative authority. This attitude proved naive in the face of an "activist" executive branch and ultimately gave way, though slowly, to a division-of-labor standing-committee system.

For assignments to committees, whether standing or select, the Speaker was charged with major responsibility. During the first week of the First Congress, committees were selected by balloting of the full House. "Almost immediately, however, this system was found unsatisfactory, and, on April 7, 1789, a rule was adopted providing that all committees [of three or fewer members] should be appointed by the Speaker, unless otherwise specially provided" (Willoughby 1934, p. 342). In the second session of the First Congress, the Speaker was granted the authority to appoint *all* committees, although the House could elect a committee whenever it chose. "Thus, if the House suspected with regard to any particular subject that the Speaker could not be trusted to conform to the custom of selecting men truly in favor of the resolution or bill, it could by majority vote take appointment away from the Speaker" (Cooper 1970, pp. 23–24). By the end of that session even the right of the full House to approve or alter the Speaker's committee-assignment choices had atrophied.

> Thus the House [in 1790], relinquishing even its right of review, gave the Speaker a prerogative which he continued to possess for nearly a century and a quarter. The power soon made the Speakership a citadel about which factional strife and party warfare continually raged. [Alexander 1916, p. 66]

Given the constraints under which he operated in the early years of the House, and the relative unimportance of committees, the Speaker's authority over committee assignments was slight in comparison to its later significance. In selecting committees he was expected to appoint only those who agreed with the general principles that emerged in Committee of the Whole debate. For standing committees he was expected to observe the practice begun under the Articles of Confederation of giving committee representation to each state. Thus, "the first [standing] committee created by the House was... made to consist of eleven members consisting of a representative from each of the eleven states which at that time had adhered to the Union" (Willoughby 1934, p. 345). Nevertheless, he did retain broad discretion within those constraints; in exercising it he provoked occasional controversies, with the effect that

> prejudice against the Speaker's authority to appoint committees never wholly disappeared. Personal resentments kept it smouldering, and some-

times fanned it into a blaze when an ambitious or subservient Speaker became offensive. [Alexander 1916, pp. 75–76]

In the early Congresses, to summarize, committee assignments were of less significance in the politics of the House than they came to be in later periods. This was so for several reasons, chief among them being the primacy of the Committee of the Whole procedure. Committees (primarily select), consequently, were not the principal decision-making units. When they were charged with producing a resolution or bill, their tasks were more those of translating guiding principles into legislative detail, collecting information, and systematizing the features of the proposal than of exercising independent judgment. With the diminished status of committees came the diminished importance of committee assignments.

Second, the Speaker, empowered to appoint committee members, was constrained in his use of that power. He was expected to appoint only those who were favorably disposed to the proposal in question and, if the matter were of great salience or involved a permanently empaneled standing committee, he was expected to secure wide geographic representation on the committee. Although the Speaker occasionally used his discretion, to the consternation of some House members, the constraints were ordinarily quite binding.[4]

Third, the absence of a "legislative program" by a dominant faction in the House moderated any systematic interest in the staffing of committees.

Finally, the brevity and discontinuity of the congressional career (see Price 1971), coupled with the brevity and discontinuity of the life of a congressional committee, reduced rank-and-file interest in committee assignments.[5]

The Committee-of-the-Whole/select committee way of doing business in the early Congresses proved to be unwieldy and unrealistic in the face of two catalysts. First, the executive branch early on asserted itself and threatened legislative autonomy. In particular, the monopoly of information by the executive departments gave them a decided advantage in their dealings with a Congress that lacked any division of labor.[6] Second, the speakership was beginning to be conceived of as a political office and its occupants had begun to assert themselves. These two catalysts produced a growing reliance on select committees which, in all but name, became permanent panels. Also, standing committees were created with growing frequency (see table 2.1). Between 1800 and 1840, twenty-five standing committees were established.

Nineteenth-Century Developments

By the beginning of the nineteenth century, the Committee of the Whole procedure was on the wane. Important matters, like the subjects in the

Table 2.1   Standing Committees, Frequency of Creation

Decade	Number of Standing Committees Created
1789–1800	4
1801–1810	6
1811–1820	7
1821–1830	6
1831–1840	6
1841–1850	1
1851–1860	1
1861–1870	7
1871–1880	4
1881–1890	3
1891–1900	9
1901–1910	3
1911–1920	3
1921–1930	2
1931–1940	0
1941–1950	1
1951–1960	1
1961–1970	1
1971–1975	2

SOURCE: Galloway (1961), pp. 66–67.

President's Message to Congress given at the beginning of each session, were only perfunctorily heard in the Committee of the Whole; they were parceled out instead to the appropriate standing or select committee for initial action. The Jeffersonian fear of primary decision-making by small groups—the principal rationale for the Committee of the Whole procedure—did not disappear; it was, however, moderated by the increasing fear of executive domination of legislative activity. A division of labor in the executive branch induced a parallel development in the legislature. "After 1809...the number of standing committees proliferated. Often the process of development was one in which a select committee gained such regularity of appointment and such general jurisdiction that it became a standing committee in everything but name and only subsequently was recognized as a standing committee in the rules" (Cooper 1970, p. 42). This proliferation intensified during the Madison and Monroe administrations. With relatively weak presidents, executive power devolved to the departments, which worked even more closely with their parallel agencies in the legislature.

Partially as a consequence of this process, and partially as an independent development, the office of the Speaker and his committee assignment powers took on a much more political flavor. As early as 1806 some House members were calling for the reinstatement of the balloting procedure for committee assignments.[7] Committees were no longer regarded as "fingers of the House" —extensions of the majority consensus. Nor were they conceived of as "little legislatures"—miniature microcosms of the House. Rather they had attained the status of independent boards and repositories of expertise, though, in fact, they were political agencies reflecting the Speaker's political tastes and the political constraints he was required to observe in order to govern.

Beginning with Clay, the Speaker systematically employed committee assignments to further his own program. Whether in behalf of his own interests, or those of the president, the Speaker used committee assignments as a bargaining resource to secure compliance with his aims and to co-opt opposition.

> Once Clay transformed the Speaker into the key political leader in the House, his prerogatives over committee appointments assumed crucial functional significance. The Speaker became the prime agent for aggregating support across particular subject areas behind a general legislative program.... In this task committee assignments furnished both a crucial resource in factional bargaining, a critical incentive and reward for individual members, and a command and communications link in the organization structure. [Cooper 1970, p. 62]

Clay, as it happened, had ideas of his own—an aggressive foreign policy and a program of internal improvements—and faced either a weak administration or one controlled by the opposition. Other Speakers, however, acted as political lieutenants for the president. Alexander (1916, pp. 71–72) refers to Speakers Stevenson and Polk, for example, as "patronage secretaries to President Jackson." Cooper (1970, p. 65) notes that Speaker Stevenson stacked the standing committees with pro-Jackson majorities in anticipation of Jackson's election in 1828.

As the salience of committees and committee assignments grew, and as the Speaker's authority over assignments became absolute, two distinct patterns emerged. Contests for the speakership became intense, and efforts to strip the Speaker of his assignment prerogatives became more frequent. Galloway (1961) reviews the history of speakership elections during the four decades preceding the Civil War. Ordinarily the political complexion of the House was obvious enough so that only a single ballot was necessary. In the early nineteenth century, however, the absence of clearly defined party coalitions (or even clearly defined factions within the major parties) led to a number of contested elections. "During the first half of the nineteenth century the election of the Speaker gave rise to several minor contests, and on at least four occasions to sharp contests that ran for days or weeks. From 1820 on, the slavery question underlay these disputes which grew more and more violent during the 1840s and 1850s" (Galloway 1961, p. 41). All of the major contests (1839, 1849, 1855, 1859) and many of the minor contests involved the issue of committee assignments and how they would affect the slavery-antislavery cleavage or other partisan controversies. Thus, "John Quincy Adams [then a member of the House], thundering against the 'iniquity' of Speaker-appointed committees, charged that the turbulent and prolonged Speakership struggle in 1839 hinged on saving slavery in the District of Columbia" (Alexander 1916, pp. 66–67). In one of the earliest explicit statements of "party government," the ultimate winner of the 1839 contest, Robert M. T. Hunter of Virginia, made clear that committee assignments had become one of the central issues in speakership elections and House politics generally. He asserted his belief that the Speaker's party should control the form of legislation and, consequently, the committees responsible for it: "The party upon which it naturally devolved to propose a question ought to have the power to present its proposition in the shape for which it is willing to be responsible" (Alexander 1916, p. 67).

As the slavery-antislavery cleavage and other partisan cleavages increasingly reinforced one another, and as the hegemony of the standing committees and the absolute control of the Speaker over committee assignments were fortified, speakership contests became bitter, protracted struggles. The contest in 1849 required sixty-three ballots extending over three weeks. "The basic issue was whether or not the District and Territorial committees were to have proslavery majorities, which would be determined by the identity of the Speaker who had the power to appoint committees" (Galloway 1961, p. 43). The speakership election of 1855 took two months and 133 ballots. "Here again the basic issue was whether the committees of the House would be organized in a manner hostile or friendly to slavery" (Galloway 1961, p. 45). The fears of the proslavery forces were confirmed: "Mr. Banks was elected above all because it was expected he would constitute the committees in favor of the Free-Soilers. He justified this expectation by putting a majority of anti-slavery men on the Kansas Investigation committee, which act practically delayed the settlement of the Kansas episode until after 1857, and thus gave time for the antislavery forces to organize" (Follett 1896, p. 59). The opening of the Thirty-sixth Congress in 1859 was the scene for the last great nineteenth-century speakership battle. After two months and forty-four ballots, William Pennington, a freshman from New Jersey, was selected. Once again the disposition of the resources of the Speaker's office and their bearing on the slavery controversy were at issue. Pennington ultimately prevailed (he had received no more than a single vote until the fortieth ballot) primarily because he was a freshman and was not known to be an active partisan on the issue.

The increasing bitterness with which mid-nineteenth-century speakership elections were contested was accompanied by numerous attempts to strip the

Speaker of his committee assignment prerogatives altogether. The Speaker's committee assignment power, originally intended to be used in an impartial fashion to expedite the business of the House, had evolved into a powerful tool "to reward friends, to cripple the competent, to humiliate the independent, to favor special interests, and to attract wide-reaching support" (Alexander 1916, p. 67).[8] Joshua R. Giddings, a distinguished abolitionist, expressed the belief in 1849 that "the Speaker, exercising his right to frame committees, exerts more influence over the destinies of the nation than any member of the Government except the President" (quoted in Alexander 1916, p. 67).

The first attempt to remove the appointment power of the Speaker occurred in 1806, when a motion to return to the ballot system for committee assignments came within two votes of passing. John Randolph's domination of Speaker Macon after the former's split with Jefferson provoked the motion by the president's supporters. "The House was out of patience with the mischief-maker" (Alexander 1916, p. 76). Little enthusiasm for committee assignments by full House election was expressed again until the Jacksonian period. Speaker Stevenson's explicit loyalty to President Jackson offended many in the House:

> By his conspicuous partiality and subserviency Speaker Stevenson had become obnoxious, and the vote to deprive him of the right of framing the [select] committee [to investigate the National Bank] stood, ayes, 100; noes, 100. Modesty did not afflict Stevenson, whose casting vote saved his privilege. [Alexander 1916, p. 76]

During the prolonged speakership contests of 1849, 1855, and 1859, removal of the Speaker's appointment power was seen as a way of breaking the election deadlocks. Motions to this effect, however, were either tabled or voted down. Further efforts to strip the Speaker of this prerogative were infrequent, raised only occasionally by members out of personal pique at being overlooked by the Speaker; the matter did not emerge again until the great revolt against Speaker Cannon in the early twentieth century.

By the time of the Civil War, then, the autonomy of the standing committees and the absolute power of committee assignments by the Speaker were firmly entrenched and had withstood several assaults. During the several decades surrounding the Civil War, a number of additional procedural practices of importance to committee assignments were established as well. The Speaker's power to appoint members to committees had always been limited in one respect. In those committees in whose reports the Speaker had a personal interest (when, for example, his own election to the House might be challenged), he was relieved of the appointment task:

> During the first half [of the nineteenth] century it was usual for such committees to be chosen by the House, but in 1843 the practice was

changed. In that year the seat of [Speaker John W.] Jones was contested; he, therefore, asked to be relieved from the duty of naming the committee on Elections. It was suggested that the appointment be given to the Speaker *pro tem.*, although it was pointed out that if there was any impropriety in the construction of the committee by the Speaker, there was exactly the same impropriety in its construction by a Speaker *pro tem.* created by him; the motion was, however, carried. The precedent thus established has since been followed. *The Speaker of course chooses a political friend to act as his substitute.* [Follett 1896, p. 219, emphasis added]

A second procedural change occurred in 1861. Until that year the term of a committee assignment was a congressional session. In the Thirty-seventh and following Congresses, however, committee assignments were made for the entire life of a Congress. Some observers regarded this procedural change as a check on the Speaker's powers.[9] However, the fact that members' committee assignments were determined once and for all at the beginning of a Congress made loyalty during the speakership election much more important on the one hand, and made committee assignments much more prized and valuable on the other. The Speaker's powers, it could be argued, were actually enhanced.

Finally, in 1858 a select committee was established to revise the then cumbersome and repetitive House rules. The resolution providing for the establishment of this committee also stipulated that the Speaker serve as a member. "This was the first time in the history of the House that its presiding officer had served on one of its committees" (Galloway 1961, p. 49). It set the stage for the further aggrandizement of the Speaker's powers in the late nineteenth century, when he assumed the chairmanship of the Rules Committee to augment his already immense control over the fate of legislation.

Further Aggrandizement of the Speaker, 1890–1910

One of the most noteworthy features of the practices of the House to emerge from the post-Jeffersonian experience—a feature perhaps second in importance only to the aggrandizement of the Speaker—is the role of party in the organization and management of conflict in that chamber. Speaker Hunter's (1839–41) early statement (quoted above) on the responsibility of the Speaker's party to promote a legislative program predates what became the prevailing attitude after the Civil War.[10] As MacNeil (1963, pp. 71–72) notes, "not until James G. Blaine became Speaker in 1869 were the intricacies of party leadership, and discipline in party ranks, given careful scrutiny." He continues:

Blaine took command of a House in which Republicans held a two-to-one preponderance over the Democrats. A dignified and courteous

Speaker with a consuming ambition to be President, Blaine boldly stated his "political" view of the office. "Chosen by the party representing the political majority in this House," Blaine addressed his colleagues, "the Speaker owes a faithful allegiance to the principles and policy of that party." He did not hesitate to carry out that implicit pledge to partisanship.... He carefully calculated the legislation he wanted, and then deliberately appointed to the appropriate committees members of the House who he knew were favorable to that legislation. It was a new ingredient of influence for the Speaker.

Other Speakers followed suit, with Randall, Keifer, Carlisle, and Reed employing the powers of the office, and especially their control over committee assignments, to pursue what they proclaimed as party policies. It was not, however, until the Reed speakership, and the promulgation of the "Reed Rules," that the Speaker possessed the assortment of instruments with which to prosecute policy partisanship effectively.

In 1879, in response to the sluggishness of the legislative process, a committee was appointed to revise the House rules. The rules revisions of 1880 were hailed as a great achievement in rendering the legislative machinery more efficient while amply providing for the protection of minority prerogatives (see Galloway 1961, pp. 51–52). The new rules, however, did not alter two minority practices which often frustrated House majorities: the "disappearing quorum" and the nongermane amendment.[11] What the rules allowed and tolerated, Speaker Thomas Brackett Reed, by fiat, forbid. Declaring it the Speaker's duty to expedite the chamber's business, he proclaimed, first, his "right of nonrecognition," according to which the Speaker could query any person seeking the floor, "For what purpose does the gentleman rise?" If the Speaker judged the purpose dilatory or otherwise nongermane, recognition was denied. Second, to cope with disappearing quorums Reed instructed the House clerk to record those present but refusing to vote as "present" and to count them as contributing to a quorum. DeAlva Alexander (1916, pp. 205–6), himself a former member of Congress and close friend of Reed, commented on the Speaker's efforts to eliminate delay and continued roll calls:

> When Reed succeeded Carlisle (1889), he determined to destroy this evil. The code-makers of 1880 boasted that they did not disturb the rights of the minority; Reed declared that a minority should not disturb the rights of the majority. The former minimized the result without abolishing the cause; the latter laid the axe to the root.... What made [the Reed Rules] famous were additions, not modifications. Having heretofore suppressed dilatory motions, adopted special orders by a majority vote, and counted a quorum, Reed now reduced the practice to written rules.

With the promulgation of the Reed Rules, the Speaker's control over legislative outcomes was virtually complete. Through his absolute authority over committee assignments, he controlled the composition of the House's primary decision-making units. His appointment of committee chairmen and his own membership on the Rules Committee insured "proper" and expeditious handling of legislative matters he favored. His authority over floor procedures, including his power to count quorums and his right of non-recognition, put in his hands the instruments to enhance the likelihood of final decisions in line with his own preferences. And finally, his power to appoint House conferees gave him an additional lever of influence.

Reed, an able parliamentarian in his own right, used these newly acquired weapons "not simply to preside over the deliberations of his fellow members, but to carry out party pledges and round up a successful legislative session" (Alexander 1916, p. x). He held to the very explicit belief that the Speaker's party had a record to make and that the Speaker was the one visible element in the chamber on whom praise or blame might be affixed.[12] He was, consequently, extremely protective of his power to make committee assignments, the principal "fountain-head of legislation" (Hasbrouck 1927, p. 2). To "carry out party pledges" and "round up a successful legislative session" depended decisively on committee assignments for, in Reed's opinion (and Alexander's words),

> legislation derives its character in large part from the complexion of committees, and the fairer, more experienced, and the better fitted is their membership, the more satisfactory must be their work. Properly to select appointees in a House membership running up into the hundreds requires an intimate personal knowledge of individual ambitions, characteristics, achievements, and peculiar fitness for service, and in Mr. Reed's judgment no one would so patiently and certainly acquire such information as the Speaker—not because the right of appointment belonged to the office, *but because upon him rested the whole responsibility of choosing men who would loyally write party pledges into legislation and give conscientious study, guided by an open mind, to all other measures. Moreover he thought the responsibility attendant to the exercise of such a delicate and significant power should be absolutely known....* Thus, when it was proposed in the Forty-seventh Congress (1881) to substitute for this purpose a board or committee of eleven members, to be selected by log-rolling processes inseparable from caucus action, he failed to find the man upon whom the responsibility for weak, sinister appointments could be fixed. [Emphasis added]

This, of course, is not to say that Reed was not a practical man. He used committee assignments varyingly to reward his friends, neutralize his competitors within his party, and immobilize the opposition. He maintained a stranglehold on the Rules Committee, which he chaired.[13] And he was not beyond consulting with "interested others" on committee assignments when he felt it suited his purposes.[14]

Reed's centralization of legislative power in the Speaker's office led to critical reaction, both from his own party and from the opposition, for, in Follett's words, (1896, p. 117) "he sought not to represent his party, but to impose his own ideas upon it."[15] The reaction, however, came at Speaker Henderson's expense. During the four years he served as Reed's successor (1899–1903), no major advances in the Speaker's powers occurred. He did, however, manage to maintain the powers he inherited from Reed, despite several assaults.

In the eight years following Henderson's retirement, Joseph Cannon of Illinois served as Speaker. Taking over where Reed left off, Cannon earned the title "Boss" for what were regarded as dictatorial uses of the Speaker's powers. Three articles in this indictment against "Cannonism" directly related to committee assignments:

1. Cannon's delay in making assignments at the beginning of a Congress in order to blackmail members (especially freshmen) into supporting his position on important issues before the House;
2. Cannon's stacking of committees to suit his own purposes (which were often at odds with those of the Republican President);
3. Cannon's violations of seniority in the making of assignments and the appointment of committee chairmen.

After the Speaker is elected there is ordinarily a brief delay of a week or so during which time the Speaker constructs the committee lists. Follett (1896, p. 231) reports that "in the early Congresses the committees were completed within a few days of the opening of the session: it was the custom of the House to adjourn in order to give the Speaker time to consider the matter. With the increased difficulty, however, in making the appointments, the time that elapses between the assembling of Congress and the announcement of the committees has also increased." Speaker Cannon's practice was to appoint a few of the important committees that immediately had to begin work and purposely to delay appointing any of the others. This had the chilling effect of forcing members to support Cannon on procedural matters as well as on any substantive issues that might come before the House early in the session.

There is no doubt that, with reference to the vast majority of assignments, the uncertainty of the situation acts as a strong inducement to party regularity on these first crucial votes. Particularly is this true with regard to a new member, for while he is not likely to understand the importance of the vote on rules, he does know that his future career in Congress depends largely upon the kind of committee assignment which he gets. Old Members can look with a fair degree of certainty to re-assignment to the committees on which they previously served, but the future of new Members is fatefully dependent upon first impressions. [Hasbrouck 1927, p. 36]

Cannon was not the first Speaker to engage in this practice, though he may well have been the most excessive. "The sixty-first Congress, for example, met on March 15, 1909. On the following day, Speaker Cannon appointed the members of the Rules and Ways and Means Committees, but he held up most of the [other] appointments until August 5, the last day of the session, after the Payne–Aldrich tariff bill had passed the conference stage" (Hasbrouck 1927, p. 37).

Cannon has, on occasion, been treated unfairly in accusations of manipulation of committee assignments for his own purposes. That he did manipulate for his own purposes (as had most Speakers who preceded him), however, is not in question.[16] He would, with some frequency, refuse to reappoint members to committees if they had crossed him in the previous Congress. Congressman Haugen of Iowa gives colorful testimony to this point in reference to the Meat Inspection Act favored by President Roosevelt:

I believe nine members of that Committee (on Agriculture) stood by the President. The other members of the Committee were against the legislation as outlined by the President, and so was the Speaker. What happened? In the next Congress when the time came for making up committees the names of seven of the nine members who had stood for the Roosevelt proposition did not appear on that Committee. The Chairman of that Committee on the morning after election found his political carcass outside of the breastworks. A new Chairman was appointed. According to the custom, the ranking member of the Committee, Mr. Henry of Connecticut, was entitled to the chairmanship, but Brother Henry had supported the meat-inspection bill, and his name did not appear on that Committee. [Cited in Hasbrouck 1927, p. 49]

Late in Cannon's speakership, when his manipulations became particularly excessive, the main objects of his wrath were the Progressive Republicans. They were denied chairmanships to which they were "entitled," and otherwise were transferred off committees on which they had sat, with considerable regularity. During the final two years of Cannon's tenure (1909–11), his conflict with the Progressives reached fever-pitch proportions, ultimately leading to his downfall.

Finally, Cannon was indicted for his frequent violations of seniority principles in his committee assignment practices. Although there is some dispute over the extent to which seniority was violated—indeed, over the extent to which seniority was a norm at all at that time[17]—there is little doubt that Speaker Cannon, like Speaker Reed, paid little heed to seniority when it conflicted with his own purposes. Both Hasbrouck (1927, pp. 48–50) and Chiu (1928, pp. 65–71) document many instances of this practice (though Chiu provides data that suggest Cannon tended to abide by the seniority principle much more frequently than his critics claimed).

Unlike Reed, Cannon was no reformer. He took the powers that Reed had amassed in the Speaker's office and put them to his own uses. He was, however, responsible for one important committee assignment reform, a reform that persists today. Speaker Cannon began the practice of consulting with the minority leader about the assignments of minority members. As he later recalled:

It was well understood between Representative [John Sharp] Williams and the then Speaker of the House that he should have his way about minority appointments, and as I recollect now there were not to exceed four cases where the minority leader did not have his way [Cited in Hasbrouck 1927, p. 44]

But when Champ Clark, who succeeded John Sharp Williams as minority leader, sought to obtain assurances that the Speaker would accept minority recommendations without alteration ("he [Clark] would not organize that minority unless his recommendations were accepted without the dotting of an 'i' or the crossing of a 't'"), Cannon demurred.

The aggrandizement of the Speaker, a process that took place almost without interruption for nearly a century, reached its apogee during the regimes of Reed and Cannon. An unbridgeable split in the Republican party, and a Speaker whose personal policy objectives exacerbated that split, brought that aggrandizement to an end in 1910. As was the case with the original accumulation of the Speaker's powers, the Speaker's relationship to the standing committees of the House and his power over committee assignments played a central role in the "revolution of 1910."

The Revolution of 1910

The revolution of 1910[18] was made possible by the election of 1908. In that election the Republican majority in the House shrunk slightly but, more important, the strength of the Progressives within the party grew. Republican "regulars" were the net losers in 1908. Between December 1908 and March 1909, during the lame-duck session of the previous Congress, reformers began organizing for an effort to curtail the Speaker's powers at the beginning of the Sixty-first Congress. Together with the 172 Democrats, if they could be held together, the 30 Progressives commanded a 202–189 majority in the new Congress.

On March 15, 1909, the Democratic-Progressive coalition defeated the motion to adopt the rules of the previous Congress.[19] A resolution was offered by the Democrats which would have stripped the Speaker of his assignment powers for all committees except Ways and Means and reconstituted the Rules Committee so as to exclude the Speaker and to insure an "insurgent" majority on that committee. Although the Progressives were prepared to support this resolution, twenty-two Democrats bolted the coalition, refusing to support a violation of the "majority control" principle. With the regular Republicans they defeated the previous question on the Democratic resolution. They substituted a resolution that restricted the Speaker's right of recognition and ultimately passed. In effect only a mild slap on the wrist, the substitute:

1. created a unanimous consent calendar;
2. allowed a motion to recommit after the previous question was called on any bill or resolution;
3. made it more difficult to set aside Calendar Wednesday.

Not only had the Progressives lost this round rather badly; in addition, Cannon made sure no Progressive secured an important committee assignment and altogether shut them out of Republican decision-making during the Sixty-first Congress.[20]

A year later the opportunity for action of a more "revolutionary" nature arose. On March 17, 1910, "Speaker Cannon sustained an attempt to set aside Calendar Wednesday by a claim of constitutional privilege for an amendment of the census act. This touched [the Democrats who had bolted the previous year in support of the Speaker in exchange for the formal assurance of a regular Calendar Wednesday procedure] in a sensitive spot. They joined in the unusual action of overruling the Speaker, in order to preserve the integrity of Calendar Wednesday" (Hasbrouck 1927, p. 6). The device of constitutional privilege was seized upon later the next day by George Norris (Rep., Neb), leader of the Progressive members. He claimed that, since the Constitution delegated internal rule-making to each chamber, reform of the House rules was a constitutional function and that, therefore, recognition to make a motion for that purpose was privileged. Cannon promised to rule on the procedural question the next day (while his lieutenants sought the votes to secure an adjournment). "Accordingly, on March 19, 1910, he held the Norris resolution not in order, and was a second time overruled by a vote of the House—162–182" (Hasbrouck 1927, pp. 6–7). Norris then moved the previous question on a resolution that increased the size of the Rules Committee from five members appointed by (and including) the Speaker to ten members elected by the House and excluding the Speaker; the motion passed. The "Revolution of March 1910" was completed with the invitation by Cannon for a motion from the floor declaring the office of Speaker vacant. The motion was offered by the Democrats but soundly defeated. Cannonism had been repudiated, but Cannon remained in the chair. He and his friends continued to dominate the Sixty-first Congress. Major reforms were not to be realized until the elections of 1910 which brought to the House a new Democratic majority.

Postrevolutionary Adjustments

The revolution of 1909–10 reduced two of the three great powers of the Speaker. It constrained his power of recognition, rendering him slightly less powerful than "Czar" Reed but still very much in control of floor procedure. Second, it removed him from membership on the Rules Committee and transferred the assignment power for that committee to the full House. It was not until the Democratic-controlled Sixty-second Congress, however, that the last, and probably the most consequential, of the Speaker's powers was withdrawn. In April 1911 the Democrats adopted several procedural revisions in the House rules (see Hasbrouck 1927, pp. 11–12). The most important of these was a rule providing for the election of all standing committees by the full House.[21]

"Election by the House," however, does not just happen. In 1910, for example, the Rules Committee was to be "elected" by the House—the major concession won by the reformers. Each party caucus decided assignments to the Rules Committee separately. The Progressives were powerless in the Republican Caucus (see note 20) and, as a consequence, received none of the new Rules slots. In fact, every member (except the Speaker) of the previous committee was "elected by the House," and one of Cannon's lieutenants became its chairman.

Beginning in the Sixty-second Congress (1911), the Democrats vested committee assignment powers in the hands of its members of the Ways and Means Committee who, in turn, were elected by the entire caucus. The party leader, by tradition, was the chairman of that committee. They immediately adopted a rule which prevented any Ways and Means member from serving on other committees, thus overcoming the objection (expressed some thirty years earlier by Thomas Reed) that a member of a committee on committees "would appoint himself chairman of a great committee" (Alexander 1916, p. 82). The chief effect of this new arrangement was to maintain the weight of the party leadership in the disposition of committee assignments, though now the principal actor was the majority leader (Oscar Underwood) rather than the Speaker (Champ Clark). Alexander (1917, p. 82) suggests that, in many respects, the reform was cosmetic:

in making its assignments the Board in no wise departed from the rules which formerly guided the Speaker. Fitness, experience, and geographical location were recognized as well as the long established custom of promoting older members and placing at the head of each committee the person entitled by long service to the chairmanship. In like manner it authorized the accepted minority leader to assign places to minority members. Indeed, the administration of the new rule made no perceptible change in the manner of making up committees, which, when finally constructed, were "elected" by receiving the formal approval of a caucus and then of the House.

The Republicans, the minority party in 1911, allowed their leader (James R. Mann of Illinois) to assign minority members to committees. In practice, Mann would draw up his slate and submit it to the majority leader, who would move its adoption. This practice continued until 1917 when, at the organizing sessions of the Sixty-fifth Congress,

the rule change recommended by Mr. Pou of the Rules Committee, and adopted by the House, was in support of the leadership of both parties. It provided that "any motion or resolution to elect the members or any portion of the members of the standing committees of the House and the joint standing committees shall not be divisible." A tendency had been noted on the part of the House to call into question certain individual nominations to committees. The new restriction, taking away the general privilege of dividing a question into substantive propositions, made sure that in the future the slates should go through precisely as authorized by the party caucuses. [Hasbrouck 1927, pp. 14–15]

Armed with this new rule, Mann began making the minority nominations himself, a practice that persists in the contemporary House.

In 1919, when the Republicans returned to power in the House, a more permanent arrangement for committee assignments was sought. Mann, the Cannon protégé, was defeated for the speakership by Frederick Gillett of Massachusetts. He managed, however, to secure a committee assignment arrangement which was controlled by his wing of the party. The method, which is still used by the Republicans today, allows for the election by each state party delegation of a member to a Committee on Committees. Each member has as many votes on the committee as there are Republicans in his state delegation.

Until 1975, the two parties maintained the above-mentioned methods of committee assignments with only minor and occasional adjustments. The controversy that most frequently had to be dealt with involved deviations from party loyalty in presidential elections. The Progressives in 1925, for example, lost many of their committees positions (see Berdahl 1949). Democratic disloyalty in 1956, 1960, 1964, and 1968 caused similar controversies, though punishments were meted out only in the latter two years.[22]

Did the revolution of 1910 and the decade of "mopping up" make a difference for committee assignments? Some twenty years later, W. F. Willoughby (1934, p. 344) was less sanguine than some of the participants in the revolution.

> The fact that the House, under the new system, would exercise little or no more independent choice in respect to committee assignments than it did under the old was brought out in the debate that took place upon the proposal to change the rules [in March 1911]. Thus, Mr. Mann, the minority floor leader of the Republican Party, in a speech to taunt the Democratic Party with insincerity in making the change, said:
>
>> You say now that you have made a great change in the rules by providing for the election of committees. You propose, you say, to elect the committees in the House; but you do not propose to elect the committees by ballot; you do not propose to give to the individual membership of the House an opportunity to pass upon the qualifications of members for committee assignments by either an open or secret ballot. What is the difference, pray, between having the gentleman from Alabama (Mr. Underwood), the Democratic floor leader, rise in his place and offer a resolution providing for the election of the gentlemen he names in the resolution as members of committees, which you have already named in your caucus, and having the Speaker of the House, as you could have done, say that the Speaker appoints the following committees which you had selected by your caucus action? The idea which went through the land as to the selection of committees by a Committee on Committees was to have a committee of the House, where both sides were represented in the committee, select the membership of the various committees. You have eliminated that. You have simply provided a different method of carrying out your caucus action, which you could have carried out under the old rule with equal facility.

Mann's taunting remarks in large measure were true; but they were also, in large measure, beside the point. The aim of the rules changes of 1909–11 was to divest the Speaker of some of the powers his office had accumulated over the previous century. That other party agents moved into the vacuum was, of course, more than coincidental. But the major objective of the rules changes—the redistribution of internal decision-making power—was in most respects successful. Three particular changes that followed from the rules reforms bear more detailed attention:

1. the strengthening of the majority leader and committee chairmen at the expense of the Speaker;

2. the increased independence of the minority party;

3. the increased reliance on a seniority norm in the naming of committee chairmen and a property-right norm in reappointing members to committees in order to protect the individual from the discretion of others.

According to Ripley's (1967, p. 16) qualitative categories, Champ Clark was a relatively weak Speaker. His style of leadership was "collective" rather than "personal" and his use of powers was "retrogressive" rather than "innovative" or "conservative." Between 1911 and 1915 the new power in the House was majority leader Oscar Underwood.[23] "He derived his personal ascendency from his control of majority committee assignments as chairman of Ways and Means, his chairmanship of the Steering Committee, and from his right to be recognized at any time on the House floor" (Galloway 1961, p. 140). The Speaker, though still in command of procedural affairs for the most part, no longer was master of the flow of legislation. Rather, the flow was determined in collaboration with the majority leader, who had direct access to the floor, and the committee chairmen (who were no longer necessarily the Speaker's allies as they had been prior to 1911). There was still some semblance of "party government," especially during the first two years of the Wilson administration. But this came to an end with Underwood's departure for the Senate, the coming of World War I, and, by the end of the decade, the termination of the practice of vesting the majority leadership and the chairmanship of Ways and Means (and the Democratic Committee on Committees) in the hands of the same person.

The second reform had its origins in the Cannon speakership. The practice of allowing the minority party to name its own committee slate was an accomplished fact in all but a few instances during the first three terms of Cannon's speakership (1903–9). This de facto practice was given substantial legitimacy by a "test case" involving the replacement of a minority member of the Rules Committee in mid-session of the Sixty-third Congress. A vacancy on Rules was created by the death of a Progressive Republican. As was the case with the ordinary filling of minority slots, the minority leader named a replacement and the majority leader moved his election. Progressive elements within the Republican party, however, sought to have a more reform-oriented member named to Rules and thus nominated an alternate candidate for the position. Many Democrats regarded this as a Republican quarrel that should have been resolved by the Republicans alone. They were prepared to abstain from the vote on filling the Rules vacancy. The majority leader, however, urged all Democrats to reject the Progressive candidate and vote instead for the minority leader's recommendation. "Although, [Underwood] reasoned, the Democratic party was in the last analysis responsible for committee personnel, the Democrats in caucus had recognized that the election of committees should be along party lines" (Hasbrouck 1927, p. 46).[24]

Both of these changes, then, were decentralizing in effect and came at the Speaker's expense. The same is true of the third change. The strict reliance on seniority for committee chairmanships and property rights for committee berths completed the devolution of authority in the House. While members still have to "go along to get along" in the modern House, they only have to go so far. The decentralization of power in the House that began with the revolution of 1910 has reached all the way to the back bench. The individual congressman of the contemporary House is, in many respects, a power in his own right. His power is committee-based (and, more recently, subcommittee-based), and this base is protected. He is much less at the mercy of party and faction than were his nineteenth-century predecessors.

Although there is still some scholarly controversy over the precise date that seniority emerged as a hard-and-fast rule for appointing committee chairmen (see Polsby, Gallagher, and Rundquist 1969; and Abram and Cooper 1968), there is general consensus that it was in place by the end of the decade following the revolt against Cannon. Actually, Speaker Cannon abided by the principle of seniority for the most part (see Chiu 1928, pp. 67–71) but chose to violate it from time to time; he was especially vindictive toward the Progressives and saw to it that they did not advance to positions of importance. Cannon used "party loyalty" (by which he meant "Cannon loyalty") as an acid test for committee advancement and would not hesitate to drop a member from a committee, or block his advancement to the chairmanship, if he failed this test. Cannon explained that such members

> failed to enter and abide by a Republican caucus, and this being a government through parties, for that as well as for other sufficient reasons, the Speaker of the House, being responsible to the House and to the country, made the appointment with respect to these gentlemen as he conceived to be his duty in the execution of the trust reposed in him. [Cited in Chiu 1928, p. 67]

By 1920 the general practice of promoting the committee member with the longest continuous committee service to the chairmanship was standard practice, a practice that remained intact until the 1970s (see the Epilogue).

Similarly, in the contemporary House a *property-right* norm is observed according to which a member, once assigned to a committee, has a claim to his committee slot in succeeding Congresses. Within the committees moreover, he has a claim to his position in the seniority queue so that, if he has accrued the most committee seniority, and his party is in the majority, he can expect to be named committee chairman. These "committee-slots-as-property" practices greatly reduce member uncertainty about their own careers and remove some of the pressure to be on the "right" side in intraparty conflicts. Since the revolt against Cannon these practices have become the rule, and violations of seniority have been the exceptions.[25]

Each of these practices was closely tied to, and in part a function of, the growing career-orientation of rank-and-file members (see Price 1971, 1975; and Fiorina, Rohde, and Wissel 1975). By the time of the revolt against Cannon, the patterns of secular decline in membership turnover and secular increase in the mean length of service were well under way (Polsby, Gallaher, Rundquist 1969). The devolution of authority following the assault on the speakership, then, was closely intertwined with the apparent increase in value of a congressional career for the rank-and-file member and his keen interest in maximizing his own discretion and reducing career uncertainty. These, in turn, have produced a concern on the part of the member for "good" committee assignments, on the one hand, and the freedom to employ the perquisites of committee membership for his own purposes, on the other.

**Committee Assignment
Practices in the
Modern House**

Committees, and hence committee assignments, remain as the primary pressure points of the modern House. The practices to which the parties conform in assigning their members to committees is the topic of the remainder of this study. It is the well-defined temporal sequence of the committee assignment process that I shall use to organize the discussion. For my purposes, the time sequence of the committee assignment process, which culminates in the creation of a committee structure for a new Congress, is characterized by the following sequence:

1. the committee structure of the previous Congress;
2. an election that "shocks" the structure;
3. requests for committee assignments from newly elected freshmen and returning members;
4. the negotiation of the new committee structure—the establishment of committee sizes and party shares—by party leaders;
5. committee assignments by the Committee on Committees of each party.

As shall be evident, the modern House is very different from the institution Speaker Clay presided over, or Speakers Reed and Cannon manipulated.

Since the revolution of 1910 and the decade of decentralization, the House has become a body with many heads. House politics is much more free-flowing and disorganized than in previous eras. Relationships are much more atomistic. It is a place with a history, however, so that traces of region, party, faction, and ideology remain and occasionally play a prominent role in the politics of committee assignments.

Part 2

Requests

Chapter 3

Seeking a Committee Assignment

The two months between Election Day in early November and the convening of the new Congress in early January are a busy period for the freshman congressman. The campaign, election, and victory celebration concluded, he must begin the task of dismantling his campaign organization, clearing up the final details and paperwork of the election, and readying himself for the move to Washington. In many instances this will involve settling business and personal financial affairs; deciding whether to move the entire family and, if so, determining what to do with his home; and, of course, looking for a place to live in Washington. As well, he must see to the establishment of an office(s) in his district and, most important, begin to assemble a staff for his Washington office.

Although the personal details of a change in career will occupy much of his time, the new congressman is faced with other matters quite consequential to his career in Washington. Chief among these is the matter of committee assignments. The centrality of the committee system in congressional life, the resources a committee position provides the member, and the long-run consequences of an initial assignment for the member's institutional career, all make the seeking and obtaining of desirable committee assignments a matter of the highest priority.

Directly after his election, each new Democrat receives a letter from the chairman of the Democratic Committee on Committees (CC) (throughout the period of this study that person was Wilbur Mills of Arkansas) congratulating him on his recent victory, impressing upon him the importance of committee assignments, and urging him to transmit to the CC, after careful consideration, his preferences for committee assignments. The letter also informs each member who his zone representative[1] on the CC is and warns the member that, despite the CC's effort to satisfy members requests, there are often too few "good" assignments available; consequently the member should submit strong second- and third-preference requests.[2]

The incumbent who survives his biennial bout with the electorate, on the other hand, returns to the Congress under circumstances far different from those of his freshman colleagues when it comes to committee assignments. The freshman seeking his initial assignment(s) is dependent on a "lottery"— the Committee on Committees—that has maximal discretion. He may receive his first-preference committee, but then again, he may be placed on a highly undesirable committee. Unless he is willing to contest a CC decision in a meeting of the full Democratic Caucus (which must ratify all CC decisions), he is completely at the mercy of the CC.[3] The nonfreshman takes comfort in the fact that he may retain the committee positions he held in the previous Congress. The *property-right norm* for committee positions held in the previous Congress insures the nonfreshman against capricious decisions by the CC. He is at its mercy only insofar as he wishes, by his own choice, to alter his committee assignments in some way.[4]

In this chapter freshman and nonfreshman request behavior is examined. Ultimately we shall be interested in who requests which committees and why. But before explanations are in order, it is useful to transmit some feel for the context in which the individual Congressman fleshes out his own interests and objectives.

Freshman Request Activities

Beginning with their arrival in Washington in the post-election period, if not earlier, most new members initiate a series of meetings with members of the CC, party leaders, state delegation colleagues, and other freshmen to discuss committee assignments. For some, the experience is not unlike that of an immigrant arriving at Ellis Island. Suffering from culture shock and the normal anxieties of a career and lifestyle change, the new member only vaguely comprehends the ways of his new home, the Washington community, and is a bit uncertain about how to proceed. Patricia Schroeder (D., Col.), for example, remarked on her arrival in Washington in late 1972:

> I came out here never having run for office before, not knowing anyone back here....I hadn't been here since my eighth grade Mariner Scouts field trip. I got here and everybody tells me it's dog-eat-dog and I think, "This will be impossible."[5]

For others the Washington community is more familiar terrain. Some have had previous terms of service in the House. The Ninety-fourth Congress freshman class included Robert Duncan (D., Ore)., Andrew Jacobs (D., Ind.), Abner Mikva (D., Ill.), Richard Ottinger (D., N.Y.), and James Scheuer (D., N.Y.), all of whom had served in previous Congresses. Others have put in time in Washington, on the Hill or in the executive branch. Ninety-fourth Congress freshman James Oberstar (D., Minn.), for example, was the former administrative assistant to John Blatnik (D., Minn.); Ninety-third Congress freshman Trent Lott (R., Miss.) had served in the same capacity for William Colmer (D., Miss.); Ninety-fourth Congress freshmen Toby Moffett (D., Conn.) and Timothy Wirth (D., Col.) each had previous executive branch experience, the former as director of the Office of Students and Youth in the Nixon administration and the latter as special asssistant to the secretary of HEW in the Johnson administration. Still others have contacts and acquaintances on the Hill from previous political activities, campaigning, candidate schools, and party gatherings.

Despite variations in familiarity with the House and linkages to it, most freshmen use the opportunity of these early meetings to accomplish two purposes regarding their requests for committee assignments: *uncertainty reduction* and *self-advertisement.*

Uncertainty Reduction

Member uncertainty is of two sorts. First, he is not always certain which committees will best serve his own interests. Committee jurisdictions are complex and committee politics is often unfamiliar to the new member. Interactions with "interested others" are sources of information on each of these matters.[6] Second, a member seeks information about appointment probabilities. In sounding out his own zone representative, the party leaders, and colleagues from the state delegation, he garners information about likely vacancies on committees and probable competition for those slots. He also elicits information about who is likely to support his request for which committees.

Consequently, members contemplating which committees to request seek advice and counsel on two questions:

1. What is the value of a particular committee to me in accomplishing my goals?
2. What is the likelihood I will be assigned to it if I request it?

Each of these considerations poses complicated estimation problems. The "value" problem requires, first of all, introspection; What committees am I interested in? Which will be most productive in terms of my goals? Which will be most useful to me in daily interactions with my colleagues and constituents? Introspection, however, is incomplete in the absence of information

—a commodity in short supply for many new members. They will need to lean on others in an effort to resolve their "value" problem. Out of these interactions emerges some sense of the relative worth of various committees to the member; preferences for some committees are beginning to take form.

While preferences are of prima facie importance in the request calculation, they are not always what, in fact, are *revealed* in the request list submitted to the CC. Preferences are modified chiefly by *expectations of successful assignment*. Thus, to take a telling example, while the Appropriations Committee is probably "valued" by most freshmen, it is rarely requested. No more than about 10 percent of the freshmen in the Eighty-sixth through Ninety-third Congresses actually revealed a preference for this committee. The reason is clear: a request for Appropriations is a bad bet for a freshman. During the seven Congresses for which request data are available, only five Democratic freshmen won assignment to Appropriations: Billie Farnum (Mich.) and Sidney Yates (Ill.) in the Eighty-ninth Congress, David Pryor (Ark.) in the Ninetieth Congress, and Gunn McKay (Utah) and J. Edward Roush (Ind.) in the Ninety-second Congress.[7]

If some committees are bad bets for a particular freshman, then we should expect him to be less likely to apply for them, even if he places high value on winning these assignments.[8] That is, most freshmen *discount* their evaluations by the conditional probability of winning the assignments they request. Here, too, the member is faced with a complicated estimation problem: what is the likelihood that I will win assignment to the ———— Committee if I request it? In this problem, as in his value problem, he must rely on introspection, intuition, and consultation with interested others.

Self-Advertisement

Despite her initial unfamiliarity with the House and its modes of operation, Congresswoman Schroeder nailed down one of the few assignments to the Armed Services Committee in the Ninety-third Congress. According to one account of her successful campaign for this assignment,

> She worked hard for the position she got. First she discussed the matter with Frank E. Evans (D., Col.), the dean of her delegation. Then she visited Speaker Albert, Majority Leader O'Neill and assignment committee members such as Al Ullman (D., Ore) and James A. Burke (D., Mass.).
>
> "Ullman was very helpful," Schroeder said. "He told me, 'What you must do immediately is see every member on Ways and Means. Talk to them and try to get their support.' I talked to [Armed Services Committee] Chairman Hebert, but he wasn't terribly receptive. That's why I did all these other things, because I didn't think he'd be too receptive."[9]

Although Schroeder was a genuine unknown to her new House colleagues, her situation is rather common for freshmen. Most freshmen have only a limited set of linkages with the House. Rarely are they very well known beyond their state borders, and often they are not even well known within the ranks of their own state delegation. Certainly those who will shortly be making assignment determinations know little about the freshmen beyond whatever gossip they have come across and the thumbnail biographical sketches with which the CC staff provides them.

Since there is a paucity of information about most freshmen in the system, and since, as a result, many early decisions about freshmen hinge on idiosyncratic, personal variables, courtesy visits are a natural device through which a new member introduces and promotes himself to those who may have impact on his committee assignments. Although uncertainty-reduction and self-promotion encourage most new members to "make the rounds"—and this is true of both the novice and the freshman with experience—there is still the occasional freshman who takes a casual approach to the matter of committee assignments, as indicated by one of the participants in a Brooking Roundtable:

> I came to Congress without any ideas about what committee I should be on. I had had enough trouble getting elected! Although I flattered myself that I was reasonably well informed and that I kept up on current problems by doing a normal amount of reading, I recognized that I had no depth of knowledge in a specific area. There was no special niche I wanted to fill. I put myself in the hands of my representative on the Committee on Committees, feeling he would obtain a decent assignment for me. [Clapp 1964, p. 208]

Said another:

> I feel that it was unfortunate for me that I came in as a member of the majority and also from a safe district. My predecessor had been here for many years and was the top man from our party on his committee. The work was of special interest to me, and I took it for granted that I would be considered for the vacancy created by his retirement. No one else on our delegation wanted the assignment. I made no organized effort to get it but rather naively thought it would fall into my lap like a ripe plum. [Clapp 1964, p. 225]

James Corman (D., Cal.), himself a member of the CC during the period of this study, confirms that one should take nothing for granted:

> When I first came here, California had no Democrat on Judiciary. And I wanted it very badly. But my man on Ways and Means said, "Don't worry about it. I'll take care of it." And I didn't get it. If I'd gone around to see all the Ways and Means members, I think I could have gotten Judiciary.[10]

*Submitting Requests
and Campaigning for
Assignment*

With whatever information and advice he has been able to extract from his interactions, the new member submits to his zone representative on the CC, in writing, a partial listing of committees in order of preference. Though encouraged to submit more than one preference, the new member is discouraged from submitting too long a list. The modal list contains two or three committees.[11] The final product that emerges—the member's request list—is a complicated mix of individual goals and ambitions, modified by newly acquired advice and information, and tempered by political realities.

Member requests are motivated chiefly by the kind of district they represent and their personal background and experiences. For some congressmen, these factors alone are determinate. Rural, midwestern, and southern Democrats, especially those with farm backgrounds, tend to seek membership on the Agriculture Committee; big-city Democrats find Banking and Currency, and Education and Labor, attractive assignments; western Congressmen request the Interior Committee in large numbers. For these members, constituency service and policy interests closely tied to reelection dictate committee requests. Former Congressman Frank Smith (D., Miss). believed that close attention to the needs of his Mississippi delta district was the sine qua non of his own legislative flexibility:

> When I came to the House of Representatives, I wanted to be a responsible member, with both a voice and a vote in historic decisions made by the Congress. If my constituents were to give me this freedom, I felt that I had to render them special service in areas of major concern to the district. This called for specialization in flood control and water resource development, which in turn required membership on the House Public Works Committee. [Smith 1964, p. 128]

For other members, especially those from heterogenous districts, constituency interests are less uniform and consequently less determinate of the particular mix of committees appearing on the member's request list. These members, that is, are suggestible. Their personal goals and ambitions do not strongly predispose them toward any single committee (though usually to some subset of committees). They are open to influence and, indeed, often seek out advice on how their reelection and policy interests might best be served. For these members, and to a lesser extent members from more homogenous districts, the availability of state committee vacancies, the needs of the state delegation, the likelihood of competition, and the predisposition of their zone representatives tend to combine with their heterogeneous district needs to produce their request list.

One thing is clear: congressmen are different. Their personal backgrounds and constituency coalitions vary; the particular mix of goals and ambitions differs from member to member; and, in their decisions to request this or that committee, different values are decisive. Committee requests reflect this diversity.[12]

In sum, member goals and objectives are given operational clarity and focus, and to some extent are modified, by the information and advice acquired during the early days preceding the organization of the new Congress. The *revealed preferences* for committee assignments that are passed on to the freshman's CC representative, then, reflect the operational compromises and tradeoffs of instrumental behavior in a context of competition for scarce committee berths.

In early January each member of the CC receives a reminder from John Martin, chief counsel to the Ways and Means Committee and the person with primary responsibility for overseeing the staff work related to committee assignments, urging him to complete the collection of requests from the members of his zone and pass them in to the CC staff for compilation.[13] Also at this time, although implicitly it has been going on all along, campaigning for committee assignments commences. While there are, of course, wide variations in approaches, most members aim their efforts at their man on the CC. He is the first major hurdle inasmuch as his failure to nominate a member for a committee berth in the executive sessions of the CC all but quashes that member's chances.

Most members solicit support in behalf of their requests, if not explicit endorsement, from their state delegations, committee chairmen, interest-group leaders, and political figures outside the House. In some cases this effort mushrooms into a full-fledged political campaign:

I called the dean of my delegation and told him my committee preference. He said he would speak to our man on Ways and Means. On the way back from my vacation, I stopped by Bonham, Texas, and spent about five hours there [with Rayburn] and let him lead the conversation. When he asked me what committee I was interested in, I told him. Then I had Adlai Stevenson, the national chairman, and some other people write the Speaker, the Majority Leader, the Whip, and the chairman of Ways and Means in my behalf, and I wrote all of these people myself. Some friends who are close to John McCormack wrote to him and went to see him on my behalf. Another important party leader wrote McCormack and my Ways and Means man about my background, which happened to be appropriate for the committee I wanted.

In addition I phoned some people once I learned they were leaving the committee. I also talked with several other members of Congress whose judgment I valued. Then I called on the committee chairman. I didn't know whether there would be competition for the committee, but I wanted the assignment very much.

.   .   .   .

I wanted a seat on the Agriculture Committee. My experience in the state legislature made me realize that you just don't get things automatically. You have to go after them. I had the support of our member on the Committee on Committees and I also sought out other influential members of that committee.[14]

The arguments members muster in behalf of their requests emphasize the approval and support they have received from others, state and regional claims including the maintenance of state representation (same-state norm), electoral needs, and previous experience. A hint of the forms these arguments take, as well as their relative frequency, may be gleaned from table 3.1, a tabulation of the letters sent to one former member of the CC during two Congresses in which he participated in the committee assignment process.[15]

Table 3.1   **Letters to a Member of the Committee on Committees, 88th–89th Congresses**

Arguments Mentioned on Behalf of Applicants	N	%
Endorsement by Others		
Reported by applicant	9	7.8
Reported by colleagues	31	26.7
Reported by interest groups	3	2.6
Total	43	37.1
Geography		
State or region replacement	14	12.1
State or region needs	18	15.5
Total	32	27.6
Electoral Needs		
District, constituency characteristics	15	12.9
Other	8	6.9
Total	23	19.8
Experience		
Personal background	11	9.5
State government	4	3.4
Other	3	2.6
Total	18	15.5
	116	100.0

Source: Achen and Stolarek (1974), p. 4.

The campaign terminates when the CC goes into executive session to make the actual committee selections, though on very rare occasions a campaign is carried all the way to the Democratic Caucus, which must ratify CC decisions.

This brief preview of the events leading up to committee assignments suggests that, for most members, committee assignments are a serious matter. They devote time and effort to the problem of defining their own interests; once they define those interests, they energetically promote them and enlist the support and assistance of their peers. Success depends, though in no straightforward fashion, on good fortune, strategic calculation, and time and energy. "No single strategy can assure the newcomer of the assignment he wants. . . . Perhaps the only certainty is that a good assignment is worth striving for" (Clapp 1964, p. 240).

Nonfreshmen Requests

The returning incumbent has several behavioral options open to him concerning his committee assignments. One which is frequently adopted is the *status-quo option*. Many members reveal, by their behavior, a desire to maintain their previous membership(s) and to acquire no additional committee assignments. A second alternative, one that only marginally alters the status quo, is the *dual-service option*. With this option a member seeks to acquire an additional committee assignment while still retaining his previous assignment. There is, finally, the *transfer option* according to which a member agrees to surrender (some of) his current committee position(s) in exchange for one or more other, presumably more desirable, committee slots. In explaining who seeks transfer and dual service assignments (and when), and who chooses to remain on his initial assignments, it is useful to regard a committee as a "queue" and to conceive of nonfreshman request decisions as involving a consideration of the benefits and costs of queue-switching.

The Costs and Benefits of the Queue

A committee, in many respects, is a *queue*: length of continuous committee service determines queue position; movement along the queue depends upon a member's own survival characteristics and those of his colleagues ahead of him in the queue; the benefits of waiting in the queue depend on one's goals and queue position, the latter of which, in turn, depends on continuous time in the queue;[16] and the real costs of waiting in the queue are the foregone opportunities offered by other queues. In considering a committee transfer, then, a rational member evaluates the benefits of securing alternative committee assignment(s) and compares them to the costs of a move, namely, the benefits associated with his current committee assignments which he must forego.

When a member reveals a transfer preference, he reveals a belief that his goals and objectives will be better served on some other committee. This belief may derive from any one of several sources. First, as is shown below, not every member receives his first-preference committee as a freshman. Indeed, some receive none of the committees they request. By their own previous behavior, then, one group of members has revealed preferences for committees other than those on which they currently sit.

Second, as we have already hinted, the committee preferences of the freshmen are often the culmination of a calculus in which "interest" is *discounted* by features in the competitive environment. Their requests are not *sincere*, that is, undiscounted, revelations of interest. In the new Congress there are new opportunities, a changed competitive environment, and the considerably reduced cost of revealing sincere preferences (because of the property-right norm).

Third, nonfreshmen are in a position to act upon their interests more effectively than freshmen. After a year or so of experience, the nonfreshman's familiarity with the House, its committees, and their jurisdictions may lead him to reassess his earlier evaluation of various committees and their utility for him. For example, as data presented shortly show, there has been a substantial egress of nonfreshmen from Banking and Currency and Education and Labor to other semiexclusive committees. There is additional interview evidence (see Fenno 1973) suggesting that service on these two committees is often frustrating and unproductive.

Fourth, and most obviously, a desire to transfer may be related to changing goals. In a few cases—due to redistricting or to demographic changes—a member's constituency has changed. More often, a member's ambition for power in the House or for higher office leads him to request a transfer to a committee more appropriate to his new objectives. ,

For any one of these reasons, or some combination of them, a nonfreshman will perceive benefits in joining a different queue. Yet many nonfreshmen remain in the queue they initially joined as freshmen. The reasons, as Jewell and Chi-hung (1974, pp. 433–34) remind us, are the costs of queue switching:

> there are costs as well as benefits in shifting committees, and these costs increase in direct proportion to the member's seniority. The most obvious cost of shifting committees is that a member must give up his seniority on one committee in order to start at the bottom of the seniority ladder on another. The member who moves usually postpones the date on which he becomes a chairman (or ranking minority member) of a committee or subcommittee. In addition to the loss of seniority, a member who shifts committees gives up at least some of the advantages

that he has gained through the accumulation of specialized knowledge in one area and the establishment of working relationships with other committee members. In other words, there are costs of "beginning again" on a committee beyond those of losing formal seniority rank.

Thus, investments—committee seniority, policy expertise, contacts in the administrative bureaucracy—and consumption, e.g., friendship ties with committee members and staff, must be sacrificed in order to effect a transfer. "Consequently, options enticing to a congressman when he is a freshman or sophomore may hold little allure after he has spent several terms on a committee" (Bullock 1973a, p. 90).

Chapters 4 and 5 focus on statistical accounts of the request behavior of freshmen and nonfreshmen, respectively. There the "discounted value problem" for freshmen and the "cost and benefits of the queue problem" for nonfreshmen are given operational content and meaning and statistical models are estimated. Freshmen and nonfreshmen are analyzed separately because their situations differ and, consequently, their calculations and behavior differ. In the remainder of this chapter some quick statistical glimpses are provided.

General Patterns of
Freshman Requests

Freshmen are not all alike. They have different interests, values, and goals; they represent different constituencies; and they may feel beholden to coalitions with very diverse concerns. The committee system—composed of jurisdiction-specific subunits[17]—accommodates this diversity. Committees have differential appeal to members. But, more importantly, *the differential appeal varies from member to member*. Consequently, "it is probably a mistake to speak of *a* or *the* committee stratification system without specifying for which particular group of Congressmen the committee ranking is assumed to hold" (Bullock and Sprague 1969, p. 496).

Committee preferences are revealed early in the committee assignment process in the form of a committee request list. Each freshman submits such a list to his zone representative on the CC. The representative, in turn, forwards these lists to John Martin, Chief Counsel to the Ways and Means Committee, who compiles a request book that is made available to the members of the CC at their formal sessions. The data of interest in this section are the request lists of Democratic freshmen in the Eighty-sixth through Ninety-third Congresses. These are presented in table 3.2.

The first thing to note in table 3.2 is the variety of revealed preferences. Only two of the twenty standing committees (Budget, Small Business, and Standards of Official Conduct are deleted throughout this analysis) received a

Table 3.2   **Freshman Requests, Frequency, 86th–93rd Congresses**
(N = 231)

Committee	Total No. of Requests	% of Members Requesting	% of Requests First Choice
Agriculture	44	19	50
Appropriations	26	11	69
Armed Services	53	24	53
Banking and Currency	59	25	57
District of Columbia	7	3	0
Education & Labor	46	20	35
Foreign Affairs	39	17	51
Government Operations	39	17	5
House Administration	6	2	0
Interior	56	24	25
Interstate	78	34	35
Judiciary	45	20	40
Merchant Marine & Fisheries	13	6	8
P.O. & C.S.	21	9	14
Public Works	65	28	34
Rules	2	1	100
Science & Astronautics	38	16	29
Un-American Activities	5	2	20
Veterans Affairs	16	7	13
Ways & Means	1	0	0
Total	659		

NOTE: N is the number of freshmen *submitting requests*. In the
86th Congress some freshmen requests were never
formally submitted.

modest number of requests—Ways and Means and Rules. In the first case, the
one request recorded for Ways and Means was misdirected—the party
caucus, not the CC, chooses members of that important committee. In the
case of Rules, the small number of requests is accounted for by the small size
of the committee, the few vacancies to be filled, the role played by the party
leadership in recruiting for this important agenda committee, and the
extremely unlikely prospect of a freshman appointment.[18] The most requested
committee, Interstate and Foreign Commerce, attracted the requests of more
than a third of all the freshmen. Closely following it, attracting the interest
of about one-fourth of all freshmen, are Armed Services, Banking and Currency, Interior, and Public Works. In fact, nearly half of all requests were
distributed among these five committees. A glance at the jurisdictions of
these committees—public housing, urban renewal, transportation and

communications, power transmission, public health, highways, water power and pollution, public lands, mineral resources, oversight of regulatory agencies, selective service, authorization for prime military contracts—reveals that, during the 1960s and early 1970s at least, this is where the action was. Some of the most salient social and political issues of the times fell within the purview of these committees.

These modal patterns, however, should not deflect attention from the fact that all committees attracted some interest from freshmen. The least-requested committees include the prestige committees—Appropriations, Rules, and Ways and Means—a fact alluded to above. Joining them are a number of "duty" or "housekeeping" committees whose jurisdictions are limited and highly specialized: District of Columbia, House Administration, Merchant Marine and Fisheries, Un-American Activities (renamed Internal Security), and Veterans Affairs.[19] In the middle range of request popularity are the remaining substantive committees.

Not only did all of the committees attract requests; with few exceptions, most committees were placed first on some freshmen's request list. Rules led the way with 100% of the requests for that committee being first-preference requests. Following it were Appropriations (69%), Banking and Currency (57%), Armed Services (53%), Foreign Affairs (51%), Agriculture (50%), and Judiciary (40%).

We have begun by conceiving of the committee system as an *opportunity structure*. For members it is their point of access to the institutional resources which may assist them in achieving their goals. The diversity of requests revealed in table 3.2 mirrors the variety of goals, interests, and concerns entertained by members that are differentially served by the committees. Moreover, even for those members who share goals in common, it is not unusual to find them revealing preferences for different committees; the imperfect demarcation of committee jurisdictions, for example, has enabled many substantive matters to be spread among several committees. Opportunity, then, is imbedded in the structure of the committee system. "House members...match their individual patterns of aspiration to the diverse patterns of opportunity presented by House committees. The matching process usually takes place as a congressman seeks an initial assignment...to a committee he believes well suited to his goals" (Fenno 1973, p. 1).

To make this point more forcefully, table 3.3 partitions freshmen according to two district characteristics—region and population density.[20] For each combination of these characteristics the most frequently requested committees are listed. Despite the fact that a number of important factors have not been controlled for in the table—factors we shall want to scrutinize more closely in the next chapter—a number of interesting patterns emerge suggesting some systematic variations in committee attractiveness.

Table 3.3   **House Committees Most Requested by Freshmen, 86th–93rd Congresses (By Region and Population Density)**

Region[a]	Density[b]	N[c]	Committees	% Requesting
South	Sparse	31	Commerce	39
			Agriculture	32
			Public Works	26
			Banking & Currency	26
Midwest	Sparse	27	Agriculture	45
			Public Works	41
			Interior	41
			Commerce	37
West	Sparse	31	Interior	71
			Public Works	39
East	Medium	20	Armed Services	40
			Public Works	35
South	Medium	17	Commerce	35
Midwest	Medium	18	Commerce	50
			Judiciary	33
East	Dense	28	Banking & Currency	54
			Commerce	54
			Judiciary	36
Midwest	Dense	13	Banking & Currency	46
			Education & Labor	39
			Judiciary	31
West	Dense	12	Banking & Currency	75
			Commerce	58
			Education & Labor	33
			Foreign Affairs	25

NOTE: I have excluded from the table those categories for which either the N is too small (fewer than 10) or no committee was requested by at least 25% of the members.

[a] East: Conn., Del., Me., Mass., N.H., N. J., N. Y., Penn., R.I., Vt.
Border: Ky., Md., Mo., Okla., W.Va.
South: Ala., Ark., Fla., Ga., La., Miss., N.C., S.C., Tenn., Tex., Va.
Midwest: Ill., Ind., Ia., Kan., Mich., Minn., Neb., N.D., Ohio., S.D., Wis.
West: Alaska, Ariz., Cal., Col., Haw., Id., Mont., Nev., N.M., Ore., Utah., Wash., Wyo.

[b] Population per square mile indicated by:
Sparse: fewer than 100 people/sq. mi.
Medium: between 100 and 1,000 people/sq. mi.
Dense: more than 1,000 people/sq. mi.

[c] N is the number of members in the category.

The two most impressive entries in the table are the Interior Committee for western congressmen from sparsely populated districts, nearly three-fourths of whom expressed an interest, and the Banking and Currency Committee for westerners from highly urbanized districts, again attracting three-fourths of these members' requests. In each of these cases, constituency service concerns, the bases of electoral support, and public policy interests neatly mesh with committee jurisdictions. At the opposite extreme is the Commerce Committee. Not only is it the most requested committee in the aggregate (table 3.2); it is highly sought-after by members in most of the categories of table 3.3.

Members do not submit a *complete* rank ordering of all standing committees to the CC. Indeed, only one member in the seven Congresses for which data are available submitted a request list with as many as nine committees on it. The modal request list contains three committees, and 90% of all freshmen include no more than four (see table 3.4). There are two forces at

Table 3.4	The Length of Freshman Preference-Orderings, 86th–93rd Congresses

Length of Preference Ordering[a]	%
1	23
2	16
3	36
4	15
5 or more	10
	100%
	(N = 231)

[a] Dual-service requests have been omitted.

work to keep request lists relatively short. First, zone representatives often instruct the freshmen for whom they are responsible to keep their request lists short. Zone representatives attempt to encourage information economies whenever feasible. A second reason why short request lists are to be expected derives from an interpretation of the information these lists transmit. A request list partitions committees into two sets: those that are desirable for the requester and those that are not. Evidence on assigments suggests that the CC goes to considerable lengths to give requesters something on their lists. In submitting requests, then, members are not "waltzing before a blind audience." The CC treats the preferences revealed on request lists as "satisfactory and sufficient" for the member and tries, for reasons elucidated below, to honor them. While the CC appears to make some slight distinction between first-preference requests and those lower on a member's list, the primary distinction made is between those committees *listed* and those *not listed*. To the extent that the CC tries to satisfy requests, it follows a path of least resistance; that is, it tries to satisfy requests for a given member in the least costly manner. Thus, for example, it is more likely to assign a member to a requested committee on which there are many vacancies to be filled and few competitors for the slots than to assign him to a committee with larger "excess demand." This will be true even if the latter is higher on the member's request list. In effect, then, the longer a member's list, the more "degrees of freedom" he gives the CC—and the greater are his chances of receiving a relatively less-preferred assignment.[21]

The interpretation of the request list as an information transmission device giving the CC "degrees of freedom" focuses on two strategic features of the request decision. The first, which we have briefly examined, revolves around *which* committees to request. The second involves *how many* committees to include on the request list. For the reasons just given, the theoretical expectation is that request lists will be relatively short, ceteris paribus. Of course, all things are not equal, and it is precisely these situational differences that permit some insight about the decision to expand or contract the request list. More precisely, variations in the member's "situation" allow for the formulation of several testable propositions about the length of the request list.

Initially let us consider the decision as faced by freshmen and nonfreshmen. These two groups of congressmen face decidedly distinct situations. The freshman has no committee assignments at all. While he desires good assignments, the only thing he knows for certain is that he will be assigned to *some* committee. Any committee assignment is possible, the range of alternatives available to the CC is maximal, and the member is entirely at the mercy of the CC. The nonfreshman, on the other hand, is protected by the property-right norm. He may retain the committee slots he held in the previous Congress. Consequently, he need never fear receiving an assignment inferior to the one he currently holds. Moreover, the range of subjectively more preferable committees is likely to be relatively limited.

From these differences in the strategic situation of the freshman and nonfreshman I hypothesize that freshman request lists will tend to be longer than nonfreshman request lists. The relative vulnerability and riskiness of his situation encourages the freshman to provide the CC with some degrees of freedom. The nonfreshman has less need for insurance of this sort.

A comparison of tables 3.4 and 3.5 confirms the expectation. The modal request-list length for freshmen and nonfreshmen is three and one, respectively. While more than nine out of every ten nonfreshmen seeking transfers

Table 3.5   **The Length of Nonfreshman Preference-Orderings, 86th–93rd Congresses**

Length of Preference Ordering[a]	%
1	84
2	8
3	5
4	2
5 or more	1
	100% (N = 130)

[a] Dual-service requests have been omitted.

submit short lists (two or fewer requests), only 39% of all freshmen behave similarly.[22]

The comparison of the distributions of freshmen and nonfreshmen in tables 3.4 and 3.5 is striking. Yet there is still some within-group variance to be explained. A more detailed treatment of nonfreshman transfer requests is reserved for Chapter 5, but it is interesting to note that none of the nine nonfreshmen with "long" lists were successful *as freshmen* in receiving any of their initial requests. Indeed, one nonfreshman who listed five committees to which he would be willing to transfer failed, as a freshman, to receive any of the four committees he requested. Instead he was relegated to two nonexclusive committees, Government Operations and Merchant Marine and Fisheries, with which he was undoubtedly displeased. Three of his five transfer requests were repeat requests.

The length of freshman request lists appears to be particularly sensitive to strategic features of the opportunity structure. From table 3.4 it is seen that 39% of all freshmen submit short lists (two or fewer requests) and 61% long lists (three or more requests). Suppose now that we partition the freshmen into two groups according to whether or not their first-preference committee has a state vacancy.[23] Within each of these groups we may examine the relationship between the length of the preference ordering and the presence or absence of state competition for that first-preference slot. The data on freshmen with first preference state vacancies are given in table 3.6. Once again a very significant statistical difference is suggested. Among those freshmen with first-preference state vacancies for which there was state competition, fewer than one in ten submitted a short list; if, on the other hand, there was no state competition for the vacancies, nearly eight out of every ten submitted short lists. It would appear that freshmen with state competition hedge their

Table 3.6   **State Vacancies, State Competition, and Freshman Requests, 86th–93rd Congresses**

Request List Length[a]	State Competition (N = 23)[b]	No State Competition (N = 28)
Short	9%	79%
Long	91%	21%

NOTE: There are 51 applicants whose *first-preference* request is for a slot vacated by a member from his state. Of these, 23 are faced with competition from some other member in his state delegation in the sense that some other member from the state has listed this committee somewhere (not necessarily first) in his request list.

a A "short" list is two or fewer entries. A "long" list is three or more.

b A member is said to have "state competition" for a state vacancy if some other member of his delegation is also applying for the slot.

bets by expanding their preference ordering. Freshmen with no state competition have no need to do so. Many of them, in fact, have the backing and endorsement of their state delegations for the assignment.

For most freshmen there is no state vacancy on their most-preferred committee.[24] Within the "no state vacancy" group those with and those without state competition differ little in the length of their preference ordering, either from one another or from the general distribution of table 3.4. Both subgroups of the "no state vacancy" group are somewhat more likely to submit modal request lists. The variance, that is, in the length of their request list is reduced.

In short, when there are state vacancies the presence or absence of state competitors appears to distort the preference-ordering length in opposite directions. With no state competitors the applicant regards his request as a virtual "lock" on the slot; when there are state competitors applicants respond to the risk by hedging their bets.[25]

While some patterns have emerged from this general examination of requests, the more basic message, I believe, is that situationally specific factors rather than cruder surrogate categories contain a more substantial chunk of explanatory power. The situational differences revealed in the comparison of freshmen and nonfreshmen in tables 3.4 and 3.5, and the competitive differences among freshmen revealed in table 3.6, begin to indicate these situationally specific factors. A more precise analysis requires a committee-by-committee inquiry.

While the number of observations and the frequency of behavior are insufficient for an examination of all committees, in the next chapter I sharpen the focus considerably by concentrating on a handful of committees. Although the situational factors will ordinarily differ from committee to committee and from member to member, the fact that committee jurisdictions do not partition policy domains perfectly, and that a member's goals may be served by any of a number of assignments, suggests that variations in request behavior will not be explained completely by variations in situation. That is, because of the richness of opportunities provided by the committee system similarly situated members may display slightly different request behavior, and differently situated members may submit request lists which overlap.

A hint of this is revealed in table 3.7. In this table I examine the interlocking

Table 3.7   **Interlocking Freshman Requests, 86th–93rd Congresses**

	Ag	AS	B&C	E&L	FA	Int.	IFC	Jud.	PW	S&A	N*
Agriculture	—	16	26	18	16	36	34	8	31	18	38
Armed Services	12	—	20	16	10	24	24	27	35	27	49
Banking & Currency	20	20	—	28	22	14	46	20	30	20	51
Education & Labor	16	18	35	—	35	25	41	23	35	12	44
Foreign Affairs	16	13	30	41	—	24	35	27	22	19	37
Interior	28	24	14	22	18	—	36	20	39	18	49
Interstate	20	17	34	25	18	25	—	25	32	14	71
Judiciary	7	34	24	24	24	24	43	—	14	14	41
Public Works	20	28	26	26	14	34	37	10	—	10	60
Science & Astro.	21	39	30	15	21	27	30	18	18	—	34

* N is the number of freshmen requesting the row committee, excluding those whose request list contains *only* that row committee. The cell entries in each row are the percentage of N requesting the column committee. Since multiple requests are permitted, rows do not sum to 100%. Cells with entries as large as 30% are underscored.

requests among most of the substantive committees.[26] A number of predictable patterns emerge: 39% of all Science and Astronautics applicants request Armed Services; 39% of all Interior applicants also ask for Public Works; 35% of all Education and Labor applicants also list Foreign Affairs; 41% of all Foreign Affairs applicants request Education and Labor.[27] I designate these relationships as "predictable" solely on the basis of the jurisdictions of these committees and the goals that service on them facilitates. The more interesting feature of this table is that, with the few exceptions just noted, there is an incredible variety of request patterns. While some requests may reasonably be expected to interlock (I have underlined all entries that exceed 30%), it is nevertheless surprising how widely dispersed these requests appear. In this respect, perhaps the only committees for which dispersion in interlocking requests is not surprising are Interstate and Public Works, whose wide-ranging jurisdictions and consequent popularity have been noted earlier.

General Patterns of Nonfreshman Transfer Request

In the remainder of this chapter I briefly anticipate the analysis of Chapter 5 with some discussion of the concepts with which nonfreshman transfer activities will be examined and some illustrative examples drawn from the data. Unlike other studies of committee transfers,[28] this one does not limit the analysis to a comparison of those who *actually* transfer (or take on an additional assignment) and those who do not. Rather, the notion of *revealed preference for transfer* (dual service) is employed:

> Committee C_1 is *revealed/preferred* to committee C_2 by a member if (1) the member *requests a transfer* from C_2 (his current committee) to C_1, or (2) the member *actually transfers* from C_2 to C_1, or both.
>
> A *dual-service preference* is revealed by (1) a dual-service *request*, or (2) the *acquisition* of a dual-service committee, or both.

The transfer and dual-service options, then, are identified either by request, actual acquisition of new committees, or both. The status-quo option is exercised when neither request nor actual transfer occurs.

The rationale for these concepts is straightforward. Neither actual transfers (dual-service acquisitions) nor requests for transfer (dual service) are, individually, comprehensive as indicators of the demand for mobility in the committee system. Actual transfers are only the tip of the iceberg. While about half of those who request transfers have their request honored (and hence may be identified by looking at actual transfers), half do not. On the other hand, those who actually transfer or accept a dual-service appointment are not selected exclusively from among those who submit requests. Some are contacted during the actual meeting of the CC and asked to transfer or to accept an additional assignment.[29] Others have only informally indicated their desire to alter their committee assignments. Their "requests" are not entered in the request book compiled by John Martin and are made known by the appropriate zone representative only at the time of the CC's meeting.

Table 3.8 tabulates all revealed transfer and dual-service preferences for the Eighty-sixth through Ninety-fourth Congresses. Each cell records the number of members who actually transferred to or requested a transfer to the column committee from the row committee. There were, for example, five revealed preferences for an Interior transfer during this period: one each from Science and Astronautics, Merchant Marine and Fisheries, and House Administration, and two from Government Operations; in addition there were twenty-five dual-service requests for Interior.[30]

The committees in this table have been ordered to minimize the entries above the diagonal in order to give some indication of relative popularity. Two notable exceptions to the otherwise strong pattern are Armed Services and Science and Astronautics. In the Eighty-sixth Congress, two members of Armed Services, Overton Brooks of Louisiana and George Miller of California, left the committee for the newly created Science and Astronautics Committee, the former as chairman and the latter as one of its subcommittee chairmen.[31] Revealed preferences for Science and Astronautics follow something of a "boom and bust" cycle that is correlated with the fate of the space program. Most "transfers to" occurred prior to the Ninety-first Congress during the height of the manned space program. As priorities shifted in the Ninety-second and Ninety-third Congresses, the frequency of "transfers from" Science and Astronautics to committees above the diagonal increased dramatically.

With these and a few other exceptions excluded, the general pattern of revealed transfers is unidirectional: committees lower down on the list serve as suppliers for those higher up. One committee, Veterans Affairs, is a universal supplier;[32] three committees, Appropriations, Ways and Means, and Rules, are universal recipients.[33] Notice that, despite this general pattern, the rank ordering, per se, does not always have an unequivocal meaning. Empirically, the aggregate revealed preference relationship is incomplete in each of two senses:

1. For some pairs of committees, no expression of revealed preference is displayed;
2. For other pairs of committees, the number who reveal prefer the first to the second equals the number who reveal prefer the second to the first.

When a cell below the diagonal and its mirror image above the diagonal are empty, condition (1) is satisfied; examples include all the pairwise comparisons of the exclusive committees, Armed Services-Judiciary, Foreign Affairs-Judiciary, Public Works-Foreign Affairs, etc. When a cell below the diagonal and its mirror image above the diagonal have the same entries, condition (2) is satisfied; examples include Interior-Science and Astronautics, and Science

Table 3.8

FROM \ TO	Approp.	W&M	Rules
Approp.	—		
W&M		—	
Rules			—
Armed Ser.	2	1	
For. Aff.	2	1	2
Jud.	1	3	1
Interst.	3	2	
Pub. Wks.	1		1
S&A	5	3	4
Agr.	6	4	1
E&L	9	2	1
B&C	6	2	1
Interior	11	2	1
HUAC	2	1	
Gov. Op.	2	2	1
MMF	6	2	
PO&CS	9	1	1
H. Adm.	2	3	1
DC	3		
VA	5		
DS Requests	—	—	—
Total	75	29	15

and Astronautics-Government Operations. Finally, it should be emphasized that preferences are *subjective*. The popularity ordering, though an aggregate indicator, does not imply any homogenity of tastes, interests, or objectives. "Different strokes for different folks" is still the order of the day.[34]

To discuss nonfreshman transfers, I focus on a special data set. Revealed preferences, as defined above, are examined for all Democrats who:

1. were freshmen in the Eighty-sixth through Ninety-third Congresses inclusive;
2. Submitted freshman requests for initial assignments,
3. were reelected at least once.

Of the 231 freshman Democrats for whom there is request data, only 57 failed in their initial reelection bids. Consequently, our data set consists of 174 Democrats elected between 1958 and 1972. Since the sophomore term is the

Revealed Transfer Preferences, 86th–94th Congresses

Armed Ser.	For. Aff.	Jud.	Interst.	Pub. Wks.	S&A	Agri.	E&L	B&C	Interior	HUAC	Gov. Op.	MMF	PO&CS	H. Adm.	DC	VA	Total
																	0
																	0
																	0
—				2													5
1	—																6
		—															5
1		1	—														7
		1	5	—													8
3	1	2	2		—		1	1	1	1	1			1			26
3	1				1	—						1					17
		2	1	1	2	1	—										19
5	1		3	1	3	1		—									23
2	4			1	1			1	—	1				1			25
										—							3
1				1		1	1			2	—		1				12
1	3		1	2	1		1	1	1		2	—		1			22
2	3	1	1	2		3	1		1		1		—				26
1	1		1	1	2		1	1		1	2			—	1		18
			3	1								4	3	—			14
1	3	1	2		3	1	1				2		2			—	21
1	3	1	2	5	7	2	2	—	25	4	15	21	17	13	23	6	
22	22	7	19	13	23	9	9	5	30	7	25	29	20	14	25	6	

first opportunity an individual has to transfer,[35] transfer activity is examined during the Eighty-seventh through Ninety-fourth Congresses inclusive. Thus, a Congressman elected in the Eighty-sixth Congress who has served in each successive Congress through the Ninety-fourth has had eight transfer opportunities in his nine terms of service. The full distribution of transfer opportunities is given in table 3.9.

The advantages of restricting the analysis to these data are two. First, transfer behavior may be examined in light of initial committee assignments and initial requests. The presumption here is that those who are more successful in receiving requested assignments are less likely to seek transfers and are more likely to seek exclusive committee transfers if they seek any at all. Second, transfer activity may be analyzed from the point of view of opportunities: the more opportunities to transfer, ceteris paribus, the more likely transfer behavior will be observed.

Table 3.9   **Distribution of Members in Committee Transfer Data Set by Terms of Service**

No. of Terms Beyond the Freshman Term	Proportion	N
1	.305	53
2	.152	27
3	.101	18
4	.067	11
5	.151	26
6	.115	20
7	.040	7
8	.069	12
Total	1.000	174

Typical and Atypical Cases

Previous studies of committee transfer behavior, with the notable exception of Jewell and Chi-hung (1974), give a very static and simplified view of mobility in the committee opportunity structure. The costs and benefits of the queue, however, are constantly changing. The behavior patterns that emerge are complex responses to these dynamics. In this section several of these patterns are examined.

To give some perspective on the multiplicity of possibilities, and to underscore the fact that transfer (dual service) behavior is not a one-shot, yes-no, decision, let us examine an abstract example. Consider a congressman who has served six terms. He has had five opportunities to reveal a preference for some alteration in his initial committee assignments. That is, at each of five decision points he may have exercised either the status quo, dual service, or transfer option. There are, then, 3^5, or 243, behavior patterns possible for a six-term congressman.[36] Some involve constant "motion"—actual or attempted changes in the member's committee portfolio; others involve a more stable set of "holdings."

Now let us breathe some life into this abstract example by focusing on a real case: a six-term New Jersey Democrat. As a freshman he revealed a preference for nine major committees and one dual-service committee, Government Operations. He received none of his major requests and instead was assigned to Government Operations and Veterans Affairs. At his first opportunity he requested a transfer from Government Operations to Interstate, Merchant Marine, or Public Works, the first and third of which he initially had requested as a freshman. He received Merchant Marine. At his second opportunity he was allowed to transfer from Merchant Marine (which he had just received) to Science and Astronautics (which had not been among his freshman requests). At his third opportunity he again sought a seat on Interstate. He was granted the request and gave up his seat on Science and Astronautics (which he had just received). At his fourth opportunity the status quo prevailed: he maintained his committee portfolio of Interstate and Veterans Affairs. At his fifth opportunity, however, he again opted for change. He gave up his seat on Interstate and his seat and subcommittee chairmanship on Veterans Affairs for a seat on the Ways and Means Committee.

While this illustration is quite unusual, it does document the potential for mobility in the committee system. Mobility involves acquisitiveness (receiving and swapping dual assignments) and actual transfer. Both forms of mobility, it turns out, are quite common. The dual service and transfer options, moreover, are employed on more than one occasion by many members, and, over time, the continuous use of the status-quo option is less and less descriptive of "managers" of committee portfolios.

The most common pattern, a result of the distribution shown in table 3.9, is that of the two-term congressman who receives one (or more) of his freshman requests, maintains the status quo at his first (and only) opportunity, and leaves the Congress before another opportunity arises.

A Maryland congressman in the Eighty-sixth Congress requested Armed Services, Foreign Affairs, and Judiciary in that order. He was assigned to Armed Services, maintained the status quo in the Eighty-seventh Congress, and ran for the Senate in the Eighty-eighth Congress.

A Connecticut Democrat in the Eighty-eighth Congress sought Armed Services and Banking and Currency, was assigned to the latter, and maintained the status quo until he was defeated for reelection to the Ninetieth Congress.

In the Eighty-ninth Congress, a New York freshman requested Agriculture, Science and Astronautics, Banking and Currency, Veterans Affairs, and Post Office. He received two requested committees—Agriculture and Veterans Affairs, sought no changes at his first opportunity, and died during his second term of office.

For the congressman who receives none of his requested committees, on the other hand, the status quo option is abandoned immediately.

Congressmen from Maryland and Minnesota who failed in the Eighty-sixth Congress to receive any of their requests each sought to transfer at his first opportunity to one of his previously requested committees. The Marylander succeeded; the Minnesotan failed.

An Eighty-eighth Congress Virginian failed to receive any requested committees. He sought, successfully, to transfer to an exclusive committee two years later. The same pattern obtained for an Eighty-eighth Congress Democrat from California.

Two Eighty-ninth Congress members who were unsuccessful in their freshman assignments sought dual-service assignments in the Ninetieth Congress. The Michigan member was successful; the South Carolinian was not.

The longer a congressman's tenure, the more complicated his pattern of transfer behavior becomes. This appears to be the case no matter what the disposition of his freshman committee requests. Because of changing objectives and changing opportunities, maintenance of the status quo becomes increasingly less viable with time for all congressmen. Of the seventy-six congressmen in the data set who served five or more terms, only four refrained from seeking transfers or additional assignments.[37] A number of members seek only to acquire an additional committee.

A Pennsylvania Democrat elected to the Eighty-sixth Congress was assigned to Banking and Currency—his first-preference committee. At his first opportunity he sought and obtained a dual-service assignment to Government Operations. He has retained both committees, without further change, through the Ninety-fourth Congress.

An Eighty-sixth Congress freshman from Indiana received his first-preference request—Education and Labor—maintained the status quo until the Eighty-ninth Congress, when he accepted (but did not request) a dual-service appointment to House Administration, and has maintained the status quo ever since.

An Eighty-eighth Congress California freshman received his first preference—Interstate—then maintained the status quo until the Ninety-fourth Congress, when he accepted (but did not request) a dual service assignment to House Administration.

Occasionally a member will seek a dual-service appointment on more than one occasion, either because he failed the first time or because he preferred to swap second assignments.

An Eighty-eighth Congress Californian unsuccessfully sought a dual-service appointment to the Merchant Marine Committee in the Ninetieth Congress. He resubmitted the request in the Ninety-first and won the assignment.

An Eighty-ninth Congress Iowa Democrat accepted a dual-service appointment to Un-American Activities in the Ninetieth Congress and swapped it for Government Operations in the Ninety-first.

Nearly two-thirds of all Congressman with five or more terms of service behave as these few examples suggest—at least once they have sought to acquire an additional committee. A number of others (indeed, more than three-fifths of all those serving five or more terms) have sought full-fledged transfers. If, as a freshman, he received his first preference, the typical move is to an exclusive committee; if he failed to receive his first preference, the typical move is to a semiexclusive committee (often one he failed to obtain as a freshman).

An Eighty-eighth Congress Democrat from Tennessee, assigned to Science and Astronautics (first preference) as a freshman, successfully won a seat on Ways and Means in the Eighty-ninth Congress.

A Ninetieth Congress Alabama member, who won assignment to his freshman first-preference committee, Banking and Currency, won an Appropriations assignment in the Ninety-third Congress.

A Ninetieth Congress Democrat from Maine who failed to receive any of his requested committees successfully obtained a transfer to Interstate in the Ninety-first Congress. This had been his freshman first-preference request.

Finally, it is not entirely unusual to observe several moves by a member over the course of a number of Congresses. The New Jersey Democrat whose institutional career introduced this section is a case in point. Other less extreme examples usually involve a member obtaining a dual assignment at one of his earlier opportunities and, a term or two later, moving to an exclusive committee.

The main point of these examples is to disabuse the reader of the belief that initial assignments lock members into particular institutional careers. Changes in committee holdings are quite common. Whether it is due to a

Table 3.10		Sources of Democratic Committee Personnel Change	
Congress	Democratic Committee Slots	New Personnel*	Proportion of New Personnel Nonfreshmen
$(t-1)-(t)$	(t)		
85–86	365	96	.239
86–87	350	51	.510
87–88	353	82	.488
88–89	407	120	.291
89–90	353	36	.583
90–91	357	61	.656
91–92	392	88	.432
92–93	387	86	.523
93–94	471	166	.265
Total		786	.397

* Number of slots on committees occupied in the 1st session of tth Congress by someone not on the committee in the 2d session of $(t-1)^{st}$ Congress.

change in goals, a change in the competitive environment, or simply a desire to remedy poor initial assignments, opportunities to alter one's committee portfolio are available and frequently taken advantage of. While a price must be paid—time, and hence seniority invested in another queue foregone—many members appear willing to pay it (early in their careers, especially).

Second, these examples hint at the highly variable and shifting nature of congressional committee personnel from Congress to Congress. Internal movements supplement the external changes due to the election of freshmen and the deaths, defeats, and retirements of incumbents in substantially altering the complexion of congressional committees. As table 3.10 details, nearly 40 percent of all committee personnel changes are due to internal movement. The examples above portray the committees of Congress as a system in flux. As in other "ambition systems,"[38] the patterns of career mobility are myriad.

In Chapter 5 a detailed examination of some hypotheses related to revealed preferences for queue-changing is presented. But first we turn to a systematic investigation of freshman requests.

Chapter 4

A Model of
Freshman
Requests

For the several weeks (or months in some cases) before the organization of a new Congress the freshman congressman is preoccupied with the politics of committee assignments. Two estimation problems are involved in his decision on which committees to request—a "value" problem and a "discounting" problem. The first involves discovering which committees will serve as useful vehicles for the accomplishment of personal goals and objectives. The second concerns how much weight he should attach to these valuations in his final request list in light of assignment likelihoods. The first follows from the general presumption that members harbor private goals and objectives, that committee activity provides opportunities and resources relevant to these goals, that member goals are served in different ways—some better, some worse—by different committees, and consequently that requests for committee assignments are conceived of in an instrumental fashion. The second follows from the fact that requests are a scarce resource for freshmen: most are encouraged to restrict their lists to no more than three or four committees; consequently, long-shot requests often fall by the way as freshmen economize in the use of this resource.

In this chapter, a theory of request behavior is articulated, operationalized, and estimated statistically. The purposes here are, first, to provide a theoretical account of why particular kinds of freshmen seek particular committees and, second, to determine the extent to which this theoretical formulation is compatible with the actual requests submitted by Democratic freshmen in the Eighty-sixth through Ninety-third Congresses. The results obtained will sustain the view articulated by Freeman (1965), Lowi (1969), Davidson (1976), and others that the congressional committee system provides arenas to which "interesteds"[1] gravitate and in which those "interesteds" (together with their counterparts in the executive bureaucracy and the private sector) hammer out public policy with only occasional outside interference. This theme is expanded in the final chapter under the heading "The Cozy Little Triangle Problem."

A Theory of Freshman Requests

Our theoretical concern[2] is with the probability that any freshman, say the ith, requests any committee, say the jth. Call $Pr(R_{ij})$ the probability that committee j appears on the request list of Congressman i. Letting a_{ij} represent the event "i is assigned to j," the two estimation problems confronting i are:

1. What value is it to me to be assigned to j?
2. How likely is a_{ij} if I request j?

Represent these two estimation problems by $f(a_{ij})$ and $g(a_{ij}/R_{ij})$, respectively. The model we examine is of the expected value genre in which the likelihood of a request is a function, Φ, of the probability-discounted value of assignment:

$$Pr(R_{ij}) = \Phi[f(a_{ij}) \cdot g(a_{ij}/R_{ij})] \tag{4.1}$$

The first step, then, of our rational calculus is the attribution to each member-committee pair of a *valuation index*, $f(a_{ij})$, giving the attractiveness to each member ($i = 1, \ldots, m$) of an assignment to each of the committees ($j = 1, \ldots, n$). Thus, whenever $f(a_{ij}) > f(a_{ij^*})$, the valuation index is representing the fact that member i has judged an assignment to committee j more attractive to him than an assignment to committee j^*.[3]

But how are we to measure the value of committee j to Mr. i? Individual value assessments are, unfortunately, unobservable. What we can hope for—and, indeed, what we shall assume—is that value judgments are based on *observable* factors. That is, it is assumed that when a member thinks about the relative worth of serving on a particular committee, his judgments are conditioned by certain observable features of his situation.[4]

One set of situation-specific features that can be used to infer valuation assessments is the set of constituency and personal background factors most closely associated with the business of the committees in question. That is,

$$f(a_{ij}) = f(v_1, v_2, \ldots) \tag{4.2}$$

where $V = \{v_1, v_2, \ldots\}$ is a set of constituency features ("percent of work force engaged in agriculture") and personal background factors ("Is i a lawyer?" or "Does i have occupation-related experience in banking and housing?").

Judgments about the value of serving on particular committees are not, as we noted earlier, the sole basis for requests. Committee attractiveness, according to our proposed calculus, is discounted by the likelihood of actually receiving an appointment. The request list in the hands of the freshman is a resource that can be put to alternative productive uses. Because it is not an unlimited resource, there are incentives to economize in its use by employing it in its most productive capacity. Freshmen can ill afford flights of fancy and wishful thinking. Thus, highly valued assignments with low success likelihoods are often avoided. On the other hand, somewhat less attractive committees accompanied by high success probabilities may show up on request lists with surprising frequency.

Subjective beliefs about the likelihood of events are, like value judgments, unobservable. Consequently, our consideration of the probability of assignment success follows the procedure laid out above for value judgments of committee attractiveness. The focus here is on the conditional probability that member i is assigned to committee j if he requests that committee, $g(a_{ij}/R_{ij})$.[5] As in our earlier analysis we assume that this number is a function of observable features of the member's situation, $P = \{p_1, p_2, \ldots\}$. The variables in P are measures of the criteria believed by the member to affect CC decision-making: the existence of a state vacancy on a particular committee, expected state competition (possibly from more senior members of the state delegation), the number of members from the requester's state already on the committee, etc. In general form the relationship giving the subjective probability of appointment is:

$$g(a_{ij}/R_{ij}) = g(p_1, p_2, \ldots) \tag{4.3}$$

All that remains is to put (4.2) and (4.3) together. Their product gives the expected value to Mr. i of requesting committee j. Once we have specified explicit functional forms for (4.2) and (4.3) an equation will be produced that can be estimated from available data with appropriate statistical techniques. It will provide a statistical accounting of the pattern of requests for various committees. Before attending to these issues, however, it is important to underscore the elementary ideas that underpin (4.2) and (4.3)—to put some substantive meat, so to speak, on our analytical frame.

The reader may have noticed that throughout this discussion little mention has been made of specific member-goals in motivating behavior. Yet surely with a decision so important to one's institutional career as his committee assignments, member goals of a more ultimate sort—reelection, policy interests, and so on—will undoubtedly loom large. In the case of freshmen, however, there is good reason to believe that the set of goals described by Fenno (1973) and others are highly collinear. First, most freshmen will be quite concerned with reelection, almost from the first day of their initial term.

The congressional term is only two years; no sooner is one elected than he has to start running again. "I devoted most of my first two-years to getting reelected," said two-termer [Bob] Bergland (D., Minn.). "I decided there was nothing in Washington as important as one constituent, and I dropped everything when one called." [6] For this reason Bullock (1973b) is able to report of freshmen in the Ninety-second Congress that "almost half of all committee preferences were explained in whole or in part on the basis that the assignment would make it easier for the congressman to win re-election. More than two-thirds of the congressmen cited this as a motive for at least one of their preferences." Of course, it should be added that, statistically, the incumbent congressmen most vulnerable to defeat are those completing their *first* terms. Reelection concerns, then, are likely to be preeminent in the minds of most freshmen, overshadowing most other, more distant objectives. [7]

Nevertheless, in more recent Congresses at least, it appears that large numbers of freshmen justify their committee requests on the basis of policy interest. In the Ninety-second Congress, Bullock (1973b) discovered, to his own surprise, that "half of all committee preferences expressed by freshmen were motivated at least partially by the desire of the member to participate in an aspect of policy making handled by the committee sought. More than three-fourths of the newcomers cited an interest in policy making." Now it seems to me (and this is my second reason for believing that ultimate goals are highly collinear for a freshman in the sense that they all point him in more or less the same direction) that "policy making" is simply one of a number of instruments in a freshman's reelection toolbag. While it is unclear that "bricks and mortar" were ever the most prominent payoffs a congressman could deliver to his constituents, if Mayhew (1974) is to be taken seriously— and I believe he should be—it is apparent that one of the more frequent reelection strategies employed by congressmen in recent years is what Mayhew calls "credit-claiming and position-taking." Constituency service and policy activity, in this view, are simply alternative (often complementary) modes for pursuing reelection. Thus, it is the rare freshman who explains a particular committee request on the basis of policy concerns independent of (much less contrary to) the interests of his electoral coalition back home. When a policy rationale is offered to explain a request, the member undoubtedly believes that these same policy concerns matter to the constituents that elected him. Position-taking and credit-claiming are the glue that holds an electoral coalition together. [8]

The consequence of my argument is this: in order to explain the relative attractiveness of a committee to a freshman, one should look to the characteristics and interests of the constituents that elected him initially or to whom he is shifting his appeal. In the absence of precise details about that electoral coalition, a "second-best" strategy focuses on the entire geographic constituency and the personal background and experience of the member. Consequently, the variables of equation (4.2) will be germane constituency and personal background factors.

The variables employed to operationalize (4.3) tap the opportunities a given committee structure and configuration of vacancies offer a freshman from the point of view of the state delegation. This choice follows from two considerations. (1) Most freshmen are not well known beyond the borders of their states. The CC knows little about a particular freshman beyond the paragraph or two of biography that appears in John Martin's request books and the first impressions they have garnered from several brief meetings with the freshman. Consequently they rely heavily on those who do know him—his zone representative, state delegation dean, and other members of the state delegation. (2) State delegations, as the research of Fiellin (1963), Bullock (1971), and Deckard (1972, 1975) suggests, often serve as informal communications networks, mutual admiration societies, and general back-scratching clubs. When it comes to committee assignments, many delegations formally caucus in order to resolve potential intradelegation conflicts and, if successful, to endorse formally one of their number for available committee slots. As Deckard (1975) notes, "the members of cohesive delegations consider committee assignments a matter of common interest. These delegations work hard to protect their positions on the choice committees and to maintain broad representation on less desirable but still important committees." As a consequence of these two points and the geographic orientation on the basis of which CC deliberations are constituted (see Chapter 8), the beliefs a freshman holds about his chances of winning a particular assignment, $g(a_{ij}/R_{ij})$, are likely to be colored by the interests and needs of his state, the extent (or lack) of representation of his state on a given committee, and the competition from within his delegation that he expects.[9] In operationalizing (4.3), then, my focus will be on the *state opportunity structure*.

In order to employ these simple theoretical notions to account for the pattern of requests in the Eighty-sixth through Ninety-third Congresses, it is necessary to assume an explicit functional form for (4.2) and (4.3). In the absence of theoretical guidance on this matter I opt for the simplest, the linear form. A number of objections[10] to this choice are accommodated by coding conventions and are discussed below.

Thus, on the linear hypothesis we have from (4.2) and (4.3), respectively,

$$f(a_{ij}) = \alpha_0 + \alpha_1 v_1 + \cdots + \alpha_s v_s = \alpha_0 + \sum_{i=1}^{s} \alpha_i v_i \qquad (4.4)$$

and

$$g(a_{ij}/R_{ij}) = \beta_0 + \beta_1 p_1 + \cdots + \beta_t p_t = \beta_0 + \sum_{j=1}^{t} \beta_j p_j \qquad (4.5)$$

The parameter α_0 in (4.4) is the average attractiveness of a given committee across members for whom the value variables are zero, with deviations from this average level dependent on each member's particular circumstances $(v_1, \ldots, v_s)$ and the weights $(\alpha_1, \ldots \alpha_s)$ attached to these circumstances. A parallel interpretation holds for β_0 and $\beta_1, \ldots \beta_t$.

Notice that (4.4) and (4.5) look something like linear regression equations. Indeed, if we had a "valuation meter" and a "subjective probability meter" which gave us independent readings of $f(a_{ij})$ and $g(a_{ij}/R_{ij})$, respectively, then (presuming the appropriate statistical assumptions were satisfied) we could assess the power of regressors $V = [v_1, v_2, \ldots]$ and $P = [p_1, p_2, \ldots]$ in explaining variations in the meter readings by the method of ordinary least squares. But, as noted earlier, $f(a_{ij})$ and $g(a_{ij}/R_{ij})$ are unobservable. Consequently, we will be unable to identify the parameters of (4.4) and (4.5).

Combining the two equations we have, according to (4.1),

$$Pr(R_{ij}) = \Phi[b_0 + \sum_s b_s v_s + \sum_t b_t p_t + \sum_s \sum_t b_{st} v_s p_t] \tag{4.6}$$

where $b_0 = \alpha_0\beta_0$, $b_s = \beta_0\alpha_s$, $b_t = \alpha_0\beta_t$, and $b_{st} = \alpha_s\beta_t$.

Equation (4.6) may be estimated from available data by the method of probit analysis. It will provide an equation which predicts the probability of a request as a linear function of selected variables and their interactions. Our theoretical calculus, then, has yielded in (4.6) an equation with which a number of interesting hypotheses may be tested. This and other methodological issues are the focus of the next section.

Freshman Requests: Methodological Discussion

Methodology...is a matter of strategy, not of morals. There are neither good nor bad methods, but only methods that are more or less effective under particular circumstances in realizing objectives on the way to a distant goal.
Homans (1962)

Let me begin the methodological discussion by noting two things. First, requests are observable (at least for the Eighty-sixth through Ninety-third Congresses). The data on freshman requests examined in the previous chapter are the actual requests submitted by Democratic freshmen to the CC. These requests are the culmination of the decision process that the model summarized in equation (4.6) purports to explain.

The second notable feature of the model is the nature of the dependent variable, R_{ij}: it is dichotomous. When $R_{ij} = 1$, i has requested committee j; $R_{ij} = 0$ otherwise. This feature proves most troublesome when traditional multivariate statistical models are employed to estimate the parameters of (4.6.)

In the next section we estimate the parameters of (4.6) for each of nine committees. While particular explanatory variables change from committee to committee, the theoretical calculus proposed in the previous section remains intact. The "standard" multivariate technique for estimating this model is ordinary least squares (OLS) regression analysis. This method, as is well known, has certain desirable statistical properties, providing that several assumptions are met. When these assumptions are violated, the virtues of OLS evaporate. Stated another way, if there are violations in the assumptions, the numbers churned out of the computer as estimates of the parameters may be misleading; their use may result in faulty inferences.[11]

There is a very serious problem with the classical regression model when the dependent variable is dichotomous. For those who believe more generally that "there ain't no such thing as a free lunch," this should not come as a surprise. When one attempts to bring a methodological tool, devised to account for variance in a *quantitative* phenomenon, to bear on a *qualitative* phenomenon (did he apply for committee j or not?), problems are to be expected. The name statisticians have given to this problem is *heteroskedasticity*. The chief consequence of this problem (and there are others as well) for estimating the parameter of our model by OLS regression is that, after the estimates are obtained from the computer, there is still great uncertainty about the true population values of the parameters; many hypotheses (even those which are in conflict with one another on substantive grounds) will be compatible with the estimates. Since the whole point of estimation is to allow us to draw inferences from the data so that we can make judgments about the proposed model, it is misleading and futile to employ inappropriate methodological tools.

Fortunately, there is an alternative multivariate statistical model more appropriate to the particular features of equation (4.6). The *probit analysis model*, which has a long history in biometrics, is relatively unknown to political scientists.[12] A concise description of this model is found in the citations given below. For my purposes a brief verbal description will suffice.

A probit equation, at first sight, looks very much like a regression equation. Some aspect of a phenomenon is written as a linear combination of independent effects, subject to random disturbances. The objective of the probit model, however, is a prediction of the *probability* that a particular observation is a one or a zero. Given a series of observations of the dependent variable (did i = 1, ..., m request committee j, in which case $R_{ij} = 1$, or did he not, in which case $R_{ij} = 0$?), as well as measures of the associated independent variables, probit analysis is a maximum likelihood estimation technique that produces parameter estimates which render the particular pattern of zeros and ones for R_{ij} that were actually observed the most probable. The parameters of the probit equation play a role analogous to those of a regression equation; consequently their estimates permit inferences about the relative importance of the explanatory variables. In the next section, equation (4.6) is operationalized for each of nine congressional committees. With our data on freshmen requests, a probit equation is estimated for each of these committees and hypotheses are tested. Before moving directly to that task, let me raise four additional methodological points.

First, from equation (4.6) it is noted that $Pr(R_{1j})$ is determined by transforming $f(a_{1j}) \cdot g(a_{1j}/R_{1j})$ by the transformation Φ. Φ is the cumulative standard normal function; its effect is illustrated in figure 4.1. The number z that

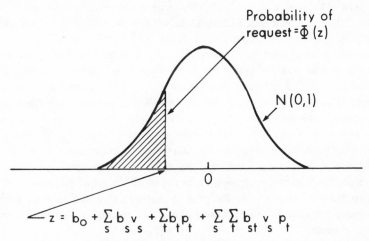

Fig. 4.1   Relationships between the probit equation and request probability.

results from estimating the model is an abscissa value of the standard normal distribution. The area under the standard normal curve, $N(0, 1)$, up to the point z gives the probability of a request. If the predicted z-score is less than zero (as shown on figure 4.1) then the probability that this particular member will request the committee under consideration is less than one-half. The maximum likelihood prediction, then, is that he will *not* request the committee. If the z-score were greater than zero, the converse prediction is made. The probit method, in brief, relates the explanatory variables to a probability prediction via the normal transformation.[13]

Second, as equation (4.6) indicates, the variables included in the equation are those assumed to measure the attractiveness of committees to members, the likelihood of appointment success, *and* the interactions among them. If equations (4.2) and (4.3) each contain three variables—[v_1, v_2, v_3] and [p_1, p_2, p_3]—then (4.6) will contain six main effects and nine interactions, thus requiring sixteen parameter estimates (including the constant term). As we add explanatory variables, we use up degrees of freedom rather rapidly. In most instances this will not pose serious problems since the sample size is sufficiently large. More serious is the potentially high correlation among explanatory variables (especially interaction variables), making it difficult to unravel their independent contributions. In addition, purists are bound to be troubled by the lack of aesthetic appeal of equation (4.6.)

The third methodological point involves the constraint on request behavior discussed earlier. Members are encouraged to keep their request lists short. The following possibility thus emerges: although a member "really" employs an expected value calculus, some committees will *not* be requested, even though their expected values to the member are "high", because of the constraint on the number of requests. It is difficult to determine how serious this problem is, though my strong suspicion is that it is of marginal significance. In any event, the chief effect of our ignoring this constraint is conservative: the goodness-of-fit of the model will be underestimated, as will the effects of the explanatory variables.[14]

Finally, I offer a methodological explanation for the particular committees I have chosen to examine in the next section. The probit model—indeed, any multivariate statistical model—is not very helpful when the event to be explained is extremely rare or extremely commonplace. What one identifies in a multivariate context is the extent to which variations in the dependent variable are accompanied by variations in the explanatory variables. With both rare and commonplace events, there is little to explain since there is little that varies.[15] In the case of committee request behavior, the problem of commonplace events is not present: even the most popular committee, Interstate, is requested by only one-third of the applicants. On the other hand, requests for a number of committees may quite reasonably be regarded as rare events (see table 3.2).[16]

Fortunately, the eight committees that have retained semiexclusive status (the major authorizing committees) throughout the entire period of analysis (1958–74), as well as the Interior Committee (which, though in fact a nonexclusive committee, has major responsibility in important substantive areas), have high enough request rates to merit further investigation. Consequently, nine probit equations are estimated, permitting hypothesis testing for the following committees: Agriculture, Armed Services, Banking and Currency, Education and Labor, Foreign Affairs, Interior, Interstate, Judiciary, and Public Works. In the next section, the results of these estimations are given, along with further discussion of the variables included and the inferences justified by the data.

Operational Models
of Freshman Requests

The Variables

Table 4.1 describes the variables that operationalize attractiveness, $\{v_1, v_2, \ldots\}$. These data have been drawn from the appropriate volumes of the *Congressional District Data Book*, its supplements, and the volumes of the *Congressional Directory*. They will be described in more detail shortly. Table 4.2 provides descriptions of the variables that operationalize the conditional

Table 4.1   **Attractiveness Variables**

Committee	v_1	v_2	v_3
Agriculture	% of work force in agriculture	Farm-related occupational background (1 = yes, 0 = no)	
Armed Services	% of work force in military/defense*		
Banking & Currency	Pop./sq. mi. (in 100's of people)	Financial/real estate occupational background (1 = yes, 0 = no)	
Education & Labor	Pop./sq.mi. (in 100's of people)	Education/labor occupational background (1 = yes, 0 = no)	
Foreign Affairs	% foreign stock		
Interior	District land area (in 100's of sq. mi.)**	% of work force in mining	
Interstate	Health/commerce occupational background (1 = yes, 0 = no)		
Judiciary	Lawyer · % foreign stock*	Lawyer · South	lawyer (1 = yes, 0 = no)
Public Works	Did predecessor serve on the committee? (1 = yes, 0 = no)		

   * Unavailable for the 86th and 87th Congresses; estimations of parameters for the 88th–93rd Congresses only.
  ** At-large districts resulting from failures to redistrict have been deleted.

Table 4.2   Likelihood of Assignment Success Variables

Variable	Description
p_1	Is there a state party vacancy on the committee? (1 = yes, 0 = no)
p_2	Is there competition from within the state party delegation for a seat on the committee? (1 = yes, 0 = no)
p_3	Is there senior competition from within the state party delegation for a seat on the committee? (1 = yes, 0 = no)
p_4	Is the state party delegation already represented on the committee? (1 = yes, 0 = no)

NOTE: These variables are the same for each of the nine committees.

probability of assignment success, $\{p_1, p_2, \ldots\}$. These data have been drawn from the committee rosters in each Congress. Finally, in table 4.3, the interaction terms of (4.6) are seen to be the product of the row p_i and the column v_j.

Table 4.3   Interaction Variables

	v_1	v_2
p_1	w_{11}	w_{12}
p_2	w_{21}	w_{22}
p_3	w_{31}	w_{32}
p_4	w_{41}	w_{42}

I will briefly comment on the operational choices reflected in these tables, leaving more detailed discussion for the committee-by-committee analysis.

1. The attractiveness variables $\{v_1, v_2 \ldots\}$ are, whenever available, measures of constituency characteristics and personal background factors related to the jurisdiction of the committee in question. A richer set of variables, as an earlier comment noted, was precluded both by high intercorrelations and by the exponential rate at which degrees of freedom would be exhausted.

Occasionally, as well, no obvious variable was available. Slightly different results will obtain, though qualitative conclusions probably will not, with a different choice of attractiveness indicators.[17] The qualitative expectation is that attractiveness enhances the likelihood of a request; in terms of the estimates of the parameters in equation (4.6), then, the hypothesis is that $b_s > 0$ for all s.

2. The availability of and competition for seats on a given committee from within the state party delegation are operational indicators of assignment likelihood. While other factors are sure to affect assignment success (for example, interzone competition), the state party delegation data are handy indicators. Moreover, given the interaction patterns of freshmen described in the previous chapter, and their need to economize on information in their uncertainty reduction activity, a focus on the state party delegation makes

Table 4.4

Committee	Constant	v_1	v_2	v_3	p_1	p_2	p_3	p_4
Agriculture[a]	−2.071	.071	1.176	—*	.597	.630	9.627	.387
	(.271)	(.019)	(.393)	—*	(.440)	(.371)	(173.740)	(.391)
Armed	−.643	.022	—*	—*	.076	.054	−1.529	−.557
Services[c]	(.175)	(.014)	—*	—*	(.423)	(.333)	(1.023)	(.285)
Banking &	−1.264	.012	1.205	—*	−.054	.511	—	.138
Currency[a]	(.181)	(.004)	(.312)	—*	(.340)	(.251)	—	(.253)
Education &	−1.145	.007	1.140	—*	—	—	—	—
Labor[a]	(.120)	(.006)	(.343)	—*	—	—	—	—
Foreign	−1.512	.038	—*	—*	.219	.917	−4.136	−.025
Affairs[c]	(.297)	(.015)	—*	—*	(.650)	(.560)	(191.745)	(.459)
Interior[b]	−1.250	.005	−.007	—*	.972	−.252	—	−.322
	(.172)	(.001)	(.068)	—*	(.325)	(.296)	—	(.305)
Interstate[a]	−.403	.967	—*	—*	.155	−.111	5.656	−.541
	(.142)	(.371)	—*	—*	(.298)	(.211)	(90.150)	(.206)
Judiciary[c]	−2.232	.019	.039	1.356	—	—	—	—
	(.385)	(.014)	(.593)	(.486)	—	—	—	—
Public	−.381	1.073	—*	—*	−.136	−.245	−.721	−.491
Works[a]	(.130)	(.634)	—*	—*	(.297)	(.238)	(.591)	(.215)

good sociological sense. The qualitative expectation is that state vacancies enhance, and state competition and representation detract from, assignment success.

3. The expected value theory that produced (4.6) entails multiplicative as well as additive effects. The estimates of b_s ($s = 1, 2, 3$) and b_t ($t = 1, 2, 3, 4$) reflect the additive effects of the v_s and p_t variables, respectively. The parameters b_{st} reflect the additional effect (if any) from the combination of v_s and p_t. Thus, the total impact of v_s and p_t on assignment success *cannot* be inferred by examining only the parameters associated with those variables; rather, for each v_s, p_t combination we must examine b_s, b_t, *and* b_{st}.

Details must await the separate analyses of the nine committees. With these brief comments, however, I will proceed to the actual models for each committee and make some general observations.

Probit Models of Freshman Requests

W_{11}	W_{12}	W_{21}	W_{22}	W_{31}	W_{32}	W_{41}	W_{42}	$\hat{R}^2$
.036	−.605	−.016	−.789	−.962	6.861	−.035	.477	
(.043)	(1.038)	(.027)	(.784)	(11.149)	(100.247)	(.028)	(.748)	.604
.000	—*	−.148	—*	.322	—*	.014	—*	
(.033)	—*	(.103)	—*	(.148)	—*	(.060)	—*	.317
−.003	−.255	−.009	.484	—	—	−.005	−.450	
(.005)	(.648)	(.004)	(.532)	—	—	(.003)	(.570)	.374
−.002	−4.424	−.004	−.259	—	—	.000	−.618	
(.002)	(41.995)	(.022)	(.505)	—	—	(.006)	(.508)	.585
.026	—*	−.057	—*	.041	—*	−.022	—*	
(.027)	—*	(.026)	—*	(5.905)	—*	(.019)	—*	.487
−.004	−.028	.004	.102	—	—	−.002	.201	
(.002)	(.091)	(.003)	(.175)	—	—	(.002)	(.171)	.585
.598	—*	.254	—*	−11.174	—*	.041	—*	
(.762)	—*	(.559)	—*	(156.110)	—*	(.566)	—*	.368
.008	.796	.009	−4.621	—	—	−.014	.219	
(.015)	(1.057)	(.012)	(72.503)	—	—	(.012)	(.652)	.501
−.255	—*	.367	—*	−4.958	—*	−5.046	—*	
(.789)	—*	(.872)	—*	(127.464)	—*	(73.575)	—*	.326

NOTE: Each cell entry is the parameter estimate associated with the column variable in the probit equation of the row committee. Standard deviations are in parentheses.
[a] N = 231
[b] N = 226
[c] N = 174
* No variable defined

*Parameter Estimates
and Discussion*

The parameter estimates for requests to each of nine committees are found in table 4.4. Since no more than one v_s variable was defined for some committees, there are a number of blank cells in table 4.4. Extremely high correlations among some explanatory variables required additional deletions as well. Each cell gives the parameter estimate and, in parentheses, the standard error. The final column of the table displays the $\hat{R}^2$-statistic, a measure of goodness-of-fit.[18]

The first thing to note in table 4.4 is that all nine constant terms are negative and highly significant.[19] This accords with common sense—if a member has no interest in a particular committee (*as measured by the v_s's*), then, no matter how propitious the likelihood of assignment, he is not very likely to request that committee.[20]

Second, note that with few exceptions the measures of interest, v_1, v_2, v_3, are positive and highly significant.[21] The theory is strongly supported in the sense that *requests reflect interests*: a man's interests characterize his behavior when it comes to committee requests. As a general proposition this appears unassailable.

The probability and interaction terms, on the other hand, defy general characterization. Because of their idiosyncrasies, further discussion of them is reserved for later. As a general mode of behavior, then, judgments on the *expected* value calculus must await more careful scrutiny. The probability terms and, consequently, their interactions with the value terms, however, do not appear to play the pervasive role that the value terms do.

Third, a glance at the $\hat{R}^2$'s suggests that the model does well with some committees, fairly well with others, and not so well with a few. The reasons, of course, vary from committee to committee, but there is one general and systematic feature that accounts for the depressed $\hat{R}^2$'s. A residual analysis was conducted for each of the equations in order to determine where the deviations occur between what the model predicts for any member—"Request" if (4.6) is positive and "No request" otherwise—and what is observed. There are two types of error possible:

Type (A): The model predicts i requests committee j, but i does not request committee j.

Type (B): The model predicts i does not request committee j, but i does request j.

For each committee, there were few Type (A) errors. That is, those who "should" request a committee according to the model in fact do.[22] The preponderance of errors are Type (B). *Many members who are not expected to apply for a committee often do so.*[23] This pattern of error is symptomatic of a problem observed earlier: committee jurisdictions are diverse, heterogeneous, and, consequently, very imperfectly correlated with particular social interests. Thus, to continue with the Agriculture Committee as an example, while those congressmen with important farming interests in their constituency are very likely to request the committee, it is also the case that a number of urban and suburban members interested in the food stamp program and the problem of rising food prices—issues of salience to *their* constituents—also apply for the committee. A variation on this theme is the Interior Committee, whose jurisdiction has been *changing* in salience for some members as environmental issues have grown in importance. At an increasing rate members from eastern, urban, and suburban districts apply for this committee.[24]

There is an important conclusion to draw from these observations: in order for a parsimonious statistical explanation of request behavior to "work," there must be a reasonably neat dovetailing of interests and committees; to the extent that member interests and the opportunities afforded by committees vis-à-vis those interests are correlated, a statistical accounting will be compelling and persuasive. If, however, member interests are ill defined or the relationship between the servicing of those interests and committee opportunities is imperfectly connected, then the explanatory power of a statistical argument will be depressed. It is precisely the heterogeneous and shifting jurisdictions of congressional committees, and the attendant imperfect relationship between committee business and member interests, that produce only moderate $\hat{R}^2$'s.[25]

Before examining the probit equations on a committee-by-committee basis,

Table 4.5   **"Worst Case" and "Best Case" Analysis for Freshman Requests**

Committee	"Worst Case" Probability	"Best Case" Probability
Agriculture	.14	.99
Armed Services	.01	.70
Banking & Currency	.23	.99
Education & Labor	.13	.99
Foreign Affairs	.27	.99
Interior	.03	.57
Interstate	.15	.87
Judiciary	.01	.90
Public Works	.13	.62

Table 4.6

Committee	Hypotheses	
	1 H_0: all variables insignificant	2 H_0: v-terms (main effects only) insignificant
Agriculture	$\ll.001$	$\ll.001$
Armed Services	.018	.05
Banking & Currency	$\ll.001$	$\ll.001$
Education & Labor	$\ll.001$	$<.001$
Foreign Affairs	.005	.005
Interior	$\ll.001$	$\ll.001$
Interstate	$\ll.001$	.005
Judiciary	$\ll.001$	.001
Public Works	.005	.08

it is useful to see just what these equations tell us about the likelihood of a request for a given committee. In table 4.5 a "worst case" and "best case" analysis is presented. In the former, the probability of a request from a freshman who has no interest in a committee ($v_s = 0$ for all s) and for whom the assignment success situation is least encouraging is determined. In the latter the probability of a request is calculated for the freshman with "maximal" interest[26] and the most propitious assignment likelihood. Ideally we should obtain great separation with these two extreme cases: "uninterested" members in difficult competitive situations should have request probabilities approaching zero, while "interested" members facing more promising competitive environments should have request probabilities near 1. Agriculture, Education and Labor, and Judiciary come closest to this ideal; Armed Services, Banking and Currency, Interstate, and Foreign Affairs are only slightly more distant; Interior and Public Works are quite inadequate.[27]

To give proper attention to the wealth of information summarized in table 4.4 it is best to focus on one committee at a time. Table 4.6 summarizes all of the results.[28]

Hypotheses about Freshman Requests

3 H_0: p-terms (main effects only) insignificant	4 H_0: p-terms and interactions insignificant	5 H_0: inter- action terms insignificant	6 H_0: constant term insignificant
.06	.01	.28	≪.001
.20	.04	.06	.001
.20	.002	<.001	≪.001
—	.18	.18	≪.001
.30	.001	.10	≪.001
.03	.005	.001	≪.001
.08	.03	.10	.002
.002	.02	.50	≪.001
.03	.02	.28	.002

NOTE: Cell entries give the probability level at which the null hypothesis (that certain b-weights are not significantly different from zero) may be rejected. The smaller the cell entry, the stronger the empirical grounds for rejecting the null hypothesis. The p-levels are determined by a likelihood ratio test which is distributed χ^2 with degrees of freedom equal to the number of parameters hypothesized to be zero under the null hypothesis. See Mood and Graybill (1963, p. 301), Theorem 12.7, for a characterization of this statistical test.

Committee-by-Committee Analysis

Agriculture

Pr(Agriculture request) =

$\Phi\left[\right.$ −2.071 + .071 [% of work force in agriculture]
    (.271)   (0.19)

  +1.176 [farm-related occupation] + .597 [state vacancy]
    (.393)   (.440)

  + .630 [state competition] +   9.627 [senior state competition]
    (.371)   (173.740)

  + .387 [state representation]
    (.391)

  + .036 w_{11} −   .605 w_{12} − .016 w_{21} − .789 w_{22} −   .962 w_{31}
    (.043)   (1.038)   (.027)   (.784)   (11.149)

  +6.861 w_{32} − .035 w_{41} + .477 $w_{42}\left.\right]$
  (100.247)   (.028)   (.748)

Two measures of "interest" in a seat on Agriculture were employed: percent of the work force in a district engaged in agriculture and whether or not a member held a farm-related occupation prior to election. The four measures of the competitive environment, and thus of the "productivity" of a request in securing an assignment, documented in table 4.2 were used.

Table 4.6 reveals that the statistical model is highly significant (col. 1). The constant term and the "interest" variables (main effects) are also highly significant and possess the correct signs (cols. 2 and 6). *Freshmen from highly agricultural districts who have farm-related backgrounds are quite likely to seek a seat on Agriculture.* While neither the p-terms themselves (col. 3) nor the interactions themselves (col. 5) are very significant, together they are (col. 4). That is, the fit is substantially improved if we append probability and interaction terms to the "interest" variables.[29]

A more detailed examination reveals that the self-interest calculus proposed in equation (4.6) works extremely well. We have already observed that the value terms affect requests as expected. Turning to the probability and interaction terms, consider the state vacancy effect: the three parameter estimates of interest are those associated with "state vacancy," w_{11} and w_{12}, namely, .597, .036, −.605 (see the above equation). When there is a state vacancy, a positive increment in the probability of an Agriculture request *always* results. To illustrate, in a modestly agricultural district (set at the national average of 6%) with the freshman having a farm-related background, the increment to the request probability (actually, to the z-score—see fig. 4.1) is: $.597(1) + .036(6) - .605(1) = .208$. Of course, a more highly agricultural district will produce an even greater increment; and, when there is *no* state vacancy, all of the variables are zero and thus do not affect the request probability.

A similar analysis may be conducted for each of the other probability effects. Thus, there are three parameter estimates of interest associated with state competition—.630, −.016, and −.789; these are attached to "state competition," w_{21}, and w_{22}, respectively. State competition produces the expected *decrement* in request probability except in the circumstance of a freshman from a relatively nonagricultural district ($w_{21} \leq 4\%$) who has no farm-related occupational background. This group of freshmen is not deterred by state competition from requesting Agriculture (but are unlikely to apply on other grounds, that is, because of lack of interest).

Similarly, senior state competition yields an expected *decrement* in the request probability in most contingencies. Owing, however, to the virtual absence of senior state competition in the Eighty-sixth to Ninety-third Congresses—very few nonfreshmen seek to transfer to Agriculture—the parameter estimates are unstable and probably are best ignored.

Finally, the presence of state representation on the committee produces the expected *decrement* in the request probability (the relevant parameter estimates are .387, −.035, and .477) for members from moderately and highly agricultural districts. It does not, however, reduce the request likelihood of members from more urban districts.

The Agriculture Committee probit, in sum, gives substantial support for the expected value calculus proposed in equation (4.6). "Interest" variables and state vacancies encourage requests; state competition and state representation discourage them.[30]

Armed Services

Pr(Armed Services request) =

$$\Phi \left[\begin{array}{l} - .643 + .022 \; [\% \text{ of work force in defense/military}] \\ \quad (.175) \quad (.014) \\ + .076 \; [\text{state vacancy}] + .054 \; [\text{state competition}] \\ \quad (.423) \quad\quad\quad\quad\quad\quad (.333) \\ -1.529 \; [\text{senior state competition}] \\ \quad (1.023) \\ - .557 \; [\text{state representation}] \\ \quad (.285) \\ + .000 \; w_{11} - .148 \; w_{21} + .322 \; w_{31} + .014 \; w_{41} \\ \quad (.033) \quad\quad (.103) \quad\quad (.148) \quad\quad (.060) \end{array} \right]$$

Only a single "interest" variable was defined for the Armed Services Committee—percent of the district work force in the military or in government employment in the defense area.[31] This is probably a poor indicator of interest, given the broad and changing nature of Armed Services' jurisdiction. Prior to 1959 the committee's jurisdiction was limited to military organization and manpower policy. It was the Appropriations Committee that both authorized and appropriated funds for specific arms and weapons systems.

In 1959, the committee assumed responsibility from the Appropriations Committee for setting ceilings on funds appropriated for the purchase of aircraft, missiles, and ships. This was a major breakthrough, giving the committee power to authorize appropriations for about 15 percent of the Defense Department's annual expenditures.

By the late 1960s, the Armed Services Committee was acting on legislation authorizing funds for the following: research, development, testing, and evaluation of weapons and communications projects; procurement of all weapons and weapons systems—aircraft, missiles, naval vessels, tracked combat vehicles and torpedoes; active duty personnel salaries; military construction programs, including family housing; and military assistance to Vietnam ... the panel does not authorize funds annually for operation and maintenance of the armed forces ..., for retired military personnel benefits and pensions ..., or for active duty military personnel benefits, all of which are approved directly by the Appropriations Committee. [*CQ Weekly Report*, February 15, 1975, p. 337]

Manpower policies and salaries (which v_1, in effect, measures) are only a very small aspect of the committee jurisdiction.

Rundquist (1973) devised a measure of prime military contracts (dollar value) per unit of capacity to perform research and development and defense production activities in the district—a measure which usefully taps the "pork barrel" aspects of the committee's attractiveness. He operationalized the measure, however, only for the Eighty-fifth Congress (a monumental task in itself), and it does not appear that the data are easily accessible for the period under consideration in this study. Even if these data were available, neither Rundquist's nor my variable captures two important aspects of "interest" in the Armed Services Committee: first, requests need not be conditioned by *prior* interest—members, that is, may to some extent convert committee membership into *future* "pork" benefits for their districts; second, membership on the committee may be used to assist members on *other* committees in *their* "pork" efforts, in exchange for assistance from those other members. Membership on the committee, that is, may be used in a quid pro quo fashion to produce both direct benefits and institutional influence for committee members. Consequently, interest in the Armed Services Committee (and the same may be said for Interstate and Public Works) is likely to be much broader than my "interest" variable indicates.[32]

Table 4.6 reveals that while the probit equation for Armed Services is quite significant, it is nevertheless a less adequate fit than those of other committees. Similarly, though the "interest" and constant parameter estimates are significant and of the correct sign (cols. 2 and 6), they, too, do not discriminate requesters from nonrequesters very well in comparison to the discriminating powers of analogous variables for other committees. The probability and interaction terms play nearly the same role they do in the Agriculture probit: neither of the factors alone is terribly significant, but together they do improve the fit significantly.

A more detailed look at the probability and interaction terms yields results compatible with the proposed self-interest calculus. The presence of state vacancies produces increments, as expected, in the request probabilities (see the parameters of "state vacancy" and w_{11} in the equation above). The presence of state competition and state representation ("state competition" and w_{21}, and "state representation" and w_{41}, respectively) results in expected decrements in request probabilities.

The senior state competition variables play an important, though limited, role. The Armed Services Committee is among the few semiexclusive committees for which there are a substantial number of transfer requests from more senior congressmen.[33] Senior state competition discourages requests so long as the "interest" variable is less than 5%. Since this is true for more than 80% of the freshmen, the senior state competition variables behave in the expected way. However, for those members who do have a high concentration of military and defense personnel in their districts, the contrary is the case: they pursue their interests despite the presence of a senior state competitor.

Even more than in the Agriculture probit, expected value calculations are revealed in the data for Armed Services. However, the model does not appear to characterize adequately the request behavior of freshmen in terms of overall fit. Both the low $\hat{R}^2$ (.317) and the relatively modest level of significance for the probit (.018) lead me to believe that the elusive quality of "interest" in the committee requires further research. Once again the issue of committee jurisdiction and its complex relationship to member goals rears its head.[34]

Banking and Currency

Pr[Banking & Currency request] =

$$\Phi \left[\begin{array}{l} -1.264 + .012 \text{ [100s of people/square mile]} \\ (.181) \quad (.004) \end{array} \right.$$

$$+ 1.205 \text{ [financial/real estate background]}$$
$$(.312)$$

$$- .054 \text{ [state vacancy]} + .511 \text{ [state competition]}$$
$$(.340) \qquad\qquad\qquad (.251)$$

$$+ .138 \text{ [state representation]} - .003 \, w_{11} - .255 \, w_{12}$$
$$(.253) \qquad\qquad\qquad\qquad (.005) \qquad (.648)$$

$$\left. - .009 \, w_{21} + .484 \, w_{22} - .005 \, w_{41} - .450 \, w_{42} \right]$$
$$(.004) \qquad (.532) \qquad (.003) \qquad (.570)$$

The Banking and Currency probit included two v-terms, population per square mile (*in 100s of people*) and whether the member had occupational experience in banking, finance, or real estate. Since housing and urban renewal fall within the committee's jurisdiction, these variables were selected as likely to tap its basically urban character. Requests, according to table 3.3, come predominantly from urban members.

As columns 1, 2, and 6 of table 4.6 reveal, the entire equation, the v-terms, and the constant term are highly significant. The constant term and both "interest" terms have the correct sign as well. While the p-terms alone are insignificant, together with interactions they are highly significant. The interaction terms, too, are highly significant, lending support to the hypothesized multiplicative effect of probabilities and utilities. However, both probability and interaction terms often mix in odd fashion.

Take "state vacancy," for example. It apparently results, unexpectedly, in a *decrement* to the probability of a request for Banking and Currency (consult the parameters attached to "state vacancy," w_{11} and w_{12}). There is, I believe, an explanation for this. A freshman from a rural district is ordinarily not going to seek a seat on Banking and Currency, even if one of his urban colleagues in the state delegation has left the committee. An urban freshman, on the other hand, because of his district's large stake in, say, housing policy, may well take a shot at a seat on the committee whether or not a state vacancy has materialized. This explanation, however, is ad hoc and not very satisfactory.

The same problem occurs with "state competition." It produces an expected *decrement* in request probability only in relatively urban districts. Only the "state representation" variables affect request probabilities in the expected direction.[35] Consequently, despite the statistical importance of the probability and interaction terms, they are occasionally in conflict with the substantive model. "Interest" is *not* always discounted by "probability of success" in the expected fashion.[36]

Education and Labor

Pr[Education & Labor request] =

$$\Phi \left[\begin{array}{l} -1.145 + .007 \text{ [100s of people/square mile]} \\ (.120)(.006) \\ +1.140 \text{ [education/labor background]} - .002\, w_{11} \\ (.343) (.002) \\ -4.424\, w_{12} - .004\, w_{21} - .259\, w_{22} + .000\, w_{41} - .618\, w_{42} \\ (41.995) (.002) (.508) (.006) (.508) \end{array} \right]$$

Two "interest" variables were employed: population per square mile (in 100s of people) and education/labor occupational background. Owing to high multicollinearity between probability and interaction terms, the probability terms were deleted from the probit equation. As in each of the preceding probits, this one is highly significant (table 4.6, col. 1). The constant term and v-terms are statistically significant, as well, and in the right direction (cols. 2 and 6). The interaction terms are quite insignificant, though all but the "state vacancy" variables operate in the expected direction. Thus Education and Labor requests, like those of Banking and Currency, appear to be motivated primarily by self-interest *undiscounted* for success probability. It is more than coincidental that there is a rather large overlap among members applying for the two committees—see tables 3.3 and 3.7.[37]

Foreign Affairs

Pr [Foreign Affairs request] =

$$\Phi \left[\begin{array}{l} -1.512 + .038 \text{ [\% foreign stock]} \\ \quad (.297) \quad (.015) \\ + .219 \text{ [state vacancy]} + .917 \text{ [state competition]} \\ \quad (.650) \qquad\qquad\quad (.560) \\ -4.136 \text{ [senior state competition]} \\ (191.745) \\ - .025 \text{ [state representation]} \\ \quad (.459) \\ + .026 \, w_{11} - .057 \, w_{21} + .041 \, w_{31} - .022 \, w_{41} \\ \quad (.027) \qquad (.026) \qquad (5.905) \qquad (.019) \end{array} \right]$$

A single "interest" variable was defined for the Foreign Affairs probit: % foreign stock. While this is a natural selection of a constituency characteristic most closely attuned to the committee's jurisdiction, it must be admitted that at the outset the Foreign Affairs Committee was believed to pose a severe test of the self-interest calculus articulated earlier. The reason for this belief is the general qualitative conclusion shared by many students of congressional committees that Foreign Affairs is one of the least useful committees for reelection purposes. Fenno (1973, pp. 12–13), on the basis of interviews, states that "in no case did a Foreign Affairs member of either party give top priority to constituency-related goals. Majority opinion was expressed by one member who said: 'Politically, it's not a good committee for me. My constituents are interested in bread and butter and there's no bread and butter on Foreign Affairs.' ... A few members see home-front advantages to be gained by pushing pro-Israeli or anti-Communist amendments on the foreign aid bill or merely by associating with the Secretary of State. But the theme is a minor one." Rather, members tend to stress the "interesting," "exciting," "controversial," and "important" subjects that fall within the committee's jurisdiction (Fenno 1973, p. 9). On the basis of interviews, then, freshmen claim they seek membership on Foreign Affairs in order to help make good public policy in areas of national significance.

For these reasons it was somewhat surprising to discover that, when it comes to Foreign Affairs requests, one ought to pay most attention to what members *do*, not what they *say*. The "interest" term in the model is significant at p = .005 and, while the probability main effects are not very significant, together with the interaction terms they are (p = .001).

Here is an excellent illustration of the collinearity of member goals suggested earlier. While many requesters believe they seek membership in order to "make good public policy," they are considerably more likely to apply for

Foreign Affairs if they come from districts whose voters *appreciate the significance of policies in the domain of Foreign Affairs*. Thus, even if the typical belief is "it's not a good [reelection] committee for me," behavior reveals it is apparently not a bad committee either![38]

A more detailed examination of the estimated model, which has an overall significance level of $p = .005$ ($\hat{R}^2 = .487$), reveals that all of the components of the expected value calculation are as expected. State vacancies increase the probability of a request; state competition reduces the request probability so long as the percent foreign stock exceeds 16 (true of more than three-fourths of all congressional districts); senior state competition and state representation, too, decrease the request probability, though the estimates associated with the former variable (those associated with "senior state competition" and w_{31}) are highly unstable owing to the infrequency of nonfreshman transfer requests. With the Foreign Affairs Committee we have a good statistical fit of the data to the theory.

Interior

Pr [Interior request] =

$$\Phi \left[\begin{array}{l} -1.250 + .005 \text{ [100s of square miles of district land area]} \\ \quad (.172) \quad (.001) \\[4pt] - .007 \text{ [\% work force in mining]} + .972 \text{ [state vacancy]} \\ \quad (.068) \qquad\qquad\qquad\qquad\qquad (.325) \\[4pt] - .252 \text{ [state competition]} \\ -(.296) \\[4pt] - .322 \text{ [state representation]} - .004 \, w_{11} \\ \quad (.305) \qquad\qquad\qquad\qquad (.002) \\[4pt] - .028 \, w_{12} + .004 \, w_{21} + .102 \, w_{22} - .002 \, w_{41} + .201 \, w_{42} \\ \quad (.091) \qquad (.003) \qquad (.175) \qquad (.002) \qquad (.171) \end{array} \right]$$

For the Interior Committee, the entire probit, the constant term, and the value terms are very significant (see table 4.6, cols. 1, 2, and 6).[39] The value terms—district land area and percent of work force engaged in mining—capture the relationship between a committee whose jurisdiction includes reclamation, general land management, and mining, and the electoral and policy interests of members. The probability and interaction terms, too, are quite significant (table 4.6, cols. 3, 4, and 5). They operate under most conditions in the expected direction. The exceptions occur only for those districts with a very large land area. In those cases the probability and interaction terms tend to cancel in their effects—undiscounted "interest" alone tends to operate.[40]

Interstate

Pr [Interstate request] =

$$\Phi \left[\begin{array}{l} - \;\; .403 \; + \; .967 \; [\text{health/commerce occupation}] \\ \;\;\;\; (.142) \;\; (.371) \end{array} \right.$$

$$+ \;\; .155 \; [\text{state vacancy}] \; - \; .111 \; [\text{state competition}]$$
$$\;\;\;\; (.298) \qquad\qquad\qquad (.211)$$

$$+ \;\; 5.656 \; [\text{senior state competition}]$$
$$\;\;\;\; (90.130)$$

$$- \;\; .541 \; [\text{state representation}]$$
$$\;\;\;\; (.206)$$

$$\left. + \;\; .398 \; w_{11} \; + \; .254 \; w_{21} \; - \; 11.174 \; w_{31} \; + \; .041 \; w_{41} \right]$$
$$\;\;\;\; (.762) \qquad (.559) \qquad (156.110) \qquad (.556)$$

The Interstate probit is among the poorest in terms of $\hat{R}^2$ because of the difficulty its jurisdiction poses for linking member interests to committee business. Nevertheless, the explanatory variables do discriminate between applicants and nonapplicants at a significant statistical level. The only v-term employed is occupational background, and it is significant at $p = .005$. The probability terms and interactions are also fairly significant (table 4.6, col. 4). Each of the probability-interaction combinations—senior competition excepted—are compatible with an expected value calculus. The estimates for the senior state competition variables are very unreliable, owing to the relative infrequency of such competition.

Despite the compatibility of the model with the expected value calculus, and the fact that it is quite significant overall ($p \ll .001$), the model for Interstate is worse than it seems! In the case of Interstate, as with no other committee, the absolute frequency of requests (34% of all members applied for this committee) renders the null model, with which the equation above is compared, particularly poor. The maximum likelihood prediction for any freshman's request behavior under the null hypothesis (that none of the explanatory variables is significant) is "no request."[41] Thus, the null model predicts "no request" for each of the 231 freshmen, and it is correct 66% of the time. The estimated model above, on the other hand, is correct in its predictions nearly 74% of the time. While this is a statistically significant improvement over the null model predictions, it is still a relatively poor predictive model. In the case of most other committees the request rate is lower so that the null model prediction ("no request") is correct with greater frequency. Thus, when our model for other committees is statistically significant, it not only is a significant improvement over the null model, its absolute level of prediction is quite high as well.

The Interstate model, then, reflects the pursuit of probability-discounted interests in request behavior; but, owing to the octopus-like quality of Interstate's jurisdiction, more members are actually interested in this committee than the rather meager set of v-terms indicates. I have returned to this theme several times, and shall have further use for it. The committee system, at its thirtieth birthday, has not maintained clear-cut jurisdictional lines. The consequence, especially for committees which capture, through jurisdictional imperialism, broader and broader policy domains, is a broadening of the set of interests impinged upon by committee decisions. An increase in the diversity of applicants is a concomitant of this phenomenon.

Judiciary

Pr [Judiciary request] =

$$\Phi \left[\begin{array}{l} -2.232 + .019 \text{ [lawyer} * \% \text{ foreign stock]} \\ (.385) \quad (.014) \\[4pt] + .039 \text{ [lawyer} * \text{ south]} + 1.356 \text{ [lawyer]} \\ (.593) (.486) \\[4pt] + .008 \, w_{11} + .796 \, w_{12} + .009 \, w_{21} - 4.621 \, w_{22} \\ (.015) (1.057) (.012) (72.503) \\[4pt] - .014 \, w_{41} + .219 \, w_{42} \\ (.012) (.652) \end{array} \right]$$

The probit equation for the Judiciary Committee has been operationalized in a slightly different manner than the others. The Judiciary Committee is one of the few committees that has a de facto occupational requirement for appointment: nonlawyers are not appointed.[42] The appropriate version of the model to estimate is one that incorporates this *necessary* condition. In particular, the "probability of success" expression (4.3) is written:

$$g(a_{ij}/R_{ij}) = \text{Pr [i a lawyer]} \cdot g(p_1, p_2 \ldots)$$

Applying this modification to (4.5) we obtain

$$g(a_{ij}/R_{ij}) = \beta_0(\text{Pr[i a lawyer]}) + \text{Pr[i a lawyer]} \cdot \sum_t \beta_t p_t$$

The product of (4.4) and (4.5), as modified, yields the appropriate probit to be estimated.

$$\Pr[R_{ij}] =$$

$$\Phi \left[b_0(\text{Pr[i a lawyer]}) + \text{Pr[i a lawyer]} \sum_s a_s v_s \right.$$
$$+ \text{Pr[i a lawyer]} \cdot \sum_t b_t p_t$$
$$\left. + \text{Pr[i a lawyer]} \cdot \sum_s \sum_t b_{st} v_s p_t \right]$$

Notice that the hypothesized necessary condition implies *no intercept term.* That is, for a nonlawyer the probability of requesting Judiciary is negligible. In the context of the probit model (recall fig. 4.1) this implication translates into an expectation of a very negative constant term.

Although we have introduced occupational background as a probability term (a dummy variable: 1 = lawyer, 0 = nonlawyer), it taps the "interest" component as well. Who, that is, but lawyers ordinarily have a general professional interest in judicial proceedings, constitutional amendments, the penal system, federal courts and judges, civil liberties, patents, trademarks, and copyrights, and immigration and naturalization? Consequently, "lawyer" is regarded as both a probability and an "interest" term.

The "interest" terms defined for this equation are % foreign stock and % nonwhite. They are, however, highly correlated in northern districts so that the latter was deleted. In order to recapture the interest of southerners with high proportions of nonwhite constituents and, more generally, to reflect the expected high interest of southerners in Judiciary (owing to the salience of civil rights legislation), a second "interest" term was defined: "Is i from the South?" (1 = yes, 0 = no). Each of the probability terms is defined as in previous probits. The same is true of the interactions. Consequently, the correctly specified model contains: (1) "lawyer" and "lawyer" interacting with "% foreign stock" and "South" as v-terms; (2) "lawyer" and "lawyer" interacting with "state vacancy," "state competition," and "state representation" as p-terms;[43] and (3) "lawyer" interacting with each of the six combinations of basic probability and interest components as interaction terms. This is the model estimated above.

The equation estimated is significant at p ≪ .001. As expected, the constant term is very negative (indeed, the Judiciary constant term has the largest negative value of all the probits) and highly significant (table 4.6, col. 6). The v-terms (which include the "lawyer" main effect variable), too, are very significant and possess the correct sign. Also as expected, the "lawyer" main effect, regarded as a p-term (table 4.6, col. 3) is very significant. The interaction terms, however, are not. Nevertheless, they affect the probability of requests in the expected direction with several noteworthy exceptions: state competition for nonsoutherners has little effect, one way or the other, on request probabilities, and southern requesters appear to be undaunted by the fact that their states are already represented on the committee—perhaps a consequence of the salience of civil rights for southern constituencies.

When all is said and done, the basic lesson of this model is this: if a freshman is a lawyer, the chances are 40 in 100 that he will request Judiciary; if he is not, the chances are less than 1 in 100. The other explanatory variables add only a little additional explanatory power; they do not help us greatly in determining *which* 40 out of every 100 lawyers will apply for the committee.

The significance of the Judiciary probit (and the $\hat{R}^2$ of .501), then, is chiefly a measure of the discriminating power of the occupational background variable, both as an indicator of "interest" and of the probability of appointment success.

Public Works

Pr [Public Works request] =

$$\Phi \left[\begin{array}{l} - .381 + 1.073 \text{ [predecessor status]} \\ \quad (.130) \quad (.634) \\ - .136 \text{ [state vacancy]} - .245 \text{ [state competition]} \\ \quad (.297) \quad\quad\quad\quad\quad\quad (.238) \\ - .721 \text{ [senior state competition]} \\ \quad (.591) \\ - .491 \text{ [state representation]} \\ \quad (.215) \\ - .255 \, w_{11} + .367 \, w_{21} - 4.958 \, w_{31} - 5.046 \, w_{41} \\ \quad (.789) \quad\quad (.872) \quad (127.464) \quad\quad (73.575) \end{array} \right]$$

The Public Works Committee is reputed to be one of the major pork-barrel committees (but see Murphy 1974). As Ferejohn (1974, pp. 49–61) notes, "Congressmen generally agree that constituency-oriented [public works] expenditures can be valuable to them. There appear to be three separate reasons why congressmen value projects in their districts. First, projects are valuable in a re-election campaign as part of an incumbent's record in office. Second, they maximize discretion over other legislative issues. Third, they ensure that a project issue will not be held against congressmen by groups who could enter or back an opposition candidate in the next election."[44] Moreover, Ferejohn (1974, pp. 137–38) discovers a statistically significant effect of committee membership on new project starts in the member's state. Thus committee membership appears to be desirable, both in principle and in fact.[45]

But desirable to *whom*? Interest in membership on Public Works is elusive precisely because it is so widespread. Nearly every district has some proposed public-works projects on the books.[46] Because public-works projects, at various stages of completion, are held to be desired by so wide a set of congressmen, "interest" variables which discriminate between requesters and nonrequesters are difficult to construct. In the absence of any obvious constituency characteristics or occupational background factors, it was believed that one group of freshmen who stood to benefit disproportionately from committee membership were those whose predecessors served on the committee. These freshmen could pick up where their predecessors left off, trading on the latter's already established good will and rapport with the Army Corps of Engineers, and expediting (and thus taking credit for) the completion of projects already on the books. Thus, the v-term employed in the Public Works probit model is "predecessor status" (1 = predecessor a member of committee, 0 = not member).

The probit is quite significant but, like that for Armed Services and Interstate, is one of the less well-fitting models. The v-term was only moderately significant and the p-terms, though statistically significant, were not always of the correct sign.[47] The interactions proved to be quite insignificant.

With Public Works, then, we must conclude that the ill-defined relationship between member interests and committee business prevents us from detecting, in a satisfactory fashion, a self-interest calculus at work. A consideration of the reasons why, as well as a general summary of the chapter, is found in the next section.

Conclusion

The empirical analysis of this chapter supports two general conclusions. First, committee requests reflect member interests and appear, in most instances, to be the product of an expected value calculus. Second, the committees of the committee system, with their overlapping, heterogeneous jurisdictions, provide numerous opportunities for members to act on their personal goals and objectives.

It is, however, the interaction of these two characteristics that makes it difficult to identify the individual importance of each. "Interest," narrowly defined and discounted for the probability of assignment success, is *sufficient* to elicit requests for a committee. This is the empirical significance of equation (4.6) and the hypothesis tests (table 4.6) for which it was employed. Although sufficient to elicit requests, probability-discounted interest is not *necessary*. By that I do not mean to deny self interest, but rather to emphasize the difficulty of identifying (measures of) interest in light of the heterogeneous nature of committee jurisdictions. Compelling evidence for this assertion is presented in table 4.7. There the results of a residual analyses for six of the nine committees are reported. From column (2) of table 4.6, in which the significance of the "interest" terms is tested, the six committees are partitioned into three groups. Agriculture and Interior have, by most casual measures, the jurisdictions most easily identified with socioeconomic interests; for Education and Labor and Foreign Affairs the task is somewhat more difficult; and, for Armed Services and Interstate, jurisdiction and constituency interest are most imperfectly matched. That is, for the three groups, "interest" variables are increasingly *less* likely to discriminate between applicants and nonapplicants. And the source of error is Type (B). Whereas

Table 4.7   Error Analysis of Equation (4.6) for Selected Committees

	% Correctly Predicted by (4.6)	% Errors*		
Committee	(1)	Type (A) (2)	Type (B) (3)	N
I				
Agriculture	86.6	2.7	10.7	231
Interior	84.1	2.0	13.9	226
II				
Education & Labor	82.7	2.2	15.1	231
Foreign Affairs	82.8	1.7	15.5	174
III				
Armed Services	79.3	1.7	19.0	174
Interstate	73.6	4.4	22.0	231
Mean	81.5	2.5	16.0	

* Type (A): i predicted to request j, but did not.
Type (B): i not predicted to request j, but did.

for all committees slightly more than 2% of the predictions err in attributing a request to a nonapplicant, there is a monotonically increasing relationship between committee type (I, II, III) and likelihood of failing to attribute a request to an applicant. For the committees with very heterogeneous jurisdictions, e.g., Interstate, or jurisdictions for which "interest" is ill defined, e.g., Armed Services, the model is *least* successful at discriminating between applicants and nonapplicants (col. 1) and *most* likely to fail to detect those who reveal their interest by their request behavior (col. 3).

A second qualification to our general conclusions deserves emphasis. Not all freshmen are "self-starters." During the influence process preceding the submission of requests, many freshmen are encouraged to apply for committees that do *not* bear the direct relationship to "interest" which we have been seeking. This is especially apparent in the residual analysis of table 4.7 in which the preponderance of errors are seen to be Type B. Self-interest does not always operate in a simple "me-and-my-constituency" and "me-and-my-background" fashion.[48] While "interesteds" do apply—and are correctly identified in the statistical analysis—a number of other applicants do not qualify as "interesteds" because the term has been too narrowly conceived.

Our analysis, then, is quite successful and appropriate for self-starters and for committees with fairly clear-cut, homogeneous jurisdictions. It is less adequate for those freshmen who "go along" in order to please others (and build up credit), or who are "inner-circle choices," and for those committees whose heterogeneous jurisdictions defy simple characterization in terms of interest. Whether these latter situations are so idiosyncratic as to defy general explanation, or whether an explanation more subtle than those offered here can improve upon our results, cannot be determined at this time. These questions surely deserve our reflection and further analysis.

Chapter 5

Nonfreshman
Revealed Preferences

In Chapter 3 it was observed that the committee system is in continuous flux, owing not only to the infusion of new personnel, but also in a nontrivial way to committee-switching and acquisition of new seats by incumbent members (see table 3.10). While most incumbent members do most of their committee moving relatively early in their careers (see table 5.1), such moves are nevertheless not all that unusual by relatively senior members.[1]

In this chapter revealed preferences for "queue-changing" are examined. Recall that a member's behavioral alternatives are (1) the status-quo option, (2) the transfer option, and (3) the dual-service option, and that he reveals a preference for a particular committee if he requests it, he transfers to it (or acquires it in the case of dual-service assignments), or both. Three factors are discovered to affect a member's revealed preferences about his committee portfolio. The first is his *initial wealth*—the status of his freshman assignment(s).[2] The second is the number of *opportunities* he has had to express (or not express) a preference. The third factor is the *status of the queue* for which he reveals a preference. These three factors interact in determining "the costs and benefits of the queue." They generate a set of propositions or theoretical expectations in accord with the intuitive cost/benefit calculus presented in Chapter 3. These propositions are listed below followed by a theoretical defense of each and an examination of the data that bear on their validity.

PROPOSITION I
(Opportunity Effect)

The proportion of members maintaining the status quo is a declining function of time (number of opportunities).

PROPOSITION II
(Wealth Effect)

The proportion of members taking the status quo option is an increasing function of wealth. The "wealth effect" is a decreasing function of time (number of opportunities).

PROPOSITION III
(Opportunity Cost
Effect)

The status of the queue for which a transfer preference is revealed is an increasing function of wealth and time (number of opportunities).

Table 5.1

Timing of Nonfreshman Revealed Preferences for Switching, 86th–93rd Congresses

Nonfreshman Term	Transfer	Dual Service
1	.685	.470
2	.148	.231
3	.065	.163
4	.055	.096
5	.028	.010
6	.010	.020
7	.010	.010
8	.000	.000
	1.000	1.000
	(N = 108)	(N = 104)

NOTE: Cell entries are proportion of *all transfer (dual service)* revealed preferences revealed in i[th] nonfreshman term. Thus, while first-term nonfreshmen comprise 30.5% of our data set (see table 3.9), they are associated with more than two-thirds of the revealed preferences for transfer and nearly half of the dual-service revealed preferences.

The Opportunity Effect

This proposition is actually rather innocuous; it would be surprising were it not true. Stated simply, it maintains that the *cumulative* prospects of change is an increasing function of time. That this proposition is to be expected, independent of particular cost-benefit information, may be demonstrated as follows:

Suppose the probability that any one member will seek to alter his committee portfolio at some opportunity is p. The status-quo probability is $(1 - p)$. The likelihood of maintaining the status quo over T periods (opportunities) is $(1 - p)^T$, and $\lim_{T \to \infty} (1 - p)^T = 0$ for any $p > 0$.

Thus, no matter how unlikely the prospect of change (no matter how small p is), the likelihood of the persistent adoption of the status-quo option diminishes with the number of terms of service (opportunities for change). For example, if p = .1 the probability that a nine-term Congressman will have left his initial freshman assignments intact is less than one-third. Since p is probably much larger for most members, an opportunity effect ought to be observed over time.[3]

Notice that Proposition I does *not* assert there is a greater likelihood of, say, a four-term member seeking change than of a two-term member (indeed, the opposite is ordinarily the case). Rather it asserts that change is a function of the number of opportunities which, in turn, is a function of the number of terms of service. Thus the proportion of four-term members who have revealed some preference for change over their careers should exceed the proportion of two-termers who have done similarly.

Three reasons (and there are probably others) may be marshalled in defense of the first proposition: acquisitiveness, changing objectives, and learning. If serving on one committee (subcommittee) is valuable to a member, then accumulating additional committee or subcommittee seats (and the privileges associated with them) is even more valuable. While the marginal utility of additional committee or subcommittee membership undoubtedly is diminishing, owing to constraints on a member's time,[4] each additional membership confers privileges that, if not directly utilized by him, are available to him for exchange. The privileges of committee and subcommittee membership—committee (subcommittee) votes, access to staff, the attention of administrative bureaucracies, influence on the committee (subcommittee) agenda—are tradeable commodities.

One should not push this line of reasoning too far, for there are constraints on acquisitiveness imposed by the Legislative Reorganization Act and/or the Democratic Caucus. Thus, with some recent exceptions, no members may serve on more than two standing committees[5] and, again with some exceptions, no member serving on an exclusive committee may possess additional assignments.[6] Nevertheless, one piece of evidence appears to lend support to the acquisitiveness hypothesis and, indirectly, to Proposition I.

Table 5.2 displays an important secular trend: there has been a monotonic growth in the proportion of nonfreshman with second-committee assignments (and this excludes Budget, Small Business, and Standards of Official Conduct). The figures are even more impressive if we exclude from the calculation those nonfreshmen prohibited from receiving a second assignment. Such a revised calculation for the Ninety-fourth Congress, for example, reveals that nearly 85% of all eligible nonfreshmen held a second assignment. While part of this growth can be explained by the fact that freshmen are receiving second assignments at a growing rate (freshmen who one Congress later become

Table 5.2   Second-Committee Assignments of Democrats, 86th–94th
                             Congresses

Congress	No. of Slots	No. of			Proportion with Second Seat	
		Fresh.	Nonfr.*	Total	Fresh.	Nonfr.*
86	365	64	219	283	.187	.281
87	350	19	243	262	.366	.295
88	353	36	222	258	.250	.355
89	407	71	224	295	.197	.387
90	353	13	235	248	.077	.408
91	357	22	223	245	.182	.448
92	392	32	223	255	.531	.489
93	387	26	217	243	.654	.535
94	471	75	216	291	.707**	.603

NOTE: Standards of Official Conduct, Budget, and Small
Business are not included in these tabulations.
* Speaker and majority leader not counted in this calculation.
** Most of those freshmen who are not recorded as having
a second assignment either were assigned to an exclusive
committee or actually had a second assignment on
Budget or Small Business. Excluding these, only 8% of
the freshmen failed to receive a second seat.

nonfreshmen), it does appear that the growing rate of nonfreshman acquisitiveness has had a relatively long history, whereas the "freshman second-
assignment phenomenon" is of more recent vintage.[7] The fact, however, that
freshman second-assignment requests are receiving increasing attention
would seem to support the view that acquisitiveness has received the sanction
of the Democratic Caucus and that freshmen are no longer discriminated
against in this regard.[8]

Given this increasingly general tendency to switch and/or acquire new
committees, it follows that the greater the number of opportunities to reveal
acquisitive tendencies the more likely they will, in fact, be revealed. Thus,
over the length of a congressional career the freshman portfolio of committees
is increasingly less likely to resist change. The likelihood of observing the
persistent use of the status-quo option declines as opportunities for change
increase.

Second, member goals are not immune to change. Institutional power
becomes increasingly more prominent among a member's objectives the
longer he remains in the House. To some extent this will be revealed in

transfers to exclusive committees. For other members, who do not wish to forego accumulated seniority on their current committee, it will be reflected, again, in acquisitiveness.

Finally, learning takes place over time. Member interests and objectives become better articulated and the instruments with which they may be served become better known as experience in the House is accumulated. The rate with which members leave Education and Labor and Banking and Currency, as observed earlier, is illustrative of this phenomenon. One Connecticut congressman sought to leave Education and Labor, his first-preference freshman committee, after one term of service; he requested a transfer to his second-preference freshman committee! Other members, after some time in the queue, discover that the actuarial tables have not produced results in accord with their hopes and expectations. Discovering that he is not advancing up the committee ladder as rapidly as he had hoped, the member learns that the costs of transferring, that is, of foregoing opportunities in his current committee, are in fact less than he had earlier believed. Thus, after fourteen years on the Armed Services Committee, Otis Pike (D., N.Y.) transferred to Ways and Means. Though the chairman of a minor subcommittee, he was only sixth in seniority on Armed Services. Moreover, there were two members ahead of him in the pecking order, Samuel Stratton (D., N.Y.) and Charles Bennet (D., Fla.), who were relatively young by congressional standards (fifty-nine and sixty-five, respectively). The chances that Congressman Pike would succeed to the committee chairmanship (he was fifty-four) had diminished considerably—so, as a result, had the cost of transferring.[9]

The evidence for Proposition I is found in table 5.3. The data persuasively demonstrate that *opportunities matter*. Independently of other factors, with

Table 5.3   **Committee Switching, Committee Acquisition, and Opportunities: Revealed Preferences in the 86th–93rd Congresses**

		No. of Nonfreshmen Terms		
		1	2–3	4 or more
	Status quo	.509	.222	.052
Option	Dual service	.208	.400	.658
	Transfer	.302	.467	.605
		N = 53	N = 45	N = 76

NOTE: Cell entries are proportion of members (column N) exercising row options at some point in their nonfreshman careers. Columns do not sum to 1.000 since some members exercise *both* dual service and transfer option.

increasing opportunities a member is less likely to maintain his "freshman wealth." He seeks either to add to it or to alter it. While more than half of all members who have had a single opportunity selected the status-quo option, only four of the seventy-six members with four or more opportunities followed suit throughout their careers. Use of both dual service and transfer options increases with opportunities as expected; indeed, the growth in the use of the dual-service option reinforces the belief that acquisitiveness is a way of life on the Hill. More experienced members have revealed dual-service preferences at more than triple the rate of their less experienced colleagues (and transfer preferences at twice the rate).[10]

The Wealth Effect

Whereas Proposition I asserts that opportunities matter, Proposition II asserts that wealth does, too. In particular, this proposition maintains that those members endowed with greater wealth as freshmen are more likely to adopt the status-quo option consistently (controlling for opportunities) than are their more poorly endowed colleagues. However, it is expected that freshman wealth effects diminish with time.

Wealth in this context is subjectively defined. The wealthier members, in light of the heterogeneity of tastes revealed in Chapter 3, are defined as those who have obtained one of their freshman requests. Since distinctions among freshman preferences—first preference, second preference—do not purchase any additional insight, and yet are costly (shrinking cell sizes), a simple dichotomy is employed here.

Wealth as we have defined it is precisely the kind of factor that mitigates the incentive to seek change. Having cashed in early in terms of committee assignments, the wealthy member faces substantial opportunity costs in seeking change, namely, accrued seniority on a committee he initially sought (and hence presumably desired) as a freshman. Unless the benefits of change are large (and Proposition III speaks to this point), the wealthy member is going to stay put. If he seeks any change at all it will be of the dual service, something-for-nothing variety.

Table 5.4 provides the evidence. In part (a) all 174 of the congressmen in the data set are divided according to their wealth, and the request options employed in their *first* nonfreshman term are tabulated. As expected, the wealthy stay put and the poor try to move. Nearly half of the wealthy maintain the status quo; nearly three-fourths of the poor opt for change. Moreover, those wealthy members who do seek change are equally divided between the dual service and the transfer options. For the poor who seek change, on the other hand, the odds are better than 6:1 that it is a transfer they seek.

Table 5.4 **The Wealth Effect, Controlling for Opportunities, 86th–93rd Congresses**

t = 1st nonfreshman term

		Wealth		
		Pref.	No. Pref.	
	status quo	.481	.256	
Options	dual service	.244	.103	(a)
	transfer	.275	.641	
		1.000	1.000	
		N = 135	N = 39	

t = 2d or 3d nonfreshman term

		Wealth		
		Pref.	No Pref.	
	status quo	.450	.375	
Options	dual service	.400	.375	(b)
	transfer	.150	.250	
		1.000	1.000	
		N = 40	N = 8	

t = 4th or higher nonfreshman term

		Wealth Pref.	
	status quo	.417	
Options	dual service	.500	(c)
	transfer	.083	
		1.000	
		N = 12	

In part (b) of the table members who sought change at their first opportunity or who failed to survive until their second opportunity were removed from the tabulation. Those who maintained the status quo at their first opportunity and survived the following election were partitioned according to their wealth as in part (a). Again the expected result obtains, though the data base is growing small. The poor are more likely to seek change and less likely to maintain the status quo than the rich. However, as predicted, the differences are not as great as in part (a). Moreover, for both the poor and the rich the dual-service option is employed increasingly at the expense of the transfer option—a sign that the opportunity costs of transfer increase with time for both groups.

Only twelve members of the sample maintained the status quo through their third opportunity and survived the following election. Their behavior is reported in part (c). Since all are wealthy, only the effects of time can be observed. They are as predicted: the "opportunity effect" is revealed in a diminished proportion who persist in maintaining the status quo; and, for those who seek change, the odds are better than 6:1 that the dual service option is employed.

The Opportunity Cost Effect

This proposition focuses on transfer behavior. The hypothesis entertained is that revealed preferences for exclusive committees are a positive function of wealth and time. Of those who seek transfers, the wealthy tilt toward the exclusive committees while the poor are willing to settle more frequently for other committees. Similarly, those who seek transfers later in their careers disproportionately reveal preferences for exclusive committees; the contrary holds for those who seek transfers early in their careers. Both of these hypotheses follow directly from an opportunity cost argument. *The rich and the senior will transfer only for the big prizes.*

Tables 5.5 and 5.6 provide the empirical support for Proposition III. The expected patterns emerge. In table 5.5 there is a monotonically increasing relationship between wealth and proportion of exclusive-committee revealed preferences. The wealthy seek the exclusive committees at a 58% rate, the moderately wealthy at a 40% rate, and the poor at a 35% rate. In table 5.6

Table 5.5   **Wealth and Revealed Preferences for Transfer, 86th–93rd Congresses**

	Wealth		
	1st Pref.	Other Pref.	No Pref.
Exclusive	.579	.400	.350
Other	.421	.600	.650
	1.000	1.000	1.000
	N = 38	N = 30	N = 40

NOTE: N is number of *revealed preferences* (not members). Cell entries are proportion of N that are exclusive or semi-exclusive.

Table 5.6   Opportunities and Revealed Preferences for Transfer,
86th–93rd Congresses

	No. of Nonfreshman Terms		
	1st	2d or 3d	4th or Later
Exclusive	.370	.458	.727
Other	.630	.542	.273
	1.000	1.000	1.000
	N = 73	N = 24	N = 11

NOTE: For each column, N is the number of *revealed preferences*
(not members). Cell entries are proportions of N that are
exclusive or semiexclusive.

the opportunity cost argument is again sustained. Nearly two-thirds of the
transfer preferences revealed at a member's first opportunity are for committees other than Appropriations, Rules, and Ways and Means. By the second
or third opportunity, only slightly more than half of all transfer revealed–
preferences are for a semiexclusive committee. And by the fourth or later
opportunity, nearly three-fourths of the requests are for exclusive committees.

Conclusions

Although our tour of nonfreshmen requests has been briefer and empirically
simpler than the tour of the freshman model, several themes have been established. The most basic of these is that the committee system is in constant flux
and that internal movements are an important component of the changing
complexion of House committees. Table 3.10 confirms the thesis of
the changing face of congressional committees—the proportion of all
Democratic committee slots *newly occupied* ranges from a low of 10.2% in the
Ninetieth Congress to a high of 35.3% in the Ninety-fourth Congress.[11] It
also documents the extent to which internal transfers and new acquisitions
contribute to this change—the proportion of new Democratic committee
personnel who are nonfreshmen ranges from a low of 23.9% in the Eighty-
sixth Congress to a high of 65.6% in the Ninety-first Congress. Although the
data suggest that committee personnel change is disproportionately nonfreshman in years of Democratic party contraction in the House, the amount
of internal mobility in every year is nevertheless impressive.

A second theme of this chapter, one argued in more detail in Chapter 3,
is the subjective quality of nonfreshman revealed preferences. House service
has a homogenizing effect on preferences only to the extent that it tends to
accentuate the benefits of serving in one of the exclusive committee queues.
Nearly half of all nonfreshman revealed-transfer preferences are for Appro-

priations, Rules, and Ways and Means. The aggregate (nonfreshman) demand for committees tabulated in table 3.8 provides a picture of a committee hierarchy with the exclusive committees at the head and the duty committees bringing up the rear. It is, however, inappropriate to read too much into this aggregate preference map. In particular, except for the general movement from the duty committee to all others, and from all committees to the exclusive committees, preferences for committees are heterogeneous. From the single revealed preference, for example, of Armed Services over Interstate, and from the absence of any contrary revealed preferences, it does *not* follow that Armed Services is, in some sense, better, more important, or more popular than Interstate. For the one person who revealed the indicated preference, *and only for him*, is the conclusion justified in its strongest form. It is justified in slightly weaker form for all the members of Armed Services, none of whom sought to move to Interstate. However, for all the remaining representatives, who expressed no preference on the matter, and a fortiori for those members of Interstate who did not seek to move to Armed Services, the conclusion is very wide of the mark. To hold otherwise is to subscribe to the hypothesis that all congressmen share a common set of interests, are faced with the same kinds of pressures, are beholden to and appeal to an undifferentiated clientele, and, consequently, have comparable tastes and beliefs about the efficacy of various committees in servicing their goals when it comes to queue-switching. In light of data on freshman requests, this hypothesis is indefensible. With the possible exception of the general gravitation toward the exclusive committees,[12] it is the *diversity* of interests, and the differing extent to which committees are believed to serve those diverse interests, that is the important point.

A third theme of this chapter, one given little attention in the extant literature on committee transfers, is the complexity of mobility patterns in the House. While it is true that many changes in committee portfolios take place early in a member's career (see table 5.1), they are very often not of the simple, single-change variety. Acquisition and switching are distinct, and to some extent independent, methods by which freshmen portfolios are changed. Members often opt for both during the course of their careers. This is especially pronounced for those with relatively long careers in the House. Thus, over half of all members with four or more nonfreshman terms in the House have opted for change on more than one occasion or in more than one fashion. The comparable statistics for those with three or four terms of service and two terms of service, respectively, are .245 and .038 (see table 5.7).

Together these themes characterize a system that is both complex and dynamic. Freshman requests are a one-shot affair; the temporal dimension plays no significant role either in affecting behavior or explaining it. The complexity of freshman requests, moreover, derives not from the heterogeneity of *objectives* (most freshmen single-mindedly seek reelection), but

Table 5.7   Patterns of Mobility, 86th–93rd Congresses

| | No. of Nonfreshman Terms | | |
Change	1	2–3	4 or more
None	.509	.222	.052
Dual service only	.151	.333	.237
Transfer only	.302	.200	.171
Multiple requests	.038	.245	.540
	1.000	1.000	1.000
	N = 53	N = 45	N = 76

rather from the heterogeneity of *interests* that endow the reelection objective with behavioral meaning. With nonfreshman transfer and dual-service behavior, on the other hand, we have a more complicated pattern of changing interests, changing objectives, multiplying opportunities, and an increased number of behavioral options. The analysis of this chapter, with its reliance on a simple cost-benefit calculus, has attempted to describe and explain the patterns that have emerged.

Part 3

Negotiated Structure

Chapter 6

Party Leaders and the Committee System: Negotiating a Committee Structure

On February 4, 1971, the following debate was reported in the *Congressional Record*:

> Mr. Boggs: Mr. Speaker, I offer a privileged resolution (H.Res. 192) and ask for its immediate consideration: Resolved, that during the Ninety-second Congress the Committee on Agriculture shall be composed of thirty-six members; the Committee on Appropriations shall be composed of fifty-five members; ...the Committee on Veterans' Affairs shall be composed of twenty-six members.
>
> The resolution was agreed to. A motion to reconsider was laid on the table.
>
> Mr. Mills: Mr. Speaker, I offer a privileged resolution (H.Res. 193) and ask for its immediate consideration: Resolved, that the following named Members be, and they are hereby, elected to the following standing committees of the House of Representatives: [Democratic Committee rosters follow.]
>
> The resolution was agreed to. A motion to reconsider was laid on the table.
>
> Mr. Ford: Mr. Speaker, I offer a privileged resolution (H.Res. 194) and ask for its immediate consideration: Resolved, that the following named Members be, and they are hereby, elected to the following standing committees of the House of Representatives: [Republican Committee rosters follow.]
>
> The Resolution was agreed to. A motion to reconsider was laid on the table.

With this neatly orchestrated procedure, the committees of the Ninety-second Congress were organized and their slots filled. The three House resolutions are deceptively straightforward for, in fact, they represent the culmination of three complex, interrelated decision processes involving the leaders of the majority and minority parties and their respective Committees on Committees. In this chapter I shall be concerned with the first of those resolutions. Part IV is devoted to the second and third.

It is suggestive to conceive of structure negotiation decisions as one side of a market-like process in which "producers" make supply decisions in response to revealed preferences for committee slots. The initial requests of new Democrats, as well as the transfer and dual-service requests of returning Democratic members, have been collected and compiled for the CC by its chief counsel, John Martin; the demand side, that is, of this assignment market is well defined at an early point in the process. Before the CC can commence its deliberations, it requires knowledge of the specific supply parameters—the number of party slots per committee. The negotiated committee structure that emerges prior to the CC's deliberations is a series of supply decisions reached by the majority party leadership in response to various pressures on it. The leadership, it is argued below, follows a *strategy of accommodation*,[1] balancing the demands by potential committee members for it to manufacture slots and the demands by those already sitting on "high-demand" committees for it to maintain scarcity. What emerges is an equilibrium committee structure that persists until the forces which created it change.

The flow of influences on the party leaders—some encouraging them to expand the number of committee slots, others to hold the line—takes place in a context governed by formal rules and practices. In the next section I examine the relevant rules. This is followed, in turn, by a theoretical formulation of the problem, some implications and theoretical expectations, and an empirical test of these propositions.

House Rules and the Supply of Committee Slots

Guidance on the question of committee size is given by Rule X of the Rules of the House of Representatives.[2] Its modern form is mandated by the Legislative Reorganization Act of 1946:

There shall be elected by the House, at the commencement of each Congress, the following standing committees:

1. Committee on Agriculture, to consist of twenty-seven Members.

2. Committee on Appropriations, to consist of forty-three Members.

3. Committee on Armed Services, to consist of thirty-three Members.

4. Committee on Banking and Currency, to consist of twenty-seven Members.

5. Committee on Post Office and Civil Service, to consist of twenty-five Members.

6. Committee on the District of Columbia, to consist of twenty-five Members.

7. Committee on Education and Labor, to consist of twenty-five Members.

8. Committee on Expenditures in the Executive Departments, to consist of twenty-five Members.

9. Committee on Foreign Affairs, to consist of twenty-five members.

10. Committee on House Administration, to consist of twenty-five Members.

11. Committee on Interstate and Foreign Commerce, to consist of twenty-seven Members.

12. Committee on the Judiciary, to consist of twenty-seven Members.

13. Committee on Merchant Marine and Fisheries, to consist of twenty-five Members.

14. Committee on Public Lands, to consist of twenty-five Members.

15. Committee on Public Works, to consist of twenty-seven Members.

16. Committee on Rules, to consist of twelve Members.

17. Committee on Un-American Activities, to consist of nine Members.

18. Committee on Veterans' Affairs, to consist of twenty-seven Members.

19. Committee on Ways and Means, to consist of twenty-five Members.

Rule X—in the 1947 version—created 484 committee slots distributed among nineteen standing committees. Over the years, however, this rule has been amended in a variety of ways. The most superficial amendments have been committee name changes. Thus, the committee on Banking and Currency is now Banking, Currency, and Housing; Expenditures in the Executive Departments has been renamed Government Operations; Foreign Affairs is called International Relations; Public Lands is now Interior and Insular Affairs; Public Works has been recast Public Works and Transportation; Science and Astronautics (created in 1958) was renamed Science and Technology; and, before it was eliminated altogether, Un-American Activities was called Internal Security.

More consequential are the amendments to Rule X that create new standing committees. Since 1947, four new standing committees have been created: Science and Astronautics (Eighty-sixth Congress), Standards of Official

Conduct (Ninety-first Congress), Small Business and Budget (Ninety-fourth Congress).[3]

Amendments involving name changes, the creation of new committees, and the elimination of extant committees are offered only infrequently. A recurring amendment to House Rule X, however, is the one offered by the majority leader at the beginning of the congressional session. Like House Resolution 192 proposed by Majority Leader Boggs, these amendments temporarily alter committee sizes. Their duration is a single Congress, after which the committee sizes revert to those stipulated by Rule X unless a new amendment to the rules is approved. On rare occasion a committee expansion is made a permanent part of the rules.[4]

Although the House rules and amendments thereto set committee sizes, there is no mention in the rules of how committee slots are to be apportioned between the majority and minority parties. Indeed, throughout the rules it is implicitly assumed that the organizational structures of Congress are the creations of its majority. Minority representation on committees is at the majority's pleasure. Since the nineteenth century, however, the minority has come to expect a fair share of the committee seats. The minority, that is, expects its proportion of seats on most committees to be approximately its chamber proportion (see table 6.1). The majority party generally maintains extraordinary majorities on the two money committees and the agenda committee—a three fifths majority on Appropriations and a two-thirds majority on Rules and on Ways and Means.[5]

Although the minority's committee allocations are at the pleasure of the majority, it should be noted that the minority, in fact, is not forced to depend

Table 6.1   **Committee Structure and Party Ratios**

Congress	Chamber Ratio[a]	Committee Ratio[b]	N[c]
86	.649	.635	575
87	.600	.600	584
88	.598	.595	593
89	.678	.676	602
90	.570	.576	613
91	.565	.592	625
92	.590	.596	658
93	.556	.576	675
94	.669	.676	697

[a] Proportion of House Democratic
[b] Proportion of committee seats (N) Democratic.
[c] Number of committee slots.

on majority altruism exclusively. While it is true that relations between majority and minority are often guided by a spirit of accommodation, it is also true that in a legislative body governed by rules as complex as those of the House a determined minority can impose rather substantial costs on a majority that is insensitive to the minority's needs. The "spirit of accommodation," then, is backed by some very real quid pro quos between majority and minority.

Two final aspects of the rules are germane to the negotiated committee structure that ultimately emerges. The final paragraph of Rule X states:

> All vacancies in standing committees in the House shall be filled by election by the House. Each member shall be elected to serve on one standing committee and no more.[6]

The practice has emerged of letting each party select its own committee members, despite the rule that requires election by the full House. After each party's CC has made its allocations, House resolutions to that effect are adopted pro forma in order to comply with Rule X. The resolutions introduced by Mills and Ford in 1971 illustrate the procedure. Thus once the majority party leaders determine the slots per committee per party, the committee assignment process is decentralized, each party being free to determine the disposition of its own committee slots.

The second sentence of the final paragraph of Rule X, however, constrains each of those allocations. It was incorporated in the House rules in response to the unmanageability of the pre-1947 House committee system. The Seventy-ninth Congress—the Congress that passed the Legislative Reorganization Act mandating Rule X—possessed a committee system containing forty-seven standing committees and in excess of nine hundred committee positions. There were, that is, more than two committee assignments per member in that Congress (one member sat on nine committees). For a legislative body that prided itself on legislative specialization and efficient, expeditious working arrangements, the overextended organization of standing committees and the plethora of legislative positions that divided a member's time and multiplied his obligations were too much to tolerate. Rules X and XI, outgrowths of the Legislative Reorganization Act, reduced the number of standing committeess, streamlined their jurisdictions, and restricted most members to service on a single committee. The one-committee-assignment constraint, however, proved to be too binding. Over the first five years of its operation, Rule X was amended modestly until, in the Eighty-third Congress, the second sentence of the final paragraph was deleted altogether.[7] From that time on, each party was constrained in its allocation only by the total number of seats put at its disposal and whatever internal rules of allocation the

Democratic Caucus and the Republican Conference chose to impose on their respective CCs.

In sum, then, the House rules affect the supply of committee slots in several respects. They prescribe lower bounds on committee sizes which obtain unless an amendment to the contrary is approved. They grant the majority party control over the disposition of committee slots, though the requirement that *every* member receive an assignment constrains the majority and protects the minority. And, until they were amended, the rules in effect restricted the supply of committee slots by restricting multiple assignments.

Although the rules by which an institution conducts its business are usually of importance in understanding that conduct, in the case of the negotiated committee structure a textual analysis of the relevant House rules has been of limited utility.[8] The ease with which the permanent rules may be changed to suit the situationally-specific features of any given Congress, and the frequency with which such changes occur (as in the House resolutions that introduced this chapter), suggest that it is those situationally-specific features, *not* the permanent rules themselves, that hold the keys to understanding. An identification of these component forces—the incentives, motives, costs, benefits, and expectations of the relevant actors—is required in order to understand and explain the equilibrium committee structure that emerges at the beginning of each new Congress.

Leadership Responsiveness

The equilibrium committee size that emerges at the beginning of each Congress is the product of two sets of forces, one pressing for expanded committee sizes, the other seeking to limit expansion. That the former has prevailed over the latter for the most part is evidenced in table 6.2. That the latter set of forces nevertheless may have been significant, though distributed differentially across committees, is indicated in table 6.3. While no committee is smaller now then it was at its creation in 1947—indeed, for most committees the 1975 majority party representation exceeds the total size of the 1947 committee—committee growth has by no means been even. Exclusive committees are the most resistant to change of any kind.[9] Semiexclusive committees increased more than 40% of the time but rarely decreased.[10] Nonexclusive committees increased less frequently and decreased more frequently than semiexclusive committees.

In this section I seek to account for the differential inflation rate of committee berths with a theory of leadership responsiveness. Before describing the two sets of influences on party leaders, I consider the situation of the leaders at the time they must negotiate a committee structure. The recently

Table 6.2   Committee Slots, 80th–94th Congresses

Congress	No. of Committee Slots
80	484
81	487
82	505
83	519
84	541
85	548
86*	575
87	584
88	593
89	602
90	613
91**	637
92	670
93	687
94***	771

  * From this Congress, Science and Astronautics (N = 25)
included.
 ** From this Congress, Standards of Official Conduct (N =
12) included.
*** From this Congress, Budget (N = 37) and Small Business,
(N = 25) included; Internal Security (N = 9) deleted.

Table 6.3   **Change in Committee Sizes by Committee Type, 80th–93rd
Congresses**

	Committee Type*		
Size Change	Exclusive	Semiexclusive	Nonexclusive
Increase	.128	.434	.289
No Change	.872	.545	.654
Decrease	.000	.021	.057
	1.000	1.000	1.000

NOTE: For each class of committee, the cell entry is the
proportion of times (at the beginning of each Congress)
a change of each kind occurred.
  * Science and Astronautics counted as semiexclusive until
the 92nd Congress, when it became nonexclusive. Post
Office counted as semiexclusive until 88th Congress, when
it became nonexclusive.

concluded election has "shocked" the committee structure, producing vacancies in committee rosters. New members, and returning members seeking changes in their committee holdings, have submitted requests to the CC and are contesting for these vacancies (as well as any others the party leaders may manufacture). The minority leader as well has transmitted to the majority party leadership the committee needs of his people. It is the imbalance between the vacancies made available by the election and the expressed preferences of those seeking assignments, as well as adjustments due to a changed party ratio in the chamber, that necessitates leadership attention to committee sizes.

Expansionist Pressures

The majority leader who, in consultation with the Speaker and the chairman of the Democratic CC, has formal responsibility for establishing the parameters of the new committee structure, is best regarded as a partisan advocate. His immediate concern is to accommodate his followers. Engaged in the early forms of coalition-building, and with an eye on his party's upcoming legislative agenda, his primary motive in seeking to accommodate member preferences is apparent:

> [He uses his] power over committee assignments variously to reward members who have been loyal and cooperative, and to reinforce the strength of [his] own position by rewarding members whose loyalty may be suspected but whose strength can no longer be safely disregarded. [Masters 1963, p. 43]

Probably the most compelling partisan pressure on party leaders is to protect the committee positions of returning members who wish to retain them. According to the property–right norm, a member may retain those committee assignments he held in the previous Congress. Owing, however, to declining party fortunes in an intervening election, the slots may simply not be there. It is quite possible, for example, for the Democrats to lose 10% of their chamber representation but to have those losses distributed in a skewed fashion across committees so that, say, only 5% of the Democrats on Armed Services fail to return. If the party shares on Armed Services are adjusted to reflect the new chamber party ratio, then there will be a handful of returning Democratic members for whom there is no room on Armed Services. Responding to the pressure to avoid bumping these members off the committee, the party leaders will push to expand the committee size. In order to keep the party ratio on the committee more or less in line with the chamber ratio, the number of seats available to both parties will have to be expanded.

A second component of total demand, and potential source of pressure on the party leaders, is freshman first-preference and nonfreshman transfer requests. Some of this demand, of course, is absorbed by the distribution of vacancies in the existing committee structure. However, to the extent that these components of total demand do not already mesh with committee berths that have become available, party leaders are likely to respond by expanding committee sizes.

The third component of total demand is composed of freshman lower-order requests and nonfreshman dual-service requests. Although the party leaders may be least likely to respond to this component of demand, it probably poses the smallest problem for the leadership since it is often directed at precisely those committees not otherwise in high demand. Moreover, the constellation of forces directed at damping the expansionist tendencies of party leaders (to be discussed below) is likely to be least intense in its effects for this group of committees.

In responding to partisan demands for committee assignments, then, the natural predilection of party leaders is to accommodate (most of) this demand by fiddling with committee sizes. As Westefield (1974, p. 1594) has noted, "The majority party leaders want compliant behavior on the part of the members. They perceive that by accommodating the followers (dispensing 'good' assignments) they, the leaders, can reward past loyalty or encourage such behavior in the future." Although the party leaders cannot literally "dispense 'good' assignments"—that is the task of the party Committee on Committees[11]—they can, and do, establish the parameters of the committee system within which follower preferences are accommodated. Observe that the committee structure is negotiated, that is, sizes and party shares are established, *after* member preferences have been submitted to the CC. The leaders, then, have a pretty good idea of who wants what. The leadership is aware of the demand schedule for committee slots.

Reinforcement emerges from other sources. Chief among these are the state delegations and their deans. As Deckard (1975) reports, "The members of cohesive delegations consider committee assignments a matter of common interest. These delegations work hard to protect their positions on the choice committees and to maintain broad representation on less desirable but still important committees. . . . Campaigning for committee assignments tends to be low-keyed. 'Everything is done behind the scene. You don't want to go after it too openly. . . .' If an important position is at stake, cohesive delegations expect all their members to do what they can to help."[12] The conflicting demands from state delegations to place their people on various committees is most easily accommodated by size expansions.

On occasion lobbyists and informal House groups seek the majority party leadership's attention on committee expansion. In the 1961 expansion of the Rules Committee, for example, prominent roles were played by the

Democratic Study Group, the southern bloc led by Carl Vinson (D., Ga.), and various labor lobbyists in support of Speaker Rayburn's move to expand the committee (MacNeil 1963, pp. 428–30).

Although partisan pressures to expand weigh heavily on the majority party leadership, they are not the only such pressures. A similar set of signals are transmitted from minority leaders. Table 6.1 suggests that quantitatively, if not qualitatively, the minority obtains its fair share of committee slots. The simple correlation between the chamber party ratio and the mean committee party ratio is .97. Given the extraordinary majorities enjoyed by the majority party on exclusive committees (generally set at three-fifths for Appropriations and two-thirds for Rules and for Ways and Means unless the chamber party proportion exceeds this amount), it follows that on many other committees the minority obtains more than its fair share of seats. Table 6.4 lends additional credence to this claim.

Table 6.4   **Growth in Seats and Slots per Member**

	Slots per member*		
Congress	Democrats	Republicans	N**
86	1.294	1.372	575
87	1.341	1.500	584
88	1.358	1.371	593
89	1.380	1.393	602
90	1.423	1.391	613
91	1.504	1.349	625
92	1.525	1.494	658
93	1.607	1.563	675
94	1.619	1.569	697

   * Party leaders holding no assignments are excluded from the calculation.
  ** Budget, Small Business, and Standards of Official Conduct excluded.

The majority party leadership, it appears, accommodates the pressures felt by the minority party leadership by granting it enough slots to satisfy the needs of minority party followers. On some occasions, for example, if the minority leader requests an additional minority seat on committee j, the request is granted outright and is "financed" by an additional expansion of the committee size.[13] On other occasions, a minority request is "financed" by a slightly larger expansion of the committee in which the newly manufactured seats are *shared* by the majority and minority.[14] In sum, the majority party leaders usually agree to grant the minority more or less what it needs; the committee-by-committee party ratio is permitted to fluctuate.[15]

The cumulative effect of all these pressures is, not surprisingly, expansion (see table 6.2.) Even excluding the creation of new committees, there has been a monotonic growth, occasionally dramatic, in the supply of committee slots. In the twenty-eight years of the modern committee system's life, the number of committee berths has increased by nearly 60%. It is rapidly approaching the expansion levels of the pre-1947 committee system, and already there is the call in some quarters for reorganization.[16]

While the range of forces that press the leaders of the majority and minority parties into partisan advocacy on behalf of the interests of their respective followers is considerable, the adjustment of the leaders to excess demand is not complete. Some excess demand for committee berths remains after committee sizes and party shares are determined. The respective party CCs, consequently, must perform their allocation tasks under a scarcity constraint. Why don't party leaders adjust perfectly to the excess demand? Why, that is, do the party leaders maintain scarcity for some committee slots, producing waiting lines, intraparty conflict for existing slots, and the need to resort to a rationing device (the CC)? In other words, what are the forces that countervail the otherwise unidirectional pressures on the party leadership to expand committee sizes?

*Counterexpansionist
Pressures*

The demand for committee slots is a major force influencing the leaders' ultimate decisions. Were it the only such force, we could expect to observe near perfect leadership accommodation of member preferences for committee assignments. If, that is, it were *costless* to manufacture precisely the right set of committee slots to satisfy member demands, then, owing to the benefit (in the form of expected compliance with and loyalty to leadership wishes) such accommodation produces, there would be no reason for the leaders to do otherwise. Indeed, they would have every incentive to produce the slots that would enable the CC to match preferences with assignments.[17] As table 6.3 demonstrates, however, the party leadership does not manufacture committee slots at will. In fact, they are least likely to manufacture slots on some of the more prominent committees. A countervailing force is at work, one distributed differentially across committees.

Consider the following anecdote conveyed by a former member of the Democratic CC:

This time [1965] I got a fine man from [my state] on Appropriations. We had one man from [my state] on Appropriations but with 10 members [in our state delegation] I thought we should have another. [Mr. X] wanted it, he's fine. Everyone likes [Mr. X]. But last time when we wanted another man on Appropriations [Mr. Y] said he didn't think we ought to. He's the dean of the delegation and he's built himself up a reputation as a god in [my state] because of his Appropriations *monopoly*. Well, I didn't tell [Y] this time. The morning [the CC] met I went around and put a note on every member's place saying I wanted [X] on Appropriations and wouldn't you help me out. ...I sat down with [X] and he asked me if he should tell [Y] about it and I told him if he did he would lose. When the vote came [X] won. We had a delegation meeting after and I could see [Y] putting the knife in a little and twisting it. He didn't say he didn't want [X] on Appropriations actually, but he said, "Well, you people always came to me on Appropriations before, now you can take your problems to [X]." [*Y*] *wanted to keep all the power for himself, he wanted to be the big man on Appropriations for* [*my state*]. I like [Y] very much but we just didn't tell him this time until it was too late. [Emphasis added.]

Committee size, at least on those committees with excess demand, is an entry barrier. Current committee members possess political leverage from their access monopoly—[Y], in the above anecdote, "had built himself up a reputation as a god in [my state] because of his Appropriations monopoly." As the barriers to entry are lowered, the influence from that monopoly is quickly dissipated.

Put another way, "currency" inflation dissipates the worth of the currently endowed. The rationale is this:·committee membership entitles the holder, among other things, to participate and vote in committee proceedings, to acquire access to relevant executive branch bureaucracies, and to employ the staff of the committee and its subcommittees for his own purposes. In addition to their value-in-use to the member, these entitlements are exchangeable commodities and are often the objects of logrolling and other forms of quid pro quo behavior. As access to these entitlements increases—the consequences, for example, of increasing the committee size—their value in exchange tends to diminish. Thus, independent of the particular policy consequences of an expanded committee, there is a very simple "economic" argument to suggest why current committee members often seek to countervail leadership expansionist tendencies: they wish to prevent the dissipation of their own monopoly on access to a policy subgovernment as well as to other material privileges of committee membership.

From time to time, of course, particular policy coalitions will oppose expansion because of their fear that it will be used in ways contrary to their preferences. This often includes the committee chairman, who seeks to protect his control over his committee's proceedings. In response to Speaker Rayburn's desire in the Eighty-seventh Congress either to prevent Congressman Colmer (D., Miss.) from keeping his assignment on the Rules Committee[18] or to enlarge the Rules Committee by three seats,[19] Judge Smith, chairman of the Committee, is reported to have said, "No purgin', no packin'." Clarence Brown (R., Ohio), senior Republican on the Rules Committee at the time and an important cog in the conservative coalition on the committee, in a statement suggestive of both his policy concerns and his "dissipation of monopoly access" fears, warned his colleagues, "If the Rules Committee can be packed to obtain political decisions, other committees of the House can likewise be packed." In another illustration Chairman Hebert (D., La.) of the Armed Services Committee opposed expanding his committee by an additional seat in the Ninety-third Congress to accommodate the demand of the Black Caucus that a black be appointed to the committee.[20]

A third group to have mixed feelings about committee expansion is the majority leadership itself. First, though the members of this leadership often instigate such expansions for their own policy reasons,[21] they appear to have grown uneasy at the increasing unmanageability of the committee system, a concomitant cost of committee size expansion. That fear is well-founded, as table 6.5 suggests. The large number of work assignments in the Ninety-third

Table 6.5	**Total Committee and Subcommittee Positions, 93rd Congress, 1st Session**		
	Committee Positions*	Subcommittee Positions*	Total*
House of Representatives	732	1,581	2,313
House positions on joint committees	61	78	139
Total	793	1,659	2,452

SOURCE: Jones (1973), p. 568.
* Includes select committees.

Congress, for example, required each member to fill an average of 5.6 slots (1.8 committee and 3.8 subcommittee).[22] If party committees and task forces are included, the figures are even larger. Not only are scheduling problems exacerbated by a more complex workload structure; the general costs of coordination, communication, and information processing for the leadership increase as well.

It should be noted, second, that the leadership bears an additional burden of currency inflation. As the leaders manufacture additional units of this congressional currency, they have more of it to distribute but each unit possesses less value in exchange. It is probably incorrect, then, to infer that a leadership accommodation strategy implies a single-minded desire to expand committee sizes to meet revealed demand. Committee assignments (to some committees) are valued precisely because they are scarce. If members had free access to any committee, then committees would play a far less consequential role in the life of the House. And, as a consequence, committee slots would be of less value to leaders as bargaining levers vis-à-vis their followers. Thus leaders, owing to their own mix of motives, will not manufacture the currency of committee slots at will.[23]

Our knowledge of the maneuvers by which committee slots are manufactured in the early days of a new Congress is quite limited. Nevertheless it appears justifiable to conclude that an equilibrium committee structure emerges from the interplay of forces that push for expanded committees on the one hand and stable committee sizes on the other. Party leaders play both a purposive and a responsive role in this equilibration process. As purposive actors they are partisan advocates for their followers. Their twin objectives of generalized influence over followers and particular legislative goals induce them to manufacture committee slots as quid pro quo bargaining chits. They are, however, responsive to the countervailing demands of the currently wealthy (and currently powerful!) to moderate their expansionist tendencies. They neither willfully press their objectives nor abjectly serve the status quo. They are (like everyone else) constrained maximizers.

Lacking additional descriptive detail,[24] I turn now to some testable implications of a theory of negotiated structure (only the broad outlines of which have thus far been articulated) and an empirical assessment of their validity. The paucity of descriptive information is, of course, both a hindrance to theoretical understanding and a call for further research.

Theory of Leadership Responsiveness

Two statistical models of negotiated structure are estimated in the next section. A third model is found in the appendix to this chapter. In each instance we seek to determine whether our expectations about leadership responses to expansionist and counterexpansionist pressures are consistent with actual observation. While one never literally proves or disproves a theory by appeals to data, his belief in the theory as an accurate characterization of real-world politics will be buoyed or scuttled. The two models in the text allow us to examine the impact of expansionist pressures directly but counterexpansionist pressures only indirectly. The model in the appendix provides a more direct assessment of the forces on the party leadership to hold the line on committee sizes.

Operational Theory

I shall be interested in accounting for variations in size changes of *majority party seats* on congressional committees. Two dependent variables, ΔN_j and ΔN_j^*, are defined. The first is the change in the number of majority party seats on the jth committee between the second session of the $(t - 1)^{st}$ Congress and the first session of the tth Congress. The second is the difference between the change actually occurring and the change that would have occurred if only the change in chamber party ratio were taken into account. The variables employed are defined formally in table 6.6. With the exception of ΔN_j^e and X_j^6 the variables are self-explanatory.

Table 6.6   **Operational Definitions of the Variables**

Variable	Definition
ΔN_j	(Number of Democratic seats on committee j in the tth Congress) − (Number of Democratic seats on committee j in the $(t - 1)^{st}$ Congress)
ΔN_j^e	$\left[\dfrac{\text{Number of Democrats in Congress } t}{\text{Number of Democrats in Congress } (t - 1)} - 1\right] \cdot N_j(t - 1)^a$
ΔN_j^*	$\Delta N_j - \Delta N_j^e$ = *actual* change in the number of Democratic seats in the jth committee − change to which Democratic majority is *entitled* as a result of the new chamber party ratio
T	Time = 1 for the 87th Congress, 2 for the 88th, ..., 8 for the 94th Congress
X_j^1	Number of freshman first-preference requests for committee j in the tth Congress
X_j^2	Number of freshman second- or lower-preference requests for committee j in the tth Congress
X_j^3	Number of nonfreshman transfer or dual-service requests for committee j in the tth Congress
X_j^4	Number of $(t - 1)^{st}$ Congress Democrats of committee j not returning to the tth Congress (due to defeat, retirement, death, resignation)
X_j^5	Number of $(t - 1)^{st}$ Congress Democrats of committee j seeking to transfer from it in the tth Congress
X_j^6	(Change in minority seats on committee j) − (Change in seats on committee j to which the minority is entitled)

^{a} $N_j(t - 1)$ is the number of majority seats on committee j in the $(t - 1)^{st}$ Congress.

The variable, ΔN_j^e, measures the change in the size of committee j to which the majority is entitled. An example illustrates its operationalization. In the Eighty-ninth Congress the Democrats increased their representation by 14.5% (from 255 seats in the Eighty-eighth Congress to 292 in the

Eighty-ninth). Since they held twenty-one seats on Agriculture in the Eighty-eighth Congress, they were *entitled* to increase their representation on this committee by

$$\Delta N^e_{Ag} = (\tfrac{292}{255} - 1)\,(21) = (.145)(21) = 3.05 \text{ seats.}$$

The "minority-needs" variable, X^6_j, measures the difference between the change actually obtained by the minority on committee j and the change to which it would have been entitled holding committee size constant. For example, in the Eighty-eighth Congress (see note 13) there was virtually no change in the party ratio from the Eighty-seventh Congress. The Republicans, therefore, were entitled to no increment (decrement) in their party representation on Banking and Currency. They received, nevertheless, one extra seat (their representation rose from 12 to 13); consequently, $X^6_{B\&C} = 1$.

The statistical models to be estimated are given in (6.1) and (6.2):

$$\Delta N_j = \beta_0 + \beta_T T + \beta_e(\Delta N^e_j) + \beta_1 X^1_j + \beta_2 X^2_j \\ + \beta_3 X^3_j + \beta_4 X^4_j + \beta_5 X^5_j + \beta_6 X^6_j \tag{6.1}$$

$$\Delta N^*_j = \beta^*_0 + \beta^*_T T + \beta^*_1 X^1_j + \beta^*_2 X^2_j + \beta^*_3 X^3_j \\ + \beta^*_4 X^4_j + \beta^*_5 X^5_j + \beta^*_6 X^6_j \tag{6.2}$$

where the estimates of β_k and β^*_k measure the impact of the respective explanatory variables on the respective dependent variables. Ordinary least squares regression is employed to estimate these parameters.

Notice that the variables of (6.1) and (6.2) measure the effects of time (T), majority supply (ΔN^e_j, X^4_j, X^5_j) and demand (X^1_j, X^2_j, X^3_j) conditions, and extraordinary minority needs (X^6_j). Owing, however, to the prospect of countervailing forces of committee size expansion, and the likelihood that these forces are *differentially* associated with committees, there is some risk that the models, (6.1) and (6.2), are misspecified.[25] I attend to this possibility in the appendix by estimating a slightly more refined model in which the countervailing forces are explicitly included. In (6.1) and (6.2) the average effect of countervailing forces may be detected implicitly. Take β_1 or β^*_1, the parameters associated with freshman first-preference requests. They measure the impact of an additional request, controlling for the remaining variables, on ΔN_j and ΔN^*_j, respectively. If the estimate of β_1 is unity, then the leadership is adjusting perfectly to freshman first-preference requests in the sense that an additional request for j would produce an additional majority party berth on j. If, on the other hand, the estimate of β_1 is less than unity, but still positive, then, even when all other (included) factors are held constant, the party leaders are not adjusting committee sizes perfectly. I choose to associate this less-than-perfect adjustment with the counterexpansionist pressures mentioned in the last section. Finally, if the estimate of β_1 is insignificantly different from zero, or even negative, then our leadership responsiveness theory is in serious trouble. While this indirect method of examining counterexpansionist pressures is inadequate for a number of technical statistical reasons, it will suffice until the more complicated statistical model is discussed in the appendix.

Theoretical Expectations

Before turning to actual estimation of (6.1) and (6.2), the theoretical consequences of the leadership responsiveness argument are tied together and some expectations for the parameters of the statistical models developed.

1. Tables 6.1 (last column) and 6.2 depict a very strong trend effect in committee sizes. Table 6.7 provides additional support. Consequently, a significant trend effect is anticipated in (6.1) and (6.2).[26]

Table 6.7 **Eligibles with Second Assignments (Democrats)**

Congress	Eligible* Nonfreshmen with Second Assignments (N)		Eligible* Freshmen with Second Assignments (N)	
86	.367	(166)	.187	(64)
87	.378	(188)	.368	(19)
88	.467	(167)	.250	(36)
89	.531	(162)	.200	(70)
90	.525	(181)	.083	(12)
91	.596	(166)	.182	(22)
92	.651	(166)	.548	(31)
93	.719	(160)	.680	(25)
94	.860	(150)	.779	(68)

NOTE: Budget, Small Business, and Standards of Official Conduct are excluded
* Those not serving on exclusive committees.

2. The number of majority party seats in a new Congress depends on the size of the majority party. Changes in committee sizes should move in tandem with changes in the party ratio. In (6.1), then, it is expected that ΔN_j will depend significantly on the increment (decrement) to which the majority party is entitled due to the change in the chamber party ratio. In (6.2) it is, in effect, assumed that there is complete adjustment to ΔN_j^e. That is, the parameter associated with ΔN_j^e is set at unity and subtracted from ΔN_j (consult table 6.6). In (6.2), then, the change in the chamber party ratio plays no explicit explanatory role; the other variables are employed to explain the deviation between ΔN_j and ΔN_j^e.

3. According to our theory of leadership responsiveness, committee size changes are expected to be related positively to freshman requests:
   (a) the leadership responds to freshman first-preference requests;
   (b) similarly, the leadership responds to lower-order freshman requests;
   (c) the former effect is expected to be stronger than the latter.

4. In a similar fashion, the leadership is expected to respond to nonfreshman transfer and dual-service requests.

5. The leadership is spared the necessity of manufacturing *new* slots to the extent that members leave the jth committee:
   (a) ΔN_j and ΔN_j^* are depressed to the extent that members of j in the $(t - 1)^{st}$ Congress fail to return to the tth Congress because of resignation, retirement, electoral defeat, or death.
   (b) ΔN_j and ΔN_j^* are depressed by expressions of desire to transfer from committee j;
   (c) the former effect is expected to have a larger impact than the latter.[27]

6. Since the theory implies majority party responsiveness to minority party "needs," and since this responsiveness is often financed by a general expansion of the jth committee (some of the slots of which accrue to the majority party—see note 14), it is expected that ΔN_j and ΔN_j^* will be affected positively by extraordinary minority party requests.

These expectations are summarized in table 6.8.

Table 6.8   **Implications of the Theory of Leadership Responsiveness**

	Theoretical Expectation	
Number	Description	Hypothesis for Parameter of (6.1) and (6.2)
1	Time-trend effect	$\beta_T, \beta_T^* > 0$
2	Change in party representation effect	$\beta_e > 0$
3a	Freshman first-preference demand effect	$\beta_1, \beta_1^* > 0$
3b	Freshman lower-order preference demand effect	$\beta_2, \beta_2^* > 0$
3c	Preference "intensity" effect	$\beta_1 > \beta_2, \beta_1^* > \beta_2^*$
4	Nonfreshmen demand effect	$\beta_3, \beta_3^* > 0$
5a	Nonreturning member supply effect	$\beta_4, \beta_4^* < 0$
5b	Transfer (potential) supply effect	$\beta_5, \beta_5^* < 0$
5c	Certainty of supply effect	$\beta_4 < \beta_5, \beta_4^* < \beta_5^*$
6	Minority-needs effect	$\beta_6, \beta_6^* > 0$

In these expectations we have done no more than operationalize a simple accounting formula. For the jth committee, party leaders begin with a base of unfilled slots available from party members of committee j not returning to the new Congress (X_j^4). They increase (decrease) that base in accord with the changed chamber ratio (ΔN_j^e), the extent of demand for that committee (X_j^1, X_j^2, X_j^3),[28] the extent to which they accommodate minority needs (X_j^6), and probabilistic vacancies due to requested transfers (X_j^5). Finally, owing to the secular trend (T) involving changing norms of acquisitiveness and an increased work load, they add an extra increment to ΔN_j.

Empirical Tests of the Theory of Leadership Responsiveness

First Empirical Test— Equation (6.1)

The parameters of equation (6.1) are estimated by OLS regression analysis. Since the exclusive committees are rarely expanded, and when they are it is usually for idiosyncratic reasons, they have been excluded from the analysis.[29] The parameter estimates, their standard errors, and the p-levels for the null hypothesis $H_0: \beta_k = 0$ are given in table 6.9.[30]

Table 6.9   **Least Squares Estimates of the Parameters in Equation (6.1)**

	Parameter	Parameter Estimate	Standard Error	p-level (t-test)*
β_0	constant	.014		
β_T	secular trend	.106	.050	$< .02$
β_e	chamber ratio change	.787	.054	$\ll .001$
β_1	freshman first-preference demand	.125	.039	$< .001$
β_2	freshman lower-preference demand	.019	.026	n.s.
β_3	nonfreshman demand	.081	.048	$< .05$
β_4	vacancies created by the election	$-.150$	.053	$< .001$
β_5	potential vacancies from nonfreshman transfers	$-.032$	.063	n.s.
β_6	minority "needs"	.485	.102	$\ll .001$
				$R^2 = .867$

* The probability of making an error in rejecting H_0: $\beta_k = 0$.

The variables of (6.1) explain a very large proportion of the variance (86.7%) in ΔN_j. The small size of β_0, moreover, suggests the absence of important exogenous effects unaccounted for in the model. Most important, most of the implications of the theory of leadership responsiveness in table 6.8 are strongly supported. The change-in-party representation effect, freshman-first-preference-demand effect, nonreturning-members-supply effect, and the minority-needs effect are all highly significant.[31] Only slightly less significant are the time-trend effect and the nonfreshman-demand effect. Interestingly, however, the majority party leaders appear to respond neither to freshman lower-preference demand nor to the potential supply resulting from nonfreshman transfer requests.[32] The two comparative hypotheses—the preference-intensity effect and the certainty-of-supply effect—require a slightly more complicated t-test,[33] so they are not reported in table 6.9. The former is significant at $p \ll .001$; the latter at $p < .03$. *On the basis of overall fit and the success of the theoretically inspired hypotheses, then, the theory of leadership responsiveness is given strong empirical support.*

Despite the temptation to quit while ahead, several observations about the parameter estimates are required. First, the changing chamber ratio accounts for a substantial proportion of the explained variance in ΔN_j. On average, the majority party takes 78.7% of the change in its committee slots to which it is entitled. For example, in the previous section it was noted that owing to good fortune in the 1964 election the Democrats were entitled to expand their representation on the Agriculture Committee, ceteris paribus, by 3.05 seats in the Eighty-ninth Congress. According to the estimate of β_e in table 6.9, the party leaders are predicted to take 78.7% of that entitlement, or 2.40 seats, as a base in their calculations.

The parameter estimate is misleading (and reflects a slight model mis-specification) in that it does not distinguish between positive and negative changes in party fortunes. On average, the party leaders adjust majority committee shares by 78.7% of the change in the party's chamber share, whether that change is positive or negative. If such a distinction had been made in the model, β_e would be close to unity for those years in which the party's fortunes improved, and close to one-half for those years in which the majority party did not fare so well. That is, the average reported in table 6.9 is misleading: in good years the party leaders take nearly all of the expansion to which the party is entitled; in bad years, however, they contract the party's representation only about half as much as they "should."

By comparison to β_e, β_1—the primary demand coefficient—is rather small. According to our estimate, if there are, for example, ten first-preference freshman requests for the Agriculture Committee, the party leaders will expand the majority party representation by approximately 1.25 seats. It would, however, be incorrect to infer that demand as reflected in request behavior is unimportant. To the contrary, since much of the demand will be absorbed by ΔN_j^o, the fact that demand, per se, has an additional significant impact on ΔN_j is testimony to the leadership's interest in accommodating the desires of new members.

Perhaps the most puzzling coefficient, at least in its interpretation, is the minority-needs coefficient, β_6. It asserts that whenever the majority leaders accommodate an extraordinary demand by the minority for an extra seat on the jth committee, they expand the committee size by nearly one and a half seats, keeping the remaining half-seat for the majority. This particular method of "financing" extraordinary minority needs is not surprising in the least. Majority altruism toward the minority is a much more compelling motive when, in addition, there is something in it for the majority! The natural causal interpretation of this coefficient, however, may be incorrect. To assert, that is, that the majority's representation is increased by a half-seat for each seat of minority extraordinary need may have the direction of causality reversed. An alternative explanation for the covariation between these two variables has the minority's extra seats as a mere by-product of the majority's desire for additional slots. However, the fact that $\beta_6 < 1$ reduces the persuasiveness of this alternative considerably.[34] In sum, the minority-needs variable is significant and substantially improves the overall fit ($R^2 = .837$ when X_j^6 is deleted). Moreover, a reasonably persuasive rationale can be established for its inclusion. Whether it really has an impact on the majority party leadership's calculus, or whether its effect is spurious, is, alas, beyond the ken of most multivariate methodologies.

*Second Empirical
Test—Equation (6.2)*

In equation (6.2) the dependent variable is ΔN_j^*, the change in the size of committee j over and above that implied by the change in the party ratio: $\Delta N_j^* = \Delta N_j - \Delta N_j^o$. Since it is very likely that these "unusual" changes are due in large measure to idiosyncratic reasons, equation (6.2) poses a much more severe test of our theory.

The OLS estimates are given in table 6.10. The low R^2 indicates that much of the variance in ΔN_j^* is explained by idiosyncrasies or other variables not included in the model. Nevertheless, both the minority needs and the primary-demand variables prove to be significant. The nonreturning members and the transfer-supply effects are somewhat less significant. The other single-parameter hypotheses of table 6.10 may be rejected. Of the two comparative hypotheses, the preference-intensity effect (hypothesis 3c) receives strong support ($p < .02$), but the certainty-of-supply effect (hypothesis 5c) does not.

Table 6.10   Least Squares Estimates of the Parameters in Equation (6.2)

Parameter		Parameter Estimate	Standard Error	p-level (t-test)
β_0^*	constant	.373		
β_T^*	secular trend	.044	.051	n.s.
β_1^*	freshman first-preference demand	.078	.041	< .03
β_2^*	freshman lower-preference demand	−.017**	.026	n.s.
β_3^*	nonfreshman demand	.049	.052	n.s.
β_4^*	vacancies created by the election	−.066	.052	< .10
β_5^*	potential vacancies from nonfreshman transfers	−.072	.068	< .15
β_6^*	minority "needs"	.510	.112	≪.001 $R^2 = .217$

** Wrong sign.

While the strong empirical support of the minority needs and the freshman first-preference demand effects stand as persuasive endorsements of the leadership responsiveness theory, especially given the subtlety of the change in committee size being measured (ΔN_j^*), the low overall fit requires the search for additional explanatory variables. Unfortunately, the theory as articulated gives no further guidance. One major source of misspecification—the one related to countervailing pressures—is examined in the appendix. The addition of this feature improves the fit considerably. Nevertheless, there appears to be much that is idiosyncratic about the change measured by ΔN_j^*.[35]

Appendix

Leadership Responsiveness and Counterexpansion Pressures

The statistical models, (6.1) and (6.2), assume that the pressures on the leadership to hold the line on committee expansion are constant across committees. The fact that the leadership does not adjust committee sizes to absorb all the revealed demand—the β_K's (β_K^*'s) associated with demand are less than unity—is consistent with the presence of countervailing pressures. However, there is good reason to believe that the assumption of *constant* pressure across committees is very wide of the mark.

One of the benefits of committee membership is the monopoly control, shared with other committee members, over the agenda and deliberations in a particular policy jurisdiction. Monopoly "rents" are earned by committee members; members capitalize these rents, that is, convert them into general institutional influence, by engaging in the quid pro quo behavior with non-members that is common in congressional life. A member of the Appropriations Committee, revealing the reasons he sought the assignment, illustrates this convertible monopoly power:

> I thought the power would be important. Like Kennedy said about the Presidency—"That's where the power is."...*The process here is one where consent must be obtained before anything gets done. If you are one of those from whom consent must be obtained, then you are an important person in the House.* When you are on the Appropriations Committee you are that kind of person. That's all. It's a question of power. [Emphasis added.] [Fenno 1973, p. 3]

The monopoly on access and influence in the committee's jurisdiction is dissipated (or is nonexistent in the first place) whenever the membership base of the committee is *permeable*. If it is relatively easy for a nonmember to become a member, either because there is large committee turnover or because new slots are created, then the "consent must be obtained before anything gets done" proviso no longer applies.[1] If, however, there are entry barriers to membership—barriers that are "binding" constraints in the sense that they produce membership waiting lines reflecting excess demand—then membership rent is preserved. There is, then, a very real incentive for the current beneficiaries of monopoly power to press for its maintenance—to countervail, that is, the leadership partiality toward committee size expansion.

Empirical Assessment
of a Respecified Model

Monopoly rents, unfortunately, are not observable. While the forces that promote the leadership's inclination to expand a committee are revealed by observable behavior—freshman requests, for example—the countervailing forces must be inferred. As a first approximation one might assume that monopoly rents and, consequently, countervailing pressures are related to committee class. They are largest for exclusive committees, smaller for semiexclusive committees, and smaller still for nonexclusive committees. Thus the extent to which leadership inclinations to expand are damped is a monotonically increasing function of committee class.

As is the case with any unobservable, the basis for inference is arbitrary and therefore controversial. The committee-class basis, however, appears to be consistent with the differential prerogatives of service on committees of each class. Service restrictions are most severe for the exclusive committees—a member may serve on no other committee; less severe for semiexclusive committees—a member is permitted a second assignment but not on an exclusive or another semiexclusive committee; and still less severe for nonexclusive committees—second assignments are permitted to any committee but the exclusive. The purpose of these restrictions, according to the monopoly-rents argument, is to reduce the disparities in rent-earning capability among members; in brief, it prevents some members from becoming "too powerful." Unfortunately, the committee-class basis for inferring the magnitude of counterexpansion pressure is too crude. In the Eighty-seventh Congress, for example, both Armed Services and Post Office and Civil Service were semiexclusive committees; yet intuitively one suspects that members of the former were far more protective of the monopoly on access to their jurisdiction than members of the latter were of theirs. There is simply too much variation within committee classes to suit my purposes.

I approach the problem in a different manner, employing an index of intercommittee movement previously used by Bullock and Sprague (1969).

Define

$$r_j = \frac{\text{number of transfers } to \text{ committee j}}{\text{number of transfers } to \text{ committee j } +}$$
number of transfers *from* committee j

This index has been computed by Bullock and Sprague (1969) for the Eightieth through Ninetieth Congresses and is displayed in table 6.11. By assuming that

Table 6.11	Index of Intercommittee Transfers, 80th–90th Congresses
Committee (j)	r_j
Ways and Means	1.000
Rules	1.000
Appropriations	.983
Foreign Affairs	.852
Armed Services	.750
Interstate	.743
Judiciary	.708
Agriculture	.541
Public Works	.485
Science and Astronautics	.480
Government Operations	.371
District of Columbia	.273
Education and Labor	.250
House Administration	.243
Interior	.241
Banking and Currency	.231
Merchant Marine	.222
Veterans Affairs	.075
Post Office	.050
Un-American Activities	.000

SOURCE: Bullock (1969)

members seek to move to committees whose monopoly access is, in some sense, worth more, and from committees whose jurisdictional monopolies are worth less, the index r_j may be used to represent the magnitude of the countervailing pressure on party leaders to hold the line on committee expansion from members currently on a committee. The pressure, according to table 6.11, is greatest for the exclusive committees and some of the semiexclusive committees and least for many of the nonexclusive committees and, again, some of the semiexclusive committees.

The following interaction terms are now defined:

$$Z_j^e = r_j \cdot \Delta N_j^e$$
$$Z_j^T = r_j \cdot T$$
$$Z_j^i = r_j \cdot X_j^i \qquad i = 1, \cdots, 6$$

The model (6.1) may now be respecified (an analogous model for (6.2) is not considered here):

$$\Delta N_j = \left[\beta_0 + \beta_T T + \beta_e(\Delta N_j^e) + \sum_{i=1}^{6} \beta_i X_j^i \right] + \left[\gamma_T Z_j^T + \gamma_e Z_j^e + \sum_{i=1}^{6} \gamma_i Z_j^i \right]$$

(6.3)

The γ's come into play whenever the Z-variables are nonzero, as they are for all committees but HUAC (see table 6.11). Their effect is understood by noting, from the definition of the Z-variables, that the impact of each of the original explanatory variables is now measured by $\beta_k + \gamma_k r_j$. For example, the effect of freshman first preferences (X_j^1) on the change in majority party seats on committee j (ΔN_j) is $\beta_1 + \gamma_1 r_j$.

If the theory of leadership responsiveness is correct, then the theoretical expectations for the estimates of the β's remain as specified in table 6.8. However, the effect of each explanatory variable is modified by its respective γ, expectations for which are found in table 6.12.

Table 6.12   **Further Implications of the Theory of Leadership Responsiveness**

		Theoretical Expectation
Number	Description	Hypothesis for Parameters of (6.3)
1	Time-trend effect	$\gamma_T < 0$
2	Change in party representation effect	$\gamma_e < 0$
3a	Freshman first preference demand effect	$\gamma_1 < 0$
3b	Freshman lower-preference demand effect	$\gamma_2 < 0$
3c	Nonfreshman demand effect	$\gamma_3 < 0$
4a	Nonreturning member supply effect	$\gamma_4 < 0$
4b	Transfer (potential) supply effect	$\gamma_5 < 0$
5	Minority-needs effect	$\gamma_6 > 0$

1. While leaders are expected to expand committees over time ($H_0:\beta_T > 0$ in table 6.8), "high rent" committees are expanded at a slower rate ($H_0:\gamma_T < 0$).

2. Leaders are expected to adjust majority seats in accord with the change in the chamber party ratio ($H_0:\beta_e > 0$), but are less responsive in proportion to the size of r_j($H_0:\gamma_e < 0$).

3. Demand induces expansion of committee berths ($H_0:\beta_1 > 0$, $\beta_2 > 0$, $\beta_3 > 0$), but inversely with the size of r_j ($H_0:\gamma_1 < 0$, $\gamma_2 < 0$, $\gamma_3 < 0$).

4. Exogenous supply reduces the pressure to expand committees (H_0: $\beta_4 < 0$, $\beta_5 < 0$), but the larger r_j is, the larger that reduction in pressure to expand ($H_0:\gamma_4 < 0$, $\gamma_5 < 0$).

5. Whenever minority needs are acknowledged ($H_0:\beta_6 > 0$), because it is important to retain majority control, the countervailing pressure against expansion is outweighed; indeed, the contrary is expected ($H_0:\gamma_6 > 0$).[2]

The parameter estimates of (6.3) are given in table 6.13. In nearly every case the parameter is of the correct sign, though its magnitude is not always

Table 6.13   **Least Squares Estimates of the Parameters of Equation (6.3)**

	Parameter	Parameter Estimate	Standard Error	p-level*
β_0	constant	−.146		
β_T	time trend	.127	.072	< .04
β_e	party representation	.824	.104	≪ .001
β_1	freshman first preferences	.192	.113	< .04
β_2	freshman lower preferences	.129	.058	< .01
β_3	nonfreshman transfers	.030	.093	n.s.
β_4	nonreturning members	−.091	.106	< .20
β_5	potential transfers	−.131	.131	< .15
β_6	minority needs	−.181**	.233	n.s.
γ_T	time trend	−.011	.136	n.s.
γ_e	party representation	−.044	.193	n.s.
γ_1	freshman first preferences	−.047	.187	n.s.
γ_2	freshman lower preferences	−.267	.124	< .02
γ_3	nonfreshman transfers	.150**	.223	n.s.
γ_4	nonreturning members	−.053	.227	n.s.
γ_5	potential transfers	.196**	.304	n.s.
γ_6	minority needs	1.295	.431	≪ .001
				$R^2 = .885$

    * The probability that the null hypothesis is true according to a t-test.
    ** Sign differs from expectations in table 6.8 and table 6.12.

significantly different from zero. No parameter with a sign in contradiction to the expectations of tables 6.8 and 6.12 is significant. Finally, there is a modest increase in explained variance as compared to table 6.9. Nevertheless, the countervailing-pressures argument is given only modest support. While there is little in table 6.13 to contradict it, the fact that most of the γ's are insignificant does not provide strong support either. The two important conclusions that do receive strong support are the following.

1. Party leaders *do* pay strong attention to freshman lower-order requests, but not for those committees with high r_j's—Foreign Affairs, Armed Services, Interstate, Judiciary (the exclusive committees have been excluded from the analysis).

2. Especially on the high r_j committees, majority party leaders rarely accommodate minority needs outright; rather their financing of these needs involves extra seats for the majority party as well.[3]

The counterexpansion argument is an intuitively plausible one; it provides an explanation for scarcity in committee berths despite powerful inflationary pressures. While the parameter estimates of table 6.13 are certainly consistent with this argument—indeed, given the number of parameters it is remarkable that the estimates are consistent with so many of the expectations of tables 6.8 and 6.12—few are statistically significant. Nevertheless a test of the gain on variance explained (a comparison of the R^2 statistics of tables 6.9 and 6.13) suggests that the joint hypothesis $H_0 : \gamma_T = \gamma_e = \gamma_1 = \cdots = \gamma_6 = 0$ may be rejected at $p < .02$ (the test is an F-test described in most econometrics texts). My inclination is to accept the counterexpansion argument provisionally; a more precise theoretical formulation and empirical operationalization should be placed on the agenda for future research.

Part 4

Assignments

Chapter 7

The Committee on Committees, I: Goals, Constraints, Strategic Premises

In early January, during the first few weeks of the new Congress, each party's Committee on Committees, sitting in executive session, determines the manner in which the newly negotiated committee structure is to be filled. The fate of many a legislative proposal rides on the decisions of these committees; the careers of individual legislators are affected as well. The committee configurations that ultimately emerge from the CC executive sessions must then receive the approval of the respective party caucuses and, eventually, of the full House.

From 1911 to 1975 the Democratic CC consisted of the Democratic members of the Ways and Means Committee. Initially, under this arrangement, committee assignments were in the tight control of the party leadership since the Democratic floor leader ordinarily served as the chairman (ranking minority member) of the Ways and Means Committee. This control, however, atrophied as a stricter reliance on seniority in the selection of committee chairman (ranking minority members)[1] produced a more explicit personnel distinction between party leaders and committee leaders. In response to the desire for more direct leadership control of committee assignments the Democratic Caucus, in 1973, added the Speaker, majority leader, and caucus chairman to the CC. In 1975 the role of the leadership was enhanced further with the shift of committee assignment responsibilities from the party contingent on Ways and Means to the leadership-dominated Steering and Policy Committee (an early assessment of which is considered in the Epilogue).

In this chapter and the next a detailed examination of the pre-1975 Democratic CC is provided. Given the rich and growing literature on the committee assignment process, it is somewhat surprising that so little is known about the CC.[2] While we have some information on its decision-making procedures (described in Chapter 8), the CC's decision-making "style," its methods of resolving intracommittee conflicts and extracommittee demands— in brief, the means by which it accommodates the sometimes conflicting goals of its members with the constraints, demands, and expectations of its external environment—have gone unreported. Our aim in this chapter is to describe the membership of the CC and the *individual objectives* they entertain, the *constraints* imposed on their goal-seeking by external actors and institutional "rules of the game," and the *strategic premises* to which they agree in order to resolve internal conflicts and to accommodate external demands. In the next chapter we discuss the *decision-making process* employed by the CC. The *decisions* that emerge from their deliberations are examined in Chapter 9.[3]

Members of the CC

The most important thing to know about the Democratic CC is that it consists of its party contingent on the Ways and Means Committee.[4] Elected by the Democratic Caucus, and usually endorsed by the party leadership, Ways and Means Democrats possess certain distinctive characteristics that affect the way that committee does its business. When they exchange their Ways and Means hats for their CC hats, many of these same characteristics predominate.

Who Gets Elected to
Ways and Means?

A statistical profile of the Democratic contingent on Ways and Means over the last twenty years produces the following composite: he[5] is elected to the committee in his fourth or fifth term; he tends to come from a relatively safe district; he has usually succeeded someone from his state or region; with rare exceptions he has the endorsement and support of the party leadership; in his floor voting he is both a party regular and a "liberal"; he does not ordinarily leave the committee for some other in the House;[6] nor does he leave the committee to seek other office;[7] and he is generally regarded as a responsible legislator—one who works hard, maintains good interpersonal relations, takes pride in his professionalism, and possesses strong institutional loyalty (Masters 1961).

Like any other composite, this one stresses central tendencies at the expense of variations and, consequently, (falsely) implies a good deal more homogeneity than actually exists. The following analysis makes the point.

1. Previous terms of service. Table 7.1 displays the data on prior service for the twenty-three members elected to Ways and Means during the Eighty-sixth

Table 7.1   Previous Terms of Service of Members Elected to the
Ways and Means Committee, 86th–93rd Congresses

Member	Year Elected to Committee	No. of Previous Terms
James B. Frazier (Tenn.)	1959	5
John C. Watts (Ky.)	1959	3.5
William J. Green, Jr. (Pa.)	1959	6
Lee Metcalf (Mont.)	1959	3
Al Ullman (Ore.)	1961	2
James A. Burke (Mass.)	1961	1
Clark W. Thompson (Tex.)	1962	8.5
Martha W. Griffiths (Mich.)	1962	3
Ross Bass (Tenn.)	1963	4
W. Pat Jennings (Va.)	1963	3
George M. Rhodes (Pa.)	1964	7.5
Dan Rostenkowski (Ill.)	1965	3
Phil M. Landrum (Ga.)	1965	6
Charles A. Vanik (Ohio)	1965	5
Richard Fulton (Tenn.)	1965	1
Jacob H. Gilbert (N.Y.)	1967	3.5
Omar Burleson (Tex.)	1969	11
James C. Corman (Cal.)	1969	4
William J. Green, III (Pa.)	1969	2.5
Sam M. Gibbons (Fla.)	1969	3
Hugh L. Carey (N.Y.)	1971	5
Joe D. Waggonner (La.)	1971	5
Joseph E. Karth (Minn.)	1972	6.5

through Ninety-third Congresses. They served an average of nearly nine years before their election to the committee. No freshman was appointed, and only two with as little as a single term of service. One of those sophomores reports the somewhat unusual circumstances surrounding his election:[8]

> I campaigned for it. I was three weeks here, a freshman, and I was at a reception at the Shoreham. A congressman from [my zone] was there, and I couldn't help it—I heard him tell a man in strictest confidence that he was not going to run for re-election. I went to McCormack and said I was interested in Ways and Means, and would he support me if a vacancy came up. He said he would. Of course he didn't know what I knew. He said I had his word, and I said, "Okay John, I'll hold you to it." Then I went to see the Speaker. He almost fell out of his chair when I said I was interested in Ways and Means. He said, "Good God, you've been here three weeks, and we don't usually put people on until they've been here three or four terms." I said I just wanted him to watch me and see if I didn't have the stability for that important position. He said

all right, but that it was extremely unlikely. Then I got to know the chairman, Wilbur Mills, and the other important members, Cecil King of California, Keogh of New York. I hung around the committee and helped when I could. At the same time I was campaigning in the rest of the House. By the time the vacancy was announced, I had the backing of four state delegations aside from [my regional] delegation. I had about seventy votes besides the ones from [my region]. There were about fifty candidates but I won in the caucus.

On the other hand, a number of members have accrued a considerable amount of service in the House before their transfer to Ways and Means: William Green, Jr., and Phil Landrum, twelve years; Joseph Karth, thirteen years; George Rhodes, fifteen years; Clark Thompson, seventeen years; and Omar Burleson, twenty-two years (and the chairmanship of the House Administration Committee and a subcommittee chairmanship on the Foreign Affairs Committee).[9]

2. Type of district. Nearly all of the members elected to Ways and Means face low electoral risks. Only one, George M. Rhodes of Pennsylvania, received less than 55% of the vote in the election preceding his transfer to the committee (see table 7.2). Six southerners actually faced no opposition in the general election and, usually, only token opposition in the primary. Some members, though their districts are now safe, have had to cultivate their electoral support. Joseph Karth, for example, weathered several competitive elections in his St. Paul, Minnesota, constituency before establishing his electoral safety. Dan Rostenkowski (D., Ill.), for another, has occasionally had his vote percentage fall below 55%.

The districts of the members elected to Ways and Means tend to be those from which the Democratic party has traditionally drawn its strength: the South and the big cities. The midwestern representation on the committee since the Eighty-sixth Congress, in fact, has come exclusively from the big cities; Thaddeus Machrowicz and Martha Griffiths (Detroit), Thomas O'Brien and Dan Rostenkowski (Chicago), Charles Vanik (Cleveland), Frank Karsten (St. Louis), Joseph Karth (Minneapolis-St. Paul).

What is more difficult to ascertain from the data, and what is probably most important from the point of view of the party leadership (whose role in recruitment for the Ways and Means Committee is recounted below), is the extent to which members are free agents. Will, that is, the member's constituents permit the occasional deviation from district sentiments and interests that may be required of a member of the Ways and Means Committee and party CC? While the testimony of others suggests that such independence is characteristic of Ways and Means members (see Masters [1961], Manley [1970], Fenno [1973]), the congressman as "trustee" or "politico"[10] cannot

Table 7.2   Proportion of Two-Party Vote of Ways and Means Members in the Election Preceding Appointment to the Committee

Member	Year Elected to Committee	% of Two-Party Vote
James B. Frazier (Tenn.)	1959	100
John C. Watts (Ky.)	1959	100
William J. Green, Jr. (Pa.)	1959	55
Lee Metcalf (Mont.)	1959	75
Al Ullman (Ore.)	1961	60
James A. Burke (Mass.)	1961	59
Clark W. Thompson (Tex.)	1962	100
Martha W. Griffiths (Mich.)	1962	58
Ross Bass (Tenn.)	1963	100
W. Pat Jennings (Va.)	1963	61
George M. Rhodes (Pa.)	1964	51
Dan Rostenkowski (Ill.)	1965	66
Phil M. Landrum (Ga.)	1965	63
Charles A. Vanik (Ohio)	1965	91
Richard Fulton (Tenn.)	1965	60
Jacob H. Gilbert (N.Y.)	1967	79
Omar Burleson (Tex.)	1969	100
James C. Corman (Cal.)	1969	57
William J. Green, III (Pa.)	1969	69
Sam M. Gibbons (Fla.)	1969	62
Hugh L. Carey (N.Y.)	1971	65
Joe D. Waggonner (La.)	1971	100
Joseph E. Karth (Minn.)	1972	74

be inferred on the basis of electoral data alone. As Fiorina (1974) has persuasively argued and demonstrated, some districts are safe *because their Congressman accurately reflects constituency interests*; these same districts that return their representative with more than 60% of the vote might not continue to do so if he were to cease toeing the line.

3. *Regional continuity and representation.* The Democratic membership of the Ways and Means Committee is among the most representative of regional party strength of all House committees.[11] Though some have chosen to emphasize its large southern component,[12] the committee is nevertheless a highly representative committee, as table 7.3 demonstrates. The large southern contingent on Ways and Means reflects the large southern representation in the Democratic party in the House.

A second pattern in the election of members to Ways and Means, however, risks running counter to the norm of geographic representation. With great

Table 7.3   Regional Representation of Democrats on the Ways and
                             Means Committee and in the House, 80th–90th Congresses

	East	Midwest	South	West
% of Ways & Means Democrats by region	20.6	20.6	47.8	11.0
% of House Democrats by region	24.7	19.1	44.3	11.9
Disproportion in committee representation	−4.1	+1.5	+3.5	−.9

SOURCE: Goodwin (1970), p. 71.

regularity, as documented in table 7.4, the Caucus replaces a member who has
left the committee with another from his region. Indeed, in sixteen of the past
twenty-one Caucus elections to Ways and Means, a member from the same
state delegation as the departing member was selected. This practice tends to
mitigate secular changes in geographic representation within the party.[13]

On several occasions the continuity norm has been put to the test, and it
has not always fared well. In the Eighty-sixth Congress, after the 1958 elections
which sent a substantial number of Democratic liberals to the House, leaders
of the newly formed Democratic Study Group sought to assert themselves.
They initiated a campaign to revamp the Rules Committee, the *bête noire* of
liberal legislation:

> While the movement was underway—letters were being sent to the new
> Democratic members, as well as to incumbents sympathetic to their
> cause—Speaker Rayburn intervened, promising to use his influence to
> prevent the Rules Committee from blocking their bills. The Speaker,
> working with Chairman Wilbur Mills of the Ways and Means Commit-
> tee and Majority Leader John McCormack, in order to demonstrate his
> willingness to cooperate with the group, offered one of their leaders, Lee
> Metcalf of Montana, an appointment to the Ways and Means Commit-
> tee...Metcalf was the logical choice in a move to head off a possible
> revolt. ...[Masters 1961, p. 44]

Thus Metcalf replaced Eugene McCarthy of Minnesota, who had moved on
to the Senate. When Metcalf followed McCarthy to the Senate, Al Ullman
of Oregon was his replacement.

In 1967, Eugene Keough (N.Y.), Clark Thompson (Tex.), and Pat Jennings
(Va.) left the committee. Owing, however, to the changed party ratio in the
chamber, the Democrats lost two committee berths. The party leadership
remained neutral in the contest between Jacob Gilbert (N.Y.) and Omar
Burleson (Tex.) for the one Ways and Means vacancy. Gilbert won in a close
vote, leaving the Texas Democrats without representation on the committee
for the first time in years.[14] In the next Congress, Texas regained its represen-

Table 7.4   **Committee Predecessors, 86th–93rd Congresses**

Member	Year Elected to Committee	Predecessor
James B. Frazier (Tenn.)	1959	Jere Cooper (Tenn.)
John C. Watts (Ky.)	1959	Noble J. Gregory (Ky.)
William J. Green, Jr. (Pa.)	1959	Herman Eberharter (Pa.)
Lee Metcalf (Mont.)	1959	Eugene J. McCarthy (Minn.)
Al Ullman (Ore.)	1961	Lee Metcalf (Mont.)
James A. Burke (Mass.)	1961	Aime J. Forand (R.I.)
Clark W. Thompson (Tex.)	1962	Frank Ikard (Tex.)
Martha W. Griffiths (Mich.)	1962	Thaddeus M. Machrowicz (Mich.)
Ross Bass (Tenn.)	1963	James B. Frazier (Tenn.)
W. Pat Jennings (Va.)	1963	Burr P. Harrison (Va.)
George M. Rhodes (Pa.)	1964	William J. Green, Jr. (Pa.)
Dan Rostenkowski (Ill.)	1965	Thomas J. O'Brien (Ill.)
Phil M. Landrum (Ga.)	1965	—*
Charles A. Vanik (Ohio)	1965	—*
Richard Fulton (Tenn.)	1965	Ross Bass (Tenn.)
Jacob H. Gilbert (N.Y.)	1967	Eugene J. Keough (N.Y.)**
Omar Burleson (Tex.)	1969	Frank M. Karsten (Mo.)
James C. Corman (Cal.)	1969	Cecil King (Cal.)
William J. Green, III (Pa.)	1969	George M. Rhodes (Pa.)
Sam M. Gibbons (Fla.)	1969	A. Sydney Herlong (Fla.)
Hugh L. Carey (N.Y.)	1971	Jacob H. Gilbert (N.Y.)
Joe D. Waggonner (La.)	1971	Hale Boggs (La.)
Joseph E. Karth (Minn.)	1972	John C. Watts (Ky.)

   * Majority party received two additional seats in the 89th Congress.
  ** Clark Thompson (Tex.) and Pat Jennings (Va.) also did not return but, owing to a two-seat reduction in majority party share on the committee, they were not replaced.

tation—Burleson replaced Frank Karsten of Missouri in another violation of the same-state practice.

These exceptions notwithstanding, the data of table 7.4 provide persuasive evidence for the practice of state and regional continuity. As a member of the Brookings Roundtable explained:

Actually, what we mean when we talk about a Pennsylvania seat or a Tennessee seat on Ways and Means ... is that we are resorting to a "don't rock the boat" technique. So many problems are involved in selecting people that it just proves easier to stick to tradition and fill the vacancy with a man from the same state. [Clapp 1964, p. 210]

4. Leadership support. The membership of the Ways and Means Committee is of special interest and importance to the party leadership. And it is not difficult to imagine why. "Year in and year out the Committee handles legislation that is vital to the administration's foreign and domestic policy," writes John Manley (1970, p. 24),

> and it is the party leader's job to get this legislation through the House ...The jurisdiction of Ways and Means, then, is enough to generate leadership concern about who is recruited to the Committee. But there is another reason too. ... The Speaker, if he is to exert any influence over the vital committee assignment process, has to work through and with the Ways and Means Democrats. Committee assignments are vital to the leadership in two ways. First, to the degree that the leadership affects assignments it has an important resource for doing favors for individual members, for rewarding members for past favors, and for establishing bonds with members that may provide some leverage in future legislative situations. Second, committee assignments are vital to the policy for which the leadership is responsible.

Although systematic, quantitative evidence is, of course, hard to come by, interview materials seem to support the thesis of active (though not always decisive) leadership intervention in recruitment for Ways and Means. All of the party leaders Manley interviewed affirmed their activity, and "thirteen of the eighteen [Ways and Means] Democrats interviewed mentioned the leadership as playing an important part in their successful candidacies. In at least six known cases ... the leadership took the initiative by asking the members to go on Ways and Means, and in the others the members made a call on the leadership first or second priority in their campaign for the Committee" (Manley 1970, p. 25). Fenno (1973, pp. 19–20), too, reports high concern and activity from party leaders on the matter of appointments to Ways and Means. Of the six committees he studied, Ways and Means, more frequently than any other, had its members recruited by leadership cooptation.

Leadership activity is often constrained by the political environment of the House and is not invariably successful. In the case of the large state delegations, for example, delegations that ordinarily maintain continuous representation on the committee, party leaders generally accept whoever the delegation chooses to propose. From time to time, of course, they seek to influence delegation deliberations. Upon the retirement of Frank Ikard (Tex.) in 1962, many believed that Walter Rogers would seek to replace him on Ways and Means. Since Rogers was unacceptable to the party leaders, it is claimed that they played a role in getting Clark Thompson to assert his seniority prerogative to seek the post.[15] Similarly, though the leadership gave the Illinois delegation free rein to nominate a successor to Thomas J. O'Brien, when the delegation selected Dan Rostenkowski, "Speaker McCormack made sure [he] was safe on medicare by asking him about it" (Manley 1970, p. 33).

On rare occasions the leaders either refrain from opposing a candidacy they do not particularly relish—A. Sydney Herlong (Fla.), though more conservative than Speaker Rayburn would have liked, was so popular that Rayburn did not oppose his candidacy—or fail to elect a member they have endorsed. Two Virginia congressmen, Burr Harrison in 1951 and W. Pat Jennings in 1963, defeated the leadership-endorsed candidacies of Wilfred Denton (Ohio) and Phil Landrum (Ga.), respectively.[16]

Leadership endorsement, then, is an important, though not always decisive, element in recruitment to the Ways and Means Committee. Political realities damp and constrain the leadership. As one current member of the committee remarked, "We are elected by the *party* as you know. You have to be acceptable to get on Ways and Means."

5. Ideological and partisan acceptability. Students of Congress have generally regarded the Democratic contingent on Ways and Means as liberal party regulars. On the basis of his analysis of those elected to the committee in the period 1955–66, Manley (1970, pp. 29–31) concludes that Ways and Means Democrats overrepresent their party's liberalism and partisanship. Fenno (1973, tables 3.1 and 3.2) discovered that Ways and Means Democrats are more partisan (as measured by *Congressional Quarterly* party unity scores) than their counterparts on any of the other five committees he examined; and though they are not as liberal (as measured by *CQ* conservative coalition scores) as the Democratic contingent on Education and Labor, Ways and Means members are more liberal than most other House Democrats.

These conclusions about central tendencies are supported by the data of table 7.5. Reported here are the scores for party support, conservative coalition support, and support for a larger federal role of all Ways and Means Democrats elected between 1959 and 1974; the scores are for the Congress preceding their election to the committee. On average, Ways and Means members vote with a majority of their party against a majority of the Republicans about 80% of the time (party-support score mean is 63); vote against the "conservative coalition" about 70% of the time (conservative coalition-support score mean of −41); and vote in favor of a "larger federal role" 85% of the time (support for larger federal role mean of 67).

Around each mean, however, there is considerable variance. Al Ullman (Ore.), at the time of his election to the committee in 1961, lay at one end of the spectrum. An ardent partisan, he voted with his party majority 94% of the time, he opposed the conservative coalition on 97% of the occasions in which it formed, and he consistently voted in favor of a larger federal role and against a smaller federal role. He is the extreme version of the liberal party

Table 7.5   Party Support, Conservative Coalition Support, and Support for Larger Federal Role of Members of the Committee on Ways and Means (Congress preceding appointment)

Member	Year Elected to Committee	Party Support[a]	Conservative Coalition Support[b]	Support for Larger Federal Role[c]
James B. Frazier (Tenn.)	1959	48	24	30
John C. Watts (Ky.)	1959	54	−20	61
William J. Green, Jr. (Pa.)	1959	48	−88	63
Lee Metcalf (Mont.)	1959	82	−80	85
Al Ullman (Ore.)	1961	88	−94	100
James A. Burke (Mass.)	1961	61	−86	66
Clark W. Thompson (Tex.)	1962	76	0	50
Martha W. Griffiths (Mich.)	1962	63	−67	100
Ross Bass (Tenn.)	1963	84	−67	94
W. Pat Jennings (Va.)	1963	83	12	66
George M. Rhodes (Pa.)	1964	89	−73	88
Dan Rostenkowski (Ill.)	1965	82	−85	83
Phil M. Landrum (Ga.)	1965	47	44	50
Charles A. Vanik (Ohio)	1965	79	−86	83
Richard Fulton (Tenn.)	1965	75	−37	89
Jacob H. Gilbert (N.Y.)	1967	84	−93	92
Omar Burleson (Tex.)	1969	−19	79	−59
James C. Corman (Cal.)	1969	63	−61	100
William J. Green, III (Pa.)	1969	85	−83	91
Sam M. Gibbons (Fla.)	1969	65	−31	82
Hugh L. Carey (N.Y.)	1971	53	−65	87
Joe D. Waggonner (La.)	1971	−17	82	−37
Joseph E. Karth (Minn.)	1972	73	−75	81

NOTE: Data drawn from appropriate issues of *Congressional Quarterly Weekly Report*.
[a] Party Support = Party Unity − Party Opposition
[b] CC Support = CC Support − CC Opposition
[c] For 85th Congress, Economy Support − Opposition Scores employed. In general, LFR Support = Support for Larger Federal Role − Support for Smaller Federal Role.

regular. At the other extreme are Omar Burleson (Tex.) and Joe Waggonner (La.). Each supported his party majority less than half the time, voted with the conservative coalition about 90% of the time (indeed, each is regarded as a leader of that coalition), and voted against a larger federal role more than 70% of the time. They are extreme versions of the conservative party irregular!

Though more of those elected to Ways and Means since 1959 are liberal party regulars, a not insignificant minority represents the conservative strain in the Democratic party. Together with committee Republicans, and under the leadership of a relatively conservative Wilbur Mills, they have moderated the liberalism of their Democratic brethren (Manley 1970, pp. 35–38).

It should also be observed that members change. Phil Landrum (Ga.) represents an interesting case (see fig. 7.1) for it appears that he purposely

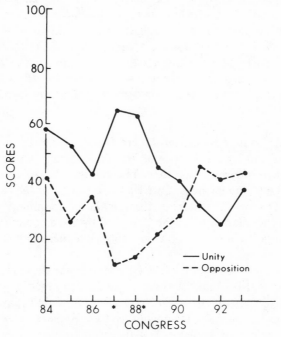

Fig. 7.1   Phil Landrum's party unity and opposition scores, 84th–93d Congresses.

sought to make himself acceptable to the Caucus in order to win election to Ways and Means. During his first three Congresses his party-support (party unity, party opposition) score dropped from an already low 20 to less than 10. In the Eighty-seventh Congress, however, it rose dramatically to 55. In an important move, he supported the party leadership in the vote to expand the Rules Committee permanently, in exchange for which he extracted a commitment from Speaker McCormack to endorse his Ways and Means candidacy. At the opening of the Eighty-eighth Congress, however, his authorship of the Landrum–Griffin bill and his past renegade party behavior proved too fresh in the minds of Caucus members. Despite McCormack's endorsement, they voted Pat Jennings (Va.), a more liberal southerner, onto the committee. Landrum persisted in his more liberal ways in the Eighty-eighth Congress and finally succeeded in obtaining committee membership in the Eighty-ninth Congress when two new seats were created. During the Eighty-eighth Congress he coauthored, and steered through the House, the Powell–Landrum bill—a bill that became the Economic Opportunity Act of 1964. Once elected to Ways and Means, however, he reverted to his renegade ways. Since the Ninety-first Congress he has supported his party less than half the time.

Although partisan and ideological acceptability tend to be the hallmarks of those elected to the Ways and Means Committee, they are not acid tests. Of the two, party support appears to be the more important. Burleson and Waggonner are genuine exceptions to this pattern. Ideological acceptability is a much weaker test reflecting a more general ideological diversity in the party.

6. Legislative professionalism. Much is made in the literature of the professionalism and legislative style of Ways and Means members. They are professionals in the sense that they are committed to the committee and to the House. Only one member, Burr Harrison (Va.), left the committee—a result of the Democrats switching from majority to minority status in 1953, necessitating Harrison's being "bumped" off the committee—and only five in recent years have left the House to seek higher office.

The characteristics typical of the Democrat newly elected to Ways and Means are important because they tend to predispose him toward certain kinds of career objectives which, in turn, have a bearing on his behavior as a member of the committee (and as a member of the CC). His several terms of accumulated House service, his knowledge of the institution and its rules, his electoral safeness that permits him to invest more time and energy in House politics, his membership (usually) in a large Democratic state or regional delegation that may serve him as a political base, his ties to the party leadership either as an ally and "regular" Democrat or as a respected representative of an important "minority within the majority," his career orientation toward the House and general lack of ambition for higher office, and his personal popularity all promote the career objective of institutional influence. Freed of major electoral concerns, generally lacking intense policy interests[17] and blessed with seniority, tied to strong state (regional) interests in the House and allied (or in a truce) with the party leadership, the Ways and Means member can devote a comparatively large portion of his energies to the brokerage activities to which his personal demeanor and legislative style lend themselves.[18] To these brokerage activities I now turn.

Goals of Ways and
Means Members

Of the three principal goals entertained by most House members—reelection, "good" public policy, and institutional influence—for Ways and Means members it is the last of these that is most frequently articulated: "If the men presently on [Ways and Means] believed that the District of Columbia Committee was the most powerful committee in the House, they would seek membership on it" (Fenno 1973, p. 4).

Chamber influence brings with it prestige, respect, the prospect of generalized brokerage activity, and the politics of quid pro quo. And these are precisely the emoluments in which the career Democrats on Ways and Means are interested. Said one member, "The only way I can interpret what I want to be is power. I don't know what I'd do with it when I got it but I want it where I can reach out and use it when I want it." Frequent references to having "reached the top" with election to Ways and Means, to the "political prestige" of committee service, and to the generally high status of the committee—"guts of government," "queen committee," "center of the House," "key committee"[19]—underscore both the abstract desire on the part of members to be regarded as important, respected and powerful, and the more practical realization that chamber influence has "value-in-exchange" as well as "value-in-use."

The authority to make committee assignments is intimately tied to the quid pro quo orientation of committee Democrats—a connection I shall explore in more detail below. The zone structure of the CC (see Chapter 8) enables a committee member to claim credit for matching one of "his people's" requests with an actual assignment. Credit-claiming, an activity Mayhew (1974) emphasized in the relationship between a congressman and his constituency, is an important element in the relationship between the Ways and Means Democrat and *his* constituency—his Democratic colleagues in the House.

A second tangible component of the Ways and Means member's logrolling arsenal is the so-called "member's bill." Members' bills, according to Manley (1970, pp. 80–81),

> are supposed to be minor, noncontroversial pieces of legislation that ameliorate the adverse or unintended impact of some small feature in the tax laws or make some "technical" improvement in the laws that come under the Committee's jurisdiction; they are regarded as "little," of no special interest to anyone other than the members that introduced them.... They are "little" favors that are large to individual congressmen.

Given the economic importance of the committee's jurisdiction, a member is in the enviable position of literally being able to create wealth for his constituents, his colleagues, and his colleagues' constituents. And favors performed are not forgotten in the accounting system of the House.

A third bargaining resource provided by membership on the Ways and Means Committee is, in a sense, the complement of the second. To create or maintain wealth for his friends, a member need not actively *promote* their interests; it often suffices for him to block proposed changes antagonistic to their position:

> Committee members make sure that nothing interrupts the "normal flow of the lumber business," they "keep oil from being used as a whipping boy" and from being "persecuted," they watch over the varied financial interests of the big cities like New York and the trading interests of New Orleans, they act as surrogates for businesses that might be affected by changes in the tax and trade laws, and so forth. [Manley 1970, p. 82]

Thus, both the basic predisposition of the committee's members—a desire for chamber influence—and the resources it places at their disposal—committee assignments, members' bills, veto power—encourage the power-broker role for Ways and Means members. But to what end? To what purposes is this generalized influence put? Are there private objectives, above and beyond institutional influence for its own sake, that members entertain? On the answers to these questions there appears to be far less consensus among the members.

For some there is a genuine concern for "good" public policy. One midwestern Democrat had presidential pens and embossed copies of Social Security amendments for which he was responsible prominently displayed on his office wall. Another waxed philosophical about the nation's energy needs and the problems faced by oil and gas producers (not uncoincidentally, he is from an oil state). A third, an economist by training, held a strong professional interest in the gasoline shortage. For the most part, however, members are attracted to Ways and Means "more by the putative 'importance' of [the Committee's] subject matter than by its content" (Fenno 1973, p. 4).

Although every congressman worries about reelection, this appears to be a decidedly subordinate goal for the Ways and Means members. Their longstanding incumbency and the safeness of their seats permit them to "nurse their ambitions inside the House because they have to expand less energy than some other congressmen on insuring their reelection" (Fenno 1973, p. 4). Many members, in fact, believe that committee membership is of no help, and perhaps even a hindrance, in seeking reelection. Both Lee Metcalf (Mont.) and Clark Thompson (Tex.), recruited by the party leadership for the committee, initially resisted the idea of running for Ways and Means. Each believed his current committee assignment, Interior, and Agriculture, respectively, was better suited to constituency service and reelection.[20]

Most members regard "getting things accomplished" as the chief requirement of their job, and they are quite free to define what it is they seek to accomplish and who the beneficiaries of their accomplishments are. For most, that is, there are "constituency" services to perform (where "constituency" is broadly conceived and subjectively defined) for which the quid pro quo resources of the Ways and Means Committee are optimally suited. A member of Congressman Dan Rostenkowski's staff illustrated this general orientation in some comments about his boss. "He represents the city of Chicago, not just the eighth district," said the staffman.

> Why just the other day we had some people from the city Department of Public Works in to see the Congressman. He took them over to see _____ on the Public Works Committee and made some calls downtown for them. You see, he needs contacts on all the legislative committees and in the Administration. We make no bones about the fact that Rostenkowski is a friend of the mayor and is intimately involved in the political administration of the City of Chicago.

*The Committee's
External Environment and
Internal
Accommodations*

Charged with legislating in areas of great national significance, expected to represent their party's position on these "great issues," and lacking any clear-cut consensus on the ultimate purposes to which they should direct the institutional influence they have accumulated, the members of the Ways and Means Committee have accommodated the demands of their external environment to their own idiosyncratic purposes through a procedural agreement. This agreement contains two imperatives (Fenno 1973, pp. 51–57):

1. prosecute partisanship in a restrained fashion;
2. write legislation that can pass on the floor of the House.

The members of the committee are leaders in the House because they are followers. With a legislative jurisdiction that contains some of the fundamental cleavages dividing the political parties, the committee's legislative deliberations take place in a charged political environment. In order to maintain their policy independence and, more important, their general brokerage roles, they must be responsive to the demands and expectations of their respective party coalitions. To do so in a manner that divides the committee, however, invites the possibility of washing the committee' dirty laundry before the full House and risks jeopardizing the committee's reputation as the repository of expertise and good judgment on complicated legislative matters. Because the committee members trade on the committee's reputation, it is that reputation that must be protected. Procedural restraint in the prosecution of partisanship fosters the reputation of technical expertise and allows for the full participation of substantive and political minorities in the committee's work. "The norm of restrained partisanship," writes Manley (1970, p. 64),

> means that partisanship should not interfere with a thorough study and complete understanding of the technical complexities of the bills under consideration. Members may disagree over what decisons the Committee finally should make, but there is a firmly rooted consensus on *how* they should go about making them. Those members who attend the protracted meetings, and attendance varies greatly, go through a laborious process of illuminating the implications of arcane tax, tariff, debt, and social security proposals. Proposed legislation is pondered line by line with the assistance of experts from the executive agencies, the House Legislative Counsel's office which helps draft the technical language, the tax staff of the Joint Committee on Internal Revenue Taxation, and at times by Library of Congress experts. The decision-making process varies somewhat from issue to issue, but, with the aid of a battery of "technicians," it is generally marked by caution, methodical repetition, and, most important, restrained partisanship.

Although partisanship is blunted procedurally, the substantive product that emerges tends to reflect the partisan preferences of the majority party. In floor debate on a Ways and Means bill, the ranking minority member will often praise the chairman's nonpartisan spirit and openness to minority input; but he also is the one who moves to recommit. This is not surprising, given the method of majority recruitment to the committee. Most Democrats, as the preceding sections detail, are party regulars with close ties to the party leadership. They are "right" on most legislative issues that come before the committee or they would not have been recruited to it in the first place.

The second strategic premise of the committee's deliberations, however, produces legislative outcomes that displease the more extreme Democratic liberals. With a majority party containing a conservative "minority within the majority," the median House member is more conservative than the median Democratic member. And it is with this median House member in mind that the committee molds its legislation.

The median-member orientation of Ways and Means reflects more than the middle-of-the-road leadership of that committee. By attending to the policy disposition of the House, and thereby maintaining the committee's track record, each member's credibility and effectiveness in "getting things accomplished" is enhanced. It is therefore in each member's interest to protect the committee's reputation as a repository of responsive legislation, for a reputation of responsiveness is also a reputation of floor success. "A good bill that cannot pass the House is a contradiction in terms for most members of Ways and Means" (Manley 1969, p. 448).

I have dwelled at length on who gets elected to the Ways and Means Committee, and somewhat more briefly on what the members' objectives are and how they accommodate them to the external constraints on their behavior. The reason is simple. The behavioral adaptations that characterize the decision-making style of members of Ways and Means are also characteristic of CC decision-making. The Democrat on Ways and Means is not schizophrenic; when he exchanges his Ways and Means hat for his CC hat, he does not alter his political characteristics, goals, or personality. He remains interested in "getting things accomplished." He still relishes playing the broker and engaging in quid pro quo politics. He continues to follow in order to lead—hence his concern with producing acceptable CC decisions. And he persists in the role of restrained advocacy, though now it is on behalf of the Democrats in his zone rather than a party position in a legislative battle. In brief, the shift in roles does not entail a shift in gears. In the following sections of this chapter and in the next chapter, I trace the transition from Ways and Means decision-making to CC decision-making.

Member Goals on the CC

The politics of quid pro quo, power, and chamber influence retain their central place in the preference map of the Ways and Means Democrat when he sits as a member of his party's CC. Although committee members can (and often do) give an abstract characterization to their goals, they just as frequently give concrete content to their chamber influence objective. They speak of "having pipelines into legislative committees," "affecting policy," "helping the freshmen get reelected," "helping the region maintain its committee representation," and "looking good in the state delegation" by getting people top assignments.

Members of the CC are not naive about the logrolling potential of their committee assignment prerogative. They tend to conceive of this prerogative more as a general source of leverage than as a specific claim for a service rendered. "They come to you and that's very important. Members are always coming to me for things and when I go to them, boy, they remember." "When you're on Ways and Means the other members smile at you. They never know when they are going to ask for your support for a committee for someone in your zone. They don't go out of their way to pick a fight with you, let's put it that way." [21] "They call you 'Mr.' and 'Sir' when you are on the Committee on Committees." [22] Others, somewhat more circumspectly, allude to an abstract exchange prospect at one step removed. They refer to "getting to know" the new members early in the new session: "The biggest plus about the job," said one former member of the CC after Ways and Means had been stripped of committee assignments, "was that you got to know the new people early on and could count on them during the session. They weren't just names up on the board." Said another, "I liked having people come around to see me. . . . I liked the power." Still others have more immediate objectives. Said one staffer about his boss, "_____ is interested in helping guys from the South. He's active as a leader on the floor so he wants to help people at the committee assignment stage so they will reciprocate when he needs them."

In addition to the explicit recognition of the quid pro quo possibilities CC membership provides, a second manifestation of the chamber influence objective is the pride members take in winning coveted slots for "their" people.[23] "You're darn right it's important to get your own people on committees they want. After all, they're *your* people. Pride and prestige are involved, too. But mostly it's loyalty to the delegation. You want to help your own out." "You know, I took the place of a very important man—Tom O'Brien. I've got to look good. He was a man who always got us boys what we wanted. . . . Luckily I only had five people and was able to get them what they wanted." Two administrative assistants reinforced the general impression that "credit-claiming" for the successful placement of members on committees they sought loomed large for "committee-makers."

> Sure it mattered to _____ to get his people on. It was personally embarrassing when he lost a vote [in the CC executive sessions].
> He always went to bat for his own people—it was important for New England. And he is proud of some of his successes—Giaimo on Appropriations and Harrington on Armed Services, for example.

A western CC member, expressing his pride in terms of regional successes, bragged, "I got a man on Appropriations this time. He was a good man and he ran very strong. What I'm trying to do is broaden us a little—last time I got _____ on Appropriations, this time _____. It used to be that my area would be represented on Interior and Public Works. Now I'm getting them on Appropriations, Space. We had no one on Space." Another CC member, after grudgingly acknowledging that "getting people what they want is no big deal, but sure you like to win," nevertheless appeared to take joy in reporting, "you know, I once beat Mills on an Appropriations slot. I told Wilbur, 'What happened? Either you don't have the clout everyone says you have or you were backing a bum horse!' We chuckled about it in the committee meeting."

Nicholas Masters (1961, p. 57), writing about "the most important single factor" affecting committee assignments, observed that "in distributing assignments the party acts as a mutual benefit and improvement society, and this for the obvious reason that control of the House depends on the re-election of party members." Securing "good" committee assignments for members who have survived difficult, close elections is, of course, another form of favor the CC has the discretion to grant.[24] Members of the CC report that they occasionally bolster their arguments in behalf of the committee requests of "marginal" congressmen in the CC executive sessions with references to their tenuous electoral circumstances. A southerner on the CC captured the spirit of the "mutual benefit and improvement society" mentality of the CC:

> The most important thing for these people is that they're only here for two years. If they want to get reelected they need to get on a committee and start getting their teeth into something for their districts. When I called _____ to congratulate him on his close victory he said, "I want Ways and Means." I said, "Hell, Harold, *I'm* on Ways and Means. It doesn't work that way around here. Not like in the [state] legislature. Why don't you try for Banking and Currency? That way you can become an expert on housing and gain some entree into the banking community. It should help you in your reelection." Let's face it. We're all Democrats and we want to keep our people in office. That's the main thing.

Though probably not as pervasive as it apparently was in the late 1950s when Masters did his fieldwork, the "reelection of peers" objective still plays a role in CC deliberations.[25]

In the early history of the House, the norm prescribed by Thomas Jefferson for committee assignments had strong policy overtones:

> the child is not to be put to the nurse that cares not for it.... It is therefore a constant rule "that no man is to be employed in any matter who has declared himself against it."[26]

In the contemporary House, policy considerations play a decidedly secondary role in the deliberations of "committee-makers." This is not to say that policy orientation counts for nothing or that, for some members, it is not quite important. Said a midwesterner on the CC:

> With some delegation deans I am very friendly, like _____ and _____.
> They come in and tell me what they need and I fight for them. We like each other—we agree on political philosophy for the most part. But if _____ or one of those types comes in, I won't give them the time of day.

I am a *policy* man. I care about getting liberals on committees. Others on the Committee on Committees, like _____, like to play politics and couldn't give a damn about policy.

A participant in the Brookings Roundtable reported the difficulty he encountered obtaining a prized committee assignment because of a policy difference with his zone representative on the CC:

> I was anxious to serve on Public Works because the St. Lawrence Seaway proposal was before the committee. I armed myself with supporting letters from Adlai Stevenson and many other national leaders. However, my regional man on Ways and Means was the author of the water diversion bill, a source of conflict between my state and his. He was not going to permit an opponent of his bill to gain a seat on the committee considering it, so I had no chance. He would not even consider anyone from my state. [Clapp 1964, p. 216]

Indeed, nearly everyone on the CC, at some time, has experienced the feeling articulated by one midwestern member, "There are just some people here who I wouldn't vote for—even if the deal was for everlasting happiness." The more common orientation, however, is that revealed by a liberal southerner on the CC: "A few sessions ago I got _____ to go on Appropriations. He and I don't vote together even half the time. But I felt we needed another Southerner on Appropriations."

All other things being equal, members of the CC attend to secondary criteria including the policy stances of requesters, their margin of election, and so on. After all, CC members are, in the main, liberal party regulars—they entertain policy preferences of their own and are concerned about maintaining the party's strength in the House. But rarely are all other things equal. Consequently, these secondary criteria rarely deflect the CC member from his primary, influence-oriented, objective. And this primary objective induces him to act as an *advocate* for the requests of the people from his zone:

> Sure it's important to get people the committees they ask for. You want to help these people out. You want them around two years from now. Also it is a matter of pride. If someone on the CC doesn't like you he's gonna take it out on your nominees. You don't want people on your own committee to be your enemies. You want them to vote for your people.

Advocacy is the principal behavioral mode induced by an orientation toward chamber influence. It is encouraged, in a restrained fashion, by the larger political environment from which the CC draws its influence. It is to these environmental constraints that I now turn.

**Environmental
Constraints**

Remember now that every member on the Committee
on Committees is a Ways and Means Member. He had
to get elected by the entire Caucus, had to build an
organization and mount a campaign. That's no cakewalk.
He has a constituency out there.
Member of the CC

The environment of the CC is party-dominated. The party elects members of
the CC, formally constrains their decisions, and ultimately must approve
them; the party leaders play an active role in the recruitment of Ways and
Means (CC) members, negotiate a committee structure which defines CC
scarcity constraints, directly lobby the CC on particular assignments, and,
since 1973, have been formal voting participants in the CC's deliberations;
state party delegations serve as conduits through which demands and expectations are signaled; and "interested others," e.g., lobbyists, the administration,
employ the party network to communicate their preferences. Since it is the
party that, in an ultimate sense, provides CC members with the instruments
enabling them to exercise chamber influence—through its restriction of the
size of the Ways and Means Committee, its maintenance of the committee's
impressive jurisdiction, and its sanctioning of the group's prerogative to
recommend the party's committee assignments—it is to the party that the
CC must attend. The party, however, is not a monolithic entity. The congeries
of interests, expectations, and demands articulated by the Democrats in the
House requires a number of strategic accommodations by members of the
CC. The variety of expectations ("constraints" is probably too strong a word)
to which the CC adjusts is the subject of this section. Their strategic accommodations are the topic of the next.

Party Caucus

The CC is the creation of the Democratic Caucus. The Democratic members
of Ways and Means are charged by the Caucus to sit as its CC[27] and to
recommend to it a slate of committee assignments which requires final
Caucus endorsement. In addition to reserving to itself the right of final
approval, serving on occasion as "court of last resort," the Caucus formally
constrains CC decisions by imposing certain rules with which CC recommendations must comply. The rules of the Ninety-fourth Congress governing
committee assignments are given in the *Preamble and Rules Adopted by the
Democratic Caucus*:[28]

E. *Rules for Making Committee Assignments.* For the purposes of this
Section the following committee designations shall apply:

(1) Appropriations; Ways and Means; and Rules Committee shall be
"exclusive" committees.

(2) Agriculture; Armed Services; Banking, Currency and Housing; Education and Labor; Foreign Affairs; Interstate and Foreign Commerce; Judiciary; and Public Works and Transportation shall be considered "major" committees.

(3) Budget; District of Columbia; Government Operations; House Administration; Interior and Insular Affairs; Merchant Marine and Fisheries; Post Office and Civil Service; Science and Technology; Small Business; and Veterans' Affairs shall be considered "nonmajor" committees.

a. No Democratic Member of an exclusive committee shall also serve on another exclusive, major, or nonmajor committee.

b. Each Democratic Member shall be entitled to serve on one but only one exclusive or one major committee.

c. No Democratic Member shall serve on more than one major and one nonmajor committee or two nonmajor committees.

d. No chairman of an exclusive or major committee may serve on another exclusive, major, or nonmajor committee.

e. Members who served as members on the Select Committee on Small Business or the Small Business Subcommittee of the Committee on Banking and Currency on October 8, 1974, shall not be deemed to be in violation of the provisions of this clause by reason of membership on the Small Business Committee.

f. Members of the Budget Committee as of December 1, 1974, shall not be deemed to be in violation of the provisions of this clause by reason of their Budget Committee membership and Members of the Appropriations and Ways and Means Committee shall be eligible for membership on the Budget Committee as provided by law, not withstanding the provisions of subsection a. Any member of the Budget Committee shall be entitled to take a leave of absence from service on any committee or subcommittee during the period he or she serves on the Budget Committee and seniority rights of such Member on such committee and on each subcommittee to which such Member was assigned at the time shall be fully protected as if such Member had continued to so serve during the period of the leave of absence. Any Member on such leave of absence shall not be deemed to be in violation of the provisions of this clause by reason of their membership on the committee from which they are on a leave of absence.

Formal election of members to committees is done according to the procedures laid out in Rule (M.I.)D of the *Preamble and Rules*:[29]

The Committee on Committees shall make recommendations to the Caucus regarding the assignment of Members to each committee other than the Committee on Rules, one committee at a time. Upon a demand supported by 10 or more Members, a separate vote shall be had on any member of the committee. If any such motion prevails, the committee list of that particular committee shall be considered recommitted to the Committee on Committees for the sole purpose of implementing the direction of the Caucus. Also, such demand, if made and properly supported, shall be debated for no more than 30 minutes with the time equally divided between proponents and opponents. If the Caucus and the Committee on Committees be in disagreement after completion of the procedure herein provided, the Caucus may make final and complete disposition of the matter.

In making nominations for committee assignments the Committee on Committees shall not discriminate on the basis of prior occupation or profession in making such nominations.

In reserving to itself the right of final approval, the Caucus, in effect, possesses an enforcement mechanism, on a committee-by-committee basis, to insure that the CC produces an acceptable slate of nominees. This formal device, however, is rather awkward and is rarely employed.[30] Of somewhat greater importance as a control mechanism are the formal allocation rules [(M.I.)E]. While still providing the CC with a large number of "degrees of freedom," the rules governing the distribution of committee slots among party members assure the Caucus that committee positions will be allocated in a reasonably equitable manner.

The formal arrangements, though awkward and "loose" as explicit instruments of control, underscore a more basic expectation. The CC is a *party* committee. In exercising its independent judgment it is expected to be responsive to the expressed preferences of party members and to resolve conflicts in an equitable manner. In a fashion directly analogous to expectations about Ways and Means legislation, the CC is expected to write a committee slate that is acceptable to the great majority of Caucus members. This expectation encourages the advocacy role for CC members alluded to earlier; but it also restrains it inasmuch as it precludes any one region or ideological interest from being too successful at the expense of other Caucus interests.

Party Leadership

> I love Speaker Rayburn, his heart is so warm,
> And if I love him he'll do me no harm.
> So I shan't sass the Speaker one little bitty,
> And then I'll wind up on a major committee.
> *Anonymous congressman*

In some of the early literature on committee assignments, much emphasis was placed on the impact of party leaders on CC decisions. "The Speaker and Majority Leader," wrote Masters (1961, p. 35), "participate extensively in the [CC's] deliberations and, of course, have considerable influence on the decisions."[31] Adds Goodwin (1970, p. 73):

> It is common knowledge that Rayburn showed a continuing interest in Democratic appointments to Ways and Means, making sure that members would favor reciprocal trade programs and would oppose any change in the depletion tax allowance granted the oil companies. Further, he is reported to have played a role in stacking the Appropriations Committee against its chairman, Clarence Cannon, and to have liberalized the membership of the Un-American Activities Committee and the Committee on Education and Labor.[32]

From these and other observations it is clear that Speaker Rayburn, by dint of personality, love of the House and its politics, and a personal organization—the so-called "Board of Education"—that included several Ways and Means people (specifically, Frank Ikard and Hale Boggs), chose to assert himself in the affairs of the CC. More recently Speakers McCormack and Albert have played decidedly less activist roles. In addition to their endorsements of Ways and Means candidates, to which we alluded above, they have concentrated primarily on appointments to the Rules Committee. A sampling of the opinions of CC members supports this view:

> The Speaker almost always gets his way on Rules. He is usually uninterested in going on the record for any other committees.
> The Speaker got his Rules preferences, but that was all he worried about.
> The leadership doesn't get involved usually. [They] can't dictate to the Committees on Committees, except for Rules—that's pretty much their choice. The Speaker and Carl Albert sit in there with us but not to lobby or pressure, just to keep informed.
> The Speaker rarely attended [CC] meetings. We would always give him his Rules requests, and that's what he was principally concerned with.
> Usually the leadership has agreed on the Rules Committee. This time it was Pepper. There is not usually any fight over the Rules Committee. The leadership just makes up its mind and sends the word down to us— mostly it just comes through informally.
> [The leaders are active] only on the Rules Committee, nothing else. They come in [to the CC executive sessions] for a minute just to let us know they were still around, but they didn't influence me one bit, not one little bit.

On the relatively infrequent occasions in which the leadership actively involves itself in CC deliberations, its track record is mixed:

> One time McCormack came in. He says he never tries to pressure us and he doesn't. But he had told some of the members, and they quoted

him as having said, that he promised the New Jersey delegation that they could have a position on a certain committee. So we honored that promise.

The leadership sits in there with us [sometimes] and this time they saw one of their own candidates for Appropriations lose! They had made a commitment, no they can't really make commitments, but it was clear who they were for.

That Speaker Rayburn chose to intervene in the committee assignment process, often successfully, whereas Speakers McCormack and Albert did not, probably reflects differences in leadership styles more than anything else. If Masters and others have overemphasized the direct influence of the party leadership on the CC (owing to the time period of their observations), they have probably not laid enough stress on indirect leadership influence. First, the leadership, through endorsements and cooptation, plays a major role in the recruitment of members to Ways and Means. Making sure that members are "right" and that they have the party's interests at heart at this initial stage obviates the need for the party leaders to play a more interventionist role. Second, in negotiating the committee structure prior to CC deliberations (but after requests have been submitted), the party leaders are in a position to relax scarcity constraints and thereby to improve the chances that their own candidates for committees will not be passed over.[33] Finally, the party leaders are often asked to write letters and make telephone calls in behalf of committee candidates. In this task they simply make their wishes known, leaving it to others—namely, delegation deans, zone representatives, and the candidates themselves—to carry the ball.[34]

Like the Caucus, the party leadership is a major element of the CC environment. Except for Rules and Ways and Means appointments, where they play a decidedly more visible role, however, the leaders do not explicitly constrain particular CC decisions. While their presence is felt and their preferences (on occasion) are known, leadership satisfaction with CC decisions is due more to the collinearity of their respective interests than to explicit intervention.

State Delegations

In 1958 Connecticut elected six Democratic freshmen to replace its previously solid Republican delegation. Two of these freshmen failed to submit committee requests. One was placed on Science and Astronautics, the other on District of Columbia and on Post Office and Civil Service. Of the four who submitted committee requests, one received no request (Government Operations), two received their third-ranked request, and only one, Chester Bowles, received his first-preference request. The Connecticut "orphans," without any senior members to take up their cause, faired poorly in the competition for committee assignments.[35]

Drawing attention to the fate of the Connecticut freshmen, Masters (1961, pp. 36–38) underscores both the interest in and activity of senior members of the state delegation in securing committee representation for fellow delegation members:

> In negotiations between the [CC] and the applicants [the state delegation dean] plays a crucially important role in securing assignments. It is his special responsibility to see that his members receive adequate representation on the various committees. In performing this task, he tries to protect or maintain the delegation's place on a major committee when a vacancy occurs and the seat has previously been held by a member of the delegation. . . .

Deckard (1975, chap. 4), too, notes the activities in which delegations engage in behalf of their members:

> Because the effectiveness with which the members of a delegation can act as allies for one another is related to the committee positions they hold, their delegation's success in the committee assignment process is of considerable importance. . . .

The state delegations, then, often act as communications and influence networks in an effort to affect the fate of their members in the decisions of the CC. Their principal point of contact with the CC is their own zone representative. Indeed, he and the delegation dean are often one and the same person. It is not unusual for state delegation deans to pay visits to most of the CC members prior to their executive session.

The major "constraining" influence of a state delegation on CC deliberations follows from its near monopoly on information about its new members and, at least for cohesive delegations, its collusive behavior according to which intradelegation conflicts are resolved internally.[36] By manipulating the information environment of the CC and restricting the CC's discretion by dissuading extradelegation competition among its members,[37] the state delegation has impact on the CC's ultimate decisions.

"Interested Others"

A number of groups and individuals outside the House are interested in the business of various committees and thus occasionally pay some attention to the committee assignment process. They tend, however, to play a relatively minor role in that process and are certainly not regarded very seriously by members of the CC unless their preferences happen to reinforce those of more important actors in the CC's environment. At any rate they do not appear to lobby openly for particular committee assignments. Reflected one CC member about Education and Labor appointments:

> Interest groups may be important. Unions and I suppose the education association back home, who supported _____, wrote letters to other people here on his behalf. But they didn't contact me; they never try to pressure members of the Committee on Committees.

Over a two-Congress period the letters of endorsement contained in the files of another CC member revealed the relative inactivity of interest groups: as few as 2.6% of the letters he received (3 of 116) were sent by organized groups.[38]

The more usual arrangement for "interested others" is to work through other members of Congress. Thus, Andrew Biemiller, chief lobbyist for the AFL–CIO, has some input into CC decisions on Education and Labor appointments chiefly through his friendship and influence with the Speaker and the chairman of the Congressional Campaign Committee. President Truman, similarly, was able to affect a more pro–St. Lawrence Seaway composition for the Public Works Committee through his collaboration with Speaker Rayburn. "Going through channels" is the standard operating procedure for outside interests. Machinations and direct intervention are apt to be resented (and disregarded) by CC members.

The environment of the CC is dominated by the party caucus, the party leadership, and state party delegations. The demands they place on CC members, however, can hardly be regarded as constraining (except, perhaps, for the formal allocation rules imposed by the Caucus) inasmuch as it is precisely those demands that CC members, given their own objectives, are most predisposed to service. In the context of CC decision-making, influence-seeking on the part of CC members begets responsiveness to the demands of their "constituents." The servicing of these demands is the basis of their quid pro quo relationship with other House members, and hence the source of their influence.

This is not to imply that outcomes are uniquely determined by the dovetailing of CC member objectives with environmental constraints. Scarcity of committee seats, with the consequences of excess demand, queuing, and intra-party conflicts, requires the CC to make choices—choices that sacrifice some interests in order to satisfy others. Here is the CC's discretion, and hence is where environmental actors have the most effect on CC decisions. Although the interests of the dominant actors in the CC's environment do little more than reinforce the CC member's basic predisposition to serve in an advocacy role, the general expectation of these actors is that the costs of scarcity should be equitably distributed. The demand that the final CC slate be acceptable to the principal regional and ideological interests of the party in the House induces restraint on the part of CC members in their more narrowly based advocacy. The interaction, then, of individual objectives and environmental constraints encourages a procedural consensus among CC members revolving around restrained advocacy on the one hand and the production of an acceptable committee slate on the other. The content of this procedural consensus is the subject of the next section.

Strategic Premises

A committee's strategic premises are the internal norms and practices to which its members subscribe in order to resolve intracommittee conflicts and to bring member goals and environmental constraints into line. Fenno (1973, pp. 46–47) conceives of them as "agreements ... designed to implement, through committee action, a given set of member goals in a given context of environmental constraints.... Agreements on strategic premises take operational form as agreements on rules for making substantive decisions."

At first glance the substance of CC decisions portends internal conflict. Each member is an advocate for his constituents and their interests. To the extent that scarcity constraints on available committee berths are binding, those individual objectives, and the larger environmental interests they represent, are incompatible. Like the parent Ways and Means Committee of which the CC is a part, the decisional context of the CC is one of pluralism. And, like the Ways and Means Committee, the consensus among CC members on strategic premises is more procedural than substantive. Rather than agreeing on particular criteria for committee assignments, the members of the CC subscribe, instead, to procedural fluidity—to "horse trading," "bargaining," "playing the game," and "negotiating."

The prospect of zero-sum conflict is further mitigated, and the likelihood of "gains from trade" enhanced, by virtue of the fact that each CC member is only responsible for a limited set of requesters. The average number of Democrats per zone is on the order of seventeen or eighteen. Of these, ordinarily fewer than half are freshmen seeking initial assignments or non-freshmen seeking transfers. The limited numbers translate into a restricted class of committees sought by the CC member for his people. This subset only partially overlaps those of his CC colleagues. Consequently, direct competition between CC members on behalf of requesters is often averted, and the prospects for internal logrolling is high.

Advocacy, then, is the agreed-upon mode of behavior for CC members because (1) it serves their individual objectives, (2) it is consistent with environmental demands, and (3) it does not entail zero sum conflict. General agreement on the advocacy role is reflected in the remarks of one CC member's

administrative assistant: "Other members of the CC don't resent _____'s
trying to get his people on committees. That's what everyone is trying to do—
that's the name of the game." Said another assistant, "_____ plays it tough
but most members of the CC respect it. Some even admit to admiring it."

To a question of CC members asking whether they regarded themselves
in competition with one another in their efforts to obtain good assignments
for those in their zone, the typical response was "no, but...," followed by
references to logrolling, bargaining, and occasional conflicts:

> No I'm not really in competition with other CC members. We try to
> work things out among ourselves.
> No, but of course there was occasionally a serious fight. Everyone
> wants to get their people on. But anyone would help if he could.
> No, but there is some horsetrading that goes on. I try to help my
> colleagues [on the CC] when I can. Sometimes there is explicit reci-
> procity, but not always. There is often a lot of headknocking in the CC
> meetings. We have arguments and it becomes a real game.

The general tone of the CC member's remarks is one of acceptance of the fact
that he and his colleagues will occasionally be on different sides of the fence,
but that is no reason not to form coalitions with them on matters from
which they may jointly profit:

> I'll talk to other members of the CC and say, "Look, I need some
> help with a good Tennessee boy on Agriculture. There are only two
> vacancies and this guy really needs to get one of them." I try to recipro-
> cate whenever I can.
> I'll say, "I have someone I'm really pushing. If you're not committed
> I'd appreciate the support." I won't twist arms and, of course, the other
> guy is likely to say, "Sure, I'll give you a hand, but I have someone I'm
> pushing, too."[39]

Advocacy, restrained by the internal requirements of building majority
coalitions within the CC, is the primary strategic premise of the CC. It fits the
style and serves the objectives of CC members. A second premise to which
members allude—"produce an acceptable slate of nominees"—appears to be
more an accidental by-product of restrained advocacy than a consciously
agreed-upon norm. Coalitions in the CC shift across regions and ideological
positions,[40] depending upon the particular mix of requesters with which each
member is endowed. A member is likely to accommodate the request of
another member to support the latter's candidate for a committee more
because he (the former) does not have a candidate of his own for that committee this time than for ideological or regional reasons. The former member's
resource—his vote—has value-in-exchange. He may either strike a specific
bargain with the member whose request he accommodates or, as is more

usually the case, bank an I.O.U. that may be drawn on at some later, unspecified time. The net result of this coalition-building process is an outcome randomized over, and consequently representative of, the distribution of regional and ideological interests in the House Democratic party.

Nevertheless, CC members make a virtue out of the inevitable and claim it as the direct consequence of their conscious efforts:

> The members try to bend over backwards to accommodate requests and desires [for committee positions]. Like the Ways and Means Committee more generally, these guys know they're doing an important job for the party and try to be as representative of the whole party and of the national sentiment as possible.[41]

Said an embittered liberal member of the CC, after a coalition of liberals in the Caucus successfully stripped the Ways and Means members of their committee assignment duty in 1975, "We asked them during the Caucus debate, 'Can anyone stand up and say they are displeased with their committee assignments and the way the current CC has handled this task?' Not one did. We've always tried to be fair."[42] Whether as the result of a conscious effort, or simply as a by-product, the fact that an acceptable slate emerged from the CC's deliberations enhanced that Committee's reputation as a responsible and responsive arm of the party (until the Ninety-fourth Congress, at least).[43]

In summary, the members of the CC have reached a procedural consensus on how to go about doing their business. That consensus emphasizes the legitimacy of advocacy, the propriety of rounding up votes, vote-trading, bargaining, and other forms of coalitional activity, and the avoidance of general principles to guide committee assignments.

Though I share with Herbert Spencer the sentiment that "only by varied reiteration can alien conceptions be forced on reluctant minds," a summary of the points in this chapter is probably unnecessary. The themes—member goals, environmental constraints, strategic premises—have been reiterated several times in the text; the underlying conceptions are no longer alien owing to Fenno's (1973) groundbreaking research; and the minds of readers ought to remain reluctant until some empirical documentation is provided in Chapter 9.

Chapter 8

The Committee on Committees, II: The Decision-making Process

Restrained advocacy is the shared strategic premise that accommodates the member's chamber-influence goal with the general expectation of responsiveness by party elements in the House. The decision-making process of the CC reinforces this premise in three distinct ways. First, "credit-claiming" is made possible by a decentralized zone system. The states with Democratic delegations are partitioned into fifteen regional zones and each of the fifteen CC members is responsible for advocating in behalf of "his people." Second, the principal CC resource—votes—is equally distributed among the members. This, together with the zone arrangement, encourages full participation in the committee's business. CC seniority appears to play only a secondary role here, though experience affects the results in some respects (see below). A third characteristic of CC decision-making that both encourages advocacy and, in the end, produces an acceptable slate of committee assignments is secrecy. CC decision-making, in its final stages, takes place in executive session. Behind the closed doors of the Ways and Means Committee Room, the CC deliberates away from the glare of publicity. The sophisticated use of bargaining, vote-trading, and coalition-building that might otherwise be misconstrued in a more public atmosphere is thereby promoted.

In this chapter I conclude my discussion of the CC. The principal aim is to describe CC decision-making. A more detailed treatment of CC decisions is found in the next chapter. The committee's internal structure and ways of doing business, as shall be seen below, serve member influence goals on the one hand, and protect the committee's integrity and autonomy by promoting responsiveness on the other. Members, consequently, have a long-run interest in maintaining the current decision-making arrangements. Indeed, until the unusual events of the Ninety-fourth Congress, CC decision-making methods exhibited a great deal of stability.

CC Decision-Making:
Preexecutive Session

Zones

Directly after the fall election, the CC staff—in effect the staff of the Ways and Means Committee headed by its chief counsel, John Martin—begins consulting with CC members on the composition of zones. The idea is to create fifteen zones each composed of geographically contiguous states containing approximately the same number of Democrats. Each CC member is then responsible for negotiating with people from his zone on their committee

Table 8.1

CC Member	86	87
Mills	Ark. Del.* Kans. Okla. (4)**	Ark. Kans. Okla. (1)
King	Alas. Ariz. Cal. Nev. Utah (6)	Alas. Cal. Haw. Nev. Utah (2)
O'Brien	Ill. Wis. (6)	Ill. Wis. (1)
Boggs	Ala. La. Miss. (1)	Ala. La. Miss. (0)
Keough	N.Y. (2)	N.Y. (4)
Harrison	Va. S.C.* (1)	Va. S.C.* (0)
Karsten	Iowa Mo. Minn. (4)	Iowa Mo. Minn. (1)
Herlong	Fla. Ga. (0)	Fla. Ga. (3)
Ikard	N.M. Tex. (2)	N.M. Tex. (0)
Machrowicz	Ind. Mich. Ohio (10)	Ind. Mich. Ohio (0)
Frazier	N.C. Tenn. (1)	N.C. Tenn. (2)
Green, Jr.	N.J. Pa. (6)	N.J. Pa. (1)
Watts	Ky. Md. W. Va. (7)	Ky. Md. W. Va. (0)

requests and, after they are submitted, seeking to accommodate them. Geographic continuity permits a regional input into CC decisions.[1] Equality in the number of Democrats in each zone, on the face of it, provides for equality of work load. However, while each zone contains about seventeen Democrats on average, the number of members seeking initial assignments or transfers varies rather dramatically from zone to zone.

Table 8.1 displays the zone arrangement for the Democratic CC in the last eight Congresses. The number of freshmen in each zone—the major work-load component for the CC members—is given in parentheses. Notice the disparities in work-load. In the Eighty-sixth Congress, for example, while Herlong (Fla.) had no freshmen and Boggs (La.), Harrison (Va.), and Frazier (Tenn.) only one each, O'Brien (Ill.), King (Cal.), and Green (Pa.) had six each, Watts (Ky.) seven, Burke (Mass.) nine, and Machrowicz (Mich.) ten.

Congress CC Zones, 86th–93rd Congresses					
88	89	90	91	92	93
Ark. Ariz. Col. Okla. Nev. N.M. (1) Cal. (10)	Ark. Ariz. N.M. Okla. (2) Cal. Nev. Utah. (3)	Ark. Ariz. Nev. N.M. Va.* Okla. (0) Cal. (0)	Ark. Mo. Okla. (4)	Ark. Mo. Okla. (0)	Ark. Mo. Okla. (4)
Ala. La. Miss. (1) N.Y. (1)	La. Miss. (1) N.Y. (9)	La. Tex. (3)	La. (1)		
Iowa Mo. Minn. (2) Fla. Ga. (5)	Iowa Mo. Neb. (7) Alas.* Fla. Haw. (1)	Iowa Mo. (0) Fla. N.C.* (1)			
Ky. Md. W. Va. (2)	Del. Ky. Md. W. Va. (3)	Ky. Md. W. Va. (0)	Ky. Md. Va. (1)		

Table 8.1—(*Cont.*)

CC Member	86	87
Ullman	Col. Id. Mont. Neb. N.D. Ore. S.D. Wash. (4)	Col.* Id. Mont. Ore. Wash. (3)
Burke	Conn. Me. Mass. R.I. Vt. (9)	Conn. Del.* Mass. R.I. (1)
Thompson		
Griffiths		
Jennings		
Rhodes		
Rostenkowski		
Bass		
Landrum		
Vanik		
Fulton		
Gilbert		
Waggonner		
Burleson		
Corman		
Green III		
Gibbons		
Carey		
Karth		

Congress CC Zones, 86th–93rd Congresses					
88	89	90	91	92	93
Alas. Haw. Id. Mont. Ore. Wash. (4)	Col. Id. Mont. N.D. Ore. Wash. Wyo. (8)	Col.* Haw. Mont.* Ore. Wash. (0)	Ariz. Col. Mont.* Nev. Ore. Wash. (1)	Ariz. Col. Nev. Ore. Wash. (1)	Ariz.* Haw. Ore. Utah.* Wash. (1)
Conn. Del.* Mass. R.I. (2)	Conn. Me. Mass. N.H. R.I. (3)	Conn. Me. Mass. R.I. (1)	Conn. Me. Mass. R.I. (1)	Conn. Me. Mass. N.J.* R.I. (4)	Conn. Me. Mass. R.I. (2)
Tex. (1) Ind. Mich. Ohio (2)	Tex. (3) Mich. Wis. (9)	Mich. Wis. (0)	Ind. Iowa. Mich. Wis. (1)	Ind. Mich. Wis. (2)	Ind. Mich. (0)
S.C.* Va. (2) N.J. Pa. (2) Ill. Wis. (0) N.C. Tenn. (1)	N.C. Va. (1) N.J. Pa. (6) Ill. Minn.* (4)	N.J. Pa. (1) Ill. Minn.* (0)	Ill. Minn.* (1)	Ill. (2)	Ill. Wis. (0)
	Ga. S.C. (3)	Ga. S.C. (2)	Ga. N.C. S.C. (2)	Ga. N.C. S.C. (1)	Ga. N.C. S.C. (4)
	Ohio Ind. (6)	Ohio. Ind. (0)	Ohio W. Va. (1)	Ohio Md. W. Va. (6)	Ohio Ky. W. Va. (1)
	Ala. Tenn. (2)	Ala. Miss. Tenn. (4) N.Y. (1)	Ala. Miss. Tenn. (2)	Ky. Tenn. Va. (1)	Md. N.J.* Tenn. Va. (0)
			La.*** (1)	La. Miss. (0)	La. Miss (2).
			Tex. (0)	N.M. Tex. Utah. (2)	Tex. (3)
			Cal. (1)	Cal. (2)	Cal. (4)
			N.J. Pa. (2)	Pa. (0)	Pa. (0)
			Fla. Haw.* (1)	Ala. Alas.* Fla. Haw* (1)	Ala. Fla. (2)
			N.Y. (4)	N.Y. (4) Iowa Kans.* Minn. Mont. N.D. S.D. Wyo. (6)	N.Y. (1) Col. Iowa. Kans. Minn. Mont. N.M. S.D. Wyo. (2)

* Noncontiguous state.
** Number of freshmen in parentheses.
*** Took over for Boggs when he was elected majority leader.

In the Eighty-eighth Congress, King (Cal.) had ten freshmen to place on committees, whereas Rostenkowski (Ill.) had none and Mills (Ark.), Boggs (La.), Keough (N.Y.), Thompson (Tex.), and Bass (Tenn.) had one each.

There are two major consequences of freshman work-load disparity. Those with few freshmen to place may devote more of their energies to caring for the transfer and dual-service requests of zone members with more seniority than can those with a greater number of freshmen. Second, those with lighter work-loads can play brokerage roles with their colleagues. Owing to the equal distribution of votes in the CC, members who are obliged to devote only a small fraction of their votes to the needs of their own people have a stockpile of votes to trade with their less well-endowed colleagues in exchange for generalized influence.

Work-load disparity, rather than overrepresentation, may be the source of southern influence on the CC. As table 7.3 indicates, the CC is very representative of regional strength in the House Democratic party. However, the work-load disparity gives the southerners a decided advantage (table 8.2).

Table 8.2   **Mean Work Load, South vs. Non-South, 86th–93rd Congresses**

	Congress							
Region	86	87	88	89	90*	91	92	93
South	1.5	1.0	1.8	1.9	2.0	1.7	0.8	2.5
Non-South	6.0	1.4	2.8	5.8	0.3	1.4	3.0	1.2

NOTE: Cell entries are the mean number of freshmen in southern and nonsouthern zones. Zones treated as southern are those represented by Mills, Boggs, Harrison, Herlong, Ikard, Frazier, Thompson, Jennings, Bass, Landrum, Fulton, Waggonner, Burleson, and Gibbons (see table 8.1).

* Southerners have maintained six or more zones in every Congress but the 90th. Owing to the loss of a Texas seat on Ways and Means, in the 90th Congress there were only five southern zones. The mean work load increased accordingly.

The randomly selected southern CC member has about 1.5 freshmen whose requests need attending to; the nonsoutherner, on the other hand, averages nearly three freshmen per zone. Higher turnover in the nonsouthern zones coupled with "one man, one vote" in CC decision-making, then, tend to give southerners on the CC greater "effective" resources with which to bargain.

On what basis are the zones created? All indications are that it is a pretty mechanical procedure in which the zones of the previous Congress are marginally adjusted to take into account the postelection pattern of Democratic representation. Said John Martin, whose task it is to recommend a zone structure to the CC:

> Zones are set up pretty much right after the elections. The old zone system is the base from which the new ones are created. It is not a very political process. We try to look dispassionately at the situation. We try to create geographically balanced and contiguous zones.

CC members tend to agree:

> John Martin would propose a zone mock-up. He'd usually call you up and try out different plans on you. But he was principally responsible for working out those details.
>
> John Martin established initial zones and this was kicked around by the members of the CC. Occasionally zones weren't established till the beginning of the new Congress, so that a lot of new people ended up coming to see me even though I turned out not to be their zone representative.

According to the books prepared for the CC that contain the zone information, on only one occasion was the staff unable to produce an acceptable zone configuration. In the Ninety-second Congress the staff recommended two alternatives from which the CC members made a choice. On all other occasions Martin was able to "look dispassionately at the situation" and make a noncontroversial decision.

In addition to its effect on work-load, the zone configuration influences the behavior and tactics of the CC member. The biggest problem for a zone representative is a zone contingent all of whose members want the same committees. Knowing full well that he will be unable to succeed in placing all of them on the committees they request, he is forced to intercede at the request stage, urging some to withdraw their requests and/or lower their expectations, and to decide to whom to throw his support in the event some intrazone competition for particular committees remains.

Ideally a CC member seeks not only a manageable work load but also one whose members display some heterogeneity in requests. To the extent that marginal alterations in the zone configuration improve his situation in either of these respects, he will prefer them. Thus, one westerner was delighted when Hawaii was taken out of his zone:

> _____ [a Hawaii freshman] could have gotten on any committee in the House. No one here would have refused [him] anything, he's so outstanding and has gotten so much publicity. So he had Education [his

first preference] sewed up. They put Hawaii in Herlong's zone because he didn't have enough and I lost Hawaii. So it was easier for me to get [another freshman in the zone] on Education.

Ordinarily, however, the zone norms of equality of size and geographical contiguity (violated on occasion—see table 8.1), together with the practices of assigning a CC member's state to his own zone and never dividing a state delegation among more than one zone, leave very little discretion. As the historical continuity of zones revealed in table 8.1 suggests, the primary sources of discretion involve the disposition of Alaska, Hawaii, and some of the Rocky Mountain states that only occasionally have Democratic representation. No amount of discretion would have cured the problems facing Cecil King (Cal.) in the Eighty-eighth Congress. Reapportionment that year produced eight new California seats and ten California freshmen. The homogeneity of their requests undoubtedly exacerbated King's heavy work load (table 8.3).

Table 8.3	California Freshmen Requests, 88th Congress	
Committee	Total number of Requests	Number of First-Preference Requests*
Banking and Currency	5	2
Education and Labor	5	1
Foreign Affairs	5	5
Interior	2	0
Interstate	5	1
Judiciary	2	0
Post Office—Civil Service	4	0

* A tenth member's first-preference request was for a committee no other California freshman sought.

The Campaign for Committee Assignments

The zone structure has not always been finalized by the time congressmen begin filtering into Washington after the fall elections. Given the historical continuity of CC zones, however, most members quickly learn whom to see about committee assignments. For the newcomer the chief objective of the courtesy visit he pays to his zone representative is to obtain a "good" committee assignment (see Chapter 3). While "objectives" such as this are uppermost in the newcomer's mind, "constraints" are the major concern of the CC member: Can I get him on the committee he wants? How many others from the zone want the committee? How many from his state [region] are already on the committee? How many vacancies are there? What about the competition from other zones?

During the campaign for assignments, some CC members play essentially a supportive role, entertaining no primary concern beyond getting their people what they reveal they want. Said the Texas CC member:

> The people in my zone come to see me and we analyze the situation. They tell me about their backgrounds and their electoral needs. We also look to see whether there is room on the committee for another Texan. Lots of people come to me saying they want Appropriations and I have to tell them that freshmen don't get on that committee too often.

Another CC member, while using "friendly persuasion" in an effort to influence the substance of requests from the freshmen in his zone, spent most of his time advising his people how to mount effective campaigns for the assignments they want:

> I'd tell my people to write evey member of the CC giving their personal background and things about their district as reasons for particular appointments. Also contact the committee chairman, Speaker, Majority Leader, and Caucus Chairman if they had time. A personal visit would help too.

Most other CC members appear to play a more activist role in determining the content of requests from their people. An administrative assistant to a southerner on the CC remarked that "members come by for a courtesy visit to _____. He tries to resolve request disputes ahead of time." Aware that the "law of scarcity" applies to committee slots, this CC member brings the information he has on the competitive environment for committee slots to bear on his discussions with his people:

> When a newcomer comes by the office _____ tells them what the state or region needs and tells them to check around to see if it will suit their purposes. He tells them, for instance, to check back home to see if an Agriculture seat would be useful to the folks back home in the district. He is very accommodating to people of all political philosophies. He is most interested in whether a person is *reasonable*, not in his political philosophy.[2]

Explaining the facts of life on the Hill during the course of the campaign appears to be the mechanism through which the CC member influences the newcomer. It is also the mechanism by which the newcomer reduces some of his uncertainty about the competitive environment (see Chapter 3) and adjusts his expectations (see Chapter 4). Most important, it is the method by which the CC member protects and enhances his reputation as an influential and accommodating person. By encouraging members to request committees for which he believes the competitive environment is propitious, by reducing intrazone competition ahead of time, and by affecting the newcomer's expectations, he magnifies his reputation by increasing the likelihood that he can deliver the goods for which he has "contracted." The campaign that precedes the CC executive session, then, is a sort of shakedown period during which objectives are clarified for the requester and the constraints on his zone representative due to the competitive environment are made explicit.

Information at the
Penultimate Stage:
CC Request Books

In late December John Martin writes each member of the CC informing him that the committee chairman has contacted the freshmen, instructed them on who their zone representative is, and urged them to submit their preferences for committee assignments at the earliest opportunity. Martin also notes that his staff is in the process of preparing the CC request books; he asks each zone representative to gather up the committee requests from the people in his zone expeditiously and return them to him for inclusion in the books. As soon as preparation is completed, a copy is forwarded to each CC member.

The CC request book contains detailed information on all of the relevant parameters, both supply and demand, of the committee assignment process.[3] Given the complex, "giant jigsaw puzzle" nature of the process, the information in the request book allows for an easy determination by CC members of what committee slots are available, who wants which, and what the consequences are of satisfying one member's request at the expense of others.

Perhaps the most important documents in the book are the request lists themselves. Two lists are given, one for freshmen and one for nonfreshmen. Each lists members in alphabetical order. Beside each name are the committee assignments requested, in order of preference. For nonfreshmen, current committee assignments are given as well. These two documents comprise a complete description of the demand side of the committee assignment process.

The request data is provided in a second format as well—on a committee-by-committee basis—that is probably more useful for actual decision-making. For each committee a separate sheet is prepared giving:

1. current members of the committee;
2. those members not returning to the new Congress;
3. the number of committee vacancies prior to any CC decisions (as negotiated by the party leaders);
4. the name, district, and state of those committee members seeking to

transfer off the committee, as well as the committee to which they have requested a transfer;

5. the name, district, and state of each requester, along with current committees (if a nonfreshman), preference rank of the request for the given committee, and the preference rank of other requests;

6. a list of endorsements of requesters by senators, outside interest groups, delegation deans, committee chairmen, and other members of Congress.

An example of this data format is displayed in figure 8.1 for the Education and Labor Committee of the Eighty-sixth Congress.[4]

The format of the request books, together with the committee-by-committee procedure employed by the CC (described below), induces a particular sort of "mind set" in CC members and reinforces their advocacy predisposition. First, in its explicit juxtaposition of supply and demand aspects on a committee-by-committee basis, the request book format encourages the members to view their task as an (almost economic) allocation process. Second, by listing members according to their preferences, as in figure 8.1, the request book information puts a premium on requests and on matching them with slots as availability permits. Thus advocacy is again stimulated and the likelihood of results acceptable to requesters (and, indirectly, "interested others") is increased. Third, by providing information about other requests (again, see figure 8.1) a "giant jigsaw puzzle" mentality is produced. The transaction costs of attempting to maximize the number of matches between requests and assignments are substantially reduced.[5]

Fenno (1973, p. 81) has observed that committee members "search for a [decision-making] structure that will help them implement their decision rules—especially as those rules reflect a strategy for achieving their personal goals." Among the members of the Democratic Committee on Committees, a prevailing consensus on individual objectives (chamber influence) and strategic premises (restrained advocacy) is further complemented by an information system (the CC request book) and a predecision institutional arrangement (the zone system) which reinforce the advocacy premise, reduce the decision-making costs of achieving personal goals, and permit "credit-claiming" by the members. In the next section we move behind the closed doors of the CC executive sessions in order to examine CC decision-making in its final stages. There, too, we shall find a decision-making arrangement conducive to member objectives.

CC Decision-making:
Executive Session

During the early weeks of the new Congress the CC meets in executive session to determine Democratic committee assignments.[6] Meeting in the

DEMOCRATIC COMMITTEE ASSIGNMENT REQUESTS BY COMMITTEES
86TH CONGRESS

COMMITTEE ON EDUCATION AND LABOR

Democratic: Vacancies 1
Surpluses

85th Congress Members of this Committee requesting another Committee: Committee requested:

George S. McGovern (1st, S. Dak.)............................ Agriculture.

Edith Green (3d, Oreg.)... Government Operations (as dual service).

REQUESTS FOR ASSIGNMENT TO THIS COMMITTEE

Name	State and District	Seniority	Assignment and Rank 85th Congress	Order of Preference This Comte.	Other Committees
	3d, Ind.	1/3/59		1	2—Interst.
	3d, Kans.	1/3/59		3	1—Pub. Wks. 2—For. Aff. 4—Ar. Serv. 5—Vet. Aff.
	7th, Mich.	1/3/59		1	2—Judic. 3—Pub. Wks. 4—Ar. Serv.
	6th, Md.	1/3/59		2	1—PO. & CS. 3—D. of Col.
	14th, N.J.	1/3/59		4	1—Interst. 2—For. Aff. 3—Judic.
	4th, Minn.	1/3/59		1	2—Pub. Wks. 3—B.&C. or F. Aff.
	2d, Kans.	1/3/59		2	(or Pub. Wks.) 1—Judic.
	3d, Conn.	1/3/59		3	1—B. & C. 2—Interst.
	5th, N.C.	1/3/57	P.O. & C.S. (10)	1	

COMMITTEE ON EDUCATION AND LABOR

LRA: 25   86th Congress: Total 30   Ratio (D/R) 20/10

(85th Congress: 17/13 = 30; Members returning: *16/10)

Democrats

1. Graham A. Barden, Chairman.........North Carolina
2. Adam C. Powell......................New York
3. Cleveland M. Bailey................West Virginia
4. Carl D. Perkins....................Kentucky
5. Roy W. Wier........................Minnesota
6. Carl Elliott.......................Alabama
7. Phil M. Landrum....................Georgia
8. Edith Green........................Oregon
9. James Roosevelt....................California
10. Herbert Zelenko....................New York
11. Frank Thompson, Jr.................New Jersey
12. Stewart L. Udall...................Arizona
13. Elmer J. Holland...................Pennsylvania
14. Ludwig Teller......................New York
15. George S. McGovern.................South Dakota
16. John H. Dent.......................Pennsylvania

*Excluding Lee Metcalf (Montana), who was elected to the
Committee on Ways and Means Jan. 7, 1959 (H. Res. 9).

Democratic Committee Members, 85th Congress, not returning:

None

Fig. 8.1   Education and Labor requests, 86th Congress.

Ways and Means Committee Room in the Capitol Building, only CC members and one or two clerks are present. Committees (with the exception of Ways and Means, whose members are selected by the entire Caucus) are taken up in quasi-alphabetical order.[7] The formal rule is alphabetical order but, since exceptions are made with some regularity, it can hardly be regarded as binding. The usual practice is to take up Appropriations and Rules first, along with the one or two semiexclusive committees, e.g., Interstate, for which there is considerable competition. After disposing of these, the remaining semiexclusive committees are taken in alphabetical order, followed by the nonexclusive committees in alphabetical order. Particular deviations from strict alphabetical order are wholeheartedly supported by CC members since it tends to reduce their uncertainty on a number of tactical dimensions. In the words of one member, "Logistics were sometimes tricky. That's why we'd often take care of the tough nuts first." Almost all CC members agreed with the description given by one of their colleagues:

> We usually take the committees where we expect senior people to want to transfer first—Appropriations, Rules, sometimes Interstate. That'll open up a lot of new slots. Then we take the major committees alphabetically. Then the minor committees. Toward the end you have a handful of people who didn't get what they wanted and a handful of slots.

When a committee is considered, nominations are the first order of business. CC members nominate in the order of their committee seniority. Thus the chairman has the first opportunity, and he may nominate one or more of his zone members or pass. After the most junior member of the CC has had his chance, the nominations are closed. A committee clerk writes the names of all those nominated on a blackboard in preparation for the balloting.[8]

Nomination practices vary among CC members. All asserted that they would never nominate a nonrequester unless they had his prior approval.[9] There was a division of opinion, however, on whether to risk splitting support by nominating more than one person from a zone for the same committee. For some the answer is decidedly negative:

> I *always* reconcile conflicts in the zone ahead of time.

> No I wouldn't nominate more than one person. But this is usually not a problem for me. The Texas delegation is a special sort of place. We resolve things most of the time.

> I would always nominate my people. If there were ever a conflict within the zone we would straighten it out early so that I didn't have to nominate two people for the same committee. I told them, "Look, if I have to nominate both of you, you'll both lose—split the votes. So get together and only one of you request the committee."

Others are willing to make multiple nominations, but they usually will reveal their priorities. Two administrative assistants remarked:

———— will nominate more than one person for a committee, but he'll tell the CC his preference if he has one.

———— always nominates people who requested, but some less enthusiastically than others.[10]

On some occasions multiple nominations are in order either because the zone has lost substantial representation on a committee or, on some other grounds, "deserves" several seats. Thus, in the Ninety-second Congress, Hugh Carey (N.Y.) placed three New Yorkers on Education and Labor. But such an event is rare.

Only one member touched on the very subtle tactical problems surrounding nominations that must concern most CC members. One source of discretion for the CC member derives from the fact that most requesters submit multiple requests. Although he ordinarily will seek to accommodate the requester's first-preference request, the CC member is occasionally faced with a dilemma caused by the prospect of the requester's second- (or lower-) preference committee appearing earlier on the agenda than his first-preference committee. Should the zone representative hold off nominating the requester for his second-preference committee and wait until his first-preference committee comes up for consideration, or should he be more conservative and nominate the requester for his second choice? On whatever basis this dilemma is resolved, "educated guesses" will weigh heavily:

> Getting back to logistics, you had to play it by ear as to whether to go for a guy's first preference. If his second-preference committee came up first you'd try to get a feel for the likely competition for the first-preference committee. In fact, during the CC meetings I would ask, "Though we're considering committee X, who's going to have candidates for committee Y?" That way I could sense whether to push my man for his second preference or hold off till his first preference came up.

Nominations are concluded with speeches in support of nominees and general discussion. The personal qualities of the nominees, their electoral needs, and geographic considerations constitute the bulk of the remarks. One member observed that in addition to talking about the personal background of his nominees, "I'd often bring in maps with little dots to indicate geographic representation for the particular committee to show how my zone was underrepresented. But only if I were behind. If you have the votes, you have the votes!"

Politicking prior to the balloting is not transparent; but it is not subtle either. Final arrangements are made at this penultimate stage, deals firmed up, last-minute appeals made. "Often you'd be voting on people you didn't even know. You read the book on them and listen to supporting speeches—but that's about all you know." At this final moment "the CC does a lot of trading, the members trade back and forth."

Voting is of the "first past the post" variety. The number of vacancies determines the number of votes by each CC member. With fifteen voting members, a nominee must secure eight votes for election.[11] One member described the voting as follows:

> Everybody gets as many votes as there are slots. The vote is secret and the ballots are collected, read off by one clerk, with another clerk putting marks next to the nominees' names on the blackboard. Sometimes, if I really want a person to get it, I'll vote for him and other *weak* candidates. Since you can't bullet vote, this is as close as you can come.

After the first round of voting, if the number of nominees receiving a majority exhausts the vacancies, then the next committee on the agenda is called up. If, however, fewer candidates are elected than there are slots, with the remaining votes spread among other candidates, a second round of voting is held. Each CC member casts as many votes as there are remaining slots. Prior to the second round, it is not unusual for a CC member whose nominee has fared poorly to withdraw his name from the competition.

By the time minor committees are reached, for which few preferences are expressed, a handful of members are still without assignments. "You get on the phone and ask them which of the minor ones they want. They usually want to know why they didn't get what they asked for. You say, 'It's simple. You didn't get the votes. Don't ask me why. Maybe they didn't like the way you parted your hair. Just don't blame me. I made a great speech in your behalf.'"

At various points in the agenda there is frequently a necessity to return to committees previously considered. This is occasioned by transfers to committees under current consideration from committees already considered. When such transfers occur, new slots are created on the previously considered committees. An attempt to minimize such discontinuities in procedure was alluded to above. Committees expected to attract a lot of transfer activity—the so-called "tough nuts"—are moved to the head of the agenda. Nevertheless, there is apparently a fair amount of jumping back and forth.

A second reason for the reconsideration of a committee is revealed in the following scenario suggested by a member:

> Sometimes there'll be a situation where we have six guys for Appropriations and only five slots. But these six people are all real solid. So Wilbur will get on the phone to the Speaker to see if maybe we can't expand the committee size. The Speaker will talk to [Appropriations Committee Chairman George] Mahon and the Republicans and get back to us.

By the time the Speaker has responded, other committees will have been considered. Both of these features underscore some of the difficulties in long-range planning for CC members. The agenda and the discontinuous serial consideration of committees promote hedging, contingency planning, and fluidity in CC deliberations.

Voting coalitions in the CC balloting are impossible to detect with confidence, given the secret ballot and the unavailability of voting tallies. Besides those that individuals build through their own entrepreneurial activity in behalf of their requesters, however, large coalitions that hold together over several votes and several committees appear quite unlikely. First, there is the simple problem of policing the coalition. The secret ballot constitutes a serious obstacle to this effort.[12] Second, there is the very real possibility of intracoalition conflicts of interest. Each coalition partner is principally an advocate for "his people." As the coalition grows in size and scope, the likelihood of intracoalition competition grows. Many members will prefer to strike their own deals. Third, the number of decisions made by the CC—perhaps as many as twenty-five or thirty votes—increases the costs of coalition maintenance. For all these reasons, the appearance of formal coalitions of any size (say, four or five people) over any duration (say, votes on three or four committees) is highly improbable. Coalitions are most likely among those with a mutuality of interests and with requesters whose preferences overlap in only a restricted number of cases. Both policing costs and conflicts of interest decline under these conditions. Especially advantaged in this regard are those with limited work load. Southerners, that is, are in the best position to take advantage of more than bilateral coalition formation (see table 8.2). Unfortunately, little evidence is available on this point.[13]

These same problems—policing, conflicts of interest, and complex decision-making—inhibit bilateral coalitions as well (the so-called "horse trading" and "vote swapping" that characterize CC decision-making), though to a greatly reduced extent. Conflicts of interest reduce the number of potential trading partners for a member; but when a trade materializes there is prima facie evidence that gains have been made for both parties. The complexity and large number of decisions discourage long-standing agreements; yet limited-duration coalitions are still very practical. The problem of policing "horse trades" remains by virtue of the secret ballot, but even here the limited number of partners and the limited duration of agreements reduce the costs of deception.[14]

At the conclusion of the CC's deliberations the results of the balloting are forwarded to the chairman of the Caucus. CC decisions must receive final approval from the full Caucus. Ordinarily this approval is granted pro forma —an indication of the acceptability of the committee slates produced by the CC—though there have been rare challenges.

The voting rules and agenda organization of the CC executive session do not eliminate the members' "conjectural variation" problems. Given the kinds of choices the CC must make, however, it is difficult to conceive of any decision-making arrangement that would. The rules, nevertheless, do place a premium on full and equal participation (a vote is a vote is a vote) and on private entrepreneurship ("horse trading"). The tactics of advocacy, therefore, are encouraged, though they are not likely to be altogether free of frustration.

An analysis of the decisions that emerge from this process—the actual committee assignments—is postponed until Chapter 9. Since I have focused here on CC advocacy, however, it is useful to examine just how successful CC members are as advocates and, overall, how responsive the committee is to member requests. The relevant data is displayed in table 8.4. The table gives the proportion of a zone representative's freshmen who have obtained a first-preference request, as well as the proportion who have obtained *some* requested committee. Starred entries are those at least as large as the column median (given in the bottom line). Overall nearly 59% of the freshmen received a first-preference committee assignment ($N = 231$), and more than 80% received at least one of the committees they requested.[15]

Some insight about the effect of seniority in the CC is also gleaned from the display in table 8.4. In any one column, note the distribution of starred entries. In the Ninety-second and Ninety-third Congresses, senior CC members appeared to be somewhat more successful in obtaining first-preference committees for their freshmen; otherwise, committee seniority does not appear to play a pervasive role. Chairman Mills, however, was uniformly successful in his efforts in behalf of his zone freshmen.[16] Indeed, his colleagues often described him as "very much *first* among equals."

I have dwelled at length in this chapter and the last on what CC members want, how their objectives are hedged and molded by external actors, what agreements they come to share in balancing objectives and constraints, and how they implement this consensus in their decision-making. *Advocacy* is the thread that unites all these strands of the committee assignment process. It is the basis upon which generalized chamber influence for CC members is built; it is the method by which the preferences of "interested others" are accommodated; it is the procedural norm observance of which CC members come to expect of one another; and it is the beneficiary of decision arrangements that provide effective resources (work load, votes), inexpensive information (request books), and the prospect of credit-claiming (zone system). The consequences of these arrangements for actual assignments is the subject of the next chapter.

Table 8.4

CC Member	% of First-Satisfied	
	86	87
Mills	67*	100*
King	25	0
O'Brien	0	100*
Boggs	—	—
Keough	100*	75*
Harrison	—	—
Karsten	0	0
Herlong	—	33*
Ikard	100*	—
Machrowicz	80*	—
Frazier	0	0
Green, Jr.	20	0
Watts	40*	—
Ullman	50*	67*
Burke	40*	100*
Thompson	x	x
Griffiths	x	x
Jennings	x	x
Rhodes	x	x
Rostenkowski	x	x
Bass	x	x
Landrum	x	x
Vanik	x	x
Fulton	x	x
Gilbert	x	x
Waggonner	x	x
Burleson	x	x
Corman	x	x
Green, III	x	x
Gibbons	x	x
Carey	x	x
Karth	x	x
Median	40	33

Performance of Zone Representatives, 86th–93rd Congresses

Preference Freshman Requests (Congress)					% of All Freshman Requests Satisfied (Congress)						
88	89	90	92	93	86	87	88	89	90	92	93
0	100*	—	—	75*	67*	100*	100*	100*	—	—	75
50*	33	—	x	x	75*	100*	70	67	—	x	x
x	x	x	x	x	50	100*	x	x	x	x	x
100*	100*	0*	x	x	—	—	100*	100*	33	x	x
0	67*	x	x	x	100*	75	100*	78	x	x	x
x	x	x	x	x	—	—	x	x	x	x	x
100*	86*	—	x	x	33	100*	100*	100*	—	x	x
40	100*	0*	x	x	—	67	100*	100*	0	x	x
x	x	x	x	x	100*	—	x	x	x	x	x
x	x	x	x	x	80*	—	x	x	x	x	x
x	x	x	x	x	0	50	x	x	x	x	x
x	x	x	x	x	40	100*	x	x	x	x	x
100*	67*	—	x	x	40	—	100*	100*	—	x	x
25	100*	—	100*	100*	100*	100*	100*	100*	—	100*	100*
50*	0	0*	75	100*	80*	100*	100*	100*	0	100*	100*
0	0	x	x	x	x	x	0	67	x	x	x
100*	33	—	100*	—	x	x	100*	67	—	100*	—
0	100*	x	x	x	x	x	0	100*	x	x	x
50*	33	100*	x	x	x	x	50	67	100*	x	x
—	75*	—	—	—	x	x	—	100*	—	—	—
100*	x	x	x	x	x	x	100*	x	x	x	x
x	33	0*	100*	75*	x	x	x	33	50*	100*	75
x	83*	—	100*	100*	x	x	x	100*	—	100*	100*
x	0	50*	100*	—	x	x	x	100*	50*	100*	—
x	x	100*	x	x	x	x	x	x	100*	x	x
x	x	x	—	100*	x	x	x	x	x	—	100*
x	x	x	50	67	x	x	x	x	x	100*	100*
x	x	x	—	25	x	x	x	x	x	—	50
x	x	x	—	—	x	x	x	x	x	—	—
x	x	x	100*	100*	x	x	x	x	x	100*	100*
x	x	x	25	0	x	x	x	x	x	25	50
x	x	x	83	50	x	x	x	x	x	100*	50
50	67	0	100	75	67	100	100	100	50	100	100

* greater than or equal to column median.
— no freshmen in zone.
x not on CC during column Congress.

Appendix

**Committee
Assignments as an
Optimization
Process**

In this brief appendix CC decision-making is characterized as a maximization process in a context of institutional constraints. A more complete presentation is found in Shepsle (1973, 1975a, 1975b).

Constraints on CC Decisions

As noted in Chapter 7, the party Caucus and the party leaders impose formal constraints on CC decisions: the Caucus imposes rules with which the recommended committee slates must comply; the party leaders define scarcity constraints in their negotiation of a committee structure. To characterize these constraints formally some notational conventions need to be established.

Let $M = [1, 2, \ldots, m]$ be the set of m applicants for committee assignments.[1] Let $C = [c_1, c_2, \ldots, c_n]$ be the set of n committees partitioned into the following subsets:

$E = [c_1, c_2, \ldots, c_e]$ is the subset of *exclusive* committees;
$S = [c_{e+1}, c_{e+2}, \ldots, c_s]$ is the subset of *semiexclusive* committees;
$N = [c_{s+1}, c_{s+2}, \ldots, c_n]$ is the subset of *nonexclusive* committees.

Finally, let $v = (v_1, v_2, \ldots, v_n)$ be the *committee vacancy vector*. The component, v_i, is the number of vacancies on the ith committee available to be allocated among the freshmen. It depends on the number of previous members of committee i who return to the committee, net transfer behavior to committee i, and the committee size negotiated by the party leaders.

Define an m × n *assignment matrix*, A, with generic element a_{ij}:

$$A = \begin{bmatrix} a_{11} & a_{12} & \cdots & a_{1n} \\ a_{21} & a_{22} & \cdots & a_{2n} \\ & & \vdots & \\ a_{m1} & a_{m2} & \cdots & a_{mn} \end{bmatrix}$$

The element a_{ij} gives the disposition of the ith freshman vis-à-vis the jth committee. If $a_{ij} = 1$ then i is assigned to j; if $a_{ij} = 0$, he is not (values of a_{ij} other than zero or unity are, as yet, uninterpreted). The assignment matrix A is a formal characterization of a CC *decision*. Its m rows are associated with the m applicants and its n columns with the n committees. Each cell indicates whether or not the row applicant is assigned to the column committee.

If zero and unity are the only permissible values for a_{ij}, then, *in the absence of any constraints*, there are 2^{mn} *possible* A-matrices.[2] The CC, however, is not unrestricted in the assignments it can make, so that the *feasible set* from which it must choose has considerably fewer than 2^{mn} elements.

The first set of constraints derives from the *scarcity* created by committee sizes:

[I] The number of assignments to the jth committee may not exceed v_j.

$$\sum_{i=1}^{m} a_{ij} \leq v_j \qquad j = 1, \ldots, n$$

If each of these n constraints (one for each committee) is satisfied as an equality, then all vacancies are filled. Empirically, as table 8.5 reveals, the class [I] constraints are *not* always satisfied as equalities.[3]

Table 8.5 Unfilled Vacancies, 86th–93rd Congresses

Congress	Democratic	Republican
86	None	Education and Labor—1 Veterans Affairs—1
87	Post Office—3 Veterans Affairs—1	D.C.—1 Post Office—1 Public Works—1
88	None	Veterans Affairs—1
89	None	None
90	D.C.—1 Education and Labor—1 Interstate—2	None
91	Public Works—1 Veterans Affairs—1	Merchant Marines—1 Un-American Act.—1
92	Science & Astro.—1	Merchant Marines—1
93	Education and Labor—1 Foreign Affairs—1 Government Oper.—1 Public Works—1	Interior—1 Merchant Marines—1

A second and third set of constraints specify upper and lower bounds on member committee service.

[II] Every congressman must serve on at least one committee.

$$\sum_{j=1}^{n} a_{ij} \geq 1 \qquad i = 1, \ldots, m$$

[III] No congressman is permitted to serve on more than two committees.[4]

$$\sum_{j=1}^{n} a_{ij} \leq 2 \qquad i = 1, \ldots, m$$

Finally there are three sets of service restrictions governing multiple assignments.

[IV] A congressman may serve on at most one exclusive committee; if he does he may serve on no other committee. A congressman serving on a semiexclusive committee may serve on at most one nonexclusive committee.

$$3 \sum_{j=1}^{e} a_{ij} + 2 \sum_{j=e+1}^{s} a_{ij} + \sum_{j=s+1}^{n} a_{ij} \leq 3 \qquad i = 1, \ldots, m$$

[V] A congressman may serve on no more than one semiexclusive committee.[5]

$$\sum_{j=e+1}^{s} a_{ij} \leq 1 \qquad i = 1, \ldots, m$$

[VI] Though multiple assignments to nonexclusive committees are permitted, a congressman may not receive a multiple assignment to the *same* nonexclusive committee.[6]

$$a_{ij} \leq 1 \qquad i = 1, \ldots, m \qquad j = s + 1, \ldots, n.$$

The linear inequalities of [I]–[VI] define the set of feasible assignment configurations as specified by the formal rules of the game. Although the feasible set is not as large as 2^{mn} (the size of the unconstrained feasible set), it is nevertheless very large.[7] For technical reasons, one additional class of constraints is included.

[VII] nonnegativity

$$a_{ij} \geq 0 \qquad i = 1, \ldots, m$$
$$j = 1, \ldots, n$$

Table 8.6 provides a guide to the substance of the constraints.

Table 8.6   Feasible and Infeasible Individual Assignment Patterns

All Allowable Assignments of a Representative to Committees*

	Exclusive	Semiexclusive	Nonexclusive
(1)	1	0	0
(2)	0	1	0
(3)	0	0	1
(4)	0	1	1
(5)	0	0	2

Some Nonallowable Assignments of a Representative to Committees

	Exclusive	Semiexclusive	Nonexclusive
(6)	2	0	0
(7)	1	1	0
(8)	1	0	1
(9)	0	0	0
(10)	0	2	0
(11)	0	0	3
(12)	0	1	2

* Constraint [VI] restricts pattern (5) in the obvious way.

The constraints need not be compatible. That is, for some combination of parameters it may not be possible to satisfy all of the constraints simultaneously (in which case the feasible set is empty). A simple condition insures against a nonempty feasible set:

THEOREM   *The condition both necessary and sufficient for a nonempty feasible set is*

$$\sum_{j=1}^{n} v_j \geq m.$$

A proof is found in Shepsle (1975b). So long as there are at least as many slots as there are members to be assigned, the constraints are mutually consistent.

CC Objectives

In this and the previous chapter it has been argued that each CC member is in the quid pro quo business. Each member, that is, seeks to match his people's requests with available vacancies. The complex coalition maneuvers that take place on each of several dozen votes, however, are difficult to model explicitly. Instead, we shall assume a zero transaction cost world in which CC members effortlessly make the internal accommodations necessary to *maximize the total number of "satisfied customers."* Because of the secret ballot, CC member uncertainty about which of his freshmen's requests to seek to accommodate, exogeneous events such as the Speaker's decision to expand a committee in the middle of the CC's deliberations—in brief, because of nontrivial transactions costs and uncertainty—the summary objective function defined below is an optimistic ideal toward which the CC aspires. Rarely is the optimum it defines actually achieved.

Define a *preference matrix* $P = [p_{ij}]$, of the same order as the assignment matrix A, where

$p_{ij} = 1$ if i lists j in his request list
0 otherwise[8]

The CC's objective is to choose an A-matrix that maximized the "correlation" between expressed preferences and actual assignments:

$$\max_{A} \sum_{i=1}^{m} \sum_{j=1}^{n} p_{ij} \, a_{ij} \quad \text{s.t. [I] through [VII]}$$

The task, then, of the CC is to select a matrix consisting of mn variables so as to maximize an objective function linear in those variables, subject to $2mn - ms + 4m + n$ constraints linear in those variables. The committee assignment process is a rather special (and technically tricky) linear programming problem.

Shepsle (1973, 1975a, 1975b) traces some of the theoretical characteristics of this linear programming problem and, along with Cohen (1974), presents some empirical evidence suggesting that actual CC decisions range between 60% and 80% of the optimality standard produced by the model. The evidence, that is, while lending support to the model, suggests that a more satisfactory model must incorporate the transaction costs and uncertainties alluded to above.

Interestingly, the model's poorest performance occurs in those Congresses associated with large Democratic contractions. In those years, e.g., 1966, the Democrats lose, both gross and net, a large number of seats. The gross losses are slightly larger than the net losses because of a small number of new seats the party wins. Thus, in large contraction years there are ordinarily very few freshmen seeking committee assignments. For that reason it was surprising that the model fared poorest in contraction years. A remark by John Martin, however, hints at an explanation:

The task before the CC is an easy one when there is a major expansion of the party's fortunes—like in the recent elections [1974]. Then you can get everybody pretty much what they want since committee sizes are increased. It's when there is contraction that the cheese gets binding and the members of the CC have to earn their pay!

In contraction years, it's every CC member for himself! The CC objective function specified above is especially unsuitable for it asserts that CC members cooperate in their concern with the *total* number of matched applicants.

The details, both theoretical and empirical, are found elsewhere, and I shall not dwell on them here. The principal purpose of this appendix has been to demonstrate the close resemblance of the problem facing the CC to more general constrained maximization problems. Further attention to institutional details in specifying the objective function should pay dividends in terms of predictions (postdictions) closer to observed results.

Chapter 9

Committee Assignments

In this, the final empirical chapter, committee assignments are examined. Several different points of view are pursued in the empirical analysis. In my first pass I shall seek to determine who is successful in obtaining requested committees and why. To avoid contamination owing to seniority, freshman initial requests and nonfreshman transfer/dual service requests are treated separately. Each of these separate analyses focuses on the basic question of whether a simple supply-and-demand argument suffices to explain the pattern of successes and failures in obtaining first-preference requests or, on the other hand, whether features peculiar to the individual, over and above the supply of seats available on his first-preference committee and the competition for that limited supply, prove important. An important conclusion of the analyses is the central role played by the "economics" of committee assignments. The not-so-simple logistics of matching requests to vacancies (see appendix to Chapter 8), underscored by the advocacy norm in the CC, explain much of the variance in success rates among different groups of congressmen. As Gertzog (1976) has recently described it, the committee assignment process has become "routinized."

My second task is an examination of committee assignments from the point of view of the committee. With a subset of committees an attempt is made to assess and explain the kinds of congressmen who populate them, the extent to which their members come from those who request the committee as opposed to those who are coopted, the extent to which nonfreshman transfer requests are given the nod over freshman initial requests, and so on.[1]

**Factors Related to
Freshman Assignment
Success**

The sophisticated self-interest calculus according to which freshmen reveal preferences for committee assignments, the apparent (partial) responsiveness of the party leadership to those requests as manifested in the committee structure it negotiates, and the advocate's role into which zone representatives on the CC cast themselves require only a modicum of coordination and rationality to produce the a priori expectation that actual assignments are closely matched to requests. The evidence from the Eighty-seventh through Ninety-third Congresses strongly supports this expectation. Table 9.1 displays

Table 9.1 **Freshman Assignment Success**

		Proportion Receiving		
Congress	First Preference	Other Preference	No Preference	N
87	.474	.368	.158	19
88	.500	.306	.194	36
89	.591	.254	.155	71
90	.308	.308	.384	13
92	.750	.144	.106	28
93	.691	.116	.193	26
Total	.585	.243	.172	193

the proportion of freshmen, by Congress, who received their first preference, some other request, or no request. Overall, the results are impressive—more than eight out of every ten freshmen during the period received some requested committee with nearly 60% receiving a first-preference assignment. Coupled with the fact that scarcity prohibits the perfect adjustment of assignments to requests, these data portray a CC that, at least in recent years, has been responsive to freshman requests.

In the absence of perfect responsiveness of assignments to requests, it becomes of interest to determine who succeeds in obtaining first-preference committee assignments and, more important, why. In the analysis to follow two broad classes of variables are employed to discriminate between those who successfully obtain a first-preference request and those who do not. The first class of variables involves characteristics of the requester. The second class focuses on characteristics of the request.

*Characteristics of
the Requester*

Personal characteristics of requesters may affect the deliberations and final choices of the CC in either of two ways. First, some personal characteristics serve as "tie breakers" in the sense that they provide reasonable criteria for choosing among contesting freshmen. Thus, for example, all other things being equal, the CC may wish to tilt in the direction of a marginally elected congressman, giving him the nod in a contest with one of his safer colleagues (the Masters/Clapp hypothesis). Second, certain personal characteristics may predispose a member's zone representative, and others as well, to work harder in his behalf and, in general, to be more inclined toward his cause. Freshmen with previous terms of service ("superfreshmen"), for example, often seek to reclaim the committee assignment they possessed during their previous term(s) of service; party leaders, members of the state delegation, and the committee chairman may choose to lend their support in this effort. In a similar fashion members of a zone representative's own state delegation may benefit from their shared group membership with him.

Let me preface the discussion of several selected personal characteristics of requesters with two observations, one methodological and one theoretical. First, a methodological warning is required in discussing the explanatory variables *one at a time*. It is dangerous, in the absence of compelling theoretical expectations, to put too much stock in simple bivariate relationships. The process by which some freshmen succeed in obtaining a first-preference committee request and others fail involves, as the bulk of this study suggests, a system of structured relationships. Motivational forces and institutional factors interact to produce final committee lists. Consequently, a focus on some single explanatory variable may be misleading since the ceteris paribus condition will rarely hold. The reader, then, is advised to resist drawing substantive conclusions until a proper multivariate model is specified and estimated.

At the theoretical level it should be observed that, at present, compelling grounds for isolating some personal characteristics while ignoring others are not available. Although a theoretical "story" accompanies the analysis of each of the variables below, and a more extensive behavioral theory motivates the multivariate analysis to follow, a general theory of interpersonal influence still eludes us. Students of Congress, journalists, and congressmen themselves continue to emphasize personality and other idiosyncratic personal features in their discussions of the House and its politics. Without denying the importance of these features, one can nevertheless correctly conclude that these discussions hardly constitute a well-grounded scientific theory. With these caveats in mind, let us turn to the relationship between personal characteristics of requesters and first-preference assignment success, looking first at the electoral security of requesters.

1. Electoral Security—The Masters/Clapp Hypothesis. Most members of the CC are, as Chapter 7 demonstrates, partisan loyalists. One component of that loyalty is a commitment to the maintenance of the party's strength in the House. By tending to the needs of marginal congressmen, the argument runs, a public interest—one highly valued by CC members—is served. Service to a public interest, however, may not be a very compelling incentive. Experience elsewhere suggests that public goods are undersupplied precisely because their production is not tied to the private motives of potential producers.[2] Thus, to the extent that the argument relating assignment success to electoral insecurity requires CC members to serve a public interest—maintenance of party strength in the House—the rationale for the expectation is rather weak.

The argument can be salvaged by two lines of reasoning. First, though public goods tend to be undersupplied because of incentive compatibility problems, the extent of undersupply is a function of group size. Small groups, for ill-understood sociological reasons, are able to overcome the suboptimality to some extent. Second, and more important, if serving a public interest (producing a public good) is compatible with serving a private interest, then the public interest is more likely to be served by individuals, chiefly as a by-product of their own private goal-seeking behavior (Olson 1965, chap. 6).

There is reason to believe that both lines of argument have some basis in fact in the case of the Democratic CC. The Democratic CC, first of all, is a small group. Over the last half-century (until 1975) its size has ranged from ten to eighteen members. Moreover, there has been considerable continuity of membership from year to year. During each of the last twenty years, for example, the membership has held between fifteen and eighteen and there has never been more than four new members. Each of these factors serves to mitigate public good suboptimality. Indeed, the CC's second strategic premise—to produce an acceptable slate of nominees for committee assignments—suggests that some conscious effort, coordinated by a committee chairman acutely sensitive to his committee's image and reputation, has been made to serve general party interests apart from the private interests of CC members.

Even in small groups, however, the incentive compatibility problem is present—whenever a member's private interest conflicts with the public interest, his "public regardingness" evaporates. Thus, a CC member is not likely to tilt toward a marginal freshman if voting for that freshman comes at the expense of someone from his own zone. In the extreme instance of direct conflict between the public interest of supporting the requests of marginal congressmen and the private interest of advocating in behalf of freshmen from the CC member's own zone, the private interest is likely to prevail. In less extreme situations, however, as when a CC member must choose between the competing requests of a member from a safe district and one from a marginal district, neither of whom are from his zone, less of a private stake is involved for him. He may, therefore, respond to a public-interest appeal.

The question remains, however, of whether anyone has any incentive to make a public-interest appeal. The answer is clearly in the affirmative. Several CC members, during personal interviews, intimated that they have invoked public-interest appeals during CC executive sessions *when some of their own freshmen would be the beneficiaries of such appeals.* And this is precisely the second line of reasoning provided above. When serving the public interest is compatible with serving a private interest, service of the public interest is a likely by-product. Thus, an effort to assist marginal freshmen is likely to be spearheaded by those on the CC whose freshmen stand to gain from it. My own strong suspicion, however, is that the large public-good component of the "help electorally insecure congressmen" criterion is so substantial that the criterion is not likely to be very important in actual CC decision-making.

Scholarly opinion on the extent to which congressmen from swing districts benefit from CC benevolence is divided. Some have argued for this proposition quite forcefully. Masters (1961, p. 50) goes so far as to assert that "the most important single factor in distributing assignments to all committees [other than Appropriations, Rules, and Ways and Means] is whether a particular place will help to insure the reelection of the member in question." A participant in Clapp's Brookings Roundtable supports Masters on this point by reference to his own unhappy experience:

> When I first came to Congress, our party went from the majority to the minority. Though I waged a strong campaign for a good committee assignment, I couldn't get one. What few decent openings were available were given to those elected from marginal districts. [Clapp 1964, p. 234]

Bullock (1972), on the other hand, disputes the Masters/Clapp hypothesis. He provides evidence revealing that marginal and safe congressmen obtain "good" assignments at about the same rate. Unfortunately, Bullock's study operationalizes the notion of "good" assignments on the basis of objective features, not the subjective preferences of requesters.

Both proponents and opponents of the Masters/Clapp hypothesis investigate the *simple* relationship between electoral insecurity and committee assignments. Democratic request data, as it happens, support the simple relationship: nearly two-thirds of the marginal freshmen (65.4%)—those receiving less than 55% of the two-party vote—obtain their first-preference request, while barely half (50.5%) of the safe freshmen are as successful. However, neither proponents nor opponents have ventured very far beyond the simple bivariate relationship (each drawing on different data sources to support his contention); both are guilty of making too much of this simple relationship. While I am inclined toward Bullock's negative judgment on the Masters/Clapp hypothesis—"public interest" is too meager an explanation— it is apparent that a more general statistical examination is required. In the multivariate model below there are strong grounds for rejecting this hypothesis.

2. Predecessor Status. One of the few pieces of personal information about a requester explicitly provided in the CC request books is the committee assignment of his predecessor. As a guide to the constituency (and hence electoral) interests of a freshman over and above the preferences he reveals in his request list, the committee status of his predecessor is probably a good one.[3] Certainly if a freshman's first-preference request is the committee on which his predecessor served, a strong case can be made by his zone representative that the freshman's district is seeking to maintain continuity of representation on the committee in question.

Table 9.2 produces two interesting conclusions. First, Fenno's warning is

Table 9.2   **Predecessor Status and Assignment Success**

		Predecessor Served on First-Preference Committee	Predecessor Did Not Serve on First-Preference Committee
First-preference assignment success	Yes	76.7	55.2
	No	23.3	44.8
		100.0%	100.0%
		N = 30	N = 163

well worth heeding. From the respective N's, it may be seen that barely 15% of all freshmen listed the committee of their predecessor as a first preference. The electoral (and policy) interests of a freshman need not coincide with those of his predecessor because the relevant constituencies from which those interests emerge need not coincide. However, a second conclusion is justified by the data of table 9.2. When there *is* a coincidence of interests between a freshman and his predecessor as reflected in the freshman's first preference request for his predecessor's committee, the CC regards that coincidence as strong grounds for honoring the request. This statistically significant difference persists in the multivariate context.

3. Previous Terms of Service. Of the 193 freshmen in the data set, only 11 were "superfreshmen." Although this is not a very large number on which to base firm conclusions, there is no evidence that "superfreshmen" are any more successful in obtaining first-preference committees than "normal" freshmen—a conclusion sustained in the multivariate model below. It should be noted, however, that five of the seven "superfreshmen" who sought to return to their old committee were successful.

4. Same State as Zone Representative. More than half of the freshmen come from a state delegation with a representative on the CC. It might be presumed that these members exploit their delegation ties with the CC, or that these state delegations are most effective in pressing their interests. Neither presumption would be accurate; freshmen with state delegation representation on the CC are no more successful in obtaining first-preference requests than are other freshmen.

5. Region. Perhaps the most anomalous relationship is that between assignment success and region. Nearly two-thirds of all nonsouthern freshmen obtain their first-preference request, while barely 40% of the southerners are successful. In Chapters 7 and 8 precisely the opposite argument was made. Because of the large southern representation on the Democratic CC, the limited work loads of their zone representatives, and the expressly regional orientation they articulate, it was expected that if any regional advantage existed it belonged to the South. Here again, however, the relationship may be spurious if the ceteris paribus condition is violated. If, for example, southerners tended to seek assignments to committees with very few vacancies and many requesters, then a success rate of 40% might be regarded as respectable. If, on the other hand, nonsoutherners sought membership on committees where the competitive situation was not severe, then a success rate of "only" 67% might be regarded as rather poor. While actual requests of southerners and non-southerners are not so different as the illustration above portrays, it does turn out that they are substantially different. Although the regional differential persists even where seat-security is controlled (see Rohde and Shepsle 1973, table 12), in the multivariate analysis below regional effects wash out entirely in the presence of supply and demand variables.

In my analysis of the effect of personal characteristics of individual requesters on assignment success, the final assessment is primarily negative. Of the three variables that appear important in the bivariate context—electoral security, predecessor status, region—only predecessor status retains its significance when supply and demand factors are controlled. And the reason is simple. *Most requester characteristics are irrelevant to the goals and objectives of CC members.* The CC member's concern is limited almost exclusively to "taking care of my people." Although occasional personal idiosyncracies may serve to intensify (or reduce) the member's activity on behalf of one of his freshmen,[4] their statistical effects are, on the whole, modest. Structural features related to the request, rather than characteristics of the requester, have a much greater bearing on assignment success. The competitive contexts in which the request is considered—both intrazone and interzone—determine the opportunities for and constraints on advocacy by the zone representative and the matching of assignments to requests by the full CC.

Characteristics of the Request

Recall that committee assignment decision-making is a two-stage process. To win appointment to a committee, a member must be nominated by his zone representative and be elected by a majority of the CC. The intrazone competitive situation is relevant to the former, while the interzone situation is relevant to the latter. I examine each of these situations separately.

1. Intrazone Competion. Since nomination is a necessary step on the way to assignment, it is expected, ceteris paribus, that any factor which enhances the likelihood of nomination by the zone representative will be revealed in actual assignments. The question thus turns on the structural features of requests that encourage nomination. To answer this question, the natural place to look is the internal competitive situation within the zone.

Table 9.3 suggests only a modest relationship between zone competition and assignment success. In this table, for each freshman's first-preference committee, the number of effective zone competitors per committee vacancy was computed. The definition of effectiveness hinges on the order in which committees are taken up by the CC. For example, consider a freshman whose first-preference request is Banking and Currency. Suppose five other people

Table 9.3		Effective Zone Competition and Assignment Success		
		Number of Effective Zone Competitors per Vacancy		
		0	0–.5	Greater than .5
First-preference	Yes	61.5	59.0	56.5
assignment success	No	38.5	41.0	43.5
		100.0%	100.0%	100.0%
		N = 109	N = 61	N = 23

(freshmen and nonfreshmen) from his zone have listed Banking and Currency on their request lists. By the time Banking and Currency assignments are the order of business, the CC will have already made assignments to Rules, Appropriations, Interstate, Agriculture, and Armed Services.[5] Suppose two of the five zone competitors who have listed Banking and Currency on their request lists have already been assigned to one of these previous committees. Then the number of effective competitors within the zone is three; if there are, say, six vacancies on Banking and Currency, then the number of effective zone competitors per vacancy is .5.

While the relationship in table 9.3 is indeed modest (though in the correct direction), the more interesting point that emerges from the table is the limited amount of intrazone effective competition that in fact exists. For nearly 60% of the freshmen there is no effective zone competition at all, a sign that the zone representatives have managed to control potential conflict and redirect requests at an earlier stage.

It is slightly misleading to look at the *absolute* level of effective competition per vacancy. The optimizing zone representative will seek to determine, whatever the absolute level of competition, whether things get better or worse as he goes down a member's request list. If there is more effective zone competition for requests lower down on a member's list, it is expected that the zone representative will be more inclined to proceed to nominate him for his first-preference request (again, whatever the absolute level of competition). If, on the other hand, it is "easier" to nominate a member for a lower-order request, the member's prospects for obtaining his first choice should decline. Table 9.4 bears out this expectation. When there is less internal competition for a first-preference committee, nearly 70% are successful in obtaining the assignment; when the circumstances are reversed, only about 30% are successful.[6]

Table 9.4   **Relative Effective Zone Competition and Assignment Success**

		Relative Competition for Lower-Order (Second or Third) Requests	
		More	Less
First-preference	Yes	69.6	30.9
assignment success	No	30.4	69.1
		100.0%	100.0%
		N = 138	N = 55

2. Interzone Competition. Factors related to the external (interzone) competitive situation complement the simple effects of intrazone competition on assignment success. Measured either as the total number of effective requests per vacancy (table 9.5) or as the number of zones per vacancy with effective (and thus potential) nominees (table 9.6), interzone competition has an important effect on the likelihood of first-preference assignment success.

Table 9.5   **Total External Competition and Assignment Success**

		Total Number of Effective Requests per Vacancy		
		Less than 1	1–2	More than 2
First-preference	Yes	94.4	67.2	30.5
assignment success	No	5.6	32.8	69.5
		100.0%	100.0%	100.0%
		N = 18	N = 116	N = 59

Table 9.6   **Zone Competition and Assignment Success**

		Number of Zones with Potential Nominees per Vacancy			
		Less than 1	1–2	2–3	More than 3
First-preference	Yes	80.4	57.8	42.9	14.3
assignment success	No	19.6	42.2	57.1	85.7
		100.0%	100.0%	100.0%	100.0%
		N = 56	N = 102	N = 14	N = 21

The multivariate analysis that follows sustains the findings of our brief inquiry into the simple effects of competitive circumstances on first-preference assignment success. Both intrazone and interzone competitive factors exert strong, independent effects on first-preference assignment success. These effects are independent of *requester* characteristics—they are true for both southerners and nonsoutherners, electorally secure and electorally marginal, those who come from the same state as the zone representative and those who do not, those whose predecessor served on the committee requested and those whose predecessor did not, and so on—and thus reinforce the argument that the principle of CC advocacy is impersonal. The constraints of committee slot scarcity, more than the personal characteristics of requesters, differentiate winners and losers. This is the message of the multivariate model that follows.

Other factors

Two other variables are examined in the multivariate model below. Since they characterize neither the requester nor the request, but rather the zone of the requester, they are discussed separately.

1. Zone Representative's Work Load. If a CC member's time and other resources are taxed by an inordinate work load, as in the case of the California CC representative in the Eighty-eighth Congress (see table 8.3), it is anticipated that his charges will not be very successful because his resource base is spread too thin. Measuring work load by the proportion of all freshmen in a given Congress belonging to a CC member's zone, however, there is no strong support for this proposition: those zone representatives with "light" work loads succeed in securing first-preference assignments for 60% of their freshmen; those with "heavy" work loads have a 56% success rate. This difference remains insignificant in the multivariate context.

2. Zone Overrepresentation. One of the strategic premises shared by members of the CC is: "Write an acceptable committee slate." Coupled with the occasionally observed practice of filling committee berths from the state delegation of the member who vacated it (the same-state norm), this translates into the presumption of geographic equity (all other things being equal, of course). A measure of *overrepresentation* of the jth zone on the ith committee was defined:

$$\begin{pmatrix} \text{number of members} \\ \text{from the } j^{th} \text{ zone} \\ \text{returning to the} \\ i^{th} \text{ committee} \end{pmatrix} - \begin{pmatrix} \dfrac{\text{number of members}}{\text{in the } j^{th} \text{ zone}} \\ \overline{\text{total number of}} \\ \text{Democrats} \end{pmatrix} \begin{pmatrix} \text{size of} \\ i^{th} \text{ committee} \end{pmatrix}$$

This index measures the difference between the actual number of members from a zone returning to a given committee and the expected number on the *new* committee (after new assignments and a possibly changed committee size) if assignments are based strictly on a proportional geographic quota. Positive index values imply zone overrepresentation. The bivariate relationship between this index and first-preference assignment success is negligible; in the multivariate context, however, it becomes more important. To examine the geographic equity norm further, the number of zone vacancies—that is, the number of berths on a given committee released by zone colleagues—was defined as a separate variable. It proved insignificant in relation to first-preference assignment success in both the bivariate and the multivariate case.

Freshmen Assignment
Success:
A Multivariate Model

The two-stage committee assignment process in which a successful applicant must clear both a nomination and an election hurdle, and in which the former hurdle must be cleared in order to attempt the latter, suggests the following simple probability model. Define the following events:

A = applicant i is nominated by his zone representative for his first-preference committee.

B = applicant i is elected to his first-preference committee.

Then, from the simple definition of conditional probability,[7] it follows that

$$Pr(B) = Pr(B/A) \cdot Pr(A) + Pr(B/\text{not } A) \cdot Pr(\text{not } A)$$

Since a requester cannot be elected to a committee if he is not nominated, i.e., $Pr(B/\text{not } A) = 0$, this expression simplifies to

$$Pr(B) = Pr(B/A) \cdot Pr(A) \tag{9.1}$$

The event B is observable from the Democratic request lists; the event A is not (see note 6). Thus we cannot estimate the two terms on the right-hand side of (9.1) separately and multiply them to solve for $Pr(B)$. We can, however, specify functional forms for each of the terms on the right-hand side, multiply the two forms, and *then* estimate the entire relationship with probit analysis techniques.

We shall specify three variables as important for the event A and four variables for the event B/A. For now the discussion can conveniently remain abstract. Let $Pr(A)$ depend on $[u_1, u_2, u_3]$ and $Pr(B/A)$ on $[v_1, v_2, v_3, v_4]$. Adopting the linear hypothesis in the same fashion that a request equation was specified in Chapter 4, we may write

$$Pr(B) = \Phi\left(\alpha + \sum_i \beta_i u_i + \sum_j \gamma_j v_j + \sum_i \sum_j \delta_{ij} u_i v_j\right) \tag{9.2}$$

where Φ is the cumulative normal function. The population parameters α, $\beta_i, \gamma_j, \delta_{ij}$ ($i = 1, \ldots, 3; j = 1, \ldots, 4$) may be estimated by the probit technique once variables are operationalized.

In table 9.7 the relevant variables are defined. These are a subset of those investigated earlier in this chapter. Several omissions (most notably electoral safeness) are included later. Table 9.8 provides theoretical expectations for the parameter estimates; these will be discussed in conjunction with the analysis of the results below.

Table 9.7   **Variables Employed in Probit Equation (9.2)**

Label	Name	Operational Definition
B	Assignment success	$B = 1$ if requester assigned to his first-preference committee; $= 0$ otherwise
u_1	Same state as zone representative?	$u_1 = 1$ if yes; $= 0$ if no
u_2	Predecessor status	$u_2 = 1$ if requester's first-preference committee is the one on which his predecessor served; $= 0$ otherwise
u_3	Internal Competitive Environment	$u_3 = 1$ if there is less competition per vacancy within the zone for a requester's lower-order requests than for his first-preference request; $= 0$ otherwise
v_1	External Competitive Environment	$v_1 = $ number of zones per vacancy with effective requests
v_2	Region	$v_2 = 1$ if requester is from South; $= 0$ otherwise
v_3	Zone overrepresentation	$v_3 = $ number of zone members returning to requester's first-preference committee $-$ (ratio of zone members to all Democrats) (size of requester's first-preference committee)
v_4	Zone vacancies	$v_4 = $ number of slots on requester's first-preference committee vacated by a (former) zone colleague(s).

The results of the probit estimation are given in table 9.9. Notice that each of the theoretical expectations reported in table 9.8 is fulfilled in the probit. Sharing a state delegation in common with the CC member (u_1), seeking the committee on which one's predecessor served (u_2), and coming from a zone with a large number of zone vacancies (v_4) have positive impact on a requester's probability of obtaining his first-preference committee. On the other hand, internal and external competition (u_3, v_1) and zone overrepresentation (v_3) detract from that probability. Moreover, with the sole exception of the "same state as CC member" variable, all the parameters are, individually,

Table 9.8

Theoretical Expectation for Each Parameter of Probit Equation

Parameter	Description	Expectation
β_1	Same state as CC member	$\beta_1 > 0$
β_2	Predecessor status	$\beta_2 > 0$
β_3	Internal competition	$\beta_3 < 0$
γ_1	External competition	$\gamma_1 < 0$
γ_2	Region	No prediction
γ_3	Zone overrepresentation	$\gamma_3 < 0$
γ_4	Zone vacancies	$\gamma_4 > 0$
δ_{ij}	Interaction terms	No prediction

Table 9.9

Maximum Likelihood Estimates of Parameters in Probit Equation ($N = 193$)

Coefficient	Represents the Effect of	Maximum Likelihood Estimate	Standard Error
α	constant	0.677[a]	0.294
β_1	u_1	0.409	0.468
β_2	u_2	2.434[a]	1.319
β_3	u_3	-0.822[b]	0.541
γ_1	v_1	-0.246[a]	0.135
γ_2	v_2	-0.843[a]	0.472
γ_3	v_3	-0.026[b]	0.021
γ_4	v_4	0.509[b]	0.333
δ_{11}	u_1v_1	-0.042	0.237
δ_{12}	u_1v_2	0.458	0.531
δ_{13}	u_1v_3	0.068	0.277
δ_{14}	u_1v_4	-0.678[a]	0.388
δ_{21}	u_2v_1	-0.359	0.550
δ_{22}	u_2v_2	-0.697	0.778
δ_{23}	u_2v_3	0.075	0.503
δ_{24}	u_2v_4	-0.979[a]	0.584
δ_{31}	u_3v_1	-0.275	0.316
δ_{32}	u_3v_2	0.477	0.614
δ_{33}	u_3v_3	-0.821[a]	0.452
δ_{34}	u_3v_4	-0.436	0.433

[a] $p < .05$
[b] $p < .10$

statistically significant. At the level of individual parameters, then, our theoretical expectations are not out of line.[8]

A more sophisticated examination of the model's performance is provided by four separate analyses: (1) some illustrative examples of the model's predictions under hypothesized conditions, (2) an examination of the overall predictive performance of the model, (3) joint hypothesis tests of the independent impact of each of the variables, and (4) a residual analysis, that is, an examination of the model's errors.

Illustrative Examples
(Table 9.10)

The cases of an advantaged and a disadvantaged freshman have been drawn from the data. While they are not the most extreme imaginable, they nevertheless display the successful manner in which the model "separates" the advantaged from the disadvantaged.

Table 9.10 **Two Extreme Cases**

Variable	Variable Description	Advantaged Requester	Disadvantaged Requester
u_1	Same state as zone representative	No	No
u_2	Predecessor status	Yes	No
u_3	Internal competition	More competition for lower requests	Less competition for lower requests
v_1	External competition	1.5 zones/vacancy with effective competitors	7 zones/vacancy with effective competitors
v_2	Region	Non-South	South
v_3	Zone over-representation	2.2 zone colleagues "too many"	.8 zone colleagues "too many"
v_4	Zone vacancies	One	None
Prediction:	Pr(assignment) =	.9903	.0003
Actual:	B =	assigned	not assigned

The advantaged freshman was a western congressman who sought an assignment to Interior in the Ninety-third Congress. Although he did not come from the same state delegation as his zone representative and although his zone was heavily overrepresented on the committee—a common fact for western congressmen and the Interior Committee—he was nevertheless advantaged in several distinct ways. His predecessor had served on the committee for four terms; the member submitted no lower-order requests; there were no other zone competitors for an assignment to Interior; for the six committee vacancies there were only nine zones with available competitors at the time of committee consideration; and a member of his zone had given up a position on the committee. The model predicts a probability of assignment for this freshman in excess of .99; he was assigned.

The disadvantaged freshman was a southerner seeking an appointment to Interstate in the Eighty-seventh Congress. He was disadvantaged in practically all respects: he did not come from the same state delegation as his CC representative; his predecessor had not served on the committee; no members of his zone had departed from the committee; his zone was already overrepresented on the committee; there were no less than seven zones with potential nominees for the single vacancy on the committee; and there was considerably less competition, both within the zone and without, for his second-choice committee (to which he was ultimately assigned). The model predicts a probability near zero for assignment; he was not assigned.

In general, the model did a good job of separating predictions on the basis of the degree of advantage or disadvantage measured by the explanatory variables. For more than seventy percent of the cases ($N = 193$), the model predicted a probability of assignment of less than .3 or greater than .7—a sign that the variables are good discriminators. Moreover, it is precisely in these prediction categories that the model's predictions are most accurate (see the residual analysis below). To gain a better grasp of the model's overall performance we turn to an examination of some summary statistics.

*Overall Predictive
Performance*

Four different measures of "goodness of fit" between model predictions and actual observations are employed. The first is the joint test of the null hypothesis that the entire probit is insignificant:

$$H_0: \beta_i = 0 \quad i = 1, 2, 3$$
$$\gamma_j = 0 \quad j = 1, 2, 3, 4$$
$$\delta_{ij} = 0 \quad i = 1, 2, 3; j = 1, 2, 3, 4$$

This joint hypothesis test uses a likelihood ratio statistic described in Chapter 4. The conclusion of this test is that the chances are less than one in ten thousand that we would err in rejecting the null hypothesis—a strong endorsement of the model.

The second measure of predictive performance is a simple one—the proportion of correct predictions. Since the model predicts a probability of assignment success, while our observations are whether a requester is success-ful or not (B = 1 and B = 0, respectively), a rule that takes us from a probability prediction to a success prediction is required. The following maximum likelihood rule was employed:

> *If model predicts*   *then predict*
> Pr(B = 1) > .5   B = 1 (assignment)
> Pr(B = 1) < .5   B = 0 (no assignment)

Thus, a prediction is correct if the probability prediction of the model exceeds .5 *and* the requester is successful, or the probability prediction is less than .5 *and* the requester fails to win appointment. According to this criterion, the model predicts correctly in 75.7% of the cases. That is, in 146 of the 193 cases, the model made the correct prediction about assignment success. The 47 "errors" will be examined in the residual analysis.

The third measure of prediction performance is the rank-order correlation between the predicted value of the dependent variable (according to the above maximum likelihood rule) and the observed value. The rank-order correlation is .466—a statistically significant value.

Finally, an $\hat{R}^2$ statistic is reported. This statistic is directly analogous to the coefficient of determination (R^2) in regression analysis (see McKelvey and Zavoina 1974). It summarizes the proportion of variance in the dependent variable accounted for by the variables of the probit. For the probit of table 9.9, $\hat{R}^2 = .509$, a relatively high figure for the kind of data used here.

By the standards of four different measures, then, the probit model estimated in table 9.9 performs satisfactorily. Measures of overall fit have held a certain fascination for political scientists, however, that is probably misplaced. Of course, it is desirable for a model to produce better predictions rather than worse. But the objective of most inquiries is not (or should not be) to explain variance but rather to assess the import of explanatory variables. To do this one looks not at measures of overall fit but at parameter estimates and the importance of their effects. This is my next task.

Joint Hypothesis
Tests

The importance of the estimates in table 9.9 is in the information they provide about the relative impact of (classes of) variables on the probability of first-preference assignment success. Since each variable has several parameters associated with it—a main effect and several interaction effects—joint hypothesis tests are required. These are reported in table 9.11.

The first hypothesis test has already been reported—the entire probit equation is extremely significant. The second and third hypotheses, however,

Table 9.11   Joint Hypothesis Tests of Probit Model (9.2)

Null Hypothesis		Probability Null Hypothesis is True*
Substantive	Joint Statistical	
1. The entire probit is insignificant	$H_0: \beta_i = 0, \gamma_j = 0, \delta_{ij} = 0,$ for all i and j	< .0001
2. All main effects insignificant	$H_0: \beta_i = 0, \gamma_j = 0,$ for all i and j	< .005
3. All interaction effects insignificant	$H_0: \delta_{ij} = 0$ for all i and j	< .40
4. Same state as zone representative is insignificant	$H_0: \beta_1 = \delta_{11} = \delta_{12} = \delta_{13} = \delta_{14} = 0$	< .50
5. Predecessor status insignificant	$H_0: \beta_2 = \delta_{21} = \delta_{22} = \delta_{23} = \delta_{24} = 0$	< .05
6. Internal competitive environment insignificant	$H_0: \beta_3 = \delta_{31} = \delta_{32} = \delta_{33} = \delta_{34} = 0$	< .0001
7. External competitive environment insignificant	$H_0: \gamma_1 = \delta_{11} = \delta_{21} = \delta_{31} = 0$	< .015
8. Region insignificant	$H_0: \gamma_2 = \delta_{12} = \delta_{22} = \delta_{32} = 0$	< .25
9. Zone overrepresentation insignificant	$H_0: \gamma_3 = \delta_{13} = \delta_{23} = \delta_{33} = 0$	< .08
10. Number of zone vacancies insignificant	$H_0: \gamma_4 = \delta_{14} = \delta_{24} = \delta_{34} = 0$	< .20

* A likelihood ratio test produces a test statistic that is distributed chi-square with degrees of freedom equal to the number of parameters hypothesized to be zero under H_0. Each entry in the last column is the probability that a rejection of the null hypothesis is in error. The smaller this entry, the more confidence one has in rejecting H_0.

suggest that it is through their main effects, not their interactions, that the variables affect the likelihood of assignment success. This casts some doubt on the multiplicative form given in equation (9.2).[9]

Hypotheses four and five examine personal characteristics of the requester that may prove relevant at the nomination stage. The expectation is that personal characteristics such as these will play a tie-breaker role for the zone representative in those situations in which he has several freshmen seeking his nomination, and all other things are about equal. The "same state" variable is very insignificant, while the "predecessor status" variable is quite significant—conclusions drawn in the earlier discussion (see table 9.2).

Two other personal characteristic variables (relevant, potentially, at either the nomination or election stage) were examined that are not reported in table 9.11: "superfreshman" status and electoral security. The variables were defined in both main effect and interaction effect form. For each, a joint test of the appropriate null hypothesis (main effect and interaction effect parameters equal to zero) was conducted. The probabilities that these null hypotheses are true (see the note to table 9.11) are .70 for superfreshman status and .30 for electoral security; thus, neither null hypothesis can be rejected.[10] (For a comparison between marginal and safe congressmen in assignment contests, see table 9.12 in note 10.)

Hypothesis eight involves the only other personal characteristic of requesters—this one potentially relevant at the election stage. Despite the strong bivariate relationship reported earlier, and the statistically significant main effect (see table 9.9), region washes out as a factor relevant to assignment success. The fact, then, that a freshman is southern has no significant impact on the likelihood of first-preference assignment success.[11]

Hypotheses six and seven focus on the internal and external competitive context within which a freshman's first-preference request is weighed both by his zone representative and the entire CC. The conclusion is clear and unequivocal: competitive characteristics of a request exert strong independent effects on the prospects for assignment success. More than any other variables, these provide the bulk of explanatory power in distinguishing successful from unsuccessful freshman requesters.

Hypotheses nine and ten examine regional equity practices in the CC. Like the personal characteristic variables for the zone representative at the nomination stage, regional representation variables are hypothesized to play a tie-breaking role for the CC at the election stage. The results indicate that the zone overrepresentation variable is moderately significant while the number of zone vacancies is not. The CC, that is, is disposed to support nominations from zones underrepresented on the committee in question and to oppose those from overrepresented zones. It is not, however, necessarily disposed to fill a committee vacancy with someone from the zone of a departing member.

In the discussion of the decision-making practices of the CC it was pointed out that freshmen, to most CC members, are virtual unknowns. Thus it is improbable that highly idiosyncratic characteristics of particular freshmen play a very significant part in either the zone representative's nomination calculations or the entire CC's election deliberations. The joint hypothesis tests suggest an even stronger conclusion. With few exceptions, committee assignments turn on impersonal competitive factors. Even though the request books provide the CC with easily accessible, objective data about each freshman, personal factors appear to play a relatively minor role. The one piece of objective information that appears to be of some importance is predecessor status. The effects of all other personal variables vanish in the presence of data on the competitive situation, the availability of committee vacancies (scarcity), and the extent to which a member's zone already has "sufficient" committee representation. The objective of advocacy and the practical realization that highly sought-after committee assignments are in scarce supply impose an attitude of economy on CC members. This pressure for allocative efficiency overwhelms personal factors.

Although the multivariate model's joint hypothesis tests support the rather strong conclusion of the last paragraph, I may have been too hasty in drawing it. The model, after all, is not perfect in its predictive characteristics. Of the 193 predictions made by the model, 47 are in error. In my last assessment of the model, I look closely at these errors to see if there is anything to be learned from them.

Residual Analysis

Figures 9.1 and 9.2 identify where the model is making prediction errors. A plot of the expected and actual rates of prediction accuracy is displayed in figure 9.1. For every probability prediction of, say, .6, the maximum likelihood rule predicts B = 1, that is, requester assigned. Thus, there will be a 40% error rate, on average, for all predictions of .6—four out of every ten such predictions will be in error. Errors, then, are highest for moderate probability predictions. Figure 9.1 confirms this fact. Errors are neither expected nor observed in the extreme prediction categories; expected and actual error frequency is much higher for the more moderate probability prediction categories. If the model's predictions are most frequently in the extreme

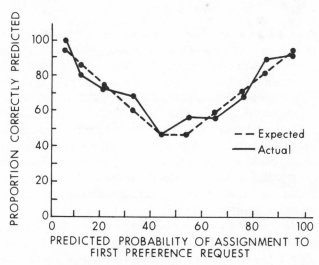

Fig. 9.1   Plot predictions from probit equation.

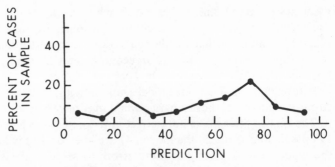

Fig. 9.2   Distribution of predictions in sample.

categories, that is, if the explanatory variables separate requesters into first-preference assignment success categories of "extremely likely" and "extremely unlikely," then the error rate will not be high. Figure 9.2, giving the relative frequency distribution of predictions across prediction categories, shows that about one-third of all predictions are in the interval [.3, .7]; two-thirds of the predictions are "extreme." Moreover, though accounting for only a third of all predictions, model predictions in this moderate category produced almost 60% of the errors (27 of 47).

The model can produce one of two types of error:

Type A: Model predicts requester is assigned to first-preference committee but he is not.

Type B: Model predicts requester is not assigned to first-preference committee but he is.

Type A errors dominate Type B errors by better than a two-to-one ratio (32 versus 15). And there is a good reason. Since the model makes only probabilistic predictions, the maximum likelihood rule must be employed to make assignment success predictions. The model does not prohibit the following circumstances from arising: a committee has three vacancies and four requesters; since the constraint that no more than three may be assigned is not an explicit part of the statistical estimation algorithm, it is not impossible for each requester to be assigned a probability of, say, .55, in which case the model predicts, according to the maximum likelihood rule, the impossible event that all four requesters are successful. This leads to Type A errors that would not occur under a model specification in which the constraint was explicitly incorporated.[12]

The Type B errors were not subject to this flaw, but another, less frequent, problem did arise. In some circumstances there is a great deal of competition for a very limited number of vacancies on a given committee. The probit model will assign very low success probabilities to all requesters in this competitive circumstance, even though some may ultimately prevail. In the Eighty-eighth Congress, for example, there were five requests (all first-preference requests from California freshmen) for Foreign Affairs. The probit model assigned a success probability for each requester ranging between .20 and .25. The maximum likelihood rule, consequently, predicted none would be successful. It was correct in four of the five cases. One California freshman did win an appointment. Since the Type B errors were fairly infrequent (fewer than 8% of the cases resulted in Type B errors), and many of them could be accounted for by the reason just given, Type A errors are the focus of the remainder of this residual analysis.

Three factors appear to account for most of the thirty-two Type A errors. In ten instances, a requester who was predicted to win a first-preference committee was assigned to a lower-preference committee considered earlier on the CC's agenda than his most-preferred committee. This confirms our earlier impression of logistical difficulty faced by the zone representative. Uncertain of the chances of first-preference success for one of his freshmen and faced with a "satisficing" alternative—a lower-order preference committee that comes up earlier—the CC representative avoids the risky course by nominating his freshman for the lower-order committee.

In five more instances of Type A errors, no freshman won assignment to the available slots on a committee. In the Eighty-eighth Congress, for example, a Texas freshman listed Government Operations as his first choice. All six vacancies were filled by nonfreshmen. This suggests that the measure of competition employed in the model should be refined in order to differentiate freshman competitors from more senior competitors.[13]

Finally, over and above the previous two sources of error, thirteen Type A errors were associated with two committees—Appropriations and Armed Services. In the case of Appropriations, freshmen for whom success was highly probable according to the explanatory variables failed to win assignment. Typically they lost to more senior congressmen.[14] The same was true of Armed Services' requesters, though they lost less frequently to senior transfers. It would appear, then, that senior competition is especially important for these two committees and, as is apparently not the case with most other committees, idiosyncratic characteristics of the requester loom large here.

Overall, twenty-eight of the thirty-two Type A errors in the model's predictions are accommodated by attending to (1) dynamic features of the CC's decision-making process, (2) senior competition, and (3) the possible importance of idiosyncratic criteria for Appropriations and Armed Services assignment success. No other variables examined—work load of zone representative, requester partisan loyalty, requester opposition to the conservative coalition, requester support of a larger federal role, requester support (opposition) of the president when he was of the same (different) party—were strongly associated with the occurrence of Type A errors.

This completes my examination of freshman first-preference assignment success. The general conclusion is that members of the CC are not, in general, idiosyncratic and arbitrary in their allocation of committee assignments to freshmen. Their own individual objectives predispose them to serve the interests of their "constituents," and physical scarcity is the principal constraint on their maximizing behavior. In the CC's effort to assign freshmen to committees they seek, the conclusion of the hypothesis tests of table 9.11 is unequivocal: it is the internal (zone) and external (CC) competitive situations that are most important is distinguishing winners from losers. With this conclusion in mind, I turn now to a parallel treatment of nonfreshman requests.

Nonfreshman
Assignment Success

My examination of nonfreshman assignment success parallels the preceding examination of freshman assignment success by focusing on nonfreshman transfers. An examination of nonfreshman dual-service acquisitions is omitted because there are too few cases and I have been unable to account for the apparent randomness of the data (but see below).

The process by which nonfreshman transfer requests are handled is similar to that for freshman requests. A nonfreshman submits his request to his zone representative; a request must receive his sanction in the sense that the full CC will not consider it without his nomination; a request, if nominated, must receive a majority of the CC votes, in competition with all other nominations, in order to win election.

There, however, the similarities to freshman requests end. First, nonfreshmen already have committee slots which they may retain. Consequently, the lottery in which they engage when they submit transfer requests has non-negative payoffs—they will either improve their situations by transferring to a more preferred committee or the status quo will prevail. As a result, 84% of all transfer requests are of the single-shot variety, that is, "Give me committee X or I'll retain the committee on which I currently serve." By comparison, only 23% of the freshman request lists contain a single committee.

Second, the nonfreshman often is the beneficiary of an informal relationship with his zone representative and others on the CC. Thus nearly one-fifth of all *actual* transfers have involved nonfreshmen who did not formally submit requests.[15] In a few additional instances a member submitted a single transfer request but accepted another. In each of these cases members revealed preferences for transfer (since they did not have to accept the reassignment) through informal means.

This raises a third important difference. The nonfreshman, to a considerably greater extent than most freshmen, is a known quantity both to his zone representative and to the full CC. His policy interests and predispositions, his personal demeanor, his voting behavior, and his electoral needs are ordinarily public knowledge. Consequently we should expect "characteristics of the requester" (to use the term employed in the freshman analysis) to loom larger in explaining nonfreshman transfer success.

The multivariate statistical model for nonfreshmen first-preference transfer success has a specification identical to that given in equation (9.2). The probability of nomination, $Pr(A)$, is a function of four intrazone and personal characteristics, $[u_1, u_2, u_3, u_4]$. The conditional probability of election, given nomination, $Pr(B/A)$, is a function of four interzone variables $[v_1, v_2, v_3, v_4]$. Thus, the probability of first-preference transfer success is simply the product of these two probabilities (in accord with equation [9.1]).

The actual statistical specification is given in equation (9.3):

$$Pr(B) = \Phi\left(\alpha + \sum_i \beta_i u_i + \sum_j \gamma_j v_j\right) \qquad (9.3)$$

The interaction terms have been deleted from the specification because of the relatively small sample size ($N = 72$). Table 9.13 defines and operationalizes the variables of equation (9.3), and table 9.14 summarizes the theoretical expectations for the parameters.

In this formulation a requester's probability of success is enhanced by the existence of zone vacancies (v_1) and a state delegation in common with his zone representative (u_3); the probability is depressed by internal competition (u_1, u_2), external competition (v_3, v_4), zone overrepresentation (v_2), and large differences in loyalty to party with his zone representative (u_4).[16] These expectations follow directly from our assumptions about CC member objectives. As in the case of freshmen, it is chiefly the competitive environment, both within and between zones, that frustrates (or constrains) the zone representative's attempts to "take care of his people" seeking transfers. Over and above these environmental constraints, however, the CC representative may choose to assist the ambitions only of certain of his people, namely, those who can bring benefits to his state and those with whom he is in agreement on party issues.

The model is estimated in table 9.15. Each of the expectations in table 9.14 is satisfied, with the magnitude of all but one of the effects (external senior competition) statistically significant. Hypothesis tests are presented in table 9.16. As in the case of freshman committee assignments, the external conditions of supply and demand conspire with CC objectives to produce the

Table 9.13   Variables Employed in Probit Equation (9.3)

Label	Name	Operational Definition
B	Assignment success	$B = 1$ if requester assigned to first-preference transfer $= 0$ otherwise
u_1	Zone competition/vacancy	$u_1 =$ Number of effective zone competitors (both freshman and nonfreshman) per vacancy
u_2	Senior zone competition	$u_2 = 1$ if there are other senior zone members seeking to transfer to requester's first-preference committee $= 0$ otherwise
u_3	Same state as zone representative	$u_3 = 1$ if yes $= 0$ if no
u_4	Party support differential	$u_4 =$ absolute value of difference between member's CQ party support score and zone representative's CQ party support score (Party Support = Party Unity − Party Opposition).
v_1	Number of zone vacancies	$v_1 =$ number of vacancies on requester's committee created by the departure of another zone member.
v_2	Zone overrepresentation	$v_2 =$ number of zone members returning to requester's first-preference committee − (ratio of zone members to all Democrats) (size of requester's first preference committee)
v_3	External competition/vacancy	$v_3 =$ number of zones with requesters per vacancy
v_4	External senior competition/vacancy	$v_4 =$ number of zones with senior requesters per vacancy

Table 9.14   Theoretical Expectation for Each Parameter of Probit Equation (9.3)

Parameter	Description	Expectation
β_1	zone competition/vacancy	$\beta_1 < 0$
β_2	senior zone competition	$\beta_2 < 0$
β_3	same state as zone representative	$\beta_3 > 0$
β_4	party support differential	$\beta_4 < 0$
γ_1	number of zone vacancies	$\gamma_1 > 0$
γ_2	zone overrepresentation	$\gamma_2 < 0$
γ_3	external competition	$\gamma_3 < 0$
γ_4	external senior competition	$\gamma_4 < 0$

Table 9.15   Maximum Likelihood Estimates of Parameters in Probit
                             Equation (9.3) ($N = 72$)

Coefficient	Represents the Effect of	Maximum Likelihood Estimate	Standard Error
α	constant	1.144	0.516
β_1	u_1	-1.984	1.316
β_2	u_2	-1.783	0.673
β_3	u_3	0.737	0.426
β_4	u_4	-0.016	0.008
γ_1	v_1	0.698	0.347
γ_2	v_2	-0.419	0.262
γ_3	v_3	-0.377	0.240
γ_4	v_4	-0.245	0.397

observed pattern of fit between transfer requests and assignments. Unlike with freshmen, however, several personal characteristics of requesters play a more substantial role at the nomination stage. All other things being equal, the zone representative appears to tilt in favor of those from his own state delegation and those with whom he is more in sympathy on policy grounds (as measured by the party support differential).

Three additional hypotheses were examined in the context of this model. First, as in the freshman case, there is no evidence of a regional bias. A parameter for a regional dummy variable (South vs. non-South) was found insignificant ($p > .20$). Southerners, that is, are neither more nor less likely to have their transfer requests honored, all other things being equal. Second, the zone representative's work load does not appear to be consequential. A parameter for a zone representative's work-load variable is not significant ($p > .50$). Finally, a measure of party support (party unity-party opposition) was examined. Since the zone representative shows a significant predisposition to support the requests of those who are most like him on a measure of party support (hypothesis 7 in table 9.16), a similar relationship was anticipated at the CC election stage. CC members are, in the main, partisan advocates, so it was anticipated that, all other things being equal, they would be most disposed to those requesters who were strong party supporters. There is no evidence to support this expectation; the parameter associated with the party support variable is insignificant ($p > .55$).

On the basis of an assessment of the estimated parameters, then, the model must be taken seriously. The supply of and demand for vacancies, zone properties, and individual characteristics all prove important in determining which nonfreshman transfer requests are honored. An investigation of the

Table 9.16 Hypothesis Tests of Probit Model (9.3)

Null Hypothesis		Probability Null Hypothesis Is True*
Substantive	Statistical	
1. The entire probit is insignificant	$H_0: \beta_i = 0, \gamma_j = 0$ for all i and j	$\ll .0001$
2. Intrazone variables insignificant	$H_0: \beta_1 = \beta_2 = \beta_3 = \beta_4 = 0$	$\ll .0001$
3. Interzone variables insignificant	$H_0: \gamma_1 = \gamma_2 = \gamma_3 = \gamma_4 = 0$	$\ll .0001$
4. Zone competition/vacancy insignificant	$H_0: \beta_1 = 0$	$< .07$
5. Senior zone competition insignificant	$H_0: \beta_2 = 0$	$< .003$
6. Same state as zone representative insignificant	$H_0: \beta_3 = 0$	$< .04$
7. Party support differential insignificant	$H_0: \beta_4 = 0$	$< .02$
8. Number of zone vacancies insignificant	$H_0: \gamma_1 = 0$	$< .02$
9. Zone overrepresentation insignificant	$H_0: \gamma_2 = 0$	$< .05$
10. External competition/vacancy insignificant	$H_0: \gamma_3 = 0$	$< .05$
11. External senior competition/ vacancy insignificant	$H_0: \gamma_4 = 0$	$< .27$

* The first three hypotheses are joint and thus are tested
with a likelihood ratio procedure. The remaining tests
examine single parameters. The ratio of the maximum
likelihood estimate to its standard error is distributed
$N(0, 1)$. Each cell is the probability that an error is made
in rejecting the null hypothesis.

predictive efficiency of the model and an examination of its errors will reinforce this conclusion. First, however, several illustrative examples are presented.

Table 9.17 provides the data on two extreme cases. The advantaged congressman is a southerner who successfully transferred to Armed Services in the Eighty-ninth Congress. He had no zone competition, came from the same state delegation as his zone representative, shared a moderate amount of party support with his zone representative,[17] sought to replace a zone member departing from Armed Services, came from a zone that was underrepresented slightly on the committee, and found himself in a situation in which there was little interzone competition for the slot and virtually no senior competition from other zones. The model predicts a probability of successful transfer near unity; he was appointed.

Table 9.17   **Two Extreme Cases**

Variable	Variable Description	Advantaged Requester	Disadvantaged Requester
u_1	zone competition/vacancy	none	0.2
u_2	senior zone competition	no	yes
u_3	same state as zone rep.	yes	no
u_4	party support differential*	13	39
v_1	number of zone vacancies	1	0
v_2	zone overrepresentation	−0.3	+0.5
v_3	number of zones with competitors/vacancy	1.0	1.6
v_4	number of zones with senior competitors/vacancy	0.4	1.2
Prediction:	Pr(assignment) =	.978	.003
Actual:	B =	assigned	not assigned

* Maximum (in principle) is 200

By way of contrast, a very popular westerner was unsuccessful in her attempt to transfer from Education and Labor to Appropriations in the Ninety-third Congress.[18] While she faced only moderate intrazone competition, it did come from another senior member (this senior competitor, by the way, prevailed in winning a slot on Appropriations). She did not come from the same state delegation as her zone representative and, while both are regarded as "liberal party regulars," she is considerably more liberal and more regular. Finally, there were no zone vacancies on the committee, her zone was already slightly overrepresented, and there was considerable external (interzone) competition for the slot, especially from other senior members. The model predicts a probability of assignment near zero (despite her personal popularity!); she was not assigned.

These illustrations are by no means representative—they were selected in order to illustrate the two extreme cases available in the data. They do, however, underscore the way in which the model works. In general the variables of the model do separate successful and unsuccessful requesters quite well, a point I examine in more detail in a residual analysis below. Before turning to that task, I will consider more generally how well the model performs as a predictive and explanatory tool.

To assess the statistical performance of the model, four summary statistics are employed. The first has already been reported as hypothesis 1 in table 9.16. There, the null hypothesis states that predictions based on no knowledge of the values of explanatory variables will be "as good" as predictions based on such knowledge. As reported, the chances are considerably less than one in ten thousand that this null hypothesis is true. In strongly rejecting this hypothesis we may strongly endorse the model as a predictive tool. Reinforcing this conclusion are three additional pieces of statistical information:

Percentage of correct predictions   = 79.2%
Rank-order correlation (predicted vs. actual) =   .576
Estimated $\hat{R}^2$ =   .560

On all four statistical dimensions, then, the model accounts for transfers at least as adequately as the model, presented in the preceding section, accounts for freshman assignments. Since the parameter estimates are in line with the expectations produced by my theoretical orientation as well, it may be concluded that the theory articulated in Chapters 7 and 8, emphasizing CC objectives, maximizing behavior, and constraints, is given strong and consistent empirical support.

Before drawing this section to a close, it is useful to examine briefly the fifteen prediction errors made by the model. Recall that two types of error are possible:

Type A: Model predicts assignment, but member not assigned.

Type B: Model predicts no assignment, but member assigned.

The estimated model produced eight Type A errors and seven Type B errors. Only two of the Type A errors were "serious" in the sense that they predicted a relatively high probability of assignment, yet the member failed to win the transfer. The first involved John Flynt (D., Ga.) who sought an assignment to Appropriations in the Eighty-seventh Congress.[19] Flynt faced no intrazone competition for the slot and, although he did not come from the same state as his zone representative, there was a zone vacancy on Appropriations, his zone was already underrepresented on the committee, external (interzone) competition was only moderate, and he was quite compatible with his zone representative on party matters (neither supported the party more than half the time). The model predicted a probability of .83 that Flynt would win the assignment. In 1961, however, a unique event transpired which interlocked with committee assignments. Prior to the CC deliberations came the classic vote on the temporary expansion of the Rules Committee, a struggle pitting Speaker Rayburn against "Judge" Smith, chairman of the Rules Committee. MacNeil (1963, pp. 440–41) recounts the impact of this event on the committee assignment aspirations of Flynt and others:

> In the final days, there were dark reports of threats coming from both sides to retaliate on party members who voted "wrong." One Rayburn lieutenant approached a freshman Democrat, who had not yet received a committee assignment. He warned him what a "wrong" vote could

mean. "If Rayburn loses this vote," he said, "you can go to 'Judge' Smith for your committee assignment." Rayburn, of course, not Smith, had a controlling voice in such assignments; and the threat was plain. John Flynt of Georgia, who had committed himself to vote with Smith, angrily protested that he had been threatened with a denial of assignment to the House Appropriations Committee, unless he voted with Rayburn. "Without a moment's hesitation," Flynt said, "I sent word that neither Jack Flynt nor Georgia wanted any assignment that badly."

There is a sequel to the story. In 1963 Jack Flynt and the Georgia delegation supported Speaker McCormack on the permanent expansion of the Rules Committee. The payoff: Flynt won assignment to Appropriations and Phil Landrum received the Speaker's endorsement for a seat on Ways and Means.

The remaining serious Type A error involved an attempt by a New Yorker to transfer from Education and Labor to Rules in the Ninety-third Congress. The requester faced no intrazone competition for the slot and shared a state delegation and a comparable policy disposition with his zone representative; but there was no zone vacancy, the zone was modestly overrepresented already, and there was a fair amount of interzone competition for the slot. The model predicted a probability of .76 for successful transfer. Two observations help to explain this error. First, the Rules Committee is the "Speaker's Committee." Rarely is there much relationship between requests for and actual assignments to this committee. Ordinarily, the Speaker coopts a member of his choosing to serve and sends his name on to the CC, which ordinarily honors his request (see Chapter 8). Rarely does the member whom the Speaker taps submit a request formally. Morgan Murphy (D., Ill.), for example, was appointed to the committee in the Ninety-third Congress without actually requesting the transfer. Thus any prediction made by the model about assignment to Rules on the basis of requests probably ought to be discounted.[20] Second, this particular Rules Committee requester was not likely to receive Speaker Albert's endorsement in any event. An extreme liberal and a member of an informal House group that often found itself at odds with the Speaker, this requester lacked the policy orientation and personal demeanor that typifies those who receive the Speaker's support for Rules.

Each of the serious Type A errors, then, involves idiosyncracies that are bound to elude any statistical explanation. The six remaining Type A errors each involved relatively weak predictions, that is, probability of successful transfer ranging between .5 and .6. Additional analysis uncovered no relationships that strongly related to these errors, with the possible exception of the fact that half of them involved exclusive committees.[21]

Similarly, all seven of the Type B errors elude understanding. Only one was "serious." It involved a southerner who successfully won assignment to

Appropriations despite a .93 probability of failure. This congressman had no zone competition, came from the same state delegation as his zone representative, was somewhat more liberal than his zone representative, and came from a zone with no zone vacancies and slight overrepresentation on Appropriations. What most affected the low probability-of-success prediction was the extreme amount of interzone competition for a very limited number of Appropriations seats in the Ninetieth Congress. No requester received a very high probability of success. Perhaps the fact that this requester's zone representative was Wilbur Mills tipped the scales in his favor.[22]

Assignment Success:
A Summing Up

The separate multivariate analyses of freshman assignment success and non-freshman transfer success (as well as the brief treatment of nonfreshman dual-service requests in table 9.18 in note 22) underscore the import of environmental constraints on CC maximizing behavior. Although personal characteristics of requesters have some impact, independently of environmental factors, on the distribution of committee slots (and this impact appears to be somewhat stronger in the case of transfers than in the case of initial assignments), the analyses indicate the considerable extent to which contextual features mesh with the individual objectives of CC members to explain the distribution of committee assignments. While neither of the models is error-free, the performance of each has passed muster according to a number of statistical desiderata, and has actually excelled according to a few.

Despite my best efforts, the statistical analyses have uncovered little evidence of CC discrimination on the basis of personal or ideological criteria. The theory articulated in Chapters 7 and 8 does not anticipate it, and the probit models presented in this chapter find some evidence for it only in the case of nonfreshman transfers (and only at the intrazone nomination stage at that). On the basis of several other observations, however, the feeling may still linger that there are grounds to suspect some sort of "ideological" bias on the part of the Democratic CC.

First, despite evidence to the contrary, the *perception* among Democrats is that freshmen have not been treated all that well by their CC. Asher (1975, p. 219) found that nearly two-thirds of the nonfreshmen Republicans he interviewed in the Ninety-first Congress believed the committee assignments of their freshmen were markedly improving. The same perception was held by less than one-third of the senior Democrats. Asher quotes one liberal western Democrat on the subject: "The Democratic establishment treats freshmen shamefully, while the Republican leadership treats them astutely."

Since Democratic freshmen in recent Congresses have been liberal on the whole, this incorrect perception among senior Democrats may translate into a belief in ideological bias by the CC.[23]

Second, there is the general belief, with some basis in fact, that the "liberal party regulars" who dominate appointments to Ways and Means either do not remain liberal as they rise in the party establishment or retain what become outdated liberal ideas. Allusion was made in Chapter 7 to Al Ullman, who was in the reform wing of his party when he was appointed to Ways and Means in 1961, but is now regarded as rather middle-of-the-road on many policy controversies. Since there is great continuity and longevity of membership on the Ways and Means Committee (and CC), it may be argued or believed that the more senior members of the committee become increasingly less disposed toward some of their newly elected liberals over time.

Third, the rumblings of reform within the Democratic Caucus, which gained momentum in the early 1970s with the creation of the Hansen and Bolling committees, and which culminated in some major revisions of committee assignment practices and other committee-related matters in the beginning of the Ninety-fourth Congress, were aimed to a considerable extent at the Ways and Means Committee. The belief was widespread that the committee's monopoly of committee assignment powers, its jurisdictional control over many salient policy areas (in the fields of energy, health, social security, tax reform, the public debt, and so on), its conservative leadership, and its cautious legislative style (reflected in the absence of any division of labor through subcommittees) constituted major roadblocks for the realization of liberal policy preferences. In the eyes of reformers, the Ways and Means Committee of the early 1970s had become what the Rules Committee of the 1950s had been—an obstructionist force.

Finally, on several occasions a furor has been raised over the committee assignments of highly visible liberals. The most prominent of these involved the recommendation of the CC to assign Representative Shirley Chisholm (D., N.Y.) to the Agriculture Commitee. She refused to accept the assignment, took her complaint to the Caucus, and ultimately forced the CC to reassign her.

In light of these observations and beliefs, one additional effort was undertaken to determine whether quantitative evidence could be uncovered as a foundation for these beliefs. In November 1974, just prior to the Democratic Caucus meeting in which CC functions were removed from the Ways and Means Committee, Common Cause polled all Democrats (including the newly elected freshmen) to determine the extent of the support for the move to strip Ways and Means of its committee assignment tasks. The staff of the CC obtained the results of this poll and a list of those Democrats who went on record as favoring the move to transfer committee assignment tasks to the

Democratic Steering and Policy Committee.[24] They prepared a memorandum for the Ways and Means Democrats summarizing action taken by the CC on the committee assignment requests of all those nonfreshmen who supported this move. I have tabulated these data in table 9.19.

Table 9.19   **The Possibility of CC "Ideological Bias," 86th–93rd Congresses**

	Freshman Requests		Nonfreshman Transfers	
	1st Pref. (N)	No. Pref. (N)	1st Pref. (N)	No Pref. (N)
Members recorded in favor of separating CC functions from Ways and Means	62.3% (69)	21.7% (69)	73.2% (56)	16.0% (56)
Members not recorded as in favor	51.0% (53)	19.0% (53)	42.8% (49)	30.6% (49)

In constructing this table, I restricted attention to those congressmen first elected since the Eighty-sixth Congress who were also members of the Ninety-fourth Congress. I then partitioned them according to whether they went on record or not in support of the move to strip Ways and Means of its CC tasks. Taking those who were recorded as supporting the move as representative of those most likely to have felt frustrated by the institutional power of the Ways and Means Committee, I compared the manner in which their assignment requests were handled by the Ways and Means Democrats to the requests of those not so recorded. These data should lay to rest any objective belief in a CC ideological bias, at least as it pertains to committee assignments. A substantially greater proportion of those who actually *opposed* the Ways and Means Committee received their first-preference freshman requests than those who were not on record against the Committee. The difference is even greater with regard to nonfreshman transfer and dual-service requests. These differences persisted (though cell sizes obviously shrank considerably) when the data were tabulated separately by Congress and by committee sought.

Conclusion

I conclude this chapter with a brief examination of the consequences of CC decisions for the committees themselves. A more detailed discussion of this topic is found in the final chapter.

There can be little doubt that biennial CC decisions have a substantial impact on the committee system. In the Eighty-sixth through Ninety-third Congresses, more than 21% of the Democratic committee slots have been filled by new personnel (see table 9.20).[25] On occasion a majority of the party slots on a committee consists entirely of new personnel, and changes at the subcommittee level, where much of the serious legislative work is done, are even more dramatic.[26]

Table 9.20   **Total Change in Democratic Committee Personnel, 86th–93rd Congresses**

Congress	Number of Newly Filled Democratic Committee Berths[a]	Number as a % of all Democratic Berths
85–86	96	26.3%
86–87	51	14.4
87–88	82	23.2
88–89	120	29.5
89–90	36	10.2
90–91	61	17.1
91–92	88	23.0
92–93	86	22.2

NOTE: Occasionally a party slot is left vacant. This slot is counted in the base for the percentage column, but not as a newly filled berth. Since these berths are ordinarily filled sometime during the Congress in which they are initially left vacant, the measure above actually *underestimates* the percentage of new committee members.

[a] Number of new committee slots—either through replacement of an old member or the creation of a new slot—summed over all standing committees.

The linkage between committee requests and assignments and its variation across committees may be gleaned from table 9.21. The request-assignment linkage varies considerably from committee to committee: 89% of all Armed Services assignments come from the pool of requesters, while none of the HUAC (HISC) assignments are stimulated by requests. On average, 56% of all assignments are nominally stimulated by requests. Since a large proportion of the assignments going to nonfreshman nonrequesters are those that involve the prior agreement or informal request (though not the formal request) of the nonfreshman in question to serve on the committee, it is not inaccurate to say that nearly five-sixths of the actual assignments made by the CC are in response to the preferences of rank-and-file Democrats.

Table 9.21   Disposition of Committee Slots, by Committee, 87th–93rd
                                    Congresses

	Requesters		Nonrequesters	
Committee (N)*	Freshmen	Nonfreshmen	Freshmen	Nonfreshmen
Agriculture (36)	61**	11	14	14
Appropriations (31)	13	48	0	39
Armed Services (28)	53	36	4	7
Banking & Curr. (28)	72	4	21	4
Dist. of Columbia (29)	7	34	11	48
Educ. & Labor (23)	61	13	17	9
Foreign Affairs (19)	31	16	16	37
Gov. Operations (19)	5	32	16	47
House Admin. (16)	0	19	19	63
Interior (42)	43	21	12	24
Interstate (21)	67	14	0	19
Judiciary (21)	72	0	19	10
Mer. Mar. & Fish. (27)	15	26	21	38
P.O. & C.S. (27)	26	4	37	33
Public Works (26)	50	12	19	19
Rules (9)	22	0	0	78
Science & Astro. (34)	41	12	26	21
HUAC (HISC) (6)	0	0	17	83
Veterans' Affairs (22)	19	5	58	18
All Committees	38	18	17	27

* N is the number of slots filled by new committee
personnel.
** Percentage of N.

The data of table 9.21 are reorganized in table 9.22 in order to obtain a
more differentiated view of the request/assignment linkage. *Requester-dominated* committees are those populated by new members drawn chiefly from
the pool of requesters. Most of the major legislative committees fall in this
category. Only Foreign Affairs is missing from the list. In addition, Appropriations and Interior new members are most likely to have requested the committees formally. *Assigned-* and *cooptation-dominated* committees are those on
which nonrequesting freshmen and nonfreshmen, respectively, land assignments. Not surprisingly, Rules and Appropriations assignments are often the
product of "inside jobs." The remaining cooptation-dominated committees
are those nonexclusive committees that serve as second assignments for
nonfreshmen. The assigned-dominated committees are typically minor
committees—the "leftovers" of the committee assignment process. An
occasional semiexclusive committee makes the list (Banking and Currency,
Judiciary, Public Works), often serving as a stepping-stone for transfer for the

Table 9.22   Committee Rank Orderings

Requester-dominated[a]	Assigned-dominated[b]	Cooptation-dominated[c]	Freshman-dominated[d]	Nonfreshman-dominated[e]
Ar. Ser. (89)	Vet. Aff. (58)	HUAC (83)	Bank & Curr. (93)	Approp. (87)
Interstate (81)	P.O.&C.S. (37)	Rules (78)	Judiciary (91)	HUAC (83)
Bank & Curr. (76)	Sci. & Ast. (26)	House Adm. (63)	Educ. & Lab. (78)	D.C. (82)
Educ. & Lab. (74)	Mer. Mar. (21)	D.C. (48)	Vet. Aff. (77)	House Adm. (81)
Judiciary (72)	Bank & Curr. (21)	Gov. Oper. (47)	Agric. (75)	Gov. Oper. (79)
Agriculture (72)	House Adm. (19)	Approp. (39)	Pub. Wks. (69)	Rules (78)
Interior (64)	Judiciary (19)	Mer. Mar. (38)	Sci. & Ast. (67)	Mer. Mar. (64)
Pub. Wks. (62) Approp. (61)	Pub. Wks. (19)	For. Aff. (37)	Interstate (67)	

NOTE: Percentage of assignments for committees in each category is in parenthesis.
[a] Table 9.21, cols. 1 and 2.
[b] Table 9.21, col. 3.
[c] Table 9.21, col. 4.
[d] Table 9.21, cols. 1 and 3.
[e] Table 9.21, cols. 2 and 4.

member to another committee in a later Congress. Finally, the lists of *freshman-* and *nonfreshman-dominated* committees suggest the mutually exclusive quality of CC decisions vis-à-vis freshmen and nonfreshmen *but not in accord with any natural prestige hierarchy.* Freshmen dominate appointments to many of the front-line legislative committees (that is, nonfreshmen rarely transfer to them), while nonfreshmen tend to dominate appointments to the exclusive committees and many of the minor committees.

The picture these data paint of CC decisions and their consequences for the committee system is quite murky. Several features, however, are worth isolating. First, it would appear that many of the minor committees tend to be highly inexpert bodies. Turnover is high; many members receive assignments to them in a dual-service capacity and can be expected to pay relatively little attention to their legislative tasks there; freshmen are typically dragged on board, kicking and screaming, and often leave at their first opportunity; nonfreshmen do not request assignment to these committees (Government Operations is an exception here), and it is not unusual for them to receive such assignments as a sweetener in those instances in which the CC is unable to honor their transfer requests; and they are almost never sought as a member's sole or main assignment.

Second, the linkage between requests and assignments is strongest for most of the substantive legislative committees (that is, semiexclusive committees). Given the already strong link between constituency interests and requests (see Chapter 4), a strong case can be made in these policy areas for what Lowi (1969), Davidson (1975, 1976), and others have called interest-group liberalism, clientelism, "cozy little triangles," and "policy whirlpools" in which the politics of distribution looms large. I shall return to this theme in the last chapter.

Third, assignments to the exclusive committees (Appropriations, Rules, Ways and Means) constitute a unique subprocess of the committee assignment process in which the interest-request-assignment pattern that dominates assignments to the substantive legislative committees does not have as much force. Only for Appropriations may it be said that the request/assignment linkage is a strong one, and even here a substantial number of assignments are prearranged, bypassing normal request channels. Ways and Means assignments, of course, are determined by Caucus election, and Rules assignments are dominated by the preferences of the Speaker.

From these data, then, and the multivariate analyses presented earlier, the following summary conclusions follow. The relationship between requests and the availability of committee slots is the principal link around which actual assignments revolve. This link emerges in its purest form for the major legislative committees (including Interior) where "interested" congressmen submit requests, CC representatives (after resolving intrazone competition) push those requests, and the entire CC responds to the extent that slot availability permits. For the minor, duty committees, deviation from this pattern takes one form; for the exclusive committees it takes another. The minor committees predominate in the cooptation and assigned categories. While requests are generally honored ("interested" congressmen who submit requests usually succeed), there are ordinarily fewer of them than there are available positions. Consequently, members must be induced to serve or, in the case of freshmen, are simply assigned (or the slots remain unfilled). While this is not true for all minor committees (Government Operations has become a genuine exception in recent years), it is the norm. For the exclusive committees, on the other hand, requests play a smaller role, not because of a shortage of members seeking these assignments, but rather because of an abundance of interest by others. Rules, in particular, receives its new assignments at the behest of the Speaker. The Appropriations assignment pattern is closer to that of the main legislative committees (61% of all assignments represent honored requests), but there is a rather large proportion of assignments that are inspired by the initiatives of others.

Part 5

Conclusions

Chapter 10

Conclusions and Implications

The empirical results and propositions of Parts 2, 3, and 4 sustain the view that most of the behavioral aspects of the committee assignment process are accounted for by a rational explanation. Behavior in this institutional context is instrumental: individual objectives evolve; members have the behavioral discretion to act at various stages of the process in accord with their objectives; both the resource base and the behavioral discretion permit an accommodation of member objectives most of the time. In the main, that is, the committee assignment process involves an *interest-advocacy-accommodation syndrome* in which interests are articulated, advanced, and accommodated in a highly institutionalized (almost routinized—see Gertzog 1976) fashion. This concluding chapter draws the empirical results together and permits some more general observations about committees in the House of Representatives.

The Interest-Advocacy-Accommodation Syndrome

Interest

The multivariate statistical models of Chapter 4 strongly demonstrate that interest—albeit in a sophisticated form—stimulates the committee request behavior of rank-and-file members. For reelection purposes, policy interests, or some mix of the two, freshmen seek assignments to those committees in which their constituents have an important stake and toward which their own previous backgrounds predispose them. For all of the major legislative committees (plus Interior), "interest" variables exert a strong independent effect on request likelihood (table 4.6, col. 2). This effect, moreover, is most pronounced in those committees for which the intuitive linkage between committee jurisdiction and constituency-clientele interests is most obvious, e.g., Agriculture. It is least pronounced (though still statistically significant) in those committees with jurisdictions of general interest to many constituencies, e.g., Armed Services and Public Works.

Unadulterated interest is revealed in actual requests for assignment to the minor committees (for which the number of requests was too small to perform a systematic, multivariate analysis). For that limited set of members for whom service on, say, Merchant Marines, District of Columbia, or Post Office is important, interest considerations need not be discounted by expectations of competition for a slot on one of these committees; the normal condition for these committees is one of excess supply of vacancies.

For the prestigious exclusive committees, on the other hand, interest is all but overwhelmed by the low likelihood of assignment success. Although interest in a seat on Appropriations, Rules, or Ways and Means is pervasive, that interest is discounted substantially for most freshmen by the low probability of competing successfully against more senior party colleagues, obtaining the nod of the Speaker, or assembling a majority coalition in the party caucus, respectively. Excess demand for these powerful committees has placed assignments to them out of reach for most freshmen.

For the remaining legislative committees, interest is modified to a significant extent by the probability of assignment success. Table 4.6 (cols. 3 and 4) reveals that the likelihood of the translation of interest in a committee into a request for that committee depends on contextual circumstances—competition from within the state delegation and the presence of state representation already on the committee reduce that likelihood while state vacancies increase it.

Nonfreshman revealed preferences for "queue-switching," too, are fashioned from personal goals. Attempts at queue-switching and/or queue acquisition are widespread, as the data of table 3.10 reveals. Nearly 40% of all new committee berths are nonfreshman-occupied, and most congressmen, given a sufficiently long career, make some effort to improve upon their initial committee portfolios. Most actual transfer activity, as indicated in tables 5.4, 5.5, and 5.6, is explained by changed or frustrated personal goals and altered circumstances. Preferences for transfer to other major (not exclusive) committees are revealed overwhelmingly by those whose freshman requests were not honored. Often they are repeat requests, underscoring the frustration of goals rather than change in goals (also see Gertzog 1976). However, owing to learning, a change in the committee assignment context, and actual changes in personal objectives and interests, goal-seeking nonfreshmen, even those who landed preferred committees as freshmen, alter their committee holdings. Typically, alterations take the form of acquiring a dual-service assignment or transferring to an exclusive committee.

Rank-and-file members are not the only ones whose interests are served in the committee assignment process. In accommodating the interests of the rank-and-file member, party leaders and members of the CC have axes to grind as well. For the party leader, rank-and-file cooperation is rewarded (or encouraged) and deviation occasionally punished by the manipulation of committee assignments (see Westefield 1974). The analysis of committee size expansion in Chapter 6 indicates that rank-and-file requests influence leadership committee structure negotiations (see table 6.9). I argued there that in responding (though not completely) to committee assignment requests by relaxing the scarcity constraints, party leaders attempt to balance competing interests, to appear accommodating, to generate good will and, therefore, to put themselves in a stronger position to hold heterogeneous coalitions together during the legislative sessions. It should also be noted that, in recent years, party leaders have had a direct part (including votes) in CC deliberations, have had their nominees for Rules rubber-stamped by the CC, and are very influential in Caucus-determined assignments to Ways and Means. In sum, committee assignments are a resource, partially controlled by the party leaders, which may be used to serve a variety of their purposes.

Similarly, though probably in a more abstract manner, committee assignments serve the CC member's generalized ambition for influence in the House. Influence derives from the ability of CC members to exercise their discretion on matters of great significance to others. From interviews with a number of Democratic CC members, it appears that they are fully aware of the fact that discretion over the committee assignments of others provides them with an important source of institutional influence. Indeed, for many of them this fact was an important reason for seeking a seat on Ways and Means in the first place. Said an unusually junior member who surprisingly landed a place on the CC, "It was a real political plum for me to go on [the CC]. It's now the power point in the House. It's where the action is. I've been able to cut deals with people I never would have known."

Others, both inside and outside the House, have interests at stake in the deliberations and ultimate decisions of the CC. Some make their presence directly felt on a regular basis.

1. State delegation deans, especially from large states, have an ongoing interest in maintaining delegation strength and representation on a wide range of committees. They often work closely with their zone representative in promoting the candidacies of "their people."

2. Committee chairmen often make their preferences among applicants for their committees known to the CC. Their interests in matters of policy and committee control motivate their efforts to influence the CC.[1]

3. Outside interest groups occasionally seek to obtain assignments for "friendly" congressmen on committees with jurisdiction in their areas of concern. Their activity usually takes the form of "campaigning" in the House in behalf of such members through letters, telephone calls, and personal visits to CC members. An extreme instance is the alleged veto-power of the AFL–CIO over Education and Labor appointments: "I always consult my good friend Andrew Biemiller on Labor committee appointments," McCormack once said publicly to mark his esteem for the AFL–CIO lobbyist (MacNeil 1963, p. 228).

Others, whose direct interests in committee assignments are less regular and enduring, or whose priorities lie elsewhere, make only occasional, unsystematic attempts to affect the CC. Often they work indirectly through the party leadership. Examples include executive interest in stacking the Public Works Committee with pro-St. Lawrence Seaway members in the 1950s, in keeping southerners off the Judiciary Committee in the early 1960s, and in liberalizing the Rules Committee, also in the early 1960s.

The committee assignment process provides many arenas and opportunities for interests to be expressed. Since committees play so decisive a role in setting the legislative agenda in the House, the committee assignment process attracts a variety of advocates—rank-and-file members, party leaders, CC members, delegation deans, committee chairmen, lobbyists, and the executive branch—who seek to have their voices heard and their preferences promoted and protected.

Advocacy

Although the rank-and-file member initiates the process of committee assignments in the sense that he resolves his "value" problem and makes his committee preferences known to the CC, and although he typically engages in a personal lobbying effort to secure a desired committee slot, to a large extent the promotion of his interests is left in the hands of others. His zone representative on the CC (and his delegation dean and other friends to a lesser extent) serves as an advocate for his committee preferences. The advocacy system "works" because of the dovetailing of CC member objectives and resources, on the one hand, and a decision-making procedure conducive to matching assignments to requests, on the other.

The CC member's quest for general institutional influence disposes him to use his discretion over committee assignments instrumentally. A decentralized system of zones, a manageable work load (except under extraordinary circumstances—see table 8.3), high-quality information (request lists and request books), a scarce supply of "high demand" vacancies, a set of party interests requiring responsiveness ("produce an acceptable committee slate"), a personal predilection toward bargaining and horse-trading, and a general desire to appear (as well as to be) influential all work to encourage the advocacy role for the CC member.

First, the *decentralized zone system* allocates individual responsibility. Although CC decisions are committee decisions, successful and unsuccessful sponsorship clearly rests with the respective zone representatives. Each CC member, that is, has a well-defined constituency "out there." Credit-claiming, as Chapters 7 and 8 of this study document, is one of the driving forces of the committee assignment process.

Second, a *manageable work load* for the CC representative permits intensive attention to a reasonably small set of interests. The sifting and sorting that characterize decision-making by the entire CC is writ small within each zone. Advocacy here takes the form of channeling interests so as to reduce intrazone competition (although this is often done at the state delegation level) and then actively pressing these claims on CC resources.[2]

Third, *high-quality information* in the form of precise counts, by committee, of how many people want which committees and how many slots are available reduces the uncertainty of the CC member and permits him to calculate and plan strategy. This information, by stabilizing both the interests he seeks to represent and his expectations about the behavior of other CC members, makes his world somewhat more predictable and, therefore, makes calculated advocacy more productive of the final results he seeks to obtain.

Fourth, *scarcity constraints* that create excess demand for some committees provide the CC with its discretionary influence. They also provide individual advocacy efforts with their payoffs. If conflicts-of-interest were eliminated ahead of time by the relaxation of scarcity constraints, then there would be less incentive for CC members to engage in extensive advocacy efforts. Scarcity sustains advocacy by providing successful advocates with the grounds for claiming credit.

Fifth, *party demands* on the CC to "produce an acceptable slate" insure that the fruits of advocacy and the costs of scarcity are equitably distributed across regions and ideological interests in the congressional party. To some extent these demands put a brake on advocacy in the name of regional and ideological comity.

Finally, the *reputational concerns* of CC members, coupled with their general taste for horse-trading, vote swapping, coalition building, and the politics of quid pro quo, encourage advocacy, while the zone system, with its credit-claiming feature, assures that successful advocacy is recognized and reputations consequently enhanced.

Accommodation   We like to give people committee assignments because
they want them and because it broadens their political
appeal.
Minority Leader Gerald Ford
cited in Davidson [1976]

Most members for most of their careers are on the committees they "want."
Most revealed preferences, that is, are accommodated—if not initially, then
eventually. Gertzog (1976, table 1), for instance, on the basis of interviews
with both Republicans and Democrats who were freshmen in the Eighty-ninth,
Ninetieth, and Ninety-first Congresses, found that while between one-quarter
and one-third of these congressmen's first-preference requests were not
honored when they were freshmen, that proportion had declined to between
14% and 26% by their third year, and to less than 10% by their fifth year
(for those who survived). It is this empirical fact that best describes committee
assignments in the modern House; it is this empirical fact with which any
theory of assignments must be consistent.

The accommodation of member preferences takes place in three stages.
The first—advocacy by zone representatives—has just been discussed. The
second stage involves the response of party leaders to revealed preferences
prior to CC deliberations. The final stage of accommodation occurs during
the decision-making of the CC.

The statistical models estimated in Chapter 6 give support to the accommodation thesis as applied to party leaders in their negotiation of a committee
structure. Table 6.9 strongly confirms this belief—even after the effects of
trend, change in party ratio, vacancies created by the election, and extraordinary minority "needs" are acknowledged, there are strong, independent
effects on changes in committee sizes due to freshman and nonfreshman
demand. Party leaders, as they negotiate a new committee structure, give
significant weight to the wishes of their followers. While the leaders cannot
accommodate follower wishes literally—that is the job of the CC—they can,
and do, relax the scarcity constraint, thereby indirectly assisting members with
their committee assignments.[3]

CC accommodation takes place at several different levels: at the one-on-
one level between a requester and his zone representative, at the zone level,
and at the level of the full CC. In the initial meetings with "his" freshman and
transfer applicants, the zone representative seeks to make their entire gamut
of request activities effective for their goals by enriching their store of information. In assisting them in fleshing out their "value" problem and in attuning
them to constraints already in effect, or likely to be in effect, the CC member
encourages the revelation of sophisticated preferences.

At the zone level, the CC member attempts to encourage a wide distribution
of requests for different committees from the people in his zone. His purpose
here is twofold: (1) at a more basic level, the CC member often finds it

personally useful to have contacts throughout the committee system—hence his preference for wide representation on committees from his zone; (2) in order to reduce conflicts of interest within the zone, which may place him in an awkward position, and/or which may decrease the likelihood that *any* of the requesters in conflict obtain the desired committee, the CC member encourages nonoverlapping requests.

At the full CC level, accommodation of committee requests is seen in its clearest form in the overwhelming proportion of freshmen who obtain a requested committee. In the six Congresses examined in table 9.1, better than eight out of every ten freshmen received some sought-after committee. Had the Ninety-fourth Congress been included (see the Epilogue) that proportion would have arisen still higher. Nearly 60% of the freshmen actually obtained a first-preference request, and it is in the analysis of which freshmen obtained these first-preference committees that some interesting conclusions follow. The results of our analysis permit the following inferences.

1. The intra- and interzone competitive environments are the most important factors in discriminating between successful and unsuccessful applicants; those in the most propitious competitive circumstances are most likely to succeed in landing a first-choice committee.

2. Personal characteristics of freshman requesters play a decidedly secondary role in determining assignment success. The one significant personal characteristic is "predecessor status"—a freshman's probability of landing his first-preference committee is significantly enhanced if his predecessor served on that committee. Of particular interest because of their *lack* of significance are the region and electoral-security variables. While southerners are decidedly less successful in obtaining first-choice committees, it is not because they are southern but rather because they seek committees for which there is extreme competition. Finally, the Masters–Clapp hypothesis that the CC tilts in favor of electorally insecure freshmen may be rejected. Rather it would appear that the higher success rate of marginal freshmen is accounted for by the fact that they seek (or are steered toward) committees for which there is only moderate effective demand relative to the supply of berths.

Our analysis of nonfreshman transfer success permits several additional conclusions.

3. Nonfreshman success, too, is highly dependent on the competitive context, but less so (relative to personal factors) than in the freshman case.

4. Personal and situational factors also play an important role. Coming from the same state as the zone representative, coming from a zone which is not already overrepresented on the committee, and coming from a zone that has recently lost some of its committee representation significantly enhance the likelihood of successful transfer. Interestingly—and in marked contrast to the freshman case—while "party support" does not endear a member with

the CC enough to influence transfer success, the similarity of party support scores between a member and his zone representative does. As in the freshman case, neither region nor electoral security appear to have a significant independent effect on assignment success.

At the level of the full CC, then, the statistical evidence is supportive of the accommodation thesis. Despite the logistical and analytical difficulties of matching assignments to requests (see the appendix to Chapter 8 and Shepsle [1973, 1975a, 1975b]), the statistical evidence portrays a CC that responds favorably to requests, restrained only by scarcity constraints.

At every stage of the committee assignment process, then, from the assistance given the freshman in fleshing out his "value" problem, to zone representative advocacy in behalf of revealed preferences, to leadership responsiveness in relaxing scarcity constraints, to the intrazone resolution of conflicts of interest, to the final decisions of the CC, there is an effort to fit the pieces of the giant jigsaw puzzle together in a responsive fashion. The matching of assignments to requests, constrained only by scarcity, is both a guiding principle and an accurate description of the committee assignment process.

The Interest-Advocacy-Accommodation Syndrome Across Committees and Over Time

Across Committees

The interest-advocacy-accommodation syndrome is most apparent (because it appears in its purest form) in assignments to the main-line legislative committees. Probability-discounted interest is strongly revealed in the freshman request data analyzed in Chapter 4. The summary of hypothesis tests in table 4.6 confirms that "value" considerations loom large in a freshman's request calculus (col. 2), but that discounting because of the competitive environment modifies those value considerations (col. 4). Evidence for the role of value considerations is weakest for the two "pork barrel" committees—Armed Services and Public Works. Although this conclusion is surprising initially, a little reflection suggests, not that "interest" is unimportant for these committees, but rather that *current* constituency and personal background factors do not discriminate between requesters and nonrequesters as well as they do for other committees. Value calculations for the remaining legislative committees (including Interior) are uniformly evident. Probability-discounting, on the other hand, is strongly indicated for all committees except Education and Labor.

Interest calculations are revealed in transfer requests to semiexclusive committees, as well, which tend to come overwhelmingly from those who were not pleased with their freshman assignments. Nearly three-quarters of these transfer requests come from those who did not obtain their freshman first-preference, and three-quarters of those were from members who obtained *no* requested committee as freshmen. Many of these requests repeated un-honored freshman requests, and they typically involved Armed Services, Foreign Affairs, or Interstate. Thus, interest prevails here as well, though probability-discounting does not. And for good reason! For the nonfreshman, requests are not the same scarce resource they are for freshmen. There is no reason for the transfer applicant to reveal other than an honest preference for some committee he prefers to his current holding. However, if he is sufficiently desperate, he will either provide the CC with several "degrees of freedom" or take the competitive situation into account. Thus, for the member who received *no* freshman requests, the likelihood of submitting a slightly longer transfer request list and not including an exclusive committee on that list is markedly higher than for his "wealthier" colleagues.

Whereas the *value* imputed to a committee and the *likelihood* of obtaining a requested committee (discount factor) contribute in similar proportion to revealed preferences for assignment to one of the semiexclusive committees (plus Interior), discounting all but overwhelms value calculations for exclusive committees and is all but irrelevant for assignment to minor committees. Hence neither group is well represented in the "requester-dominated" category of table 9.22. The former committees tend to be populated by "non-freshman coopteds" while the latter are dominated by "freshman assigneds."

Advocacy by the CC members, like interest, varies across committees in expected ways. Again like interest, it manifests itself in its purest form in the assignments to the main substantive committees. These committees are "requester-dominated" (see table 9.22) in two senses: assignments to them come chiefly from requesters, and the number of requesters exceeds the number of available berths. The role played by the CC member in pushing his candidates and making the trades that produce their election is pivotal. In assignments to neither exclusive nor nonexclusive committees does the CC member play the same uniquely pivotal role. In the former case, though advocacy can be important, it is usually the activities of others in the House that are more crucial:

1. the CC plays no direct role in the appointment of Ways and Means members—they are chosen by the Caucus;
2. the CC "rubber stamps" the Speaker's preference for Rules appointments; and
3. though the CC member's advocacy plays a more instrumental role in Appropriations assignments as compared to other exclusive committees, it is nevertheless the case that the role of "interested others"—

party leaders and state delegations, chiefly—takes on added importance here.

In the case of nonexclusive committees, excess supply reduces the import of
CC advocacy, at least for freshmen. In obtaining second assignments for
nonfreshmen, however, CC members do play a more central part.

Variations across committees in accommodating requests are detected in
the decisions of party leaders in negotiating a committee structure and in the
committee assignment decisions of the CC. Exclusive committees are rarely
increased in size, and when they are it constitutes an event of great political
import.[4] The nonexclusive committees are increased more than twice as
frequently—nearly 30% of the time—but they are also decreased in size on
occasion. Since the Legislative Reorganization Act of 1946, contractions in
committee size are associated, when they occur, about 75% of the time with
nonexclusive committees. Semiexclusive committees are expanded at about
four times the rate of exclusive committees.[5] Table 6.9 strongly supports the
accommodation thesis for this latter class of committees. Party leaders make
their structure negotiation decisions with an eye to accommodating freshman
and nonfreshman demand on the one hand, and minority "needs" on the
other. Finally, there is some slight indication that party leaders' responses to
demands to relax the scarcity constraints on committees vary according to the
"rent-producing" capacity of committees. Leaders appear to be less responsive
to demand for the high-rent committees, thereby accommodating the desires
of the currently advantaged not to have their monopoly rents dissipated.

CC accommodation differences across committees derive mainly from
factors exogenous to their deliberations. For both freshman and nonfreshman assignments, competition per vacancy is the key factor. And this factor
depends upon the requests submitted by rank-and-file members and the
vacancies generated by leadership structure decisions. Given these constraints,
the CC accommodates the requests of freshmen at an 83% rate (see table 9.1)
and nonfreshman transfers at nearly a 65% rate (see table 9.18). Moreover,
when the CC must pick and choose among competing requesters, it picks and
chooses in a fairly predictable fashion, discriminating (usually) neither on
idiosyncratic personal factors nor seniority but rather on the basis of how
easy it is to take care of "losers" in some other fashion. There appear to be
few differences across committees in CC accommodation behavior, over and
above the exogenous effects of supply and demand. Rather, the main variations
appear over time, my next topic.

Over Time

Because of the relatively short time period to which the empirical side of this
study has been restricted (1958–74), there has been little opportunity to do

more than glimpse at the "over time" changes in the interest-advocacy-accommodation syndrome. Nevertheless, some changes in patterns are apparent.

Overall, requests for most committees have not varied significantly over time. For three committees, however, a shift in demand has occurred. In the case of Interstate, which has always been a popular committee, that popularity has grown. This growth in requests probably reflects the growing importance of the jurisdiction of the Commerce Committee to a wider set of constituencies. To some extent the same is true of the Interior Committee, where the composition of requests, if not total demand, has changed. Since the Ninetieth Congress, there has been some growth of interest from non-westerners with the growing salience of environmental issues. Perhaps the most striking demand shift over time is found in the boom-and-bust pattern of the Science and Astronautics Committee. During the 1960s there was considerable interest in the committee. With a shift in budget and policy priorities at the end of that decade, interest in the committee dried up. Indeed, there was a substantial egress from the committee. Since it has been reclassified as a minor committee, making it possible for a member of this committee to sit on another semi-exclusive committee as well, interest has again picked up somewhat.

Beyond the most casual empiricism, little analysis of the changes over time in requests for committee assignments has been conducted. Future inquiries on this subject should attend to the crucial link between member goals and committees as instruments for the realization of these goals. This entails an examination of changes in member orientation—for example, toward a more conscious desire for influence in policy-making (see Mayhew [1974] and Bullock [1973b]); changes in the salience of committee jurisdictions—for example, the growing interest in the Interior Committee's jurisdiction over some environmental issues; actual changes in committee jurisdiction—for example, consolidating most transportation matters in Public Works or placing authority over general revenue-sharing in the Government Operations Committee; as well as structural changes in the rules classifying committees and governing dual assignments—for example, the demotions of Post Office and Science to nonexclusive status. That is, on the basis of the propositions established in this study, it is anticipated that changes in the demand for assignments to particular committees, over and above those that derive from changes on the supply side, depend on changes in member goals and/or changes in the instrumental value of committee vis-à-vis those goals.

Changes over time in the advocacy behavior of the CC have been relatively invisible not necessarily because they have not taken place but rather because CC behavior, itself, is not directly observable. When the findings of this study are compared with the earlier observations and speculations of Masters (1961), Clapp (1964), and Goodwin (1970), it appears that the 1960s and early 1970s have witnessed a growth in the CC's autonomy, as the influence of party leaders and other power centers in the House over committee assignments has declined. CC advocacy, that is, has grown in importance during the period of this study as compared to the period studied by Clapp, Goodwin, and Masters. The CC during the Rayburn years seemed to be much more responsive to the Speaker's wishes, perhaps because that Speaker sought to assert himself more than recent Speakers or because that Speaker's personal retinue included a number of Ways and Means Democrats. In order to reestablish the influence of party leaders on committee assignments, the Democratic Caucus has made two recent structural changes. In 1973, the Speaker, majority leader, and Caucus chairman were added to the CC as voting members. In 1975, committee assignment duties were shifted to the Speaker-dominated Steering and Policy Committee. Now, according to a member of the CC in 1975, "if [Speaker] Albert or [Majority Leader] O'Neill spoke up in behalf of a nominee, he had it greased!"

The empirical analysis gives indication of a noticeable secular trend in the accommodation of committee requests. Committee assignments per member have risen from nearly 1.3 slots in 1959 to better than 1.6 slots in 1975. The proportion of eligible freshmen (those not on an exclusive committee) with second assignments has risen smoothly from .187 to .779 during that period; the comparable figures for nonfreshmen are .367 and .860. There is a final piece of evidence: party leaders have been increasing continuously over time the stock of vacancies from which the CC allocates assignments. By relaxing scarcity constraints as a matter of general practice over time, party leaders have made it easier for the CC to honor requests. Indeed, one scholar (Gertzog 1976) has recently noted that the honoring of requests has become almost routine in the last few years.

The assignment data of table 9.1 support this observation. While the proportion of freshmen receiving no requested committee has remained in the 10%–20% range, the proportion obtaining a first-preference committee has risen from about half to nearly three-fourths. In the Ninety-fourth Congress, nearly every freshman received some requested committee, and nearly every nonfreshman transfer request (save Ways and Means) was honored (see the Epilogue). Accommodation of requests by the CC has increased over time, not because of a change in attitudes or motivations of CC members, but because binding scarcity constraints have been relaxed over time. This is most apparent in the Ninety-fourth Congress in which the Democratic Caucus passed a "two-thirds plus one" rule requiring that all committees have Democratic majorities of at least two-thirds plus one. This resulted in the creation of a large number of new seats on most committees. As the director of the Ways and Means staff noted, "The task before the CC is an easy one when there is a major expansion of the party's fortunes.... Then you can get

anybody pretty much what they want since committee sizes are increased."
The Democratic CC has been a mutual admiration society all along, as the
description in Chapters 7 and 8 suggests. Their objectives have become easier
to achieve over the years because, thanks to party leaders, scarcity has become
less of a problem.

**Committee Assignment
Practices and the
Functioning of the
Committee System**

To this point my concluding comments have focused on the committee
assignment process, itself, and the consequences of the interest-advocacy-
accommodation syndrome for actual committee assignments. In this and the
next section a wider focus is sought. Committee assignment politics is one of
the pressure points of the House precisely because its ramifications have a
ripple effect on a wider set of phenomena. The consequences of committee
assignment politics cannot be sealed off from the wider net of institutional
and interinstitutional politics. The purpose of this section is to examine the
impact of the interest-advocacy-accommodation syndrome on the management of the committee system, clientele politics, legislative innovation,
legislative oversight, and committee representativeness. Since these topics
require (and have received) monographic treatments of their own, the
discussions that follow are no match for the complexity of the subjects. What
these discussions should demonstrate, however, are the prospects for cumu-
lativeness where the analysis of one aspect of institutional life sheds light on
and stimulates research questions about other institutional phenomena.

*Management of the
Committee System*

The interest-advocacy-accommodation syndrome, while serving the objectives
of relevant actors, has a number of unintended or unexpected side effects. To
oversimplify, they entail time and complexity problems for members and
scheduling, synchronization, and jurisdiction problems for leaders. These
problems do not yield easily to simple "reforms" and, like the other topics
examined in this section, are best understood as concomitants of an arrangement that has evolved to handle a more basic interest aggregation; they are
the costs that must be borne in order to realize other objectives.

Coordination, at both the individual and the "system" level, is complicated
by the interest-advocacy-accommodation syndrome. In the words of one

congressional scholar, Nelson Polsby, in his testimony before the Bolling Committee:

> To my mind, the most difficult organizational problem faced by this Committee is to reconcile the clear and overwhelming advantages of decentralization of responsibility in the House structure with the necessity for coordination. [*Panel Discussions*, 1973, p. 10]

For the individual congressman, his committee activities impose upon his time and other resources. While many of these activities are directly useful for serving constituents back home, for taking an active role in the policy process, and for cultivating influence within the House, there is much time- and staff-consuming drudgery—attending hearings, reading committee reports, reading agency reports. To the member these activities often do not appear to serve any of his more immediate objectives. The effects of committee assignment practices on individual member's allocation problems are several. When members are assigned to committees they perceive as useful to their career objectives, the likelihood is enhanced that the members will allocate their scarce resources—principally time and staff—to committee-related activities. Conversely, members assigned to committees whose activities do not mesh well with their individual goals are likely to shift resources at their disposal to activities unrelated to committee work. The increased accommodation of committee requests witnessed in recent years should be accompanied by an increased conscientiousness, on average, in the performance of committee work, not because congressmen have discovered how to be good public servants but because "public service" is a by-product of a more narrow, goal-seeking self-interest that is served by committee work. However, because accommodation has been uneven—across members and across committees—its effects are likely to be uneven. In particular, the following hypotheses may be derived from this line of reasoning.

1. Members whose committee requests have been honored by the CC are expected, ceteris paribus, to allocate a greater proportion of scarce resources at their disposal to committee-related activities than those assigned to unrequested committees.

2. Committees composed chiefly of requesters are likely to have fuller participation in their activities than are those committees populated by "coopted" and "assigned" members, ceteris paribus.

The ceteris paribus condition is important, for many other secular changes have accompanied the increased accommodation of committee requests. Great care in research design will be required to untangle the effects expected in these hypotheses from other changes. One which can be underscored here might be labeled the "too much of a good thing" condition. Not only has the CC been receptive to freshman and nonfreshman major assignment requests, it has responded to requests for *second* assignments as well. As has been noted (see table 6.7), 78% of the eligible freshmen in the Ninety-fourth Congress had second assignments; the same was true of 86% of the nonfreshmen. Comparable figures hold for the minority members so that, with the general growth in committee assignments per member, there has been an exploding growth of committee-based responsibilities per member. This fact may confound the effect specified in the second hypothesis above because those who *did* request a committee as a second assignment will nevertheless find their resource base sorely tried. A number of minor committees, then, may be plagued by inadequate participation, unequal work load shares, and domination by a small minority for whom the committee's business is especially important. Ogul (1976, pp. 59ff, 182) provides some evidence of this effect for the Post Office Committee.

If the multiplying committee-based obligations of the individual member as a consequence of CC accommodation pose difficult allocation problems for him, then the allocation and coordination problems of party leaders are at least as complicated. The majority party leadership has broad responsibilities for overseeing the flow of legislation—from the initial assignment of bills to committee, to the loose coordination of their progress (from hearings through markup) with the activities of other committees, to the scheduling of committee products for House action. The growth of the committee-based responsibilities of members, coupled with the increased decentralization of decision-making via subcommittees, and the growth in the sheer magnitude of the legislative task, has created jurisdictional conflicts, scheduling problems, and, consequently, legislative logjams.

The Bolling Committee hearings are sprinkled with references to these coordination problems, assigning responsibility to two principal factors: (1) overlapping and disintegrated committee jurisdictions; (2) overextended committee obligations of rank-and-file members.

In large measure these problems are the result of short-term accommodation decisions made by the party leadership (see Chapter 6 and Westefield 1974). The Bolling Committee solution, a solution rejected by the Democratic Caucus in 1974, involved reducing the number of committees, reorganizing their jurisdictions along functional lines, and restricting the number of assignments a member could hold (a so-called "modified one-track system"—see Peabody 1973).

Since the Legislative Reorganization Act of 1946, the House has witnessed a number of changes which have caused difficulties for the smooth functioning of the committee system. The most important of these has been the rapid and uneven growth in the public sector; the categories of public policy that underlie the current jurisdictions of committees are now more than thirty years out of date. The congressional response to this change has been slow, limited, and unsystematic. The "Congressional response to the twentieth century," to use Huntingdon's (1965) phrase, is the response typical of most social and political institutions wedded to an out-of-date status quo. Aiding and abetting this institutional sluggishness is a committee assignment process that encourages members to behave "myopically" vis-à-vis this relatively fixed set of jurisdictional arrangements and leaders to accommodate their wishes. Each behavioral response has its roots in the 1910 revolt against Speaker Cannon that produced a leader-follower relationship in the House in which exchange replaced, or at least constrained, authority. The long-run impact of a leadership tied to its followers by exchange, followers concerned with cultivating the independence with which to exercise individual discretion, and leaders consequently accommodating that concern by assigning members to committees they seek, is a membership whose interests are ill-served by large-scale institutional rearrangements. Exogenous change takes its toll through institutional friction, and the institution's response is only partial and limited until infused with new personnel less committed to an outdated status quo.[6]

The "Cozy Little Triangle" Problem

In his book *The Political Process: Executive Bureau-Legislative Committee Relations*, Freeman (1965) focused attention on a "pluralistic leviathan," a governmental arrangement in which policy emerged from interactions within subgovernments. Subgovernments, inhabited by executive agency decision-makers, interest-group lobbyists, and members of relevant congressional committees and subcommittees, are arenas in which specialized policy is hammered out by "interesteds." "The leading members of these subunits are the major, constant participants in a process through which special issues are discussed and policy solutions are formed" (Freeman 1965, p. 120). Subgovernment policy solutions are often decisive, even though their effects are felt beyond the subgovernment, because "the multiplicity of types of special groups of people promoting and defending particular values in American life results in selective concentration of public interest and attention in politics" (Freeman 1965, pp. 119–20). According to this view, then, policy demands are processed in a routinized fashion by subgovernments of "interesteds"; the policy solutions that emerge from their interactions are ordinarily decisive since access to the subgovernment and challenges to its decisions are discouraged both by the current participants in the subgovernment and by the extraordinary costs of entry.

The subgovernment focus of Freeman, complementing studies of a similar nature by Cater (1964) and Griffith (1961), has received some recent attention by congressional scholars under various guises—clientelism, interest-group liberalism, policy whirlpools, reciprocal noninterference, the "unholy trinity," and "cozy little triangles."[7] As Davidson (1976, pp. 1–2) notes:

> The organizational features of Congress—in particular, its accessibility to outside influences, its weak central leadership, its decentralization, its bargaining ethos, and its norm of specialization and reciprocity—form an ideal setting for the conduct of clientele politics.

In the House, in particular, where committees play a much more conclusive role in insulating policy agendas, interesteds gravitate to appropriate committee and subcommittee arenas to influence policy. Davidson (1974, pp. 2–3) continues:

> If it is true that war is too important to be left to generals, it follows equally that it is unwise to leave agricultural policy to the farmers, banking regulation to the bankers, communications policy to the broadcasters, or environmental protection to the environmentalists. Yet this is what frequently passes for representative policy making [in the House].

The committee assignment process described in this book conspires with other factors—the career orientation of congressmen, weak party and House leadership, the seniority system, and reliance on committees as the principal gatekeepers for the House—to keep subgovernments in business. The accommodation of interests at the stage in which members seek committee assignments is the necessary first step in the creation of enduring relationships among legislators, lobbyists, and agency personnel in particular policy areas. A reelection-oriented legislator, on a committee in which he may preserve or promote projects and interests in his district, is in a position to collaborate with interest groups and agency bureaucrats. In exchange for lobbying/bill drafting services, research, and campaign contributions from interest groups, and the expediting services for district projects and interests by agency personnel, the strategically located legislator provides "good public policy" for the former and authorizations and appropriations for the latter.

References to clientelism and the support it receives from the process by which committee assignments are allocated are found throughout the hearings of the Bolling Committee (see *Panel Discussions*, 1973). Perhaps the most radical reform recommended by that committee, a reform that accepted the interest-advocacy-accommodation syndrome as a given, was one that would have created a limited number of broad-jurisdiction committees. The intent was to institutionalize *intra*committee conflict, to bring the glare of publicity to extant clientele relationships, and therefore to remove debates over national priorities from the subgovernment arena. "A reshuffling of jurisdictions, in other words, would 'unplug the wires' that bind the cozy triangles together" (Davidson 1976, p. 20). But would it? Limited experience with jurisdictional changes along the lines proposed by the Bolling Committee suggests not.

Ornstein and Rohde (1976, pp. 39–40), for example, note that clientelism in agricultural policy has not been altered by an expansion of the Agriculture Committee's jurisdiction to include consumer interests:

> The lack of a major urban or consumer focus on agricultural policy is ... related to the nature of subcommittee assignments on Agriculture. Through a process of *self-selection*, the few urban-oriented members ... have avoided the commodity subcommittees and have chosen operational subcommittees like Domestic Marketing and Consumer Relations for their first assignment option and their major time commitment. Thus the agricultural legislation which goes through the commodity subcommittees remains dominated by legislators who represent particular commodity interests. [Emphasis added.]

Intracommittee comity and "cozy little triangles" may persist in the face of jurisdictional devices aimed at mitigating their effects by the same self-selection and interest accommodation that have characterized committee assignments in the first place.

Committee assignments are, on the legislative side, at the root of the "cozy little triangle" problem. A system that permits "interesteds" to gravitate to decision arenas in which their interests are promoted provides the fertile environment in which clientelism flourishes. Short of total disruption of current committee assignment practices (in which case clientelism would probably emerge in some other guise), cozy little triangles are likely to dominate the policy process. The interest-advocacy-accommodation syndrome provides the legislative underpinnings for these relationships.

Policy Innovation

Writing in 1970 when discussions of the decline of Congress were the vogue, Moe and Teel (1970, p. 462) found that "Congress continues to be an active innovator and very much in the legislative business." They examined case histories of laws over a twenty-seven-year period (1940–67), updating an early study by Chamberlain, and discovered that the Congresses of the late 1960s retained a central place in the policy-formation process:

> Congress provides innovation in policy through "successive limited comparisons." As an institution Congress shies away from an architectonic role and prefers its public policy interventions to be corrective and supplemental. Its decentralized committee system permits it to be simultaneously involved in many policy fields and to develop the expertise necessary to compete with the bureaucracy.

In rejecting Huntington's (1965) "decline of Congress" thesis, Moe and Teel nevertheless acknowledged the limited nature of congressional policy innovation. Except on rare occasions, congressional innovations were limited and incremental, and often were responses to or alterations of executive initiatives.

Recently, scholars of both the House and the Senate have discovered a more substantial impact on policy from the Congress.[8] Price (1972, p. 322), for example, sees "policy entrepreneurship" in the Congress as a more frequent phenomenon: "initiatives taken [are] best seen not as a response to group demands but as an anticipation or projection of group interests and a stimulation of their active concern." Similarly, Ornstein and Rohde (1976, p. 74) note an increasing activism by House committees and subcommittees:

> the 94th Congress has seen an increasing aggressiveness by Congress toward the Executive, and a correspondingly greater friction between the two branches. . . . [A]ctivist subcommittee chairmen, unleashed by reforms [of the past six years], have investigated federal agencies like the IRS, the Federal Reserve Board, the CIA, and the Federal Trade Commission; subpoenaed executive and Presidential documents; and moved to cite a number of cabinet members for contempt of Congress. Recent congressional activity and aggressiveness has been particularly marked in foreign affairs, where the House's role has traditionally been weak.

Finally, Dodd and Shipley (1975, pp. 21–31) find not only that the volume of committee hearings has generally increased in the post-war period (1947–70), especially for committees with domestic policy jurisdictions, but also that the focus of these hearings has been overwhelmingly programmatic rather than agency-oriented.

Why, in recent years, has the Congress taken on a more active policy-innovation role, a role previously assumed principally by the executive branch? There are several factors at work. First, congressional resources have greatly expanded over the past thirty years. Once referred to as the "broken branch" and the "sapless branch," the Congress was recently termed "the bloated branch."[9] Allowances for staff, travel, stationery, office space, computer facilities, and general operation have increased dramatically. A second kind of resource has also increased substantially—committee positions generally and subcommittee chairmanships in particular. At this writing nearly one of every two majority party members holds a party or committee leadership position.

Increasing the resources that may be employed for policy innovation purposes does not, of course, insure that they will be used in those ways. There are substitution as well as income effects from resource expansions. If the objectives of congressmen differ from those which motivated the resource expansion, and if the resources are fungible and hence can be substituted for other purposes, then it is likely that some of those resources will be siphoned off for those other purposes. Indeed, for years increases in committee staffs and budgets were earmarked for oversight with little apparent effect (see the next section).

Three additional factors, however, have combined to produce a congressional interest in policy in the last few years. First, divided leadership has provided congressional Democrats with the opportunity (not always seized) to be the chief spokesmen for the congeries of interests that seeks refuge in federal largesse. As well, there is the strong electoral incentive to play the "credit-claiming—position-taking" game by charting a set of policy directions distinct from those of the executive branch.

Second, as Bullock (1973b) has discovered, congressmen increasingly are giving policy rationales for their committee assignment requests. In Chapter 3 it was argued that a new interest in policy innovation does not imply a changed motivational structure—congressmen, especially freshmen, are still seelection-oriented. What it does suggest, though, is the increased utility of the policy role for the pursuit of reelection. With the increased decentralization of the committee system, the opportunity to mold policy and to claim credit credibly for the results has been enhanced. Congressional motivations, namely seelection, have not changed; rather, instrumental rationality in pursuit of that objective has promoted policy activity.

Third, with the increased responsiveness of the CC to committee assignment requests, congressional committees (and subcommittees), especially the main authorizing committees, are dominated by "interesteds." As a consequence, reelection activities and policy interests are happily married. Ornstein and Rohde (1976, pp. 75–76) conclude:

> With more congressmen in positions to have an effect on public policy, as subcommittee chairmanships have expanded in number and in influence, policy innovation has become more likely in a number of different areas, including consumer affairs, environmental protection, and mass transportation. The House may well become a major congressional *incubator* of policy initiatives in the society, a role which, until now, has been played much more frequently by the Senate.

Policy activity, according to most observers, has increased in the Congress. The net product of this increased activity, however, is often stagnation, not from failure of intent or effort but from failure of coordination. With the increased decentralization of congressional structure, which has multiplied the opportunities of rank-and-file members for policy innovation, has come an often bizarre combination of jurisdictional arrangements. The inability to coordinate across jurisdictional bailiwicks has produced frustration, despite the increased effort and resources devoted to policy initiative. The accommodation of member interests, through decentralization and the honoring of committee assignment requests, has produced (with exceptions, of course) private success and collective failure. Thus, the reputation of the Congress continues to decline in public opinion polls and, at election time, members "run for Congress by running against Congress" (Fenno, 1972).

Oversight

[*Congressman Dave*] *Martin*: I would like to throw out this thought, if I might. We have found in the course of hearings . . . that there is a great weakness among many committees with regard to oversight, oversight being the follow through on programs in which the committee has enacted the legislation. They are not following through with the reports from downtown as to how that particular program is operating. Do you have any suggestions as to how we can improve this committee problem?

[*Professor John*] *Bibby*: Mr. Martin, I think this is a matter of incentive. The regularization of oversight will not take place until the Members think it is worth their while to invest time, staff, and other resources in it. . . . It is the political incentive, I think, that counts.
Panel Discussions (1973, 2:14–15)

From among twenty-three Congressmen interviewed on this issue all but three indicated they considered committee review of agency activity a time-expensive, low priority concern except when there was likely to be something "big" in it.
Scher (1963, p. 532)

Oversight is often shunned not only because it is regarded as unglamorous and unrewarding, but because it may be antithetical to committee norms and interpersonal comity within the House.
Davidson (1976, p. 6)

Since the Legislative Reorganization Act of 1946 enjoined congressional committees to engage in "continuous watchfulness" of executive agencies and programs, legislative oversight has been the banner around which numerous reformers have rallied. Some have seen in it the means by which the legislative branch could reassert its coequal status with the executive branch. Others regard it as a way to keep an extended bureaucracy in check. Still others conceive of it as a device with which to prosecute policy partisanship in an era of divided national leadership. Whatever the purpose, if the Bolling Committee hearings are indicative, many believe that "continuous watchfulness" is not being adequately maintained.

Four factors account for the general impression that the Congress has failed in its oversight mission: resource inadequacy, lack of will, malcoordination, and misidentification.

1. Resource inadequacy. Since the LRA of 1946 (PL 79–601), four additional pieces of legislation have provided committees with the resources— legal authority, staff, money—with which to perform oversight: the

Intergovernmental Cooperation Act of 1968 (PL 90–577), the Legislative Reorganization Act of 1970 (PL 91–510), the Congressional Budget and Impoundment Control Act of 1974 (PL 93–344), and the Committee Reform Amendments of 1974 (H. Res. 988). These pieces of legislation, together with budget authorizations and appropriations, have provided individual committees, as well as the parent House, with such considerable resources that one scholar could conclude in 1973:

> Legal authority, staff, and money are all important prerequisites to congressional action, but none of these are grossly lacking now. Genuflections before the trilogy of authority, money, and staff do not reach the basic problem. [Ogul 1973, p. 706][10]

The definition, of course, of "continuous watchfulness" is problematic, so that what constitutes "adequate resources" is difficult to determine. For those who believe, however, that resources, "are not grossly lacking now," it is evident that their concern is not with the adequacy of current resources but rather with their utilization.

One of the "basic problems" to which Ogul alludes follows from the multiple uses to which oversight resources may be put. Consider the subcommittee chairman authorized to hire staff. In addition to oversight activities for the subcommittee, these staff people can be assigned to other tasks, e.g., personal casework for the subcommittee chairman. The subcommittee chairman allocates man-hours of staff time in accord with his preferences for different mixes of casework and oversight activity. In figure 10.1 his preferences, given by the indifference contour II, and the resource constraint on total man-hours available, given by the solid line, dictate the choice of the point x, providing x_1 man-hours of oversight activity and x_2 man-hours of casework for the chairman's constituents.

In figure 10.2 the effects of an expansion in resource endowment are displayed, where there is no effective means by which to supervise how the chairman assigns the new staff to activities. The new equilibrium, x', entails increases in both oversight (x_1') and casework (x_2'). Thus, legislation endowing subcommittees with additional resources for oversight, but lacking mechanisms to insure they will be invested in oversight, are likely to witness those resources (partially) siphoned off for other purposes.

This same effect will be observed, though its magnitude damped, in the event there is some way to "earmark" the resource expansion for oversight purposes. This is shown in figure 10.3. The resource expansion in this figure is earmarked so that the maximum amount of casework activity is unchanged from the initial resource constraint. The maximum amount of oversight activity possible, however, has been increased. Nevertheless, notice that in the new equilibrium, x^*, both oversight (x_1^*) and casework (x_2^*) activities have

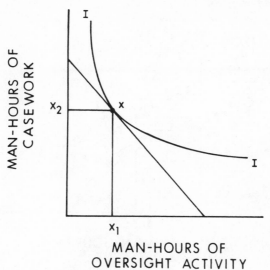

Fig. 10.1   Allocation of subcommittee staff man-hours: mix of
casework and oversight activity.

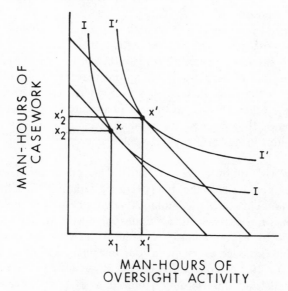

Fig. 10.2   Allocation of subcommittee staff man-hours: effect
of an expansion in resource endowment.

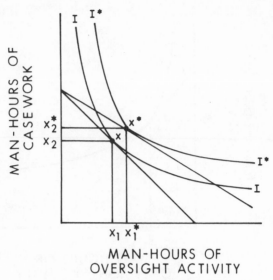

MAN-HOURS OF
OVERSIGHT ACTIVITY

Fig. 10.3   Allocation of subcommittee staff man-hours: effect of
an earmarked expansion in resource endowment.

increased. In effect, the subcommittee chairman has siphoned off some of the
"unearmarked" man-hours, previously allocated to oversight, for his own
casework purposes.

The point of these illustrations is that it is difficult to build walls around
multiple-purpose resources. To the extent that it is costly or otherwise
infeasible to monitor resource use, even if there is in-principle earmarking for
particular legislative purposes, it will appear that the resources available are
inadequate to the task. In fact, it is the preferences for various mixes of
oversight and other activities of those who allocate the resources, and the de
facto discretion they possess, that produces seemingly suboptimal oversight.
"It is," to quote Professor Bibby, "the political incentive, I think, that counts."

2. Lack of will. Bibby (1973, p. 532), in his presentation to the Bolling
Committee, noted that "the 1946 Reorganization Act's admonition that
committees should exercise 'continuous watchfulness' of agencies under their
jurisdiction is not self-executing." Endowing an institution whose members
lack the will to be continuously watchful with oversight resources will not
automatically produce oversight (as our imaginary subcommittee chairman
of figures 10.1–10.3 demonstrates). Oversight, according to some observers, is
"unglamorous and unrewarding"; indeed, it is often offensive to fellow
congressmen and the cozy little triangles in which they are enmeshed. Nevertheless, the Ninety-fourth Congress has witnessed some aggressive oversight

by a number of subcommittees.[11] Several factors that are at work here suggest some conditions under which tradeoffs in favor of oversight are forthcoming.[12]

First, personnel changes in the House, beginning dramatically in the Eighty-ninth Congress and continuing throughout the late 1960s and early 1970s, have infused the majority party with a vocal activist contingent. The attrition of conservative Democrats and all shades of Republicans has resulted in a large contingent of more activist Democrats. Many of these new congressmen have survived later elections and, through the inexorable workings of the seniority system, moved to high positions in committee and subcommittee queues. Bob Bergland (D., Minn.), for example, was first elected to the Ninety-second Congress in 1970, defeating the ultraconservative Odie Langen (R., Minn.). Assigned to the Agriculture Committee, Bergland had become, by the Ninety-fourth Congress, thanks to the retirement of a number of southerners ahead of him on the committee, the ninth-ranking Democrat on the full committee and the chairman of the Conservation and Credit Subcommittee. The effect is described by Ornstein and Rohde (1976, p. 37):

> the only subcommittee [of Agriculture] which has experienced a marked increase in activity is Conservation and Credit, which went from four meetings and hearings in the first part of the 93rd Congress to fifteen in the first part of the 94th. The replacement of Robert Poage as subcommittee chairman by Robert Bergland . . . is the apparent cause of this upsurge in activity. The Conservation and Credit meetings and hearings in the Congress have been on a wide range of subjects, including the Consolidated Farm and Rural Development Act, the Commodity Futures Trading Commision, and livestock credit.

Not all moribund subcommittees have been transformed into activist legislative and oversight entities, of course. But the effects of ten years of personnel turnover, in conjunction with the workings of seniority, have had decided impact.

Second, since 1971 there have been important alterations in the internal distribution of power in the House. Chief among them is a rules change implemented by the Democratic Caucus limiting subcommittee chairmanships to one per member. This has made it necessary to drop farther down committee seniority lists to fill subcommittee chairmanships, exaggerating the impact of the personnel turnover of recent years.[13]

Third, subcommittees and their chairmen have been granted considerable freedom from the authority of chairmen of full committees. In addition to being permitted to hire professional staff, the subcommittee is given wide discretion to hold hearings, call witnesses, receive evidence; it is given a fixed jurisdiction and is authorized to receive all relevant legislation in that jurisdiction referred to the full committee; and it is provided with an adequate budget.[14]

Fourth, the tendency for earmarked oversight resources to be siphoned off for other purposes has been diminished in recent years by the increases in personal privileges for House members. One need only compare Clapp's (1964, chap. 2) data for the early 1960s with Gwirtzman's (see note 9 below) discussion of the mid-1970s to discern the increases in salary, personal staff budgets, and allowances for travel, district offices, stationery, telephone and telegraph, and franking. Consequently, there is less need to monitor resources earmarked for oversight since their deployment for oversight purposes may now constitute their highest valued use. The marginal value of "siphoning" has declined.

Fifth, again referring to Bullock's (1973b) interviews, there does appear to be a genuine increase in the belief among congressmen that policy activity makes for good reelection politics. An interest in oversight—especially of bureaucratic abuses—is increasingly compatible with taking care of the folks back home. Moreover, the credibility of credit-claiming, especially for the ombudsman tasks that are associated with subcommittee oversight activity, has been enhanced by the devolution of authority to small work groups.

Finally, the multiplied committee and subcommittee assignments of most congressmen provide large numbers of members with access to committee and subcommittee resources. Coupled with the recent influx of more activist members, this means that, increasingly, members who wish to engage in oversight activity have access to the institutional resources with which to do so.

What may we conclude, then, about the recent upsurge of oversight[15] on the one hand, and the "lack of will" to perform "unglamorous" and "unrewarding" oversight functions on the other? The former, I believe, for the reasons just cited, contradicts the latter. New policy-oriented personnel, endowed with the personal resources with which to handle reelection tasks, and outfitted with the institutional resources of authority, staff, and money to engage in the "surveillance" of executive programs, lack neither the will nor the capacity to engage in oversight.

Neither "resource inadequacy" nor "lack of will" provides a satisfactory explanation for alleged failures in oversight performance, at least in recent Congresses. The sources of perceived failure, I believe, lie in the highly decentralized fashion in which oversight is conducted and in the unacknowledged oversight that passes unrecognized.

3. Malcoordination of Oversight. In their study of the growth of committee surveillance of the executive branch between the Legislative Reorganization Act of 1946 and the Legislative Reorganization Act of 1970, Dodd and Shipley (1975, p. 43) conclude:

a. The volume of surveillance practically doubled;

b. The surveillance process moved from one conducted largely in full Committee to one conducted largely in Subcommittee;

c. The preoccupation of House Committees with policy rather than agency surveillance ... increased ... ;

d. The average number of House Committees conducting hearings in the [same] discrete agency and policy areas rose dramatically.

As expected from our earlier discussion, they discover the devolution of oversight-related activities to the subcommittee level and, with the multiplication in the number of these panels over the twenty-four years of their study, the consequent expansion in the volume of activity. The increases in the sheer volume of surveillance, and the number of panels involved, would, in itself, pose coordination problems. Complicating matters are the jurisdictional arrangements of committees and subcommittees. Current jurisdictional lines neither match up very well with the contemporary executive bureaucracy nor are they internally neat and clear-cut. Rather, they are replete with overlaps, gray areas, and dead areas. Consequently, what oversight does take place is not only unsystematic; it is often repetitive as well. Dodd and Shipley (1975, p. 44) suggest that "the growth in multi-Committee surveillance [in the same policy area] should raise doubts either (a) about the adequacy of the 1946 Reorganization Act in establishing clear jurisdictional lines for Committees that parallel the agency/policy divisions of the Federal Government, or (b) about the adequacy of existing procedures for enforcing these jurisdictional lines."

Subcommittee-initiated and -implemented oversight will remain haphazard and idiosyncratic so long as jurisdictional anomalies persist, and so long as neither party nor institutional leaders take an active role in damping the centrifugal effects of decentralization. It is this absence of central coordination that produces concern, both inside and outside Congress, about legislative oversight performance.[16]

4. *Latent Oversight.* In his testimony before the Bolling Committee, Morris Ogul noted that

When many of us talk about oversight we talk about formal oversight. Much oversight is going on in the Congress under different labels, for which I use the term "latent oversight." It is there in a lot of places but not highly visible. [*Panel Discussions*, 1973, 2:232]

The Congress has many eyes and is "continuously watchful" not in its formal oversight activity but in the day-to-day activities of its members in their legislative and casework capacities. By focusing exclusively on the missions of official oversight agents, some observers have underestimated the actual amount of legislative intervention in policy execution. If anything, however, latent oversight exacerbates the decentralization already apparent in the more manifest forms and thus is an additional source of dissatisfaction with the overall oversight performance of the Congress.

Having argued that oversight—both manifest and latent—suffers from neither a paucity of resources nor a lack of will but from being conducted under conditions of extreme decentralization and lack of central coordination, I may now inquire into the effects of committee assignment practices on this situation. In doing so, an apparent inconsistency in my argument needs to be cleared up.

In an earlier section I argued in support of the dominant role of subgovernments and "cozy little triangles" in the policy process; in this section, I have supported the view that a substantial amount of legislative oversight and other forms of legislative surveillance in fact takes place. Are these two positions compatible? The answer is in the affirmative for two different reasons.

First, although oversight often connotes aggressive follow-up on the implementation and administration of executive programs, it is often aimed at buoying up existing cozy little triangles or laying the groundwork for new policy subgovernments. Oversight activity is not exclusively a remedy to "unplug" the wires that bind a cozy little triangle together.

Second, cozy little triangles survive "between the cracks." Since so much oversight is partial and idiosyncratic, often the consequence of some particular abuse catching the attention of an interested committee member or of his staff, much of the real relationship among congressmen, bureaucrats, and interest groups in a policy subgovernment remains intact.

Recent committee assignment practices in the House are both a symptom and a cause. As a cause, these practices are Cannon-Taberism in reverse.[17] By allowing members to gravitate to committees where they can actively pursue the interests of their constituents, and by liberating them from backbench obscurity through the expansion of subcommittees and the redistribution of power within committees, the interest-advocacy-accommodation syndrome contributes to the politics of clientelism in both its cozy little triangle and its oversight forms. Highly fragmented committees, which increasingly look like holding companies for their subcommittees, can accommodate these diverse expressions of self-interest:

> the committee system aids congressmen simply by allowing a division of labor among members. The parceling out of legislation among small groups of congressmen by subject area has two effects. First, it creates small voting bodies in which membership may be valuable.... Second, it creates specialized small-group settings in which individual congressmen can make things happen and be perceived to make things happen. [Mayhew 1974, p. 12]

As a symptom, committee assignment practices, like many other practices and relationships in the modern House, have been shaped by sixty-five years of decentralization and leadership impoverishment. CC members, in the absence of externally imposed constraints or leadership guidance, have been relatively free to put the resources of their institutional position to work for their own personal objectives. The interest-advocacy-accommodation syndrome is the product of this arrangement.

Committee Representativeness	Committees and subcommittees perform essential legislative functions, but they are not little legislatures: they distort the full range of societal interests as articulated in the political system or even as manifested in the parent houses. *Davidson (1976, p. 3)*

An important consequence of the interest-advocacy-accommodation syndrome is the unrepresentative committee composition it produces. Responding to a distinctive set of institutional interests—the so-called "interesteds"—in their assignment decisions, the CC determines committee makeups that provide a basis for the policy subgovernments Freeman (1965) and others have described. Accommodation of revealed preferences, not representativeness, is the operating premise of the CC. And because the CC responds favorably to expressed preferences for committee assignments, it also inadvertently samples other characteristics, correlated with committee preferences, in a distorted fashion. Thus, many congressional committees are not only deep in "interesteds" but are also unrepresentative of regional, ideological, and seniority groupings in the House.[18]

Representation on House committees of regional, ideological, and seniority groups of the parent chamber is not, in its own right, important or commendable. As Bibby observes in his testimony before the Bolling Committee,

> The most important consideration should not be representativeness of committee membership, but whether or not the Members have a real incentive to participate in the work of the committee and become specialists. I think you encourage that incentive only by allowing Members the freedom to try and get on committees where they have a special interest. [*Panel Discussions*, 1973, 2:4]

Any attempt to engineer representativeness contrary to the committee preferences of rank-and-file members would probably produce the same dominance of committee affairs by "interesteds," as others turned their attention and activity to other arenas. Moreover, owing to anomalous jurisdictional arrangements in which policy domains often cross committee jurisdictions, the cost of unrepresentative committee membership is reduced.

If energy and environment legislation were the sole preserve of the western-dominated Interior Committee, for example, then the cost to other regions in terms of inattention to their policy problems might be substantial. Energy and environmental matters, however, by my count, are handled by nineteen sub-committees of thirteen House committees, by two special committees, two joint committees, and innumerable congressionally created commissions. Jurisdictional overlaps, then, moderate the effects of committee membership unrepresentativeness, a point to which Polsby alludes in his testimony before the Bolling Committee:

> A certain amount of overlap, and consequently political competition among subcommittees—especially in emerging areas of concern—is probably a good thing, and not wasteful since it permits a wider range of forces in society to participate in the shaping of the way issues come before Congress. (*Panel Discussions*, 1973, 2:10)

This point is important in light of recent scholarly and political interest in committee jurisdictions realigned along functional lines.[19] Functionally re-organized jurisdictions, in the absence of any changes in the interest-advocacy-accommodation syndrome, would serve to entrench whichever configuration of interests came to dominate a particular policy domain. With overlapping jurisdictions on the other hand, one cozy little triangle with its legislative base in one subcommittee may be counterpoised by another cozy little triangle in a different subcommittee.

In sum, committee unrepresentativeness, a product of the way in which committee assignments are made, is not a serious normative matter when committee jurisdictions overlap. The important concern is that a variety of interests have legislative access to policy subgovernments. The self-selection that typifies the interest-advocacy-accommodation syndrome, together with otherwise anomalous jurisdictional arrangements, permits an "interested" to gravitate to one of *many* policy pressure points in the issue area salient to him. Jurisdictional realignment that does not take account of rival interests competing for legislative access is liable to witness considerable intra-House conflict, extreme competition for committee assignments, and, perhaps, the emergence of a dominant interest in many policy areas with a virtual mono-poly on legislative access.

Committee assignment practices, as my examination of their implications for the functioning of the committee system suggests, play a pervasive and impor-tant role in determining the kind of political institution the House is. They produce the raw material from which committees and subcommittees are fashioned and, consequently, contribute to a whole series of relationships—between leaders and followers, between committees and their parent chamber, among participants of policy subgovernments, and between members and their constituents, to name a few. While producing a number of important effects, some of which I have investigated here, they, in turn, are the product of both long-term secular trends, e.g., decentralization, and short-term shocks to the system, e.g., personnel turnover. The many pieces of the giant jigsaw puzzle have been interwoven, over time, with other practices, processes, and phenomena in the House of Representatives. But that is what an institution is all about, isn't it?

**Recent Reforms
in Committee
Assignment
Practices:
Revolutionary or
Cosmetic?**

One difficulty with the study of political institutions is that they will not hold still for very long. This is especially true of the recent House. While internal arrangements in the House have long been the object of reformist passions (see Wilson 1885; MacNeil 1963; Bolling 1965, 1968, 1974), only during the last few years have a number of reform efforts been successfully concluded.[1] My task in this epilogue is to survey those reforms that bear on committee assignment practices and, on the basis of Democratic committee assignments in the Ninety-fourth Congress, to determine whether these procedural alterations have had substantive import. Of course, the experience of a single Congress is too limited to make this determination with confidence; yet some early signs of impact (or lack thereof) due to changes in the rules emerge.

Committee Assignments and Reform in the 1970s

In the decade following the revolt against Speaker Cannon, both parties developed their modern committee assignment practices; there was little alteration in those committee assignment procedures until the Ninety-second Congress. The Democrats, in particular, vested exclusive nomination authority for committee assignments in its contingent on the Ways and Means Committee, reserving for its Caucus final approval of the Ways and Means recommendations (as well as the actual nomination and election of Ways and Means members). In practice, the Caucus rubber-stamped the recommendations of its Committee on Committees.

By 1970, despite a considerable opening-up of committee assignment practices elsewhere,[2] the Democratic CC was still regarded as a powerful, independent force in the organizational politics of the House. In some quarters its independence from the party leadership and its alleged unresponsiveness to the dominant reformist wing of the congressional Democratic Party was lamented.[3]

In the Ninety-second Congress, after several elections in which the reformist ranks in the Democratic House contingent had increased, some modest reforms were enacted by the Caucus. The monopoly hold of CC zone representatives over the fate of the members of their zones was weakened by a Caucus decision permitting a state delegation to place one of its members directly before the full CC for consideration.[4] A second reform, aimed primarily at committee chairmen but nevertheless striking at some of the powers of the CC, made it possible to challenge the CC's nominations of committee chairmen. In submitting its committee selections to the Caucus for formal approval, the CC lists committee members in order of seniority, the person at the top being designated the chairman. According to a 1971 change in the Caucus rules, any ten members could demand a separate Caucus vote on a committee chairman proposed by the CC.

In 1973 reforms were ratcheted up another several notches. Voting on committee chairmen proposed by the CC became automatic; at the request of one-fifth of the Caucus, these votes were by secret ballot. Proposals by the CC for other committee assignments were ratified (or rejected) by the Caucus one committee at a time and, on a demand supported by ten Caucus members, a vote could be taken on any particular assignment recommended by the CC. Second, the Caucus added the Speaker, majority leader, and Caucus chairman to the CC as official voting members in an effort to involve the party leadership more directly in CC deliberations. Third, the Caucus constrained the CC by requiring that every member be appointed either to an exclusive committee or to a semiexclusive committee; no longer could the CC assign a member to two (or less) minor committees.[5]

Other signs of reform were visible during the Ninety-third Congress. Two important developments had a later bearing on Democratic committee assignments. The Democratic Caucus, in early 1973, significantly upgraded the importance of the Steering and Policy Committee. Of special consequence were the central place of the party leadership on this committee[6] and its relative geographic representativeness.[7] In both leadership importance and geographic spread, the Steering and Policy Committee provided an alternative to Ways and Means as the party CC. Although probably not forseen, the availability of a Steering and Policy Committee possessing both strong leadership input and wide geographic representation proved decisive two years later when Ways and Means lost the right to make Democratic committee assignments.

The second important development occurred on January 31, 1973, with the passage of House Resolution 132. This resolution, which evoked some controversy (the vote on final passage was 282–191), created the Select Committee on Committees for the purpose of surveying and making recommendations for changes in the structure and operation of the committee system in the House. Speaker Albert appointed ten members to this committee, equally divided between the parties, and named Richard Bolling (D., Mo.) its chairman.[8] For the next year and a half (but principally between September 1973 and March 1974), the Bolling Committee, as it came to be known, held numerous hearings and committee meetings.[9]

In December 1973, it released a working draft of its report, containing plans for a major realignment of committee jurisdictions: three committees would be eliminated; Education and Labor would be separated into two committees; Interior would be recast as an energy and environment committee with much of its former jurisdiction over national parks, forests, public lands, territories, and Indians allocated to other committees; Interstate would acquire new exclusive jurisdiction over health-related matters while losing jurisdiction in transportation and energy; Public Works would aquire jurisdiction over rail, air, and water transportation; Agriculture, Foreign Affairs, Government Operations, and Science would all have additional areas of responsibility; finally, and perhaps most significantly, Ways and Means would lose a number of its substantive responsibilities in health, the public debt, renegotiation, and revenue sharing.[10]

On March 13, 1974, the Bolling Committee unanimously reported a resolution that restructured House committee jurisdictions. Despite a flood of protest, the Select Committee stuck pretty much to the changes that appeared in its December 7 working draft.[11] The relevance of the resolution for committee assignments was twofold. First, and most obvious, major jurisdictional realignments altered the relative attractiveness of committees for members. In the wake of its passage, one would expect a change in the flow of "interesteds" as reflected in transfer and freshman request activity. Second, the resolution offered by the Bolling Committee insisted on a "modified one-track" system for committee assignments, according to which most House members would be restricted to a single committee assignment and only a handful of members would receive a second assignment to one of the surviving minor committees. Since 71% of the Democrats held two assignments in the Ninety-third Congress, a major shuffling of committee personnel at the beginning of the Ninety-fourth Congress would have been required. Bolling himself acknowledged the controversial nature of the modified one-track arrangement but felt that it was central to the overall proposal. The proposal did allow those members who would have to give up a committee to make the choice themselves.

On May 9, 1974, the Democratic Caucus voted 111–95 to send the Bolling Committee Report (HR 988) to a Caucus committee—the Hansen Committee on Organization, Study, and Review—for further consideration. This was a major setback for supporters of HR 988. The Hansen Committee, many of whose members sat on committees scheduled to lose jurisdiction under HR 988, reported back to the Caucus on July 17. It proposed a different plan in which the status quo would, in effect, be preserved for both committee jurisdictions and committee assignments. The major new thrust of the Hansen Committee plan involved restrictions on the Rules Committee—a further slap at Bolling and Martin, who sat on that committee.

The Caucus, on July 23, voted to direct the Rules Committee to send both plans to the floor under an open rule making the Bolling report the vehicle for debate and permitting the Hansen report to be in order as a substitute. The Rules Committee held hearings in early September and voted on September 25 to follow the directive of the Caucus. Debate in the House commenced on September 30 and continued until October 8. On that date the House voted to substitute a slightly modified version of the Hansen report for the Bolling report; the vote was 203–165. The Hansen substitute won final approval, 359–7. A major reform effort had been thwarted but, in the wake of the 1974 elections, the stage was set for another run at reform in the Ninety-fourth Congress.

The Ways and Means Committee had been a constant source of frustration to reformers during the Ninety-third Congress. Owing to frequent absences by Chairman Wilbur Mills (D., Ark), and the lack of a subcommittee structure, the committee became bogged down in trade reform, and consequently failed to make much headway in areas of high priority to many Democrats—health insurance and tax reform, in particular. The committee, nevertheless, managed to survive the radical jurisdictional surgery proposed by the Bolling report, though the Hansen substitute did require the creation of subcommittees beginning in the Ninety-fourth Congress. Bitter feelings toward the committee remained, and reformist ranks were swelled by the November elections.

Adding to the political problems of the committee was a bizarre series of events involving Mills. On October 9 Mills, apparently drunk, was detained by the Washington Metropolitan Police at the Tidal Basin in the company of Fanne Fox, a local stripper. The so-called Tidal Basin incident, though embarrassing, might have been forgotten; Mills, however, compounded the problem by appearing on stage in Boston with the stripper on November 30. "We could overlook the Tidal Basin incident," said Sam Gibbons (D., Fla.), a Ways and Means member, "but not Mills' antics in Boston. He's flipped." [12] On December 3 he entered Bethesda Naval Hospital for treatment of exhaustion. [13]

The Democratic Caucus of the Ninety-fourth Congress convened on December 2, 1974. The combined effects of pent-up hostility towards the Ways and Means Committee, the addition of seventy-five freshmen to the Democratic ranks, most of whom held reformist sentiments, and the symbolism of the Mills affair were dramatic. First, a number of Ways and Means members, probably in an effort to head off further attacks on the committee, made it clear that they would not support Mills in his attempt to retain the committee chairmanship (he later withdrew). This failed in its purpose for, second, the Caucus voted, 146–122, to strip Ways and Means Democrats of their power to make committee assignments for other Democrats. The Steering and Policy Committee, strengthened two years earlier, assumed this responsibility. Third, the Speaker was granted the authority to nominate Democratic members of the Rules Committee, subject to Caucus ratification. Fourth, the Ways and Means Committee was expanded from twenty-five to thirty-seven members and all other committees were required to have a "two-thirds plus one" Democratic majority. (This, in effect, necessitated expansion of other committees.)

Other notable changes were produced by the Caucus, but they were not directly related to committee assignments and so will not be discussed here. Two additional modifications, though, were adopted by the Caucus in February 1975. One, sponsored by Larry McDonald (D., Ga), banned discrimination in committee assignments based on previous occupations. He was miffed at being denied a seat on the Internal Security Committee (which was later abolished) because he was not a lawyer. A second change barred major committee chairmen from serving on other committees.

In the remainder of this Epilogue, an assessment of the impact of these rules changes on committee assignments in the Ninety-fourth Congress is made. Before moving to this assessment, let me note that, as of this writing in late 1976, a number of additional changes in committee assignment practices are being contemplated.

They include:

1. Direct elections as the method of filling vacancies on Appropriations and Ways and Means.

2. All nominations to the Budget Committee to be made by the Democratic CC. Under current procedure the chairmen of Appropriations and of Ways and Means are permitted three nominations each.

3. Reduction of the number of Speaker-appointed members on the Steering and Policy Committee (the Democratic CC) from nine to three.

4. Prohibition of members from serving simultaneously on the Democratic Campaign Committee and the Steering and Policy Committee.

These changes are supported by the Democratic Study Group and Common Cause. They have been presented to the Ninety-fifth Congress Democratic Caucus in December 1976.

Democratic Assignment Procedures in the Ninety-fourth Congress

According to the "Preamble and Rules Adopted by the Democratic Caucus, 94th Congress," the Steering and Policy Committee (S & P), which is the new Democratic CC, consists of the Speaker (who serves as its chairman), the majority leader, the Caucus chairman, twelve members elected by the respective caucuses of twelve compact and contiguous zones (designed by the Speaker), and nine appointees of the Speaker.[14] The membership for the Ninety-fourth Congress, plus other pertinent details, is found in table E1. Although the zones are compact, contiguous, and approximately equal in size, the large number of appointed or mandated members distorts geographic representativeness. Note, for example, that both Texas and California have three representatives each, while New York has only one. Also note the turnover on the committee. The members who will not return to S & P in the Ninety-fifth Congress include: Albert (retired), Burton (failed to be elected majority leader), McFall (failed to be elected majority leader), Fulton (resigned from House), Matsunaga (elected to Senate), Hebert (retired), Patman (died), Mezvinsky (defeated for reelection), and Stanton (ran for Senate). There also will be changes in the four Speaker-appointed members, and the remainder of the regionally-elected members (who must be returned by their regional caucuses and who are limited to two two-year terms) is in doubt. This membership instability on S & P is substantial and may affect its long-run performance and style when it sits as its party's CC.

The data in table E2 compare the current and former CCs on partisan and ideological dimensions. While Ways and Means members are accurately characterized as liberal party regulars (supporting party majorities about two-thirds of the time and opposing the conservative coalition nearly 60% of the time in the Ninety-third Congress), S & P members are even more liberal and partisan (supporting party majorities nearly 80% of the time and opposing the conservative coalition on 70% of the votes on which it formed in the Ninety-third Congress).

There are other dimensions on which the current and former CCs differ— for example, S & P people tend to be middle- and lower-seniority members to a greater extent than were the Ways and Means members—but I shall not dwell on them here. Instead I turn to the new procedural arrangements for making committee assignments.

Table E1   **Democratic Steering and Policy Committee, 94th Congress**

Name	Zone (No. of Democrats) if elected	Reason (if nonelected)
Albert (Okla.)	—	Mandated by Rules—Speaker
O'Neill (Mass.)	—	Mandated by Rules—Majority Leader
P. Burton (Cal.)	—	Mandated by Rules—Caucus Chairman
McFall (Cal.)	—	Mandated by Rules—Whip
Brademas (Ind.)	—	Mandated by Rules—Chief Dep. Whip
Fulton (Tenn.)	—	Mandated by Rules—Dep. Whip
Matsunaga (Haw.)	—	Mandated by Rules—Dep. Whip
Wright (Tex.)	—	Mandated by Rules—Dep. Whip
Brodhead (Mich.)	—	Appointed—Represents 1st termers
Davis (S.C.)	—	Appointed—Represents 2nd and 3rd termers
Jordan (Tex.)	—	Appointed—Represents women
Metcalfe (Ill.)	—	Appointed—Represents Blacks
Bingham (N.Y.)	New York (27)	—
D'Amours (N.H.)	Conn., D.C., Guam, Mass., N.H., P.R., R.I., V.I. (21)	—
Hebert (La.)	Ala., Fla., La., Miss. (23)	—
Mathis (Ga.)	Ga., N.C., S.C., Tenn. (29)	—
Mezvinsky (Ia.)	Ark., Ia., Kans., Mo., Okla. (23)	—
Moss (Cal.)	Calif. (28)	—
Obey (Wis.)	Mich., Minn., Wis. (24)	—
Patman (Tex.)	Texas (21)	—
Price (Ill.)	Ill., Ind., Ky. (27)	—
Stanton (Ohio)	Ohio, Pa. (22)	—
Thompson (N.J.)	Md., N.J., Va., W. Va. (26)	—
Udall (Ariz.)	Ariz., Col., Haw., Mont., Nev., N.M., Ore., Utah, Wash., Wyo. (23)	—

Table E2   **Ways and Means and Steering and Policy Compared**

	Mean Scores (standard deviation)	
	Party Support[a]	Conservative Coalition Support[b]
Ways and Means[c]	36.6	−13.4
	(44.7)	(59.7)
Steering and Policy[d]	58.9	−40.8
	(32.3)	(47.1)

SOURCE: Based on 93rd Congress votes. See *Congressional Quarterly Weekly Report*, January 24, 1976, pp. 172–73, 182–83.

[a] Party Support = *CQ* Party Unity − *CQ* Party Opposition.

[b] Conservative Coalition Support = *CQ* Conservative Coalition Support − *CQ* Conservative Coalition Opposition.

[c] Based on thirteen members returning to 94th Congress.

[d] Speaker Albert and the two freshmen, Brodhead and D'Amours, deleted.

The most important thing to observe about the committee assignment procedures of S & P is that they are nearly identical to those followed by the Ways and Means Committee.[15] Freshmen and returning members desiring transfers submit requests to S & P, the party leaders negotiate a committee structure, and then the CC meets in executive session to decide on the recommendations it will make to the Caucus. The similarities between previous and current practice, however, may be a temporary phenomenon since:

1. The switch to S & P as the CC came in the middle of the assignment process—for example, freshmen requests had already been submitted. S & P had little opportunity to strike out in new procedural directions.

2. The staff of the Ways and Means Committee assisted S & P in the latter's first run-through. In future Congresses, the staff of S & P and the party leadership will come to play a more significant role.

There are a few variations in procedure worth noting. First, only twelve of the twenty-three members of S & P have regional constituencies. Compared, then, to the Ways and Means Committee, the impact and import of "taking care of my people" is blurred considerably. To the extent that it still has meaning, a CC member's constituency is no longer determined exclusively by geography. Policy, partisan, and ideological aspects may be more pronounced under the newly constituted arrangements.

Second, the impact of the party leadership is more significant now. This, of course, was one of the motivations for switching committee assignments to S & P.[16] There has, however, been some concern expressed about a too-powerful party leadership and this has stimulated the move to reduce the number of Speaker-appointed members on S & P in future Congresses.

In sum, committee assignment procedures in the Ninety-fourth Congress followed the pattern established by the Ways and Means Committee in previous years. CC members still served as advocates but, except for those elected from regional caucuses, there was a good deal more discretion in choosing a clientele "out there." My expectation is that, more than in previous years, success in obtaining requested assignments in the Ninety-fourth Congress hinged on idiosyncratic and individual characteristics of requesters, but only marginally more. I examine this prospect and others in the next three sections.

Committee Requests in the Ninety-fourth Congress

The committee assignment process for the Ninety-fourth Congress was well under way when, early in December of 1974, the Caucus voted to remove this function from the Ways and Means Democrats. Newly elected Democrats had already been contacted by the "old" CC and many of them had met with their zone representatives and had submitted requests. Thus, any changes in requests were due more to changes in the opportunity structure and freshman background characteristics than to the changes in the assignment process itself.

The distribution of freshmen requests across committees is given in table E3. For comparative purposes, the percentage of freshmen requesting each committee in the Eighty-sixth through Ninety-third Congresses is also tabulated. In the Ninety-fourth Congress, as in previous Congresses, Interstate and Public Works were the two most requested committees; each appeared to be even more popular among Ninety-fourth Congress freshmen. In addition to these two committees, several others attracted increased requests in 1974—Agriculture, Appropriations, Government Operations, House Administration, and Ways and Means. The increased popularity of Agriculture followed from the midwestern Democratic success in the 1974 elections; a similar phenome-

Table E3   **A Comparison of Freshman Requests**

Committee	% of Members Requesting	
	86th–93rd Congresses (N = 231)*	94th Congress (N = 75)
Agriculture	19	28
Appropriations	11	19
Armed Services	24	8
Banking & Currency	25	19
Budget	—	4
D.C.	3	1
Education & Labor	20	23
Foreign Affairs	17	8
Government Operations	17	27
House Administration	2	9
Interior	24	29
Interstate	34	43
Judiciary	20	17
Merchant Marine	6	7
P.O. & C.S.	9	5
Public Works	28	31
Rules	1	3
Science	16	12
Small Business	—	5
Un-American Activities	2	—
Veterans' Affairs	7	9
Ways and Means	0	20

* Data drawn from Table 3.2.

non occurred in 1958 and 1964. Government Operations and House Administration requests grew, I suspect, for two reasons:

1. For the first time, freshmen were asked to submit separate request lists for major and minor committees, with the expectation that most freshmen would receive two assignments.
2. Both of these committees were upgraded in the previous Congress—oversight activities were emphasized in both the Bolling and Hansen reports, as well as in Caucus deliberations, with Government Operations given major new responsibilities; campaign finance and other federal election reform matters are handled by House Administration.

The popularity increases of the two exclusive committees reflected the increased likelihood of freshman success in these formerly exclusive domains of high seniority and, of course, the fact that Ways and Means assignments no longer depended on open election in the Caucus. Major popularity declines were associated with Armed Services and Foreign Affairs. It is fair to conclude that committee preferences in the Ninety-fourth Congress, as in previous Congresses, mirrored the continued effects of interest and assignment likelihood. The procedural changes of the Ninety-fourth Congress probably had only minor impact here, simply continuing the trend of opening up opportunities (both in number of assignments and on particular committees) for freshmen.

In previous years, as was documented in tables 3.4 and 3.5, freshman requesters typically submitted "long" request lists (three or more committees requested) while nonfreshman requesters tilted toward "short" lists. In the Ninety-fourth Congress these tendencies were even more pronounced (see table E4). And, although the numbers are small, competitive factors appeared to influence the decision of a freshman to submit a long or short list in the expected direction (see table E5).

Table E4 **Length of Request Lists**

Length of Preference Ordering	86th–93rd Congresses		94th Congress	
	Freshmen*	Transfers**	Freshmen	Transfers
1	23%	84%	13%	100%
2	16	8	19	0
3	36	5	29	0
4	15	2	23	0
5 or more	10	1	16	0
	100%	100%	100%	100%
	(N = 231)	(N = 130)	(N = 75)	(N = 20)

    * From Table 3.4.
  ** From Table 3.5.

The procedural changes in committee assignments in the Ninety-fourth Congress had no noticeable impact on requests. While mine has hardly been an exhaustive analysis,[17] the comparisons made provide no firm basis for tracing any differences in request patterns to changes in procedure. Part of the explanation, I suspect, lies in the fact that the procedural changes occurred at about the time that requests were being submitted. Thus, in future years additional differences may emerge. The procedural changes were well in place, however, by the time party leaders had to negotiate a new committee structure. And, as we shall see, the effects were substantial.

Table E5   State Vacancies, State Competition, and Freshman
                                            Requests, 94th Congress

Request-List Length	State Competition	No State Competition
Short	9%	57%
Long	91%	43%
	100%	100%
	(N = 11)*	(N = 7)**

* Eleven freshmen had competition for their first-preference
  request—a committee from which a state delegation
  member had departed (state vacancy)—from another
  member of their delegation.
** Seven freshmen had no state competition for their first-
  preference request for a committee from which a delegation colleague had departed.

Structure Negotiation in the Ninety-fourth Congress

The Democratic Caucus, in its December 1974 meetings, instructed its party leaders on two aspects of structure negotiation. First, it endorsed a "two-thirds-plus-one" rule according to which the majority party would receive two-thirds plus one of the seats on each standing committee (except Standards of Official Conduct). Second, it required an expansion of the Ways and Means Committee from twenty-five to thirty-seven members.[18] As a consequence most committees were increased in size (see table E6).

To see whether the Caucus-mandated changes in committee sizes and party ratios have affected the actual structure negotiated by party leaders in the Ninety-fourth Congress, the regression equation estimated in table 6.9 to *explain* structure negotiation in the Eighty-seventh through Ninety-third Congresses is employed to *predict* (actually postdict) the Ninety-fourth Congress structure. Since the independent variables of that equation—measures of supply, demand, and minority party "needs"—explain most of the variance in ΔN_j, the change in the number of Democratic slots on committee j ($R^2 = .867$), and since the rules governing negotiated structure remained fixed over the period covered by that data, prediction errors for the Ninety-fourth Congress may be attributed to the Caucus-mandated changes or to something else that has changed in the environment. As a basis for further discussion, table E7 provides the actual size-change in Democratic slots and those predicted by equation 6.1. Notice that in every case equation

Table E6   Committee Sizes, 93rd and 94th Congresses

Committee	Committee Size (Dem., Rep.)	
	93rd	94th
Agriculture	36 (20, 16)	43 (29, 14)
Appropriations	55 (33, 22)	55 (37, 18)
Armed Services	43 (24, 19)	40 (27, 13)
Banking and Currency	40 (24, 16)	43 (29, 14)
D.C.	25 (14, 11)	25 (17, 8)
Education and Labor	38 (22, 16)	40 (27, 13)
Foreign Affairs	40 (22, 18)	37 (25, 12)
Government Operations	41 (23, 18)	43 (29, 14)
House Administration	26 (15, 11)	25 (17, 8)
Interior	41 (23, 18)	43 (29, 14)
Internal Security	9 (5, 4)	—
Interstate	43 (24, 19)	43 (29, 14)
Judiciary	38 (21, 17)	34 (23, 11)
Merchant Marine	39 (22, 17)	40 (27, 13)
P.O. & C.S.	26 (15, 11)	28 (19, 9)
Public Works	39 (23, 16)	40 (27, 13)
Rules	15 (10, 5)	16 (11, 5)
Science	30 (17, 13)	37 (25, 12)
Standards of Official Conduct	12 (6, 6)	12 (6, 6)
Veterans' Affairs	26 (15, 11)	28 (19, 9)
Ways and Means	25 (15, 10)	37 (25, 12)
Budget	—	25 (17, 8)
Small Business	—	37 (25, 12)

6.1 predicts a ΔN_j *smaller* than the actual change, and in a number of instances the residual is substantial. A comparison of residuals (see table E8)—Ninety-fourth Congress vs. Eighty-seventh through Ninety-third Congress means—suggests that factors not operating in the earlier period have produced Democratic slot increases considerably larger than expected.

There are, in fact, two different questions buried in these numbers. First, why does the model systematically underestimate Democratic committee slot increases in the Ninety-fourth Congress (that is, why is every residual negative)? And second, why is the absolute size of the prediction error so "large"?

The answer to the first question may rest on factors other than Caucus-mandated procedural constraints. In both the Eighty-ninth and Ninetieth Congresses, a similar phenomenon occurred: in the former the residuals are negative for sixteen of seventeen committeess, while in the latter the residuals are positive for sixteen of the seventeen committees. In each of these Congresses, as well as in the Ninety-fourth Congress, there was massive turnover

Table E7   **Democratic Structure Negotiation Predictions for the 94th Congress**

Committee (j)	Change in Democratic Slots (ΔN_j)	
	Predicted	Actual
Agriculture	3.99	9
Armed Services	2.08	3
Banking and Currency	3.92	5
District of Columbia	1.51	3
Education and Labor	3.66	5
Foreign Affairs	1.31	3
Government Operations	2.72	6
House Administration	1.80	2
Interior	2.81	6
Interstate	3.35	5
Judiciary	1.46	2
Merchant Marine	2.03	5
Post Office and Civil Service	1.69	4
Public Works	3.02	4
Science	2.65	8
Veterans' Affairs	1.63	4

NOTE: The exclusive committees—Appropriations, Rules, Ways and Means; newly created committees—Budget, Small Business; a recently eliminated committee—Internal Security; and Standards of Official Conduct have been deleted.

involving a major swing in the party ratio in the chamber. It would appear, then, that major swings in party representation generate more than the usual amount of uncertainty about the pieces of the giant jigsaw puzzle for party leaders. Their ability to fine-tune in response to endogeneous supply and demand factors is taxed by this "noise."[19]

Even in the Eighty-ninth and Ninetieth Congresses, however, the absolute size of the prediction error was considerably smaller than in the Ninety-fourth Congress. The mean residuals over committees in the Eighty-ninth and Ninetieth Congresses, respectively, are −1.2 slots and 1.6 slots; for the Ninety-fourth Congress, the mean residual is −2.1 slots. I suspect that the size of the prediction error (though not its sign) may be traced to the "two-thirds-plus-one" rule mandated by the Caucus.

Two model misspecifications, then, appear to have produced major prediction errors in the negotiated structure model as applied to the data of the Ninety-fourth Congress. Majority party leaders respond appropriately to

Table E8   Residual Analysis of Negotiated Structure

| | Residual* | |
| | 87th–93rd Congress Mean | 94th Congress |
Committee		
Agriculture	.85	−5.01
Armed Services	.44	− .92
Banking and Currency	−.24	−1.08
District of Columbia	.26	−1.49
Education and Labor	.21	−1.34
Foreign Affairs	.37	−1.69
Government Operations	−.13	−3.28
House Administration	.43	− .20
Interior	−.22	−3.19
Interstate	.61	−1.65
Judiciary	.36	− .54
Merchant Marine	.33	−2.97
Post Office and Civil Service	.11	−2.31
Public Works	.12	− .98
Science	−.04	−5.35
Veterans' Affairs	.21	−2.37

* The residual is the difference between the growth (decline) in Democratic seats predicted by equation 6.1 (see table 6.9) and the actual growth in Democratic seats. For Agriculture, for example, the model averaged a .85 seat overprediction in the 87th–93rd Congress, while it underpredicted by more than 5 seats in the 94th Congress.

changes in the party ratio in their structure negotiations (see the parameter estimate for β_e in table 6.9). But the effect of this factor takes two forms, depending upon whether the change benefits or harms the majority party. The model understates structure negotiation decisions in good years (1964, 1974) and overstates them in bad years (1966).

The second misspecification involves the constraints imposed on party leaders in their committee structure decisions. These constraints are of no consequence for the model estimated in Chapter 6, since they remained fixed over the period for which the model was estimated. In the Ninety-fourth Congress, however, the "two-thirds-plus-one" rule was imposed. While it is impossible to trace the larger than normal residuals in this Congress to the Caucus-mandated rule with confidence, this possibility is strongly suggested. In the wake of a large influx of new "committee-seekers," the requirement that each committee's composition be "two-thirds-plus-one" Democratic, and the desire not to bump returning Republicans, party leaders expanded Democratic slots on each committee more than they "should." Two consequences flowed from these decisions.

1. More freshmen than ever received second-committee assignments (and the match between requests and assignments for second committees was poor owing to an oversupply of slots on some minor committees).
2. With greater frequency than in past years, slots provided by structure negotiation decisions have been left vacant.

And these two remarks lead me to my concluding topic.

Committee Assignments in the Ninety-fourth Congress

Committee assignments in the Ninety-fourth Congress were, for the first time, handled by the Steering and Policy Committee. Despite this major departure, advocacy continued to characterize CC decision-making and a strong emphasis continued to be placed on matching requests and assignments. Its performance in this task is provided in table E9.

Compared to CCs of previous years, the Ninety-fourth Congress CC assigned freshmen to first-preference committees at about the average rate of the previous CC (though less than in either the Ninety-second or Ninety-third

Table E9   **CC Performance in the 94th Congress, Freshmen**

Assignment Success	Proportion
Received first preference	.595
Received other preference	.351
Received no preference	.054
	1.000
	(N = 75)

Second-Committee Success (Eligibles)*	Proportion
Received more than one requested committee	.328
Received more than one committee	.910
	(N = 67)

* An eligible freshman is one not sitting on an exclusive committee.

Congresses). However, a smaller proportion of freshmen received no requested committees, a considerably larger proportion received a second assignment,[20] and a surprisingly large number of freshmen actually received two requested committees.

Those nonfreshmen who sought to transfer from one major committee to another received extremely accommodating treatment from the CC—only four members actually submitted requests, all of which were honored.[21] There was much more interest in exclusive committee positions.

1. Five nonfreshmen transferred to Appropriations. Six had requested the transfer, and four of these were honored by the CC; a nonrequester transferred as well.

2. Two nonfreshmen moved to Rules. They were the only ones to submit a request for this committee, and they must have been supported by the Speaker since his nomination was required.

3. Ways and Means, with twelve vacancies, evoked the most interest. Six of the eight nonfreshmen who requested the committee won assignment. Four other nonfreshmen, along with two freshmen, also were appointed.

In order to make some assessment of the effect on actual committee assignments of switching CC responsibilities to Steering and Policy, I focus on freshman assignments. The probit model (9.2), estimated in table 9.9, does not perform very well for Ninety-fourth Congress freshmen in predicting first-preference assignment success. Whereas the model predicts correctly in 75.7% of the cases (146 of 193) in the Eighty-seventh through Ninety-third Congresses, it predicts correctly in only 58.7% of the Ninety-fourth Congress cases (44 of 75).

The model was reestimated in two different ways in order to include the Ninety-fourth Congress freshman data. In the first instance the model was simply reestimated from a data set that included all freshmen in the Eighty-seventh through Ninety-fourth Congresses ($N = 268$). The inferences from the hypothesis tests of table 9.11 remain intact, though the significance levels were not quite as decisive and the overall goodness of fit declined slightly. The suggestion of this exercise, then, is that the statistical relationships discovered in table 9.11 are disturbed somewhat by the addition of the Ninety-fourth Congress data but not enough to lead me to alter my substantive judgments about committee assignments over the entire period.

This conclusion is not very satisfactory, for it does not permit a direct assessment of the precise ways in which these statistical relationships have been "disturbed." Consequently, the following probit model was estimated:

$$Pr(B) = \Phi\left\{\alpha + \sum \beta_i u_i + \sum \gamma_j v_j + \sum \delta_i(d \cdot u_i) + \sum \varepsilon_j(d \cdot v_j)\right\}$$

where the u_i- and v_j- variables are the same as those defined in table 9.7 and

$d = 1$ if the member was a freshman in the Ninety-fourth Congress
0 if otherwise

With this model, then, we may determine, for each independent variable, the way in which the statistical relationship was altered under the new procedures of the Ninety-fourth Congress.[22] The parameter estimates for δ_i and ε_j will allow us to determine how the relationship between assignment success and u_i and v_j, respectively, has changed in the Ninety-fourth Congress. The results are reported in table E10.

Table E10   **Maximum Likelihood Estimates of Assignment Success Probit Model with 94th Congress Effects ($\mathrm{N} = 268$)**

Coefficient	Represents the Effect of	Maximum Likelihood Estimate	Standard Error
α	Constant	1.068[b]	.223
β_1	u_1	.042	.207
β_2	u_2	.663[a]	.324
β_3	u_3	−1.005[b]	.229
γ_1	v_1	− .325[b]	.097
γ_2	v_2	− .520[a]	.236
γ_3	v_3	− .227[a]	.124
γ_4	v_4	− .118	.185
δ_1	$d \cdot u_1$	.088	.423
δ_2	$d \cdot u_2$	− .314	.600
δ_3	$d \cdot u_3$	− .382	.443
ε_1	$d \cdot v_1$	− .700	.461
ε_2	$d \cdot v_2$	− .014	.577
ε_3	$d \cdot v_3$	.275	.208
ε_4	$d \cdot v_4$	.811[b]	.346

[a] $p < .05$
[b] $p < .01$

First, note that the β_i's and γ_j's are, for the most part, statistically significant and in the expected direction—predecessor status (u_2) enhances the chances of assignment success while internal competition (u_3), external competition (v_1), coming from the South, (v_2), and zone overrepresentation (v_3) detract.[23]

Second, while all but one of the Ninety-fourth Congress dummy variables are insignificant, the joint hypothesis

$H_0: \delta_i = 0$ and $\varepsilon_j = 0$ for all i and j

may be rejected at p = .05. That is, although the statistical relationship between any one independent variable (with one exception) and assignment success probability is the same in the Ninety-fourth Congress as it was in previous Congresses, the joint statistical relationship has changed.

Third, the overall predictive performance is quite satisfactory—the probit is significant at $p \ll .0001$ and the prediction accuracy is 75%.

A more intuitive feel for these numbers is provided by an illustration. In table E11 I have collected information for three Ninety-fourth Congress

Table E11 **Assignment Success Illustrations from the 94th Congress**

| | | Requester | | |
		Advantaged	Toss-up	Disadvantaged
Variable	Description			
u_1	same state as zone rep.	yes	yes	yes
u_2	predecessor status	yes	no	no
u_3	internal competition	more competition for lower-ordered request	more competition for lower-ordered request	less competition for lower-ordered request
v_1	external competition	.5 zones/vacancy with effective comp.	1.0 zones/vacancy with effective comp.	1.3 zones/vacancy with effective comp.
v_2	region	non-South	non-South	South
v_3	zone overrepresentation	underrepresented	appropriately represented	underrepresented
v_4	zone vacancies	2 vacancies	none	none
Model Prediction = Pr(B)		.990	.577	.016
	Actual	assigned	assigned	not assigned

freshmen, representing the range of assignment-success prospects. The model predicts that the advantaged, toss-up, and disadvantaged requesters are, respectively, nearly certain, slightly probable, and highly improbable to win assignment to their first-preference committees. If these same people—with the same personal characteristics and environmental circumstances—had been elected to some Congress other than the Ninety-fourth, then the prediction probabilities would change to .963, .755, and .326, respectively. Thus, while no single parameter associated with the Ninety-fourth Congress makes a dramatic difference, the total effect can nevertheless be substantial.

A closer look at the numbers in table E10 does not produce greater clarity. The strongest conclusion one might draw—and this is stretching the statistical analysis—is that competition, both internal and external, played an exaggerated role, and zone-related characteristics, overrepresentation, and vacancies, a more muted role in the Ninety-fourth Congress committee assignment process than in previous years.[24] These patterns, however, are tenuous. One thing is clear: the Ninety-fourth Congress data introduced more "noise" so that the process, as it is currently arranged, is no longer as comprehensible as it once was. The extent to which the process "shakes down" and begins to display clearer patterns as the Steering and Policy Committee acquires more experience, or the extent to which the "noise" and the concomitant uncertainty persist, remains to be seen.

Conclusion. Things have not remained the same in the Ninety-fourth Congress, but the changes are hardly revolutionary.

Chapter 1

1. The veto power to which Wilson alluded is given literary force by the playwright Ibsen. "When the devil decided that nothing be accomplished, he appointed the first committee."

2. A partial list includes Carroll (1958), Fenno (1962, 1963, 1966, 1973), Ferejohn (1974), Ferejohn and Rundquist (1974), Green and Rosenthal (1964), Jones (1961), Kaplan (1968), Manley (1965, 1970), Murphy (1974), Robinson (1959, 1963), and Rundquist (1973).

3. Scholarship on committee assignments in the House includes Achen and Stolarek (1974), Bullock (1969, 1971, 1972, 1973a, 1973b), Bullock and Sprague (1969), Clapp (1964, chap. 5), Cohen (1974), Gawthrop (1966), Gertzog (1976), Goodwin (1970, chap. 4), Masters (1961), Mezey (1969), Rohde and Shepsle (1971, 1973), Shepsle (1973, 1975a, 1975b), Uslaner (1971, 1975), and Westefield (1974).

4. Professor Robert Salisbury made the Eighty-Sixth Congress data available to me. These data, by the way, were described and used by Masters (1961) in his classic paper on committee assignments. Professors Richard Fenno and John Manley provided me with the request data for the Eighty-seventh, Eighty-Eighth, and Ninetieth Congresses. A current member of the Ways and Means Committee opened his committee assignment files to my inspection and permitted me to extract the preference data for the Eighty-ninth, Ninety-second, and Ninety-third Congresses. Finally, a current member of the Democratic CC provided me with the Ninety-fourth Congress data. In order to employ these data, I have agreed to abide by the usual anonymity guarantee. Consequently, I shall not associate particular requests with particular identities.

5. Additional interviews with members of the Democratic CC conducted by John Manley and Richard Fenno during the Eighty-Ninth Congress and by Barbara Deckard during the Ninetieth and Ninety-first Congresses were kindly made available to me. As with the request data, I have deleted from the quotations that are used the explicit

identities of those interviewed. Also, as a matter of convention, I have not distinguished the interviews I conducted from those conducted by Deckard, Fenno, and Manley unless a particular quotation has already appeared in their written work.

Chapter 2

1. I have relied on Abram and Cooper (1968), Alexander (1916), Berdahl (1949), Bolling (1965, 1968), Chiu (1928), Cooper (1970), Follett (1896), Galloway (1961), Hasbrouck (1927), MacNeil (1963), McConachie (1898), Polsby (1968), Polsby, Gallaher, and Rundquist (1969), Price (1971), and Willoughby (1934).

2. "The committees were not seen as sifters of the business for the House but as fingers of the House. As a result, it was assumed that committees would report back, even if their report was unfavorable" (Cooper 1970, p. 24).

3. This committee was charged with deciding contested elections and other issues of House membership. It remains today as a standing subcommittee of the Committee on House Administration.

4. Follett (1896, pp. 220–21), for example, notes that "since the Speaker always owes his election to the dominant faction of his own party, he naturally gives to that faction the preference in the construction of the committees." Though parties were only in nascent form in the early Congresses, factional politics abounded.

5. The select committees, as noted earlier, were discontinued as soon as they completed their appointed task. The standing committees were appointed anew at the beginning of each congressional session, often with new personnel.

6. Fisher Ames expressed his concern over the organizational inefficiency of the House in the Fourth Congress: "We are a mere militia. There is no leader, no *point de railliement*. The motion-makers start up with projects of ill-considered taxes and, by presenting many and improper subjects, the alarm to popular feelings is rashly augmented." Cited in Hasbrouck (1927, p. 70).

7. The Speaker, Nathaniel Macon, was loyal to John Randolph, who split with the Jefferson administration in 1806. Jeffersonian loyalists in the House feared Macon's handling of committee assignments would be detrimental to the president's objectives. The motion for balloting failed by only two votes.

8. By the time of the Polk speakership, the traditional practice of the House at the end of a Congress of passing a resolution thanking its Speaker for his "impartial" leadership was often used to embarrass the Speaker for his *lack* of impartiality. Of the eleven Speakers that served from the time of Polk until the Civil War, seven failed to be honored by the adjective "impartial." See Alexander (1916, pp. 71–72). Many received the further humiliation of receiving fewer votes for the resolution of thanks than they had received in their original election to the speakership.

9. Follett (1896, pp. 218–19), for example. The rationale is the following: most Congresses had a lame-duck third session, and not infrequently the Speaker would schedule consideration of important legislation for this short session. He would, naturally, stack the committees appropriately for that last session.

10. Actually, sentiments for "party government" appear even earlier than Speaker Hunter's 1839 statement. When Speaker Stevenson reorganized the standing

committees in 1827, placing pro-Jackson majorities on each, Adams supporters saw nothing illegitimate in this practice. One minority member stated:

> I do not think, after two parties have been struggling for power, and one of them succeeds, it can reasonably be expected, that, in the distribution of honorable stations in this House, the victorious party shall select their adversaries. This ought not to be required.... If the party which has now the majority here, has placed its friends in stations where they can be useful to the country, while they do honor to themselves, I hope we who are of the minority, will never complain of it. If they have the honor, they have the responsibility too. [Cited in Cooper 1970, pp. 65–66]

Also see Bogue and Marlaire (1975) on the role of state party delegations as early as 1821–22 and Cooper (1970) on party organization during the Jeffersonian period.

11. In order for business to be transacted, a quorum must participate, a quorum defined as a majority of the membership. The minority could frustrate a majority effort to pass a bill by refusing to vote. Since it was inevitable that some majority members were absent, in a closely divided House the minority's nonparticipation reduced the number of *voting* members to less than a quorum. Thus a bill might "pass" overwhelmingly but, because less than a quorum had actually participated, the bill technically did not carry. A quorum call was then in order to which the minority members responded. With a quorum present to do business, a new vote was called. But again the quorum would disappear.

> Again and again, this procedure would be followed: a roll-call vote, followed by a quorum call, followed by another roll-call vote, followed by another quorum call. On occasions, the House clerk grew hoarse from constantly calling the member's names. In 1850, on a bill to admit California into the Union, the House polled its members thirty-one times during a single day. In 1854, there were 101 such roll calls in a single, long legislative day. Needless to say, the House made no progress on enacting the bills then under consideration. [MacNeil 1963, p. 50]

12. Reed subscribed to the philosophy of party government, but a government led from the Speaker's chair rather than the White House. This ultimately led to a very cool relationship with President McKinley, once one of Reed's House allies, and to Reed's resignation from the House in 1899.

13. Reed appointed two Democrats along with the chairman of Appropriations, the chairman of Ways and Means, and himself to the Rules Committee. He and his two Republican colleagues would meet privately, decide on a course of action, and only then call a meeting of the full, five-man committee. To his Democratic colleagues on the committee he would announce, "Gentlemen, we are about to perpetrate the following outrage!"

14. He was, from time to time, accused of visiting with the "gentlemen of the lobby," especially Boston textile interests, to consult on committee assignments. And Chiu (1928, p. 78) suggests that, at least on one occasion, a discreet visit to the Speaker's office by a congressman's wife changed Reed's mind on an assignment:

> Both Mr. Dolliver and his wife were in hopes that Mr. Reed would place him on the Committee on Ways and Means. When Mr. Dolliver learned his name was not on the list of this important committee, he "sorrowfully" communicated the fact to his wife, "who immediately proceeded to Reed's office, and when she returned, her husband was on the Ways and Means Committee."

15. A disgruntled Republican, one Mr. Struble of Iowa, accused Reed of "sitting in the chair with his feet on the neck of the Republican party."

16. See Abram and Cooper (1968) for a discussion of this issue.

17. See Chiu (1928, table on p. 70), Abram and Cooper (1968), and Polsby, Gallaher, and Rundquist (1969).

18. See Hasbrouck (1927, pp. 1–20).

19. Many of the Progressives refused to go the one step further of voting against their nominal party's nominee for Speaker. Thus, Cannon was easily elected to a fourth term as Speaker in 1909.

20. It is interesting to note the somewhat different circumstances in which reformers of the 1960s and 1970s have found themselves. The Progressives of 1909–11 had a working majority (on some votes at least) on the House floor through coalition with the Democrats. They were, however, a small minority in the Republican party in the House. The dilemma for the Progressives was that their point of strength in terms of votes—the House floor—was also the arena in which a powerful Speaker, through his control over procedure, could obviate that strength. For the Democratic reformers of the 1960s and 1970s, on the other hand, their numbers were most effective in the Democratic Caucus. There they often had a working majority while, on the House floor, they did not. Throughout the late 1960s and early 1970s they succeeded in securing reforms through the Caucus. In 1975, with larger numbers than ever, their successes were quite impressive. See the Epilogue. For the Caucus orientation of the reformers, see Bolling (1968).

21. The Speaker retained the power to appoint members to select and conference committees.

22. In 1957, Adam Clayton Powell's support of the Eisenhower–Nixon ticket led to a call in some quarters for his being demoted or removed from his second-rank position on the Education and Labor Committee. In 1961, a similar situation involving southern Democratic support for Nixon occurred. For a time there was talk of removing Representative Colmer (Miss.) from the Rules Committee as part of an effort to liberalize that committee. In 1965, Albert Watson (S.C.) and John Bell Williams (Miss.) were stripped of their committee seniority for their support of the Goldwater candidacy. Watson resigned his seat immediately and ran successfully as a Republican in a special election. Williams resigned his seat a year later and was elected to the Mississippi governorship. In 1968, John Rarick was similarly stripped of seniority for his lack of support for the Humphrey–Muskie ticket. However, he was already the most junior member of Agriculture, his only committee assignment, so the penalty was without substance.

23. In 1915 he moved to the Senate.

24. By the end of the decade the Speaker was also consulting with the minority party on minority appointees to select and conference committees.

25. Thus, in a speech to the freshmen in 1913, Speaker Clark remarked ,"A man has to learn to be a Representative just as he must learn to be a blacksmith, a carpenter, a farmer, an engineer, a lawyer, or a doctor. As a rule, the big places go to old and experienced members." Cited in Galloway (1961, p. 34).

Chapter 3

1. The fifteen members of the Ways and Means Committee served, until 1975, as the Democratic CC. Each member was responsible for a geographic zone, usually composed of his own state and several geographically contiguous states.

2. In recent years a seminar for new freshmen has been conducted during the period between the election and the convening of the new Congress. Initiated by a bipartisan group of congressmen, and occasionally cosponsored by the American Political Science Association, this seminar attempts to familiarize the new member with the practical details of congressional life. In addition to practical matters, the seminar focuses on teaching freshmen how to become nonfreshmen (not noncongressmen!). In discussing the seminar preceding the Ninety-fourth Congress, a *Washington Post* article reports, "Newly elected House Democrats, proudly bearing their mandates, were in town yesterday for some straight talk from incumbents on what they should do now to be effective and get re-elected." Committee assignments were among the topics discussed. "The new members were urged to get in requests quickly for committee assignments and to make strong second choices because new members can't always get what they want." See Richard L. Lyons, "Freshman Democrats in Town for Seminar on How to Stay," *Washington Post*, November 21, 1974, A6. Also see Tacheron and Udall (1966).

3. Rarely are CC decisions contested. The only two cases in recent years involved New York City Democrats (Shirley Chisholm and Herman Badillo) who were assigned to the Agriculture Committee.

4. In a year in which there is a dramatic change in party fortunes, it is likely to affect party representation on committees differentially. Thus, it is entirely possible, on any given committee, for the number of returning party members to exceed the number of slots to which the party is entitled. In this case the property-right claim cannot be enforced for all members. The "usual" practice is to bump the member with the least committee seniority. This person has first claim on existing vacancies on other committees. The "usual" practice, however, is not very usual: the committee structure negotiated by the party leadership protects the committee slots of returning members, even in the years in which there is a large change in party representation.

5. Reported in *CQ Weekly Report*, February 10, 1973, p. 282.

6. One Ninety-fourth Congress freshman from New York expressed a strong policy interest in the field of health and thus originally requested the Committee on Interstate and Foreign Commerce. He learned, however, that "the Health subcommittee was the sexiest subcommittee on that Committee. Everybody wants it. Even if I get assigned to the full committee—and I think my chances are pretty good—it's very unlikely that as a freshman I would land the Health Subcommittee. I decided that I did not want to end up reading reports about the electric utility industry for the next few years. So I'm pushing hard for one of the New York seats on Judiciary instead. After all, I'm a lawyer and have been especially interested in civil liberties and the penal system."

7. Each of these cases has something "special" about it. Yates and Roush were "superfreshmen"—both had prior terms of service. Yates left the House (and the Appropriations Committee) to run unsuccessfully for the Senate in 1962. He was returned to the Congress in 1964 and successfully sought his old seat on Appropriations. Roush was defeated for reelection in 1968, but was returned in 1970. Though he did

not previously sit on Appropriations, in many respects his request was treated very much like a nonfreshman transfer request. Pryor, too, was technically a "super-freshman." The member he replaced resigned shortly after the election, permitting Pryor to be sworn in early and have a seniority "jump" over other Ninetieth Congress freshmen. More than anything, however, Pryor's appointment to Appropriations was indicative of the influence of Chairman Wilbur Mills. Farnum's appointment came about because of a Michigan vacancy on Appropriations. As a former member of the Committee on Committees put it, "I think it was because of the respect and affection for Mrs. Griffiths [Michigan representative on the CC]. She pins you down. She came around and asked me point blank if I would vote for Farnum and what do you say to a woman? The thing was they [the other Michigan members] were all happy with what they had. Martha assured me she had checked with all of them and that no one else wanted it. Michigan didn't have anyone on Appropriations at all so they had to get the seat, and Farnum was the only one who wanted it." Finally, in the case of McKay, the Ninety-second Congress request books reveal that he did not even request Appropriations. Rather his zone representative on the CC took it upon himself to push hard for the appointment of a Rocky Mountain states representative to Appropriations. Since there were only five requests for the six slots on Appropriations, McKay won appointment. The zone representative "seen his opportunity and he took it."

8. It is a bad bet not only because of a low probability of success, but also because there are opportunities foregone by placing the bet. Freshmen are encouraged by the CC to keep their request lists short. Most freshmen, therefore, list only two or three requests. Given this constraint, low-probability requests often fall by the wayside.

9. *CQ Weekly Report*, February 10, 1973, p. 282.

10. Ibid.

11. With the growing tendency of the CC to assign members to *two* committees, in the Ninety-fourth Congress the CC asked each freshman to submit two lists, one for his major assignment and one for his minor.

12. For this reason it is misleading to refer to a committee prestige hierarchy. While it may be the case that some committees are regarded as generally superior, and others as generally inferior, for most committees there is little consensus among members on preferences. The fascination in the congressional literature with prestige rankings, therefore, is probably misplaced.

13. On occasion a zone representative has chosen to keep the committee preferences of his charges to himself. During the 1940s and 50s, Thomas O'Brien (D., Ill.) would keep his CC colleagues in the dark about the committee requests of Illinois Democrats. He would appear at the executive sessions of the CC with the Illinois preferences jotted down on the back of an envelope!

14. Both of these quotations are drawn from Clapp (1964, pp. 223–25).

15. These letters were made available to Professors Richard Fenno and John Manley by the former member.

16. This, of course, in no way denies that "half the fun is getting there." Waiting in the queue, that is, has *consumption* as well as *investment* aspects: friendships are established, policy expertise developed, and constituency services performed while moving through the queue. In some committees even the relatively junior members play an

important role in molding legislation and guiding it through to passage. Joseph L. Fisher (D., Va.), the most junior Democrat on the Ways and Means Committee in the Ninety-fourth Congress (and an economist by training), for example, has had a major role in hammering out legislation in the tax and energy areas (see *CQ Weekly Report* during February and March 1975). A former member of the Education and Labor Committee, a southern liberal, reported that as a very junior member he was frequently called upon to defend committee legislation on the House floor. "The party leaders knew that a speech defending an education bill cast in a sweet southern accent was worth a few votes!"

17. It should be noted that the current committee system, mandated by the Legislative Reorganization Act of 1946, is past its thirtieth birthday—and it is beginning to show its age. Jurisdictional lines established just after World War II have not always meshed very neatly with changes in the executive branch and the emergence of new public policy concerns. Recently a Select Committee on Committees (the Bolling Committee) and a committee appointed by Democratic Caucus chairman Olin Teague (the Hansen Committee) focused on jurisdictional reorganization. Some modest changes were made in the committee system during the Ninety-third Congress.

18. The only freshman appointee to Rules in recent Congresses was Clem Rogers McSpadden (Okla.) in the Ninety-third Congress. McSpadden's district bordered that of Speaker Carl Albert and his appointment has generally been regarded as Albert-inspired. Said one member on the scene, "All McSpadden has to do is go along when Albert calls him up on something. We didn't put him on there to exercise independent judgment on substantive questions of legislation." See *CQ Weekly Report*, February 10, 1973, pp. 279–83. Gillis Long (La.), a "freshman" with previous service, was also appointed to Rules in that Congress.

19. Since the duty committees are in low demand, discounting of interest by the probability of assignment success assumes decidedly less importance, that is, there is little competition for these committees. Consequently, requests are based almost entirely on "value" considerations. Thus, of the seven freshman requests for the District of Columbia Committee, three were from freshman in the Maryland suburbs. Two additional requests were from southerners. Because of the capital's large black population, the governance of Washington, D.C., has long been a symbolic issue for southern constituencies (and has become increasingly important for congressmen with large numbers of black constituents). More obviously, suburban Washington constituencies have a direct economic, social, and cultural interest in the affairs of the capital city. Looking at all nineteen requests for the D.C. Committee (from both freshmen and nonfreshmen), fourteen came from members of suburban Washington, or southern districts, or districts with a large percentage (above 30%) of blacks. Merchant Marines and Fisheries requests display a similar pattern: the thirteen freshman requests came from members in whose districts were the ports of Philadelphia, New York (two), Seattle, Baltimore, Cincinnati, Boston, and Houston; there were also requests from two members whose districts bordered on the Mississippi River, one whose district lies on the Great Lakes, and four whose districts border the Atlantic or Pacific oceans. In all, twenty-two of the twenty-five requests for this committee came from members with obvious district-related interests in the committee.

20. These surrogate variables will be replaced by specific characteristics, more closely matched with committee jurisdictions, when I turn to particular committees. For now, they will serve to distinguish regional and demographic differences in districts.

21. On the other hand, the member may believe that a very long list, say five or more committees, will minimize the probability of his receiving a highly undesirable appointment. As the data of the next chapter suggest, however, the likelihood of receiving *some* requested committee appears to be nearly independent of the length of the preference-ordering.

22. This comparison is all the more compelling when it is observed that two "biases" in the data have *reduced* the number of nonfreshmen with short lists. First, and most important, most nonfreshmen do not submit requests at all. They are not interested in transferring to some other committee (at least, that is what their behavior reveals). Second, I have excluded dual-service requests from the computations of table 3.5. With very few exceptions, no more than one committee is listed by a nonfreshman as his dual-service request. In both these instances, then, table 3.5 understates the proportion of nonfreshmen with "short" lists.

23. A freshman's committee request has a state vacancy associated with it if a member of his state party delegation served on that committee in the previous Congress but failed to return to it in the current Congress. That freshmen often use a "same state" rationale in arguing in behalf of their requests is documented by Bullock (1971) and Achen and Stolarek (1974). See table 3.1.

24. Of the 231 freshmen 180 are faced with no state vacancy on their first-preference committee.

25. Several additional intuitive hunches, some of which may have occurred to the reader, have provided no explanation of variations in request-list length. The behavior of marginally elected freshmen is indistinguishable from that of their safer colleagues. Similarly, those who believe that "what you get depends on who you know" will be disappointed: freshmen from the same state delegation as their zone representative have neither longer nor shorter request lists than their less fortunately situated colleagues (they are no more successful in winning preferred appointments either). A slight pattern emerges when first preferences are partitioned according to committee *type* (exclusive, semiexclusive, nonexclusive): those whose first preference is non-exclusive disproportionately submit "short" lists (the relationship becomes substantially stronger when the Interior Committee is excluded).

26. I have excluded all exclusive committees since they are rarely requested by freshmen. For similar reasons I have excluded all the nonexclusive committees with the exception of Interior. The idea of examining interlocking requests came from David Rohde in some earlier research on which we collaborated.

27. See Fenno (1973, p. 10), for some possible reasons underlying this relationship.

28. Bullock and Sprague (1969), Bullock (1973a), Goodwin (1970), Jewell and Chi-hung (1974), and Westefield (1974).

29. For example, in the Ninety-first Congress the Democrats had difficulty filling some of their slots on Agriculture (owing to the poor performance of midwestern Democrats in the 1968 election). The CC asked B. F. Sisk (D., Cal.) to swap his dual-service assignment on the D.C. Committee for Agriculture, and he complied. The Democrats still had to leave one Agriculture slot unfilled in this Congress.

30. A table like 3.8 can be constructed in a variety of ways. I have observed the following conventions in my construction.

    1. When a congressman left two committees (or revealed a willingness to do so) and joined one, the one to which he was switching was counted as revealed

preferred to *each* of the initial assignments. Thus, a congressman who gives up his seats on Interior and D.C. for a seat on Appropriations is considered to have revealed a preference for Appropriations over Interior *and* for Appropriations over D.C.

2. When a congressman leaves a single committee for two new ones, only the *major* committee which he has joined (or indicated a willingness to join) is counted as revealed preferred to the single initial committee; the second committee joined is tabulated in the dual-service row.

3. When a congressman leaves two committees for two new ones (or expresses a willingness to do so), *four* entries are recorded in table 3.8. This last pattern occurred very infrequently.

31. Brooks gave up second rank on Armed Services for this chairmanship. It was rumored that this was arranged in order to remove Brooks from the running to succeed an aging Carl Vinson as chairman of the important Armed Services Committee. Miller gave up fourteenth rank on Armed Services and no better than fourth rank on any subcommittee for third position and a subcommittee chairmanship on Science.

32. With the partial exceptions of Government Operations and Interior, the nonexclusive committees are primarily suppliers. Few members are willing to give anything up in order to acquire a seat on one of them. Indeed, most of the demand for these committees is of the something-for-nothing dual-service variety.

33. Appropriations is the only committee to be revealed preferred to all others (excluding Ways and Means and Rules). This however, is probably a consequence of its size and turnover, and of the special way in which preferences are revealed for Rules and Ways and Means. Rules is the "Speaker's committee." The CC generally acts favorably upon the Speaker's recommendations for this committee; rarely is it explicitly requested by members despite its desirability. Vacancies on Ways and Means are filled through election by the Democratic Caucus (until the Ninety-fourth Congress—see the Epilogue). Entries, through the Ninety-third Congress, in table 3.8 are only the actual transfers to Ways and Means, since "requesters" who fail to win elections are not always publicly known. In the Ninety-fourth Congress, the Steering and Policy Committee made committee assignments. Since requesters who failed to win appointment *are* known in this Congress, they have been included in the tabulation.

34. Numerous measures of committee popularity or prestige have been suggested. Among them are:

1. Percent freshmen (Dyson and Soule 1970),
2. Mean House seniority of committee members (Dyson and Soule 1970),
3. *Net* transfers to as proportion of committee size (Goodwin 1970),
4. Percent of all transfer activity that is favorable to the committee (Bullock and Sprague 1969; Bullock 1973a).

Most of these measures had been suggested earlier in a still unpublished study by Warren Miller and Donald Stokes, "Representation in the American Congress." These aggregate measures of popularity have too often been used as preference indicators, improperly implying a homogeneous set of tastes among members.

35. Only transfers occurring at the opening of each new Congress are considered. These account for the overwhelming proportion of transfers.

36. Actually there are more if we allow for the fact that members, at any one time, may make multiple requests. Thus, a member's primary request may be a transfer and his

secondary request a dual-service slot. A "mixed strategy" of this sort is occasionally observed in the data. For our purposes here we need make no more than a passing reference to this possibility.

37. All four received their first-preference requests as freshmen.

38. See Schlesinger (1966), Fishel (1971), Mezey (1970), Black (1972), Hain and Smith (1973), and Rohde (1974) for theoretical and empirical insights about electoral systems as arenas of ambition.

Chapter 4

1. The term is Bullock's (1973a).

2. It is common, at this point, for the author to advise the nontechnical reader to skip over technical discussion and go right to the results. This is absurd, for the nontechnical reader will then have no basis on which to assess those results. In methodology and theory, as in nutrition, we are what we eat! I have, therefore, written the next two sections with the nontechnical reader in mind.

3. Inequalities of the form $f(a_{ij}) > f(a_{i^*j})$ have no meaning in this formulation. The "natural" interpretation of such an inequality is that member i judges service on committee j more valuable to him than does member i*. Judgments, however, are subjective, being based on personal "value" yardsticks. These judgments are not comparable in an interpersonal sense.

4. While I think this assumption is reasonable even if a member relies only on his own introspection, its descriptive accuracy is enhanced by the fact that a member's value judgments typically emerge from his interactions with "interested others." In proffering advice, these "others" will rely on observable features of the member's situation.

5. Let me emphasize that $g(a_{ij}/R_{ij})$ is a *conditional* probability. This observation is more than a theoretical nicety. It underscores several assumptions: that requests matter; that members seeking assignment believe they matter; and, more specifically, that members believe the likelihood of receiving an assignment to any of the more popular committees is practically zero if a member does not ask for one of them. *Why* requests matter is a separate issue that turns on the motives of and environmental constraints operating on the CC, a topic covered in Chapter 7.

6. Quoted in Richard L. Lyons, "Freshman Democrats in Town for Seminar on How to Stay," *Washington Post*, November 21, 1974, A6.

7. In this sense, other goals don't matter. That is, they add no additional information or explanatory power regarding freshman congressional behavior. Reason no. 1, then, is that goals inconsistent with reelection are pushed off of stage center by the all-consuming concern with reelection. They are of future relevance, heavily discounted, and consequently of little immediate importance as explanations of *freshman* request behavior. This is an unadulterated argument a qualified version of which is probably more nearly true. Reason no. 2 provides some of this qualification.

8. Fenno (1972) observes of congressmen that "foremost is their desire for reelection. Most members of Congress like their job, want to keep it and know that there are people back home who want to take it away from them. So they work long and hard at winning reelection. Even those who are safest want election margins large enough to discourage opposition back home and/or to help them to float further political

ambitions. *No matter what other personal goals Representatives . . . wish to accomplish —increased influence in Washington and helping to make good public policy are the most common—reelection is a necessary means to those ends."* (Emphasis added.)

9. It should be noted here that a persuasive case may also be made for the *zone* as the basis for these sorts of expectations. Happily, many freshmen come from the states which are dominant in their zones, so the distinction may not make much difference. Unhappily, this fact makes it difficult to distinguish empirically between the "same-state norm"—the alleged practice of trying to fill vacancies in committees from the same state as the member whose departure created the vacancy (see Bullock [1971])—and what might be called the "same-zone norm."

10. Since probabilities are bounded, they cannot be linear throughout the entire domain of the independent variables. The same point applies to the value function; according to economic reasoning about value judgments, utility functions in general are bounded and, for most economic goods, increase at a diminishing rather than a constant rate.

11. For a good discussion of the assumptions and possible violations, see Goldberger (1964, chap. 4).

12. An excellent discussion of the relevance of the probit model and other generalizations of regression to many political studies is found in Zavoina and McKelvey (1969). An earlier discussion of its relevance to economic survey data is Tobin (1955). A recent application of the technique to some aspects of committee assignments is found in Achen and Stolarek (1974). The classic statement of the probit model is Finney (1971). Also consult Aldrich and Cnudde (1975), McFadden (1974), McKelvey and Zavoina (1974).

13. This nonlinear transformation resolves the heteroskedasticity problem that required us to abandon the ordinary regression method.

14. Since the model will "expect" an $R_{ij} = 1$ when the explanatory variables are of the "correct" order of magnitude, the fact that $R_{ij} = 0$ in those instances where a member fails to request a committee because of the constraint will be regarded as error. Goodness-of-fit decreases as a consequence. Similarly, the efficacy of explanatory variables will also decrease. What we have is an instance of model misspecification. In principle, the constraint should be built into the estimation procedure. In the context of regression analysis, this possibility is discussed in Judge and Takayama (1966). Intriligator (1971, p. 42) discusses this problem from the perspective of the Kuhn–Tucker theory of concave programming. There are both theoretical and practical reasons for ignoring this model misspecification. First, our model is of the single-equation variety. For each committee for which there are adequate data, equation (4.6) is estimated. In order to specify the constraint on request lists explicitly, a simultaneous equation system is required, since the constraint links responses *across committees*. Since the theoretical problems of simultaneous equation systems are complex and largely unknown (at least to me) in the probit context (but see Schmidt and Strauss [1975]), I ignore the constraint. The practical problems are (at least) two: how to specify the constraint in a usable form, and where to find the computer program (either of the regression or the probit variety) that allows constraints to be incorporated.

15. In most uses of the probit model, the rule-of-thumb definitions for "rare" and "commonplace" are 10% and 90%, respectively, for the frequency of "1's."

16. Three of these committees, Appropriations, District of Columbia, and Merchant Marines, with request rates of 11%, 3%, and 6%, respectively, have already been examined seat-of-the-pants fashion in notes 7 and 13 of Chapter 3.

17. Special note should be made of the Judiciary variables. For all intents and purposes, a legal background is a *necessary* condition for assignment to this committee. Consequently, this condition was incorporated into the model, necessitating a slight departure in variable definition. See below.

18. The parameter estimates and $\hat{R}^2$-statistic were produced by NPROBIT, a computer program made available to me by Richard McKelvey and described in McKelvey and Zavoina (1971). Discussion of the $\hat{R}^2$-statistic, which is similar but not identical to the coefficient of determination in regression analysis, is found in McKelvey and Zavoina (1974) and Zechman (1974). I shall not make extensive use of this statistic, and include it for descriptive purposes only.

19. For any *single* parameter, the hypothesis that it is not significantly different from zero may be tested by dividing it by its standard deviation. The result is a Z-score; consultation with a table of areas of the normal curve provides the probability that this hypothesis is true. To test hypotheses about *groups* of parameters requires a likelihood ratio test described in McKelvey and Zavoina (1974) or Mood and Graybill (1963). Recall in the probit model that a prediction of a highly negative number is a prediction of a very low probability (see figure 4.1).

20. All of these coefficients are significantly different from zero at $p \ll .001$, except for Interstate and Public Works. They are significant at $p = .002$—still highly significant. It is nevertheless interesting that the two most popular committees have the least significant constant terms. That is, a member is more likely to apply for one of these, even if he has no interest *as measured by the v_s's*, than for any of the other committees. My own suspicion is that these two committees, and Armed Services as well, are very difficult to characterize in terms of interest. Interstate has so heterogeneous a jurisdiction that no handful of indicator variables is likely to partition freshmen successfully into "interesteds" and "uninteresteds." Similarly, since Public Works and Armed Services are likely to be of interest to those who seek future public works projects and prime military contracts for their districts, current constituency characteristics are likely to prove poor surrogates for "interest"; other members may seek either of these committees for reasons other than the pork barrel. See Ferejohn (1974), Rundquist (1973), and Ferejohn and Rundquist (1974). The relatively smaller negative values for these three committees is indicative of the fact that they are committees with very heterogeneous constituencies.

21. All of the hypotheses are formally summarized in table 4.6, where precise levels of significance are reported.

22. Recall that in earlier discussion I mentioned the possible difficulties of failing to incorporate explicitly the constraint on request-list length in a simultaneous equation structure. There I suggested that there was some basis for discounting those difficulties. The low frequency of type (A) errors provides the supporting evidence for this claim, for if the constraint were inhibiting requests from people who, on other grounds, "should" submit requests, the frequency of type (A) errors would be much higher.

23. The Agriculture Committee is illustrative: For the 231 freshmen that constitute the data set, the model correctly predicts request behavior in 201 of the cases. Of the 30 errors in prediction, 6 are Type (A) and 24 are Type (B).

24. This observation is supported by the fact that more than 60% of the Type (B) errors associated with the Interior equation occur *since the Ninetieth Congress*. That is, with the growing salience of environmental issues that began in the late 1960s, the variables of the Interior probit are increasingly imperfect indicators of "interest." Also, see Fenno (1973, Epilog).

25. It is noteworthy that the three poorest fits—Public Works, Armed Services, and Interstate—are committees whose jurisdictions are salient to a diverse set of congressmen. In constructing the data at the outset, I had difficulty determining appropriate indicator variables for these three committees.

26. In this calculation, the variables involving percent of work force in agriculture, military, and mining activities, as well as the percent foreign-stock variable, have been set at 50%. Population per square mile is set at 99,999 and land area is also set at 99,999.

27. The nonexclusive status of Interior may be at work here: even those one would "expect" to request Interior often have bigger fish to fry.

28. The hypothesis tests of table 4.6 are of the following form:

Column Number:	H_0:
1	$b_s = b_t = b_{st} = 0$, all s and t
2	$b_s = 0$, all s
3	$b_t = 0$, all t
4	$b_t = b_{st} = 0$, all s and t
5	$b_{st} = 0$, all s and t
6	$b_0 = 0$

In essence, the likelihood ratio test employed to determine the significance of several parameter estimates simultaneously involves running two separate probits, one including and the other excluding the variables whose parameters are hypothesized to be zero under H_0. If the probit that excludes the variables under examination performs about "as well" (according to the test statistic) as the one which includes the variables, then we have no basis for rejecting the null hypothesis.

29. The reason neither the p-terms nor the interaction terms, by themselves, are terribly significant is that they are quite highly correlated. Thus, with one set included in the probit, the other set is not very well correlated with the resulting residuals.

30. The exceptions alluded to in the text qualify this conclusion, of course. But in almost every case they involve extrapolations to extreme values of the variables—a dangerous basis for drawing inferences.

31. A combination of two categories of the *Congressional District Data Book*. These data were unavailable for the Eighty-sixth and Eighty-seventh Congresses.

32. No background variable was computed for this committee since the biographies in the *Congressional Directory* were ambiguous in discriminating between those who had some military experience and those who pursued military careers.

33. Thus, nearly 9% of the freshmen had senior members of their delegation seeking to transfer to Armed Services. By comparison, only 1% of the freshmen had senior state competition for Agriculture.

34. In an effort to fix more nearly on "interest" in the Armed Services Committee, a second probit model was run in which an additional "interest" variable was defined: v_2 = did member's predecessor serve on Armed Services? It was believed that this

variable would measure a member's stake in getting on Armed Services. Though the number of members whose predecessor served on the committee is small, half of them requested the committee as compared to only 20% of those whose predecessor was not a member. The resulting equation has an $\hat{R}^2 = .589$—a considerable improvement over the model presented in the text.

35. Due to little variation in the "senior state competition" variables—very few non-freshmen seek transfers to Banking and Currency—they are deleted.

36. A disproportionate number of Banking and Currency requests—nearly 10% of the total demand for this committee—came from one state during one Congress: California, in the Eighty-eighth Congress, had ten freshmen whose committee assignments had to be negotiated. Half of them submitted requests for Banking and Currency. California Democrats, though ordinarily a very cohesive delegation (see Deckard 1975), apparently were unable to resolve conflicts over committee assignments ahead of time. Instead the members appear to have simply acted independently, submitting requests according to "interest" (and the "interests" of ten California freshmen happened to be quite similar). This same phenomenon is true, to some extent, of New York Democrats—a notoriously uncohesive delegation. Consequently, though we must take the data as it comes, this one unusual feature may well account for the sometimes bizarre ways in which the p-terms affected requests.

37. Fenno (1973, pp. 9–10) comes to the same conclusions about the similarities of applicants for these two committees.

38. As one member of the CC put it, "Most of the men on the Foreign Affairs Committee have very cosmopolitan districts *and they think it has an appeal there.* Like _____ with the city of Miami and all the Cubans down there. Look at the members of the Foreign Affairs Committee and you'll see that most of them come from the *large urban centers with minority groups or ethnic groups in them.* This time we put on a man from Colorado. We don't know how he'll fare in his reelection, but he was personally interested in it." (Emphasis added). Note: the Colorado Democrat referred to was defeated in his reelection attempt rather handily.

39. The second v-term has the wrong sign, but it is not statistically different from zero.

40. The Interior Committee is generally regarded as a "western" committee. The proportion of committee members from districts west of the Mississippi River has historically been large. However, that proportion has been falling: it stood at a remarkable 80% in the Eighty-sixth Congress; it is down to 59% in the Ninety-fourth Congress. Moreover, the two top Democrats in the Ninety-fourth Congress are from the East. This trend reflects, as I noted earlier, the changing salience of parts of Interior's jurisdiction. Thus we may expect the particular "interest" variables employed in the model to discriminate between applicants and nonapplicants less successfully as time passes. See Fenno (1973, Epilog).

41. The null model maximum likelihood guess is the modal behavior pattern—"no request."

42. Whether because of this policy or because of the highly technical nature of legislation considered by this committee, few nonlawyers ever apply. In the Eighty-sixth through Ninety-third Congresses, only one of the 103 nonlawyers requested Judiciary. This practice, by the way, officially came to an end in the rules changes of the Ninety-fourth Congress. "The [Democratic] caucus adopted by voice vote a

resolution sponsored by Larry McDonald (D.Ga.) that banned discrimination based on a representative's prior occupation or profession in making committee assignments." See *CQ Weekly Report*, February 8, 1975, p. 302.

43. Since the p-terms, that is, "state vacancy"·"lawyer,"..., are so highly correlated with other variables they had to be deleted. Moreover, since fewer than 5% of the freshmen had senior state competition for Judiciary, the "senior state competition" interaction terms, w_{31} and w_{32}, were deleted.

44. With the growing concern about environmental impact, and the political organization of environmentalists, this third reason has lost some of its force.

45. Murphy (1974), on the basis of interviews with members of the Public Works Committee, reports that most believe their committee membership has helped them to serve constituency needs and, consequently, has benefited them electorally.

46. The Army Corps of Engineers goes to considerable lengths to establish a good relationship with the Congress. It does this by maintaining an active file of feasibility studies for projects in districts all over the country. Contrary to the wishes of the Office of Management and Budget, but pleasing to congressmen, it employs a discount rate in its cost-benefit analyses which tends to exaggerate benefits and understate costs.

47. The "state vacancy" variables, contrary to expectation, discourage requests. This is especially surprising given that Public Works is often cited as a committee on which states seek to maintain representation. Ferejohn (1974, pp. 270–71) arrives at a similar conclusion: "There is some indication of state 'claims' to committee seats, but there are so many exceptions that it cannot be regarded as a firm rule." State competition discourages requests, as expected, though those freshmen whose predecessors served on the committee are likely to apply even if there is state competition. Senior state competition and state representation affect request probabilities in the expected direction.

48. I would like to thank Richard Fenno for raising this point.

Chapter 5

1. Omar Burleson (D., Tex), Edith Green (D., Ore.), and Otis Pike (D., N.Y.) are three extreme examples. Burleson moved to Ways and Means in his twenty-third year in the House; Green transferred to Appropriations in her nineteenth year; and Pike switched to Ways and Means in his fifteenth year.

2. Recall that unlike the practice in the previous research of Bullock and Sprague (1969), Bullock (1973), Goodwin (1970), Jewell and Chi-hung (1974), and Westefield (1974), committee status is *not* based on an aggregate popularity index. Rather it is based on *actual requests*.

3. This "proof" is deceptively simple. The crucial hidden assumptions are that p remains constant over time—$p(t) = p = $ constant—and that each opportunity is an independent trial. However, so long as p is not zero, the same qualitative behavior, namely, the decreasing frequency of persistent maintainers of the status quo, will emerge.

4. In order to be a conscientious participant in the proceedings of the dozen or so subcommittees of which he was a member, the late Senator Everett Dirksen is reputed

to have declared the dire necessity of a pair of roller skates! The story, though probably apocryphal, is to the point.

5. The Committee on Standards of Official Conduct, created in the Ninety-first Congress in the wake of the scandals surrounding Adam Clayton Powell, has served as a *third* assignment for some members. In the Ninety-fourth Congress, a freshman, Butler Derrick (D., S.C.), received three committee assignments—Banking and Currency, Budget, and Small Business.

6. A number of members holding dual assignments in violation of service constraints prior to the 1946 reorganization were permitted to retain their seats nevertheless. Until the Ninety-fourth Congress, the only other violations of the service constraints that I have been able to detect involved members of the Rules Committee. They were the assignments of James W. Trimble (D., Ark.) to the District of Columbia Committee during the Eighty-eighth and Eighty-ninth Congresses, Spark Matsunaga (D., Haw.) to Agriculture in the Ninety-second and following Congresses (Matsunaga served on Agriculture in the Eighty-eighth and Eighty-ninth Congresses, was elected to Rules in the Ninetieth and Ninety-first Congresses, and took on a second assignment—Agriculture—in the Ninety-second Congress), Claude Pepper (D., Fla) to the Internal Security Committee in the Ninety-first and succeeding Congresses (Pepper moved from Banking and Currency to Rules in the Eighty-ninth Congress, the latter his sole assignment until the Ninety-first Congress), and B. F. Sisk (D., Cal.) to the District of Columbia Committee in the Eighty-eighth Congress (he was elected to Rules in the Eighty-seventh Congress) until the Ninety-first Congress, when he swapped it for Agriculture In the Ninety-fourth Congress, the Committee on the Budget was created as a new standing committee. Many members on Appropriations and Ways and Means received a second assignment to this committee, reflecting a change in the constraint on acquisitiveness. At the same time, however, the Caucus reimposed the single-committee constraint on members of Rules. Sisk and Matsunaga were required to give up their seats on Agriculture (Pepper, too, returned to single-seat status with the elimination of the Internal Security Committee).

7. For additional details consult Gawthrop (1966) and Westefield (1974).

8. In the Ninety-fourth Congress freshmen were encouraged to submit two preference-orderings—one for "major" committees and one for "minor."

9. Since the competitive environment for committee slots changes over time, there is still another reason to expect an increase in the proportion of members revealing, sometime during their career, a preference for change. In Chapter 4 we discovered that, independent of and in interaction with "interests," competitive factors influenced freshman requests. Over time it is to be expected that some members who were discouraged from initially requesting particular committees because of these factors will later seek to transfer to them as the competitive environment becomes more favorable.

10. The figures for dual-service revealed preferences in the second and third columns of table 5.3 are conservative since greater proportions of the N for these columns (as compared to the N of column one) are *ineligible* for dual-service appointments, that is, many of these members sit on exclusive committees.

11. Changes in personnel at the subcommittee level, where much of the work of committees takes place, is even more dramatic. This fact would seem to cast some doubt on one common defense of the committee system—the argument that specialization

of labor encourages the development of substantive expertise, the skills of oversight, and the evolution of reciprocity norms between committees which expedite the chamber's agenda. With changes in subcommittee personnel exceeding 50% on occasion, even on some of the major committees, highly specialized work groups is perhaps too generous a characterization of the committee system.

12. Indeed, it is not even clear that the pecking-order hypothesis is accurate in the comparison of exclusive and nonexclusive committees. It is reported, for example, that only under great pressure from the party leadership did Lee Metcalf finally agree to run for a Ways and Means seat in the Eighty-sixth Congress. Apparently he regarded the opportunity costs of giving up a seat on Interior (his committee in the Eighty-fifth Congress) to be quite high for a congressman from Montana.

Chapter 6

1. See Westefield (1974) for an excellent empirical study, based on slightly different data from those of this study, of the leadership strategy of accommodation. This chapter may be taken as a modest extension of the reasoning initially proposed by Westefield. The data on committee requests employed throughout this study permit us to focus more accurately on an important set of pressures on the leadership than Westefield's reliance on the public record permitted. They do not, however, allow for the scope of analysis found in Westefield—in particular, this chapter in no way improves upon Westefield's interparty analysis or on his comparative analysis of structure negotiation before and after the Legislative Reorganization Act of 1946.

2. See Lewis Deschler, ed., *The Constitution, Jefferson's Manual, and the Rules of the House of Representatives*, House Document No. 769 (Washington, D.C.: Government Printing Office, 1947, pp. 303–7). This document, with permanent amendments and other commentary, is reissued from time to time. This particular edition is the first to incorporate the permanent changes of the Legislative Reorganization Act of 1946.

3. Also, in 1975 a standing committee, Internal Security, was eliminated.

4. Such a rare occasion was the permanent expansion of the Rules Committee in 1963. This committee had been expanded temporarily to fifteen members in a classic parliamentary struggle between Speaker Rayburn and Howard Smith, chairman of the Rules Committee, in 1961. See Cummings and Peabody (1963), Bolling (1965), pp. 210–20, and MacNeil (1963), pp. 412–47, for excellent descriptions of the temporary expansion. On the 1963 permanent expansion, see Peabody (1963) and the *Congressional Record*, January 9, 1963, pp. 13ff.

5. In both the Eighty-ninth and the Ninety-fourth Congresses, the Democratic majority was so large that its extraordinary majorities on the three exclusive committees were made slightly larger. Also, since the Ninety-first Congress, the Committee on Standards of Official Conduct has been evenly divided between majority and minority, reflecting the sensitive nature of its jurisdiction.

6. Deschler (1947, p. 306). The paragraph goes on to specify certain exceptions to the single assignment rule, but they are very limited. See note 7 below. It should be noted that the second sentence of this paragraph limits the majority's discretion toward the minority; that is, each member must receive *an* appointment.

7. Galloway (1961, p. 81) notes that "under the one-committee-assignment rule adopted in 1946 all the standing committees of the House were 'exclusive' committees, except that members who were elected to serve on the District of Columbia Committee or on the Un-American Activities Committee might be elected to serve on two committees and no more, and members of the majority party who were elected to serve on the Committee on Government Operations or on the Committee on House Administration might be elected to serve on two standing committees and no more. These exceptions were made so that the majority party could maintain control of all the committees. In the Eighty-third Congress, however, when the Republicans had a 'paper thin' majority of only seven seats in the House, eighteen Republicans were given second committee assignments so as to enable them to control all the standing committees of the House. This necessary departure from the one-committee-assignment rule apparently marked the beginning of the breakdown of that rule."

8. An excellent, though now somewhat dated, analysis of the House rules related to committees and committee assignments in the post-1947 system may be found in Riddick (1949, pp. 152–71).

9. For the period in question, Ways and Means remained the same size throughout, Rules was increased once and Appropriations was increased in size four times. None was ever decreased. In the Ninety-fourth Congress, both Rules and Ways and Means were increased. While the increase in the former was due to a technical restriction imposed by the Democratic Caucus (the "two-thirds-plus-one" rule—see the Epilogue), the increase in the size of the Ways and Means Committee—from twenty-five to thirty-seven—was the result of pent-up jealousy of the Ways and Means Committee jurisdiction and of frustration with the relatively conservative leadership of that committee.

10. Indeed, in only two instances—both involving Agriculture—has a semiexclusive committee been reduced in size. In both cases I expect the reason is a dramatic excess of available slots over requests. Unfortunately, these reductions occurred in Congresses for which request data are unavailable.

11 Until the Ninety-third Congress, Democratic party leaders were *not* members of the CC, though their influence was often felt. The Republican CC, on the other hand, is chaired by its party leader.

12. See also Bullock (1971).

13. For example, there was virtually no change in chamber party ratios between the Eighty-seventh and Eighty-eighth Congresses. The size of the Banking and Currency Committee was nevertheless expanded from thirty to thirty-one. In the former Congress the seats were shared in the ratio 18:12; in the latter the ratio was 18:13. The majority party leaders, that is, expanded the size of this committee by one and awarded the entire expansion to the minority in order to accommodate its "need" (even though it did not "deserve" the expansion according to the objective chamber ratio.)

14. In the Ninety-first Congress the Commerce Committee had thirty-seven seats divided between majority and minority in the ratio 21:16. Owing to the new chamber ratio in the Ninety-second Congress, the majority party leadership might have chosen to reflect the change, while keeping the committee size constant, by the distribution formula of 22:15. Alternatively, if they chose not to penalize the minority party leadership by reducing the committee slots at its disposal, the majority leaders might have chosen to reflect the change in the chamber ratio by expanding the committee

by two seats and distributing them in the ratio 23:16. They chose neither course, deciding instead to increase the committee by *six* seats and distributing them in the ratio 25:18. While some of this expansion is due to intraparty pressure on the majority party leaders, that they chose to grant the minority party two additional seats, despite a decline in their numbers, evidences a strategy of interparty accommodation.

A more explicit instance of majority accommodation of minority needs occurred at the beginning of the Eighty-ninth Congress. Gerald Ford, the newly elected minority leader, sought to protect the committee positions of returning Republicans after the Goldwater debacle. Although congressional Republicans suffered a major setback, a rather large proportion of the Republicans sitting on the Foreign Affairs committee were returned to the Eighty-ninth Congress. Ford fought to have the committee expanded in order to avoid bumping junior Republicans. See *CQ Weekly Report*, January 8, 1965, p. 36.

15. For example, in the Eighty-sixth Congress the Democrats held nearly 65% of the House seats yet claimed only 61% of the slots on semiexclusive committees.

16. For example in a paper presented to the Select Committee on Committees of the House of Representatives, Ninety-third Congress, Professor Robert Peabody has proposed a "consolidation of the standing committees which would reduce them to eight major committees, plus two special committees . . . the Committee on the Budget and the Committee on Agenda. These would [all] be exclusive committees. . . . A member would be assigned to one committee only." See Peabody (1973). Westefield (1974) first drew the analogy between committee slots and a monetary currency, arguing that one of the long-run consequences of steady currency inflation is the occasional necessity of a currency revaluation.

17. The fact that the credit for accommodating member preferences would have to be shared with the CC reduces that incentive somewhat. It also explains why the Speaker and majority leader (as well as the chairman of the Democratic Caucus) sought, successfully, to be added to the Democratic CC in the Ninety-third and ensuing Congresses.

18. He had not supported the Kennedy–Johnson ticket in the 1960 election.

19. Either outcome would have accomplished Rayburn's objective of liberalizing the Rules Committee and thereby clearing the way for President Kennedy's legislative program.

20. See "Politics of House Committees: The Path to Power," *CQ Weekly Report*, February 10, 1973, pp. 279–83.

21. Speaker Rayburn apparently pushed for an expansion of the Public Works Committee in the early 1950s in order to expedite passage of St. Lawrence Seaway legislation. He is also reported to have consistently increased the size of the Education and Labor Committee during the 1950s in order to liberalize its composition.

22. The creation of two new committees in the Ninety-fourth Congress has increased the per capita work load.

23. The increasing success in recent years of freshmen in landing prestigious committee assignments is testimony not only to the increasing influence of junior members in recent Congresses, changing attitudes toward freshmen, a reassessment of the apprenticeship norm (see Asher 1975), and the increased necessity of relying on freshmen as the Congressional work load has expanded; it also reflects the inflated value of currency.

24. The only *public* aspect of the negotiation of the committee structure is the actual structure that emerges. Descriptive detail of other aspects of structure negotiation is sketchy. An occasional bit of information emerges from journalistic accounts of momentous events, e.g., the 1961 expansion of the Rules Committee. A few additional details were obtained by me in my interviews of the members of the Democratic CC in December 1974–January 1975.

25. For example, the time trend on exclusive committees may be insignificant whereas that same trend on nonexclusive committees may be very high. The estimates of β_T and β_T^* will be averages of these two patterns. Thus they will underestimate the trend for nonexclusive committees and overestimate it for exclusive committees. An even more misleading result occurs if, for example, the impact of one of the variables is positive for one class of committees and negative for another. Aggregating the two effects in a single parameter may produce an estimate that is statistically indistinguishable from zero—a serious specification error.

26. It is something of a copout to use "time" as an explanatory variable since it is change over time that I wish to explain. Elsewhere I have alluded to the growing "acquisitiveness" of congressmen over time, but this, too, is no explanation for the change I am interested in here. That is, I would need to account for the change in attitudes toward acquisitiveness in order to provide a satisfactory explanation. The time variable, however, does tap an important secular change imposed on the Congress—*work load*. As the Congressional work load has increased over time, along with most other aspects of government, the sharing of the burden has encouraged committee-size expansion. Although a more explicit measure of work load, e.g., number of bills processed, is preferable to our measure T, the latter is an acceptable surrogate.

27. Effect (5a) is expected to be larger than (5b) because of the *certainty* of the former as compared to only the *possibility* of the latter. A *certain* supply of slots is produced by members not returning to Congress. This supply may or may not be increased by transfers, depending on decisions by the CC.

28. The linear specification does not accommodate the possibility of important interactions. For example, the leadership response to freshman demand for committee j may depend on the magnitude of nonfreshman demand for that committee. It may be more responsive to the former if the latter is small than if the latter is large. This possibility, suggested to me by Professor David Grether of the California Institute of Technology, has been tested statistically and proven insignificant. A similar result obtained for the potentially complementary supply variables. Thus the linear specification, with interactions deleted, appears appropriate.

29. A note on the data: ΔN_j, ΔN_j^e, X_j^4, and X_j^6 are obtained from first-session committee listings which appear in various volumes of the *Congressional Quarterly Almanac*. The Congresses for which the committee changes were calculated are: Eighty-sixth–Eighty-seventh, Eighty-seventh–Eighty-eighth, Eighty-eighth–Eighty-ninth, Eighty-ninth–Ninetieth, Ninety-first–Ninety-second, Ninety-second–Ninety-third, Ninety-third–Ninety fourth. For all of these Congresses the demand variables (X_j^1, X_j^2, X_j^3) and the potential supply variable (X_j^5) are obtained from the freshman and nonfreshman request data used throughout this study. Since the Internal Security Committee was eliminated in the Ninety-fourth Congress, I have seven observed changes for each of sixteen semi-exclusive and nonexclusive committees and six observations for a seventeenth nonexclusive committee: $N = 118$. The committees on Budget, Small Business, and Standards of Official Conduct, as well as the exclusive committees, have been excluded.

30. Though I use OLS regression, my observations are a mix of cross-sectional and time series data. In effect, I have pooled seventeen different time series—one for each committee. There is, then, the possibility of interdependent disturbances, a violation of the regression assumptions. The main consequence of this "flaw" in the data is that the standard errors of table 6.9 are underestimated somewhat. Thus, the t-statistic is overestimated. With ordinary time series the extent of underestimation can be quite serious. Since our data are only partially time series, the underestimation problem is probably not too serious. Nevertheless, it is probably wise to be suspicious of any parameter that is only marginally significant. See Goldberger (1964, pp. 238–42).

31. The hypothesis $H_0 : \beta_k = 0$ is tested with a t-test in table 6.9, where $t = b_k/s_k$, b_k is the parameter estimate, and s_k is its standard error.

32. The estimates of both β_2 and β_5 are of the correct sign, but the p-levels are only .20 and .30, respectively.

33. In both cases I test $H_0 : \beta_1 - \beta_1' > 0$. The test statistic is

$$t = (b_1 - b_1')/\sqrt{\mathrm{var}(b_1 - b_1')}$$

where $\mathrm{var}\,(b_1 - b_1') = \mathrm{var}\,(b_1) + \mathrm{var}\,(b_1') - 2\,\mathrm{covar}\,(b_1, b_1')$.

34. It is one thing to argue, according to this latter interpretation, that majority party acquisitiveness is the "causal" force, and that the minority receives additional slots only in order to keep party ratios on committees from getting too far out of line. But why, under this interpretation, would the minority get *more* seats than the majority, that is, why should β_6 be *less* than unity?

35. For example, the two committees that were demoted from semiexclusive to non-exclusive status—Post Office and Science—grew slower or actually shrunk in size (as compared to other committees) for the Congress or two preceding their change in status. There was, that is, an excess supply of seats. Few members wanted either of these committees as their major assignment. Also, from time to time, the leadership appears to respond to expectations about committee work load. Thus, despite little change in party representation from the Eighty-seventh to the Eighty-eighth Congress, the Science and Astronautics Committee grew by 24%, partially in response to President Kennedy's expressed desire to beef up the manned space program and the consequent leadership expectation of an increased committee work load. Indeed, in that latter Congress the subcommittee structure of the committee was radically reorganized to handle the increased work load. Finally, on occasion and for policy purposes, the party leadership takes an active role in generating additional committee slots by forcing or "persuading" sitting members to release their seats. In the late 1940s and 1950s Speaker Rayburn engaged in this practice. MacNeil (1963) reports that the Speaker was instrumental in having two members of the Un-American Activities Committee removed after they brought embarrassment on the House with some of their wild antics under the klieg lights. Former Congressman Frank Smith (1964) indicates that Rayburn, in alliance with President Truman, "persuaded" four anti–St. Lawrence Seaway Democrats to leave the Public Works Committee in the early 1950s. In Chapter 3 I note a similar occurrence involving Overton Brooks' departure from the Armed Services Committee in the Eighty-sixth Congress.

Chapter 6, Appendix

1. If the committee membership is permeable because of high turnover, there is very little that sitting members can do to prevent "rent dissipation." Indeed, the absence of

waiting lines to get on the committee is prima facia evidence of the limited amount or complete absence of monopoly rents. What members can do in principle, though this is rarely observed in practice, is lobby the leadership to *contract* the committee size, thereby creating the scarcity (and rents) that did not previously exist. Two committees, however, were reduced from semiexclusive to nonexclusive status, thereby increasing demand for them as dual-service assignments.

2. In effect, the hypotheses suggest that the impact of the demand variables are damped and the supply variables exaggerated for those committees with strong counter-expansionist pressures (high r_j values). While these hypotheses are fairly straight-forward, the last one is not. It suggests that if extraordinary minority party needs are accommodated, the importance of majority party access to a committee's jurisdiction *increases* with r_j. That is, on the high "monopoly rent" committees, minority needs will rarely be financed by a simple expansion of their representation without a compensating expansion for the majority party. The contrast between Banking and Currency and Commerce in notes 13 and 14 of this chapter illustrates this point.

3. The fact that $\beta_6 < 0$ suggests that, for lower r_j committees, the normal form of financing in minority representation owing to "extraordinary need" is simply to transfer a majority party seat to the minority or add an extra seat to the minority side without a compensating addition for the majority. Again, the Banking and Currency illustration of note 13 is suggestive.

Chapter 7

1. See Abram and Cooper (1968), Polsby, Gallaher, and Rundquist (1969).

2. Masters (1961) devotes little more than a paragraph to the CC; Clapp (1964) and Goodwin (1970) no more than a page or so.

3. As the italicized concepts above reveal, I have chosen to adapt the mode of analysis employed by Fenno (1973) in his comparative study of six *legislative* committees to analyze the CC—a nonlegislative, task-oriented, party committee. The flexibility and general utility of Fenno's approach derives from its very close resemblance to models of constrained maximization found in economics and operations research. For a more explicit recognition of this resemblance, see the appendix to Chapter 8, Shepsle (1975a, 1975b), and Ferejohn and Fiorina (1975).

4. This section relies heavily on Fenno (1973) and Manley (1965, 1969, 1970).

5. Until the Ninety-fourth Congress, Martha Griffiths (D., Mich.) was the only "she"; in 1975, Martha Keys, a freshperson from Kansas, was elected.

6. Burr Harrison (D., Va.), under unusual circumstances, did so. Both John McCormack and Hale Boggs (D., La.) left the committee upon election to party leadership posts.

7. Lee Metcalf (D., Mont.) and Eugene McCarthy (D., Minn.) were elected to the Senate; Hugh Carey (D., N.Y.) became the governor of New York; Richard Fulton (D., Tenn.) became the mayor of Nashville; and William Green (D., Pa.) ran unsuccessfully for the Senate.

8. Cited in Deckard (1975).

9. In the Ninety-fourth Congress, Otis Pike (D., N.Y.) gave up sixteen years of com-mittee service on Armed Services in order to switch to Ways and Means.

10. See Eulau et al. (1959).

11. See Fenno (1973, table 3.3).

12. See Manley (1970, pp. 36ff and figure 2.4). Manley's point in emphasizing the large southern flavor of the committee is to underscore the a priori prospect of the emergence of the "conservative coalition" in the affairs of the committee, not to challenge its geographic representativeness.

13. This practice has benefited southerners, who have maintained strong representation on the committee despite declining numbers within the Democratic party. A case in point: upon the resignation of Richard Fulton (D., Tenn.) from the committee in 1975, the Caucus elected Harold Ford (D., Tenn.).

14. Riegle (1972, p. 189) suggests that though Burleson had the votes, Gilbert won 115–113 because the Alabama delegation had not yet returned from the inauguration of Governor Lurleen Wallace.

15. The Texas Democratic delegation follows a strict seniority rule in settling committee assignment conflicts. See Deckard (1975).

16. On the Jennings–Landrum contest, see Peabody (1963, p. 161), Bolling (1964, p. 75), Manley (1970, pp. 34–35).

17. This is not always the case. In my interviews with Ways and Means Democrats, one member was the exception that proved the rule. He strongly resented the fact that so many of his committee colleagues "play politics" and "don't give a damn about policy."

18. Ever since Masters (1961, pp. 46–47) first articulated it, "legislative responsibility" has been considered the most important criterion for appointment to Ways and Means. Committee members, according to this view, are respectful of the legislative process and of their colleagues, are moderate or gradualist in approach and personal style, and are House-oriented. They are regarded by other House members, according to the respondents in Fenno's study (1973, pp. 20–21), as "cooperative," "popular," "reasonable," "sober," "easy to work with," and not as "screwballs," "running around kicking everyone in the teeth," "shooting their mouths off," "going off half-cocked." I have always felt that "legislative responsibility" lacked clarity as a theoretical concept, though apparently congressmen (and Congress scholars) "know it when they see it." Rather than regarding it as a criterion (Masters called it "the most crucial test"), I think it should be viewed as a concomitant of other personal and situational characteristics. In the absence of serious electoral risks, strong policy concerns, and progressive ambition, the legislator is free to attend to matters of style, can afford to be gradualist, does not have to "go off half-cocked," and so on.

19. See Manley (1970, pp. 53–58).

20. A current member of the committee believes that the political parties should devote more resources to trying to defeat opposition members of Ways and Means. "It's not a good committee for running back home. Knowing what I know now, I don't think it would be too difficult to run against many of the people on the committee." This view is, perhaps, a bit extreme. While the committee may not be "a good committee for running back home," most members are not pushed in their elections in the first place.

21. As quoted in Manley (1970, p. 77).

22. Cited in Fenno (1973, p. 3).

23. The CC decentralizes its deliberations by organizing itself according to geographical zones. Each CC member is responsible for nominating people from his zone. Because of this arrangement, winners and losers on the CC are identifiable. This fact has important consequences for the strategic premises which CC members share and for the style of their decision-making process. See above and Chapter 8.

24. There is only modest evidence in support of the hypothesis that marginal congressmen are more successful in obtaining requested committee assignments than safe congressmen. See Rohde and Shepsle (1973, tables 12 and 13), and Chapter 9 of this study.

25. My conversations with members of the CC lead me to believe that the "reelection of peers" objective plays a more telling role at the request stage than at the assignment stage. The CC member attempts to dissuade the marginally elected requester from seeking long-shots (see the previous quotation), encouraging him instead to obtain a constituency-oriented committee that he (the CC member) feels confident he can secure for the requester.

26. See Lewis Deschler, ed., *The Constitution, Jefferson's Manual, and the Rules of the House of Representatives*, House Document No. 769 (Washington, D.C.: Government Printing Office, 1947). It should be noted (see Chapter 2) that, in Jefferson's time, *standing* committees were not all that common. Rather, once the "will of the House" had been revealed in debate, a *select* committee was appointed to draft legislation reflecting that will.

27. A charge rescinded in the Ninety-fourth Congress.

28. Doc. No. 45–789–h (Washington, D.C.: Government Printing Office, 1975), Rule (M.I.)E. I would like to thank the former Caucus chairman, Philip Burton (D., Cal.), for making a copy of these rules available to me, and his predecessor, Olin Teague (D., Tex.) for doing the same for the Ninety-third Congress rules.

29. The major change in constraints on the CC contained in the 1975 rules regards the Rules Committee. The Speaker is empowered to recommend Rules Committee candidates directly to the Caucus. In the past, the CC nominated *all* committee members (excepting those for Ways and Means), though, in fact, it followed the Speaker's lead on Rules nominees (see next section, "Party Leadership").

30. The formal authority relationship between Caucus and CC is, like most formal relationships, an incomplete representation, for it neglects the very real possibility of CC retaliation against those who challenge it. Consider the case of Shirley Chisholm (D., N.Y.): Elected to the Ninety-first Congress, she was furious at being assigned to the Committee on Agriculture. She resigned from the committee and appealed to the Caucus for a new assignment (her first preference was Education and Labor). The caucus so instructed the CC. Instead of assigning her to one of her requested committees, however, the CC placed her on Veterans Affairs. She had to wait two years until she could transfer to Education and Labor. Several liberal members of the CC with whom I spoke in 1975 still smarted from the "Chisholm Affair."

31. Throughout this seminal essay Masters reiterates this point: "The Democratic and Republican leaders not only play the principal role in the selection of the members of their respective [CC's], but their personal judgments also tend to become the norm for major committee assignments" (p. 43); "Party leaders, working in conjunction with their [CCs], use assignments to major committees to bargain with the leaders of

party groups or factions, in order to preserve and fortify their leadership positions and conciliate potential rivals, as well as to reward members who have cooperated" (p. 57).

32. Goodwin (1970, p. 77) notes that Representative John Flynt (D., Ga.) denounced the Speaker after he failed to win an appointment to Appropriations in 1961. He had voted against Rayburn on the expansion of the Rules Committee and claimed that that was being held against him. In 1963 he supported Speaker McCormack on the permanent expansion of the Rules Committee. He also won his Appropriations assignment that year.

33. It has been suggested that this was the principal technique used by Rayburn to liberalize Education and Labor. It was also used to increase the responsiveness of the Rules Committee in 1961.

34. In the Ninety-fourth Congress, under a reconstituted arrangement (see the Epilogue) the Speaker presides over CC executive sessions. Despite his formal inclusion in committee assignment decision-making, his intervention is strikingly minimal. Said one participant, "He leaves most of the decisions to us. He really doesn't play that much of a role. But we give him pretty much what he wants. When he speaks in favor of some guy, that guy's got it greased!"

35. Their performance was even poorer than these remarks suggest. Of the three requesters who failed to do well, in at least two of the cases scarcity of openings on their first-preference committees could not be faulted. In only one case, that is, were the vacancies of a Connecticut freshman's first-preference committee filled with other requesters. The other two were passed over despite the absence of excess demand.

36. It should be noted that "delegation preferences" are recorded in the CC files and are regarded as important endorsements.

37. For example, one member of the CC "had great difficulty resolving disputes among state and regional members, so he essentially delegated request decisions to the [regional] Caucus in the last two Congresses. Whatever request decisions they jointly made, he went to bat for them."

38. See table 3.1 above and Achen and Stolarek (1974).

39. Occasionally the mix of advocacy and accommodation takes on an unusual flavor, as the experience of a border state CC member reveals:

> I had a man who wanted to go on Interstate and there was a lot of competition for it this time. Mills and Boggs said they understood that he wanted to go on Science, implying that they wanted someone else for Interstate. Even with them against me, my man got a tie vote. Then I offered to withdraw if they would put him on Science unanimously. This made me look good to Mills and Boggs and my man was happy to go on Science anyway—there were a lot who wanted Science this time.

40. Said one administrative assistant about a CC member: "Though he is a liberal and generally goes to bat for other liberals, even those outside his zone, he is accommodating to *all* his fellow members of the CC. That's true in the House generally."

41. From an interview with the chief counsel to Ways and Means (who oversees CC activities).

42. Prior to the Caucus debate of December 1974, the CC staff prepared for its members a report giving the Committee's disposition of the committee assignments of those

Democrats who were already on record as favoring the removal of the assignment task from the Ways and Means contingent. Of the 85 nonfreshmen in favor of stripping Ways and Means of its CC task,

> 13 either did not make their committee assignment preferences known to the Committee on Committees at the beginning of their service, or their service dates from before the 83rd Congress (the earliest records of the Committee on Committees). Of the 72 members for whom detailed information is available:
>> 45 received the assignment of their first choice....
>> 13 were assigned to committees of their second choice....
> Only 8 requests for assignment have not been accommodated, either initially or in subsequent Congresses (and some of these were apparently satisfactorily resolved since the request was not repeated).

The report goes on to speculate about the majority of Ninety-fourth Congress freshmen who, at the time, were apparently predisposed against the Ways and Means members:

> As to the 40-odd new Democratic Members without prior term service who [favor transferring the committee assignment task], the question arises: On what basis [have] these new Members decided to vote affirmatively in this regard? Are they aware of the record of service of the Democratic Committee on Committees in accommodating the interests of all Members as demonstrated in the attached pages? If so, what possible reason could they have for thinking this function should be transferred to some other group?

43. One aspect of the "acceptability" objective that does appear to be conscious, rather than coincidental, is related to the continuity of membership and staff on the Ways and Means Committee. Several members, and the chief counsel to the committee, emphasized the "organizational memory" of the committee, a consequence of membership and staff stability. In contrast, the Steering and Policy Committee, owing to its limited-term membership and (probably) more volatile staff, is likely to fall short on this dimension. Said one member, "Because Ways and Means has continuity we would remember if a guy tried to get on a committee last time and tilt toward him this time. On Steering and Policy they get elected every four years and, hell, they're gonna have new people on all the time—won't be able to take advantage of continuity." The chief counsel to Ways and Means added:

> The Steering and Policy Committee has unstable membership and staff. Hell, in two or four years four-fifths of that Committee could be different. And all the staff could be gone. They won't have any memory. They're all around the Speaker's Office. Even he could be different in two years and the whole group of staff will disappear. I don't even know if they're going to keep any records. The point is, they won't have very long memories. Here at Ways and Means we did. Our staff and committee membership had great continuity.

Chapter 8

1. One member delegated many of his decisions to the regional caucus of Democrats comprising his zone.

2. The Illinois delegation, noted for its cohesiveness, is perhaps most explicit in its occasional imposition of "delegation preferences" on its newcomers. The delegation dean and the CC representative survey the delegation's "needs" and attempt to match newcomers to needs accordingly. Ordinarily this matching process is compatible with the newcomer's preferences. If, for example, Illinois needs someone on Agriculture,

it is likely that one of the downstate members is interested in going on the committee. On occasion, however, delegation preferences take precedence over member desires. One junior delegation member reported:

> The delegation didn't have anyone on Banking and Currency, so I was put on. Seeing that the delegation has a man on all the major committees is Rostenkowski's job. He has to see that Illinois has good representation. He'll put a new man on a committee where Illinois doesn't have a member regardless of his qualifications. He can learn. [Cited in Deckard, 1975, chap. 4.]

3. The request book for the Eighty-sixth Congress was made available to me by Professor Robert Salisbury. Request books for the Eighty-seventh through Ninety-third Congresses were provided by a current member of the Ways and Means Committee. The Ninety-fourth Congress request book was shown to me by a sitting member of the Steering and Policy Committee, now the Democratic CC. The striking feature of these books is their similarity. In the sixteen years covered by these books their organization is identical, reflecting the continuity of staff for the CC (and, in the Ninety-fourth Congress, the willingness of the old CC staff to lend assistance to the inexperienced Steering and Policy staff).

4. Identifications have been removed to preserve anonymity.

5. For example, in figure 8.1 members may tilt in their voting on applicants for the Education and Labor Committee toward those whose other requests are much more difficult to satisfy (due to scarcity, competition, and so on); on the other hand, they may bypass those whose other requests are easier to satisfy, especially if they are higher-ranked by the applicant. For a general model of CC optimization, see Shepsle (1975a, 1975b) and the appendix to this chapter.

6. In 1974 House Resolution 988 was passed instructing congressmen to return to Washington between December 1 and December 20 in election years for the purpose of organizing the new Congress *before* it convenes.

7. It is appropriate at this point to make mention of the classes into which committees are partitioned. Three committees are designated as *exclusive*: Appropriations, Rules, Ways and Means. No member sitting on an exclusive committee may sit on any other committee. This rule has been relaxed on occasion (some Rules members have had second appointments, and the legislation creating the House Budget Committee requires that its membership be composed partially of Appropriations and Ways and Means members). Eight committees are designated as *semiexclusive* or *major*: Agriculture, Armed Services, Banking and Currency, Education and Labor, Foreign Affairs, Interstate and Foreign Commerce, Judiciary, and Public Works. In addition, until the Eighty-eighth Congress, Post Office and Civil Service was semiexclusive, as was Science and Astronautics until the Ninety-second Congress. Any member sitting on one of these committees may sit on no other exclusive or semiexclusive committee. The remaining House committees are designated as *nonexclusive* or *nonmajor*: Budget, District of Columbia, Government Operations, House Administration, Interior and Insular Affairs, Internal Security (deleted in the Ninety-fourth Congress), Merchant Marine and Fisheries, Post Office and Civil Service (since the Eighty-eighth Congress), Science (since the Ninety-second Congress), Small Business, and Veterans Affairs. Any member sitting on one of these committees may hold at most one additional semiexclusive or nonexclusive assignment (with several minor exceptions). One additional committee, Standards of Official Conduct, created in the wake of the scandals surrounding Adam Clayton Powell, is unclassified and often serves as a

third assignment for members. A more detailed treatment of committee classes and the rules for multiple assignments is found in the appendix to this chapter.

8. Until 1970, the only way in which a member might be considered for a committee assignment by the CC was through nomination by his zone representative. In that year the Democratic Caucus ruled that a majority of a state delegation could directly nominate one of its own and charged the CC chairman with insuring that people so nominated were brought to the CC's attention.

9. Thus, the request lists are occasionally inaccurate. At the last moment a change in the competitive environment may make the prospects for appointment more propitious for a member, even though he has not requested the committee. After checking with him, his zone representative may choose to nominate him.

10. One or two members mentioned that they go through the motions of nominating one of their people (while throwing their weight behind someone else from the zone) for fear that it might "get out" that they didn't nominate him.

11. With the addition of the Speaker, majority leader, and Caucus chairman to the CC in 1973, ten votes were required for election.

12. Said one member, "I trust you if you say you'll vote for Sam Jones but I trust you all the more if I can see you write it down."

13. One modest piece of evidence points in this direction. Very few comments were made to me about CC objectives (beyond those relating to restrained advocacy) in my interviews with CC members, except by the southerners. On a number of occasions, southern CC members volunteered their concern about making sure that the South was well represented. Moreover, two CC members, Omar Burleson (Tex.) and Joe Waggonner (La.), are active floor leaders for the southern contingent in the House and are regarded as linchpins of the "conservative coalition," both in the Committee and in the House, when it forms. For additional observations on the possibility of a "southern strategy" in the committee assignment process, see Bullock and Sprague (1969). That this strategy may not always have been used exclusively by southerners is suggested by the following evidence. One member, talking about the "old days," noted that "Massachusetts, New York, Illinois, and Pennsylvania would get together beforehand and trade—two positions for you, two for me, and so forth. They would protect their own interests. They would go into the meeting and vote their own interests, and [only] after that they'd help out someone."

14. Several members made passing references to an agreement-policing practice called "peeking". "When you are marking your ballots, some members may look over your shoulder and say, 'You aren't voting for my man?' and so you'll change your ballot." "Peeking! One [guy] is just wonderful at this, _____. It's embarrassing! _____ will say, 'You voted for my man, didn't you? Let me see!' Marvelous! Then, of course, if you voted the way he wants, you tell him yes, and he says, 'Let me see, you s.o.b.,' and so you show him. You don't do this all the time. You do it once, you have to do it just once." A third member said that *he* often shows his ballot to someone else in order to demonstrate good faith on his part, but that it was rare for him to be *asked* to show someone his ballot.

15. This is a conservative measure of CC responsiveness to requests since scarcity constraints prevent all requests from being satisfied. See the appendix to this chapter.

16. In the Eighty-eighth Congress he had a single freshman for whom he obtained a second-preference committee assignment.

Chapter 8, Appendix

1. The complexity of the problem is greatly reduced if attention is restricted to *freshman* committee assignments. To handle nonfreshman transfer phenomena, a considerably more complicated set of features needs to be incorporated.

2. Since each cell may assume either of two values, and there are mn such cells, there are 2^{mn} possible configurations of 1's and 0's. For even modest values of m and n, the number of A matrices is quite large. This number might be called the *Cannon number* in honor of Speaker Joseph Cannon who had virtually unlimited committee assignment powers (see Chapter 2).

3. There are several reasons why [I] is not always satisfied as an equality for all j. First, it is occasionally *infeasible*—to do so, that is, violates other constraints. A second reason was called to my attention by Professor Charles Bullock. The CC often leaves vacancies unfilled to accommodate expected intra-Congress changes in demand for committee seats. These changes are associated with intra-Congress personnel turnover due to death, retirement, appointment or election to other office, and party switching, e.g., Donald Riegle (Mich.), John Jarman (Okla.), Ogden Reid (N.Y.), Albert Watson (S.C.). Third, in negotiating a committee structure, the party leaders occasionally *oversupply* seats on particular committees, either because of error, because expected demand does not materialize, or because of accommodations with the minority.

4. There are several violations of the class [III] constraints that are easily accommodated. Some members who held third assignments prior to the Legislative Reorganization Act of 1946 were "grandfathered" in and permitted to retain those assignments. Assignments to several recently established committees—Standards of Official Conduct and Budget—have not been required to satisfy [III].

5. This set of constraints is redundant if *integral* assignments are explicitly required, for then the largest integer in the middle term of [IV] would be 1. We have not imposed an integral restriction because it follows as a logical consequence of maximizing behavior. See Shepsle (1975a, 1975b).

6. Multiple assignments to the same exclusive or semiexclusive committee are already proscribed by [IV].

7. In Shepsle (1974) a computing formula, parameterized in m, n, and the v_j's, is derived. To take an illustrative case, in the Eighty-seventh Congress there were nineteen Democratic freshmen to be assigned to thirty vacancies distributed among eleven committees. The constraints define a feasible set containing 1.28×10^{19} assignment configurations.

8. Notice that in this representation the CC member regards *any* committee appearing on a freshman's request list as "satisfactory and sufficient" to the freshman. The CC member does not distinguish the order in which requests are reported. The request list, therefore, is regarded as a device with which a freshman partitions the committees into "acceptable" and "unacceptable" subsets. Attempts have been made to cardinalize freshman request orderings so as to reflect the information of preference orders, but these cardinalizations appear to have little effect on the results.

Chapter 9

1. The data base for these analyses consists of the Democratic request lists for the Eighty-seventh through Ninety-third Congresses. The Eighty-sixth Congress request

list has been deleted because a substantial proportion of freshmen failed to submit requests that year; this failure does not affect our earlier results on requests but would bias results on assignments.

2. See Olson (1965) for a classic statement.

3. Fenno (1975) cautions us not to be too indiscriminate in our characterizations of the congressional constituency. In fact, he argues, there are really four constituencies: (1) the geographic, (2) the reelection, (3) the primary, and (4) the personal. Although a congressman shares the geographic constituency with his predecessor (except in cases of massive redistricting), there may be only limited overlap of the last three constituencies. To the extent, then, that a congressman's electoral interests only partially overlap those of his predecessor, the latter's committee assignment may only be of limited utility as an indicator of the interests of the former.

4. Eugene Keough, Ways and Means Democrat from New York, for example, was reputed to have gotten along poorly with many New York City Reform Democrats. He would not always give their committee preferences his strongest endorsement.

5. The assumption employed here, derived from Chapter 8 and the personal interviews with CC members conducted by the author, is that committees are taken up in the following order: Rules, Appropriations, Interstate, remaining major committees in alphabetical order, minor committees in alphabetical order. The results reported in these tables are not very sensitive to slight alterations in this assumption.

6. The kind of sentence we would like to utter is, "If the relative zone competition for lower-order requests is greater than it is for first-preference requests, then X% are successfully *nominated* for their first-choice committee; if the circumstances are reversed, then only Y% are *nominated*." The internal zone competition situation, that is, is relevant to *nomination* which, in turn, is crucial for ultimate election. Unfortunately, nominations are unobservable. The CC keeps no records of actual nominations. The marginal impact of relative zone competition on nomination, however, should translate into actual election success, that is, a higher nomination success rate produces a higher election success rate. And this is precisely what table 9.4 indicates.

7. The expression $\Pr(y/x)$ means "the probability that event y occurs given that event x has occurred." The expression $\Pr(x)$ is simply the unconditional probability that the event x occurs.

8. The reader is cautioned against drawing statistical inferences about each of the variables on the basis of the significance of the main effect only. To assess the statistical impact of a given variable it is necessary to perform a joint statistical test of the main effect and all of the interactions in which the variable in question appears.

9. The model was respecified with v_1, v_2, v_3, and v_4 main effects deleted. In fact, this is probably a more appropriate specification on theoretical grounds. The rationale is the following. The u_i variables are relevant to nomination and therefore have main effects. The v_j's come into play *only if* a requester is nominated, that is, only if the u_i's are "high enough." Consequently, the v_j's should be represented only as interactions. The respecified model is

$$\Pr(B) = \Phi\left(\alpha + \sum_i \beta_i u_i + \sum_i \sum_j \delta_{ij} u_i v_j\right)$$

Under this specification, the null hypothesis $H_0 : \delta_{ij} = 0$ for all i and j may be rejected at the p-level of $< .04$. In this latter model all of the conclusions inferred from table

9.11 are retained (though some at slightly lower statistical levels). The goodness-of-fit measures are all depressed—hence our primary reliance on the model estimated in table 9.9. The insignificance of the interaction terms in table 9.9, then, is primarily due to the high correlation between the interaction terms and their respective v_j variables. Their independent effect cannot be disentangled from the v_j main effects.

10. Since the Masters/Clapp hypothesis is given much currency in many discussions of committee assignments, and since the discussion above has indicated that, according to the request data, there is a strong bivariate relationship between electoral marginality and first-preference assignment success, it is useful to adduce some additional evidence for my conclusion that electoral marginality is spuriously related to that assignment success. The multivariate model hypothesis test indicates that the simple relationship between assignment success and electoral marginality is spurious—that, when other factors are controlled for, the relationship vanishes. Achen and Stolarek (1974) have devised an ingenious way to control for many "other factors" in a rather straight-forward fashion. Their empirical focus is on the *assignment contest*, a paired comparison between two members seeking an assignment to the same committee. Examining contests between marginal and safe congressmen, they conclude, on the basis of Democratic request data for four Congresses, that "marginally elected Congressmen and safe Congressmen fare about equally well in contests against one another." An adaptation of their table 8 provides the supporting evidence (see table 9.12).

Table 9.12   **Contests for Assignments: Marginal vs. Safe Freshmen**

Congress	N^a	% of Contests Won by Marginal[b] Freshmen
86	86	45.3
87	13	84.6
88	50	50.0
90	10	40.0
Total	159	49.7

SOURCE: Based on Achen and Stolarek (1974, table 8).
  [a] N is number of *contests*, not number of freshmen.
  [b] A marginal freshman is one with less than 55% of the vote.

11. The Achen–Stolarek (1974, table 7) "contest" analysis supports my conclusion. Over the four Congresses of their data, nonsoutherners won 53% of all assignment contests with southerners—a statistically insignificant percentage.

12. A similar problem was encountered in Chapter 4. In practice it is awkward and difficult to accommodate constraints in many multivariate statistical methodologies.

13. Achen and Stolarek's contest analysis again supports this conclusion. They discovered (see their table 5) that nearly 80% of all contests between a freshman and a nonfreshman for a given committee slot were won by nonfreshmen.

14. These instances were not counted among the five cases above in which no freshman won assignment.

15. Since there is no way of knowing who sought a transfer via this informal route but failed, our analysis focuses exclusively on those who submitted requests.

16. After this model is estimated, several additional effects are examined. We shall conclude that neither region, zone representative's work load, nor member's party support (to be distinguished from differences he might have on this variable with his zone representative) is significant.

17. The member supported his party on *CQ* party-unity roll calls about half the time. His zone representative supported the party about two-thirds of the time.

18. In my own interviews with CC members, her name came up on several occasions, without prompting. On each occasion she was warmly praised as a competent, capable, thoughtful representative; her name was given to me as an illustration of someone "who could have anything she wanted."

19. Anonymity is not maintained in this illustration because the case is well documented in the public record.

20. During the entire period of this data there were only a handful of Rules Committee transfer requests. None was successful and only the New Yorker's request was handled incorrectly by the model.

21. A dummy variable for type of committee (exclusive vs. not exclusive) did not improve the error rate.

22. An analysis of nonfreshman dual-service acquisitions has been deleted because of my own inability to uncover any regularities relating to success. One thing may be said, however. In table 9.18 it is revealed that 58% of all dual-service requesters obtain *some* dual-service committee, with about 41% receiving their first-preference requests. There is some variation around this seven-Congress average *by Congress*. In those Congresses in which *freshman* success rates (assignment to some requested committee) are high, dual-service requests by nonfreshmen are honored, too. On the other hand, when it is not possible to satisfy freshman requests, then many of the minor committees that would otherwise go to nonfreshmen dual-service requesters are given to the disappointed freshmen as "sweeteners" instead.

Table 9.18   **Nonfreshman Assignment Success: Transfers and Dual Service**

	1st. Pref.	Other Pref.	Other	None	Total (N)
Transfer	52.8	5.0	4.7	37.5	100.0% (72)
Dual Service	40.9	5.0	12.1	42.0	100.0% (66)

23. According to a preference-oriented measure of freshman assignment success (see table 9.1) and an ad hoc measure of the "prestige" ranking of freshman assignments (see Asher 1975, table 3), it appears that committee assignments have improved rather steadily over the last twenty years for freshman Democrats.

24. No one has ever questioned the accuracy of this poll. In fact, the Common Cause poll predicted the aggregate vote result in the Caucus with perfect accuracy.

25. The Republican percentage for the same period is 26.5. Thus, in total, nearly one-quarter of all standing committee positions in the House are filled by new committee members each Congress.

26. At the committee level, massive personnel changes ordinarily involve minor committees; however, Democratic representation on Armed Services in the Eighty-ninth Congress and Ways and Means in the Ninety-fourth Congress consisted of a majority of new committee members, so major committees are not immune to substantial personnel changes. At the subcommittee level, shifting personnel, shifting jurisdictions, and the general birth and death of subcommittees are considerable. I have examined these phenomena for two Congresses (the Eighty-sixth and the Ninety-first), one involving a large Democratic freshman class and the other a small one. Defining a new subcommittee member as one sitting on a given subcommittee for the first time (note that this is an underestimate since it does *not* include members sitting on a new subcommittee that resulted from merging their old subcommittee with another), the instability of subcommittee membership is startling. In the Eighty-sixth Congress fully 46.7% of all subcommittee slots were newly occupied; in the Ninety-first Congress the number is 30.0%. And this change often involves major committees. In the Eighty-sixth Congress the following committees head the subcommittee instability list (percentage of all subcommittee slots filled by new members in parenthesis): Armed Services (63.3%), Judiciary (57.1%), Veterans Affairs (56.9%), Interstate (54.5%), Post Office (54.2%), Agriculture (52.0%). Even Appropriations subcommittees had a substantial injection of new blood—30.6%. A comparable list could be supplied for the Ninety-first Congress, though the levels are lower. These numbers should qualify the impression one has from casual observation that committees and subcommittees are stable work groups in which specialization and the accumulation of expertise develop. This entire subject area requires some intensive research.

Chapter 10

1. Their influence, by the way, is difficult to discern. In recent years several "powerful committee chairmen" have gone public in their opposition to particular appointments and lost. Former Chairman Hebert's failure to deny a seat on Armed Services to Congressmen Dellums and recent failures of Chairman Mahon to exclude liberals from the Appropriations Committee are cases in point. The liberalization of Education and Labor, Un-American Activities, and Rules in the 1950s and 1960s, over the objections of conservative chairmen, provides an additional basis for questioning the systematic influence of committee chairmen.

2. The bivariate statistical analysis of Chapter 9 gives only modest support to the impact of work load on actual assignment success. That is, variations among zone work loads are not significantly correlated with variations in assignment success, ceteris paribus. The important feature to emphasize, however, is the gross impact of *decentralization* itself. In no Congress did the number of freshmen in any one zone exceed ten, and rarely did it rise above seven. Thus, even though variations in our particular measure of work load failed to account for variations in assignment success, the simple fact that the work load was so light permitted the CC representative to invest intensively in advocacy for the interests of his zone.

3. Elsewhere in that chapter, there is some modest support for the idea that party leaders also accommodate the wishes of members of especially powerful committees

who prefer not to have their monopoly power dissipated by size expansion. The leaders tend to be less responsive to the supply and demand variables of those committees.

4. For example, consider the expansion of Rules in 1961 and the expansion of Ways and Means in 1975.

5. Only Agriculture in the Eighty-third and Eighty-fourth Congresses was contracted.

6. One troublesome fact for this discussion is the Legislative Reorganization Act of 1946 itself. Why did the Congress, in the absence of massive transfusions of new blood (which did occur in the 1946 elections *after* passage of the Act), reform itself? Westefield (1974) suggests that the principal impetus for reorganization in the House was an inflated exchange currency in that chamber—committees and committee slots were too numerous to command very much in exchange. I suspect this is a very incomplete explanation because, in order for the reorganization to pass, the support of many who stood to lose their institutional advantages was required. Side payments were needed—and they were forthcoming in the form of a large congressional pay raise, increased travel expense-accounts, and increased personal and committee staffs. Interestingly, in the Senate (there were no roll-call votes on the Monroney-Lafollette bill in the House), chief opposition to the bill came from the South (sixteen of the twenty-two southerners voted against, joined by only three others), allegedly because of opposition to the pay raise but conceivably because of the loss of institutional perquisites or the opportunity to obtain them in the future.

7. See, among others, the studies by Davidson (1974, 1976), Davidson and Oleszek (1975), Lowi (1969, 1972), Ripley (1973), and Ripley and Franklin (1976).

8. See, among others, Dodd and Shipley (1975), Orfield (1975), Ornstein and Rohde (1976), Price (1972), and Ripley (1965).

9. See Milton S. Gwirtzman, "The Bloated Branch," *New York Times Magazine*, November 10, 1974, pp. 30ff.

10. For a general statement, see Ogul (1976).

11. For example, the Subcommittee on Investigations of the Commerce Committee, chaired by John Moss (D., Cal.), and the Subcommittees on Commerce, Consumer and Monetary Affairs, and Government Information and Individual Rights, both of the Government Operations Committee, chaired, respectively, by Benjamin Rosenthal (D., N.Y.) and Bella Abzug (D., N.Y.), were especially active in the Ninety-fourth Congress. See "Congress May Step Up Oversight of Programs," *CQ Weekly Report*, March 22, 1975, pp. 595–600. Also see Ornstein and Rohde (1976).

12. For an early case study covering some of these matters, see Bibby (1966). Also consult Ornstein and Rohde (1975, 1976).

13. Bergland, for example, replaced Poage as chairman of Conservation and Credit when Poage moved to the chairmanship of the Livestock and Grains Subcommittee and was not permitted to retain the Conservation and Credit chairmanship.

14. For more on these and other provisions of the so-called "Subcommittee Bill of Rights," see Rohde (1974).

15. For empirical details on the volume of oversight, its scope, and so on, consult Dodd and Shipley (1975).

16. Evidence of this concern is found in the Committee Reform Amendments of 1974 where each House committee with twenty or more members is required to create an oversight subcommittee and, during the first two months of each Congress, the Government Operations Committee is charged with surveying and coordinating the oversight activities of these panels. Also, the Democrats have supported the upgrading of their party's Caucus and Steering and Policy Committee, the two instruments most likely to play a coordinating role in the future. Finally, there has been discussion recently of computerizing casework activity in order to pinpoint persistent bureaucratic trouble spots that might warrant formal congressional inquiry.

    A related source of dissatisfaction involves the lack of comprehensive oversight. A recent interest in across-the-board "sunset laws" is a symptom of this dissatisfaction. But "comprehensive" oversight is unrealistic and contrary to common sense: "Congress has to decide, the committees have to decide, what it is that they see as most important for oversight purposes rather than trying to meet this broader expectation that somehow all activities can be systematically overseen" (Ogul, *Panel Discussions* [1973], p. 231). Also consult *CQ Weekly Report*, November 27, 1976, pp. 3255–59.

17. During the 1950s and early 1960s, Clarence Cannon (D., Mo.) served as chairman of Appropriations and John Taber (R., N.Y.) as ranking minority member. They determined subcommittee assignments for their respective party contingents, following the practice of assigning members to subcommittees in which their constituents had little "interest." The objective of this practice, known as the Cannon–Taber norm (see Fenno 1966), was to eliminate conflicts of interest, thereby encouraging subcommittees to reduce executive budget requests.

18. The one dimension on which committees are quite representative is the partisan, this being mandated by House rules and historical practice. For evidence of regional bias, see Fenno (1973, table 3.3). On ideological bias, see Fenno (1973, tables 3.1 and 3.2), and Goss (1975, figures 3 to 22). On seniority bias, see the discussion in Chapter 9, especially that attached to table 9.23.

19. See Brock (1974) and Peabody (1973) for statements endorsing realignment of committee jurisdictions along functionally homogeneous lines. The final recommendation of the Bolling Committee, too, endorsed functional jurisdictions but in a form that permitted bill consideration by several House panels, either simultaneously, jointly, or sequentially, in recognition of the "continuously shifting sands of policy issues."

Epilogue

1. For a survey of reforms during the 1970s and an early assessment of their impact, see Davidson and Oleszek (1975), Ornstein (1974), Ornstein and Rohde (1976), and *Panel Discussions* (1973). Also consult *Inside Congress* (Washington: Congressional Quarterly, Inc., 1976).

2. In the Senate, the operation of the Johnson rule and a liberalization of the Steering Committee (charged with making committee assignments) greatly improved the committee prospects of junior Democrats. In the House there was a general perception that the back-bench Republican received more generous treatment by his CC than his Democratic counterpart received, and that minority leader Gerald Ford, as well, was especially concerned with the fate of his junior colleagues (see Asher 1975).

3. See the 1974 revision of Bolling (1968), particularly Chapter 7. Recall, however, the analysis of Chapter 9 above which qualifies the unresponsiveness charge.

4. This procedural change came in the wake of a highly publicized conflict between Congressmen Vanik and Stokes of Ohio. Vanik, the CC member for Ohio, refused to place Stokes' name in nomination for a seat on Appropriations because the latter endorsed Vanik's opponent in a primary.

5. In the Ninety-fourth Congress, Herbert Harris of Virginia requested and received assignments to the District of Columbia Committee and the Post Office and Civil Service Committee, both of which are minor.

6. The Speaker was made its chairman, the majority leader its vice-chairman, and the Caucus chairman its second vice-chairman. In addition, the Speaker could appoint eight additional members, five of whom were the whip and the four deputy whips.

7. The eleven leadership-appointed slots were supplemented by twelve elected positions, one each from twelve regional caucuses of state party delegations.

8. The Democrats serving on the committee were Bolling, Stephens (Ga.), Culver (Iowa), Meeds (Wash.), and Sarbanes (Md.). The Republicans were Martin (Nebr.), Frelinghuysen (N.J.), Wiggins (Cal.), Steiger (Wis.), and Young (Fla.).

9. See Davidson (1976) and Davidson and Oleszek (1975) for historical details of the Bolling Committee.

10. A detailed account is found in *CQ Weekly Report*, December 22, 1973, pp. 3358–66.

11. On the opposition to the working draft, see ibid., February 2, 1974, p. 195. On the March 13 resolution and its similarity to the working draft, see ibid., March 16, 1974, p. 688.

12. Cited in ibid., December 7, 1974, p. 3274.

13. For a freshman's view of these events, see James M. Naughton, "The Lost Innocence of Congressman AuCoin," *New York Times Magazine*, August 31, 1975, pp. 9ff.

14. In effect, only four of these nine were unrestricted, since the rules required that five of the appointees consist of the whip and the four deputy whips. The rules, by the way, also required that "consideration shall be given to reducing the number of appointive Members"—hence proposal 3 above, considered at the beginning of the Ninety-fifth Congress.

15. This account is based on interviews with several members of S & P, including one, Richard Fulton (Tenn.), who also served on the old CC.

16. It is also the reason behind giving the Speaker the exclusive power to nominate members of the Rules Committee.

17. An examination of the revealed preference for transfers by nonfreshmen, not reported in detail here, showed little deviation from the patterns reported in Chapter 5. Perhaps the only pattern worth underscoring is the large proportion of revealed preferences expressed for exclusive committees—especially Ways and Means. This, in turn, is a result of the new way in which Ways and Means appointments are made *and* the large number of vacancies that were created by the expansion of the committee's size.

18. The Caucus also supported the establishment of two new standing committees— Budget and Small Business. The Internal Security Committee was not eliminated until

after Democratic committee assignments were made. The Democratic CC made no new appointments to that committee, and, of the members returning from the Ninety-third Congress, reappointed only its chairman, Richard Ichord (D., Mo.).

19. These patterns for the residuals raise the very real prospect of model misspecification. Positive and negative swings in the party ratio need to be discriminated in the model, and landslides for the parties need to be explicitly incorporated. This point is made in Chapter 6.

20. By the second session of the Ninety-fourth Congress, five of the seven eligible freshmen who failed to receive second assignments initially had been given additional committee positions, so that 97% of the freshmen had two assignments!

21. Only one other nonfreshman exchanged major committees. He had unsuccessfully sought a seat on Appropriations. A number of other nonfreshmen obtained dual-service committees.

22. Notice that the interaction terms, $u_i \cdot v_j$, have been excluded since hypothesis (3) of table 9.11 tells us that they are highly insignificant. Direct comparisons, then, between the estimates of this model and those of table 9.9 are inappropriate.

23. Neither coming from the same state as the zone representative (u_1) nor the number of zone vacancies (v_4) is significant.

24. The negative competition parameters, β_3 and γ_1, are rendered more negative in the Ninety-fourth Congress by amounts δ_3 and ε_1, respectively. The negative zone parameters, γ_3 and γ_4, are less negative in impact in the Ninety-fourth Congress by amounts ε_3 and ε_4, respectively.

Abram, Michael and Joseph Cooper. "The Rise of Seniority in the House of Representatives." *Polity* 1 (Fall 1968): 53–86.

Achen, Christopher H. and John S. Stolarek. "The Resolution of Congressional Committee Assignment Contests: Factors Influencing the Democratic Committee on Committees." Delivered at the Annual Meeting of American Political Science Association, Chicago, 1974.

Aldrich, John and Charles F. Cnudde. "Probing the Bounds of Conventional Wisdom: A Comparison of Regression, Probit, and Discriminant Analysis." *American Journal of Political Science* 19 (August 1975): 571–608.

Alexander, DeAlva Stanwood. *History and Procedure of the House of Representatives.* Boston: Houghton Mifflin, 1916.

Asher, Herbert B., "The Changing Status of the Freshman Representative." In Ornstein (1975), pp. 216–40.

Berdahl, Clarence A. "Some Notes on Party Membership in Congress." *American Political Science Review* 43 (1949): 309–21, 492–508, 721–35.

Bibby, John F. "Committee Characteristics and Legislative Oversight of Administration." *Midwest Journal of Political Science* 10 (February 1966): 78–96.

———. "Reforming the Committees While Retaining the Unique Role of the House." In *Panel Discussions* (1973), pp. 525–34.

——— and Roger Davidson, *On Capitol Hill.* 2d ed. Hinsdale, Ill.: Dryden, 1972.

Black, Gordon. "A Theory of Political Ambition: Career Choices and the Role of Structural Incentives." *American Political Science Review* 66 (March 1972): 144–59.

Bogue, Allan G. and Mark Paul Marlaire. "Of Mess and Men: The Boardinghouse and Congressional Voting." *American Journal of Political Science* 19 (May 1975): 207–30.

Bolling, Richard. *House Out of Order.* New York: Dutton, 1965.

Bolling, Richard. *Power in the House*. New York: Capricorn, 1968.
———. "Committees in the House." In Ornstein (1974), pp. 1–14.
Brock, Bill. "Committees in the Senate." In Ornstein (1974), pp. 15–26.
Bryce, James. *The American Commonwealth*. Rev. ed. New York: Macmillan, 1911.
Bullock, Charles S., "Committee Assignments in the U.S. House of Representatives." Ph.D. dissertation, Washington University, 1969.
———. "Apprenticeship and Committee Assignments in the House of Representatives." *Journal of Politics* 32 (November 1970): 717–20.
———. "The Influence of State Party Delegations on House Committee Assignments." *Midwest Journal of Political Science* 15 (August 1971): 525–46.
———. "Freshman Committee Assignments and Re-election in the United States House of Representatives." *American Political Science Review* 66 (September 1972): 996–1007.
———. "Committee Transfers in the United States House of Representatives." *Journal of Politics* 35 (February 1973a): 85–120.
———. "Motivations for Congressional Committee Preferences, Freshmen of the 92nd Congress." Presented at 1973 Annual Meeting of the Southwestern Political Science Association, Dallas (1973b).
——— and John D. Sprague. "A Research Note on the Committee Reassignments of Southern Democratic Congressmen." *Journal of Politics* 31 (May 1969): 483–512.
Carroll, Holbert N. *The House of Representatives and Foreign Affairs*. Pittsburgh: University of Pittsburgh Press, 1958.
Cater, Douglass. *Power in Washington*. New York: Random House, 1964.
Celler, Emanuel. "The Seniority Rule in Congress." *Western Political Quarterly* 14 (March 1961): 160–67.
Chiu, Chang-wei, *The Speaker of the House of Representatives Since 1896*. New York: Columbia University Press, 1928.
Clapp, Charles. *The Congressmen: His Work as He Sees It*. Garden City, N.J.: Doubleday–Anchor, 1964.
Cohen, Michael. "The Importance of Member Preferences in Committee Assignments: An Assessment Against Optimal Standards and a Simple Process Model." Presented at MSSB workshop on Mathematical Models of Congress, Aspen, Colorado, 1974.
Cooper, Joseph. *The Origins of the Standing Committees and the Development of the Modern House*. Rice University Studies, vol. 56, no. 3 (September 1970).
Cummings, Milton C. and Robert L. Peabody. "The Decision to Enlarge the Committee on Rules: An Analysis of the 1961 Vote." In Peabody and Polsby (1963), pp. 167–95.
Davidson, Roger H., "Breaking Up Those 'Cozy Triangles': An Impossible Dream?" Presented at Symposium on Legislative Reform and Public Policy, Lincoln, Nebraska, 1976.
———. "Representation and Congressional Committees." In Ornstein (1974), pp. 48–62.

Davidson, Roger H., and Walter J. Oleszek, "Adaptation and Integration: Structural Innovation in the House of Representatives." Delivered at the Annual Meeting of the American Political Science Association, San Francisco, 1975.

Deckard, Barbara, "State Party Delegations in the U.S. House of Representatives—A Comparative Study of Group Cohesion." *Journal of Politics* 34 (February 1972): 199–222.

————. "Cohesion and Conflict: State Party Delegations in the House of Representatives." Manuscript, 1975.

Deschler, Lewis, ed. *The Constitution, Jefferson's Manual, and the Rules of the House of Representatives.* House Document no. 769. Washington, D.C.: Government Printing Office, 1947.

Dodd, Lawrence C. and George C. Shipley. "Patterns of Committee Surveillance in the House of Representatives, 1947–70." Delivered at the Annual Meeting of the American Political Science Association, San Francisco, 1975.

Dyson, James W. and John W. Soule. "Congressional Committee Behavior on Roll Call Votes: The U.S. House of Representatives, 1955–1964." *Midwest Journal of Political Science* 14 (November 1970): 626–47.

Eulau, Heinz, John C. Wahlke, Leroy C. Ferguson, William Buchanan. "The Role of the Representative: Some Empirical Observations on the Theory of Edmund Burke." *American Political Science Review* 53 (September 1959): 742–56.

Farquharson, Robin. *Theory of Voting.* New Haven: Yale University Press, 1969.

Fenno, Richard F. "The House Appropriations Committee as a Political System: The Problem of Integration." *American Political Science Review* 56 (June 1962): 310–24.

————. "The House of Representatives and Federal Aid to Education." In Peabody and Polsby (1963), pp. 195–235.

————. *The Power of the Purse.* Boston: Little–Brown, 1966.

————. "If, As Ralph Nader Says, Congress Is 'The Broken Branch,' How Come We Love Our Congressmen So Much?" Delivered as part of a Time, Inc. editorial project, "The Role of Congress: A Study of the Legislative Branch," Boston, 1972, 16 pp. Reprinted in Ornstein (1975), pp. 277–88.

————. *Congressmen in Committees.* Boston: Little–Brown, 1973.

————. "Congressmen in Their Constituencies: An Exploration." Presented at the Annual Meeting of the American Political Science Association, San Francisco, 1975.

Ferejohn, John A. *Pork Barrel Politics.* Stanford: Stanford University Press, 1974.

———— and Morris P. Fiorina. "Purposive Models of Legislative Behavior." *American Economic Review Papers and Proceedings* 65 (May 1975): 407–15.

———— and Barry S. Rundquist. "Observations on a Distributive Theory of Policy Making: Two American Expenditure Programs Compared." in Craig Liske, John McCamaut, and William Lehr, eds. *Comparative Public Policy: Theories, Methods and Issues.* Beverly Hills, Calif.: Sage, 1974.

Fiellen, Alan. "The Functions of Informal Groups: A State Delegation." In Peabody and Polsby (1963), pp. 59–79.

Finney, D. J. *Probit Analysis.* 3d ed. Cambridge: The University Press, 1971.

Fiorina, Morris P. *Representatives, Roll Calls, and Constituencies*. Lexington, Mass.: Lexington Books, 1974.

———, David W. Rohde, Peter Wissel. "Historical Changes in House Turnover." In Ornstein (1975), pp. 24–58.

Fishel, Jeff. "Ambition and the Political Vocation: Congressional Challenges in American Politics." *Journal of Politics* 33 (February 1971): 25–56.

Follett, Mary Parker. *The Speaker of the House of Representatives*. New York: Longmans–Green, 1896.

Freeman, J. Leiper. *The Political Process: Executive Bureau–Legislative Committee Relations*. Rev. ed. New York: Random House, 1965.

Froman, Lewis A., Jr. "Organization Theory and the Explanation of Important Characteristics of Congress." *American Political Science Review* 62 (June 1968): 518–26.

——— and Randall B. Ripley. "Conditions for Party Leadership: The Case of the House Democrats." *American Political Science Review* 59 (March 1965): 52–63.

Galloway, George B. "The Operations of the LRA of 1946." *American Political Science Review* 45 (March 1951): 41–68.

———. *History of the House of Representatives*. New York: Crowell, 1961.

———. "Leadership in the House of Representatives." *Western Political Quarterly* 12 (June 1959): 417–41.

Gawthrop, Louis C. "Changing Membership Patterns in House Committees." *American Political Science Review* 60 (June 1966): 366–73.

Gertzog, Irwin N. "The Routinization of Committee Assignments in the U.S. House of Representatives." *American Journal of Political Science* (November 1976): 693–713.

Goldberger, Arthur S. *Econometric Theory*. New York: Wiley, 1964.

Goodwin, George. *The Little Legislatures*. Amherst: University of Massachusetts Press, 1970.

Goss, Carol F. "House Committee Characteristics and Distributive Politics." Delivered at the Annual Meeting of the American Political Science Association, San Francisco, 1975.

Green, Harold P. and Alan Rosenthal. *Government of the Atom*. New York: Atherton, 1964.

Griffith, Ernest S. *Congress: Its Contemporary Role*. 3d ed. New York: New York University Press, 1961.

Groennings, Sven and Jonathan P. Hawley, eds. *To Be a Congressman: The Promise and the Power*. Washington: Acropolis Books, 1973.

Hain, Paul and Terry Smith. "Congressional Challenges for the Office of Governor." Delivered at the Annual Meeting of the American Political Science Association, New Orleans, 1973.

Hasbrouck, Paul DeWitt. *Party Government in the House of Representatives*. New York: Macmillan, 1927.

Healy, Robert. "Committees and the Politics of Assignments." In Groennings and Hawley (1973), pp. 99–120.

Hinckley, Barbara, "Seniority in the Committee Leadership Selection of Congress." *Midwest Journal of Political Science* 13 (November 1969): 613–30.

Hinckley, Barbara. "Policy Content, Committee Membership, and Behavior." *American Journal of Political Science* 19 (August 1975): 543–58.

Homans, George C. *Sentiments and Activities*. New York: Macmillan, 1962.

Huntington, Samuel P. "Congressional Responses to the Twentieth Century." In David B. Truman, ed. *The Congress and America's Future*. Englewood Cliffs, N.J.: Prentice-Hall, 1965, pp. 5–32.

Intriligator, Michael D. *Mathematical Optimization and Economic Theory*. Englewood Cliffs, N.J.: Prentice–Hall, 1971.

Jacobs, Andy. *The Powell Affair: Freedom Minus One*. Indianapolis: Bobbs–Merrill, 1973.

Jewell, Malcolm E. and Samuel C. Patterson. *The Legislative Process in the United States*. 2d ed. New York: Random House, 1973.

———— and Chu Chi-hung, "Membership Movement and Committee Attractiveness in the U.S. House of Representatives, 1963–1971." *American Journal of Political Science* 18 (May 1974): 433–43.

Jones, Charles O. "Representation in Congress: The Case of the House Agriculture Committee." *American Political Science Review* 55 (June 1961): 358–67.

————. "The Role of the Congressional Subcommittee." *Midwest Journal of Political Science* 6 (November 1962): 327–44.

————. "Joseph G. Cannon and Howard W. Smith: An Essay on the Limits of Leadership in the House of Representatives." *Journal of Politics* 30 (August 1968): 617–46.

————. "Congressional Committees and the Two-Party System." In *Panel Discussions* (1973), pp. 564–72.

Judge, G. G. and T. Takayama. "Inequality Restrictions in Regression Analysis." *Journal of the American Statistics Association* 61 (March 1966): 166–82.

Kaplan, Lewis A. "The House Un-American Activities Committee and Its Opponents: A Study in Congressional Dissonance." *Journal of Politics* 30 (August 1968): 647–71.

Kessel, John H. "The Washington Congressional Delegation." *Midwest Journal of Political Science* 8 (February 1964): 1–21.

Kravitz, Walter. "Evolution of the Senate's Committee System." In Ornstein (1974), pp. 27–38.

Lowi, Theodore J. "American Business, Public Policy, Case-Studies, and Political Theory." *World Politics* 16 (July 1964): 677–715.

————. *The End of Liberalism*. New York: Norton, 1969.

————. "Four Systems of Policy, Politics, and Choice." *Public Administration Review* 32 (July-August 1972): 298–310.

MacNeil, Neil. *Forge of Democracy*. New York: McKay, 1963.

McConachie, Lauros G. *Congressional Committees*. New York: Crowell, 1898.

McFadden, Daniel. "Conditional Logit Analysis of Qualitative Choice Behavior." In Paul Zarembka, ed. *Frontiers in Econometrics*. New York: Academic Press, 1974, pp. 105–41.

McKelvey, Richard D. and William Zavoina. "An IBM Fortran IV Program to Perform N-Chotomous Multivariate Probit Analysis." *Behavioral Science* 16 (March 1971): 186–87.

McKelvey, Richard D. and William Zavoina. "A Statistical Model for the Analysis of Ordinal Level Dependent Variables." Mimeo. University of Rochester, 1974.

Manley, John F. "The House Committee on Ways and Means: Conflict Management in a Congressional Committee." *American Political Science Review* 59 (December 1965): 927–39.

――――. "Wilbur D. Mills: A Study in Congressional Influence." *American Political Science Review* 63 (June 1969): 442–64.

――――. *The Politics of Finance*. Boston: Little–Brown, 1970.

Masters, Nicholas A. "Committee Assignments." *American Political Science Review* 55 (June 1961): 345–57. Reprinted in Peabody and Polsby (1963), pp. 33–58.

Mayhew, David. *Congress: The Electoral Connection*. New Haven: Yale University Press, 1974.

Meller, Norman. "Legislative Behavior Research." *Western Political Quarterly* 13 (March 1960): 131–53.

Mezey, Michael L. "A Multivariate Analysis of Committee Assignments in the House of Representatives: 1949–1967." Ph.D. dissertation, Syracuse University, 1969.

――――. "Ambition Theory and the Office of Congressman." *Journal of Politics* 32 (August 1970): 563–79.

Moe, Ronald C. and Steven C. Teel. "Congress as Policy-Maker: A Necessary Reappraisal." *Political Science Quarterly* 85 (September 1970): 443–70.

Mood, Alexander M. and Franklin A. Graybill. *Introduction to the Theory of Statistics*. 2d ed. New York: McGraw–Hill, 1963.

Morrow, William L. *Congressional Committees*. New York: Scribner's, 1969.

Murphy, James T. "Political Parties and the Porkbarrel: Party Conflict and Cooperation in House Public Works Decision-Making." *American Political Science Review* 68 (March 1974): 169–86.

Nelson, Garrison. "Assessing the Congressional Committee System: Contributions from a Comparative Perspective." In Ornstein (1974), pp. 120–32.

Ogul, Morris J. "Legislative Oversight of Bureaucracy." In *Panel Discussions* (1973), pp. 701–10.

――――. *Congress Oversees the Bureaucracy*. Pittsburgh: University of Pittsburgh Press, 1976.

Olson, Mancur. *The Logic of Collective Action: Public Goods and the Theory of Groups*. Cambridge: Harvard University Press, 1965.

Orfield, Gary. *Congressional Power: Congress and Social Change*. New York: Harcourt Brace Jovanovich, 1975.

Ornstein, Norman J., ed. *Changing Congress: The Committee System*. Philadelphia: The Annals of the American Academy of Political and Social Science, 1974.

――――. *Congress in Change: Evolution and Reform*. New York: Praeger, 1975.

――――. "Towards Restructuring the Congressional Committee System." In Ornstein (1974), pp. 147–57.

―――― and David W. Rohde. "Seniority and Future Power in Congress." In Ornstein (1975), pp. 72–88.

Ornstein, Norman J. and David W. Rohde. "Shifting Forces, Changing Rules and Political Outcomes: The Impact of Congressional Change on Four House Committees." Delivered at Symposium on Legislative Reform and Public Policy, Lincoln, Nebraska, 1976.

Panel Discussions before the Select Committee on Committees, House of Representatives, Ninety-Third Congress, First Session on Committee Organization in the House. 3 vols. Washington D.C.: Government Printing Office, 1973.

Peabody, Robert L. "The Enlarged Rules Committee." In Peabody and Polsby (1963), pp. 129–67.

————. "Research on Congress: A Coming of Age." In Huitt, Ralph K. and Robert L. Peabody. *Congress: Two Decades of Analysis.* New York: Harper and Row, 1969, pp. 3–73.

————. "House Leadership, Party Caucuses and the Committee Structure." In *Panel Discussions* (1973), pp. 573–81.

————. "Committees from the Leadership Perspective." In Ornstein (1974), pp. 133–46.

———— and Nelson W. Polsby, eds. *New Perspectives on the House of Representatives.* Chicago: Rand McNally, 1963.

Pennock, J. Roland. "The 'Pork Barrel' and Majority Rule: A Note." *Journal of Politics* 32 (November 1970): 709–16.

Polsby, Nelson W. "The Institutionalization of the U.S. House of Representatives." *American Political Science Review* 62 (March 1968): 148–68.

————, Miriam Gallaher, and Barry Spencer Rundquist. "The Growth of the Seniority System in the U.S. House of Representatives." *American Political Science Review* 63 (September 1969): 787–807.

Price, David. *Who Makes the Laws?* Cambridge, Mass: Schenkman, 1972.

Price, H. Douglas. "The Congressional Career—Then and Now." In Polsby, Nelson W., ed. *Congressional Behavior.* New York: Random House, 1971, pp. 14–28.

————. "Congress and the Evolution of Legislative 'Professionalism.'" In Ornstein (1975), pp. 2–24.

Riddick, Floyd M. *The United States Congress: Organization and Procedure.* Manassas, Va.: National Capitol Publishers, 1949.

Riegle, Donald. *O Congress.* New York: Popular Library, 1972.

Ripley, Randall B. "Congressional Government and Committee Management." *Public Policy.* (Winter 1965): 24–48.

————. *Party Leaders in the House of Representatives.* Washington, D.C.: Brookings Institution, 1967.

————. "Party Leaders and Standing Committees in the House of Representatives." In *Panel Discussions* (1973), pp. 552–64.

———— and Grace F. Franklin. *Congress, the Bureaucracy and Public Policy.* Homewood, Ill.: Dorsey, 1976.

Robinson, James A. "The Role of the Rules Committee in Arranging the Program of the U.S. House of Representatives." *Western Political Quarterly* 12 (September 1959): 653–69.

————. *The House Rules Committee.* Indianapolis: Bobbs–Merrill, 1963.

Rohde, David W. "Risk-Bearing and Progressive Ambition: The Case of Members of the United States House of Representatives." Delivered at MSSB Workshop on Uncertainty, Political Processes, and Public Policy, San Diego, 1974.

———. "Committee Reform in the House of Representatives and the Sub-committee Bill of Rights." In Ornstein (1974), pp. 39–47.

——— and Kenneth A. Shepsle. "The Committee Assignment Process in the House of Representatives: A Case Study of Social Choice." Presented at the Annual Meeting of the American Political Science Association, Chicago, 1971.

——— and Kenneth A. Shepsle. "Democratic Committee Assignments in the House of Representatives: Strategic Aspects of a Social Choice Process." *American Political Science Review* 67 (September 1973): 889–905

Rundquist, Barry S. "Congressional Influences on the Distribution of Prime Military Contracts." Ph.D. dissertation, Stanford University, 1973.

Scher, Seymour. "Conditions for Legislative Control." *Journal of Politics* 25 (August 1963): 526–51.

Schlesinger, Joseph. *Ambition and Politics: Political Careers in the United States.* Chicago: Rand McNally, 1966.

Schmidt, Peter and Robert P. Strauss. "Estimation of Models with Jointly Dependent Qualitative Variables: A Simultaneous Logit Approach." *Econometrica* 43 (July 1975): 745–55.

Sharkansky, Ira. "An Appropriations Subcommittee and Its Client Agencies: A Comparative Study of Supervision of Control." *American Political Science Review* 59 (September 1965): 622–28.

Shepsle, Kenneth A. "A Model of the Congressional Committee Assignment Process: Constrained Maximization in an Institutional Setting." Delivered at the Annual Meeting of the American Political Science Association, New Orleans, 1973.

———. "Counting the Pieces and Measuring the Effects of the Giant Jigsaw Puzzle." Mimeo, 1974.

———. "Congressional Committee Assignments: An Optimization Model with Institutional Constraints." *Public Choice* 21 (Summer 1975a): 55–78.

———, "An Optimization Model of Congressional Committee Assignments." Delivered at the Joint National Meeting of the Operations Research Society and the Institute for Management Science, Las Vegas, 1975b.

Smith, Frank E. *Congressman from Mississippi.* New York: Capricorn, 1964.

Sokolow, Alvin D. and Richard W. Brandsma. "Partisanship and Seniority in Legislative Committee Assignments: California after Reapportionment. *Western Political Quarterly* 24 (December 1971): 740–60.

Staats, Elmer B. "General Accounting Office Support of Committee Oversight." In *Panel Discussions* (1973), pp. 692–701.

Swanson, Wayne R. "Committee Assignments and the Nonconformist Legislator: Democrats in the U.S. Senate." *Midwest Journal of Political Science* 13 (February 1969): 84–94.

Tacheron, Donald G. and Morris K. Udall. *The Job of the Congressman.* Indianapolis: Bobbs–Merrill, 1966.

Tobin, James. "The Application of Multivariate Probit Analysis to Economic Survey Data." Cowles Foundation Discussion Paper no. 1, New Haven, 1955.

Uslaner, Eric M. "Congressional Committee Assignments: A Linear Programming Technique." Delivered at the Annual Meeting of the American Political Science Association, Chicago, 1971.

————. "Congressional Committee Assignments: Alternate Models for Behavior." *Sage Professionnal Papers in American Politics*. Beverly Hills: Sage Publications, 1975.

Vardys, V. Stanley. "Select Committees of the House of Representatives." *Midwest Journal of Political Science* 6 (May 1962): 247–65.

Vogler, David J. "Patterns of One-House Dominance in Congressional Conference Committees." *Midwest Journal of Political Science* 14 (May 1970): 303–20.

Westefield, Louis P. "Majority Party Leadership and the Committee System in the House of Representatives." *American Political Science Review* 69 (December 1974): 1593–1605.

White, William S. *Home Place: The Story of the U.S. House of Representatives*. Boston: Houghton–Mifflin, 1965.

Willoughby, W. F. *Principles of Legislative Organization and Administration*. Washington, D.C.: Brookings, Institution 1934.

Wilson, Woodrow. *Congressional Government*. Boston: Houghton–Mifflin, 1885.

Wolfinger, Raymond E. and Joan Heifetz. "Safe Seats, Seniority, and Power in Congress." *American Political Science Review* 59 (June 1965): 337–49.

Wright, Jim. *You and Your Congressman*. New York: Coward, McGann and Geoghegan, 1972.

Zavoina, William and Richard McKelvey. "A Statistical Model for the Analysis of Legislative Voting Behavior." Delivered at the Annual Meeting of the American Political Science Association, New York, 1969.

Zechman, Martin J. "A Comparison of the Small Sample Properties of Probit and OLS Estimators with a Limited Dependent Variable." Mimeo, University of Rochester, 1974.

Index